P9-EEF-436

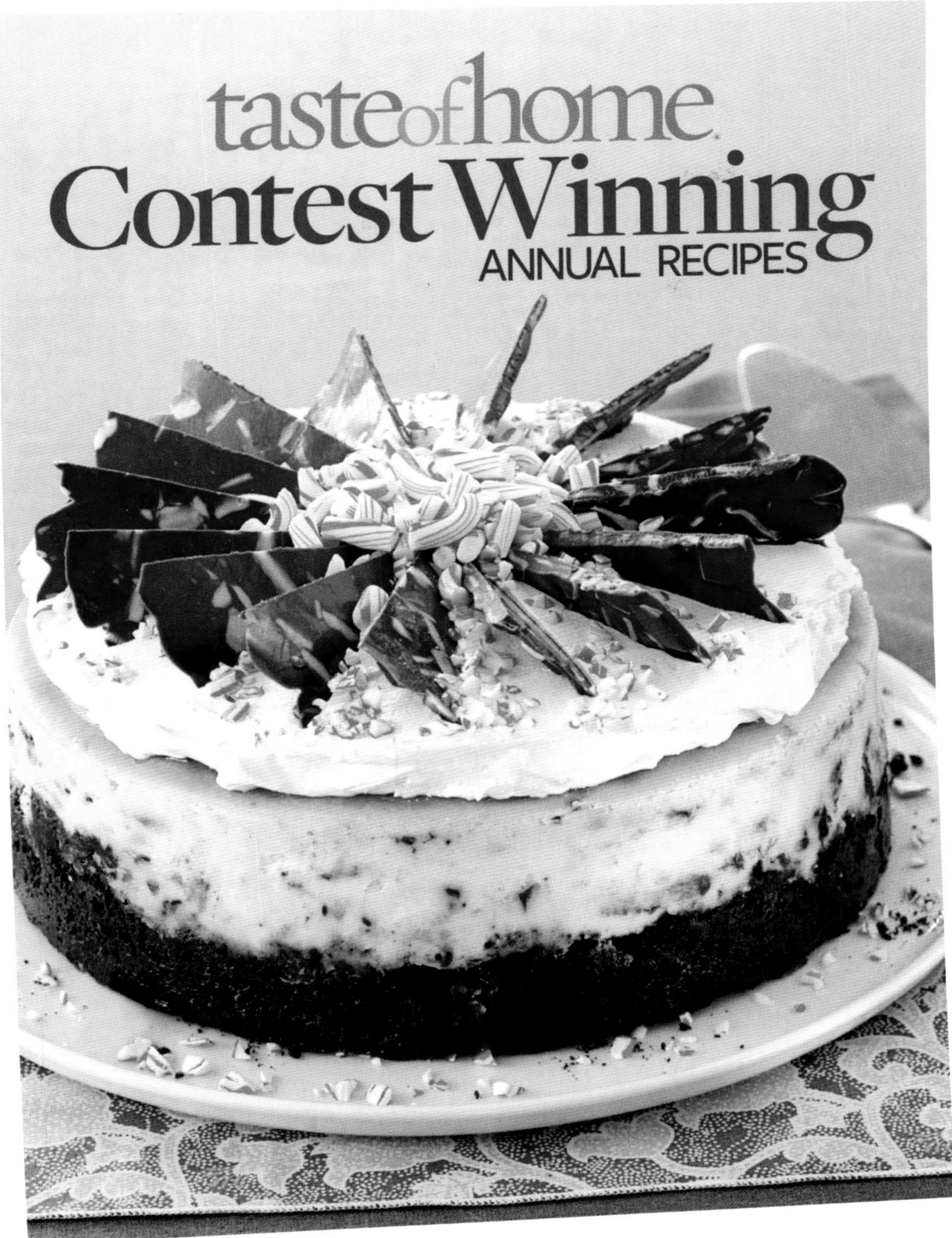
tasteofhome
Contest Winning
ANNUAL RECIPES

tasteofhome
Contest Winning
ANNUAL RECIPES

EDITORIAL
EDITOR-IN-CHIEF Catherine Cassidy
CREATIVE DIRECTOR Howard Greenberg
EDITORIAL SERVICES MANAGER Kerri Balliet

MANAGING EDITOR/PRINT & DIGITAL BOOKS Mark Hagen
ASSOCIATE CREATIVE DIRECTOR Edwin Robles Jr.

EDITORS Amy Glander, Ellie Martin Cliffe, Christine Rukavena
ART DIRECTOR Jessie Sharon
EDITORIAL PRODUCTION MANAGER Dena Ahlers
LAYOUT DESIGNER Nancy Novak
COPY CHIEF Deb Warlaumont Mulvey
COPY EDITOR Mary C. Hanson

CHIEF FOOD EDITOR Karen Berner
FOOD EDITORS James Schend; Peggy Woodward, RD
ASSOCIATE FOOD EDITOR Krista Lanphier
ASSOCIATE EDITOR/FOOD CONTENT Annie Rundle
RECIPE EDITORS Mary King; Jenni Sharp, RD; Irene Yeh
CONTENT OPERATIONS MANAGER Colleen King

TEST KITCHEN AND FOOD STYLING MANAGER Sarah Thompson
TEST KITCHEN COOKS Alicia Rooker, RD (lead); Holly Johnson; Jimmy Cababa
PREP COOKS Matthew Hass (lead), Nicole Spohrleder, Lauren Knoelke
FOOD STYLISTS Kathryn Conrad (senior), Shannon Roum, Leah Rekau
GROCERY COORDINATOR Molly McCowan

PHOTOGRAPHERS Dan Roberts, Grace Natoli Sheldon, Jim Wieland
SET STYLING MANAGER Stepanie Marchese
SET STYLISTS Melissa Haberman, Dee Dee Jacq

BUSINESS
VICE PRESIDENT, PUBLISHER Jan Studin, jan_studin@rd.com

GENERAL MANAGER, TASTE OF HOME COOKING SCHOOLS Erin Puariea

VICE PRESIDENT, BRAND MARKETING Jennifer Smith
VICE PRESIDENT, CIRCULATION AND CONTINUITY MARKETING Dave Fiegel

READER'S DIGEST NORTH AMERICA
VICE PRESIDENT, BUSINESS DEVELOPMENT Jonathan Bigham
PRESIDENT, BOOKS AND HOME ENTERTAINING Harold Clarke
CHIEF FINANCIAL OFFICER Howard Halligan
VICE PRESIDENT, GENERAL MANAGER, READER'S DIGEST MEDIA Marilynn Jacobs
CHIEF MARKETING OFFICER Renee Jordan
VICE PRESIDENT, CHIEF SALES OFFICER Mark Josephson
GENERAL MANAGER, MILWAUKEE Frank Quigley
VICE PRESIDENT, CHIEF CONTENT OFFICER Liz Vaccariello

THE READER'S DIGEST ASSOCIATION, INC.
PRESIDENT AND CHIEF EXECUTIVE OFFICER Robert E. Guth

COVER PHOTOGRAPHY
PHOTOGRAPHER Jim Wieland
SENIOR FOOD STYLIST Kathryn Conrad
SET STYLIST Melissa Haberman

5400 S. 60TH ST., GREENDALE WI 53129

INTERNATIONAL STANDARD BOOK NUMBER: 978-1-61765-223-3
INTERNATIONAL STANDARD SERIAL NUMBER: 1548-4157
COMPONENT NUMBER: 118400026H

PRINTED IN U.S.A.

1 3 5 7 9 10 8 6 4 2

PICTURED ON THE FRONT COVER Peppermint Cheesecake, pg. 228.

TABLE OF CONTENTS

OVER 350 PRIZE-WINNING RECIPES & TIPS

Thumb through your big box of recipes and you're sure to find a gem or two that always wins you compliments. Now it's your turn to take a glimpse into the recipe files of other great family cooks from across the country. *Contest Winning Annual Recipes* brings you 319 prize-worthy recipes, all winners in the monthly recipe contests featured in *Taste of Home* and her sister publications.

Now in its tenth edition, this brand-new, can't-miss collection serves up a big helping of first-rate favorites and expert kitchen tips to guarantee success. You'll find everything from main dishes, soups, starters, salads and sides to breads, rolls, desserts, breakfast, brunch and more...so you won't have to look far for a blue-ribbon meal from start to finish!

Wondering how these recipes received high honors in their respective contests? First, home cooks from all around read our request for entries and sent in their culinary creations—the must-have dishes their family and friends ask for time and again.

Then our test kitchen professionals sorted through the many entries we received and prepared the most promising selections for our judging panel of experienced food editors. After much delicious sampling, the judges selected a Grand Prize winner and the runners-up.

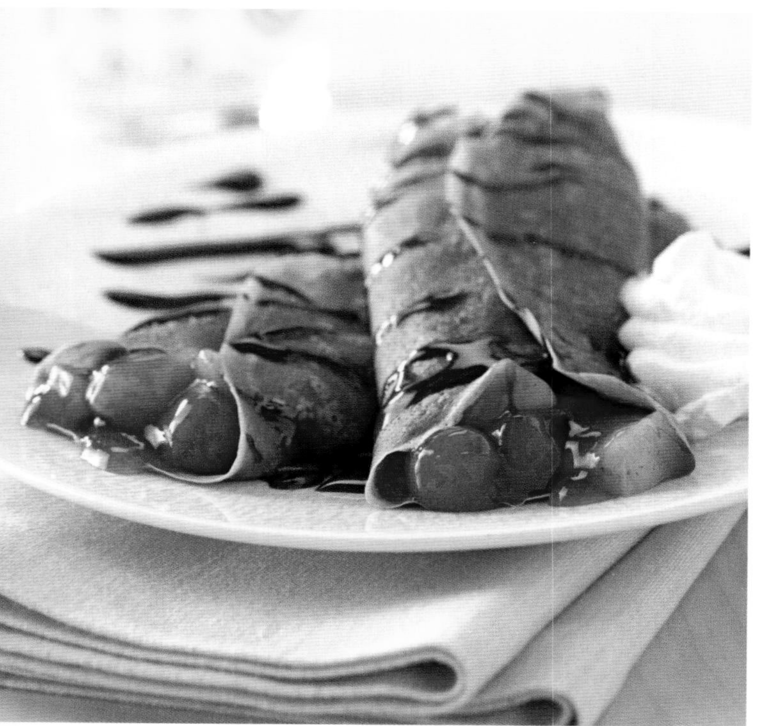

Winners from Dozens of Contests

The contests spotlighted in this cookbook cover a wide range of recipes—snacks and beverages; salads and dressings; soups and stews; entrees; side dishes and condiments; breads and rolls; brownies, bars and cookies; cakes and pies, and special desserts. No matter what type of recipe you're looking for, you're sure to find the perfect offering in this mouthwatering collection.

For a complete list of chapters, see the Table of Contents on page 3. Here's a quick glance of the year's worth of contests in this book and the top prize winner of each competition:

APPEALING APPETIZERS

Bite-sized and big on flavor, Gorgonzola Figs with Balsamic Glaze (page 11) made our judges' "A-list" of hors d'oeuvres.

SUPER SUPPER SALADS

Many sensational medleys were tossed into the bowl of entries, but Shrimp 'n' Scallops Tropical Salad (page 35) was declared the judges' favorite. These refreshing main dish delights raise the "salad" bar!

CORN IS KING

The pick of this contest crop was Tomato Corn Salad (page 44), beating out almost 3,000 entries! Enjoy this refreshing salad and a cornucopia of other recipes calling for this versatile summer veggie.

BEST LIGHT BURGERS

Add some spark to your next cookout with Terrific Teriyaki Burgers (page 55). Once folks sink their teeth into this grilled masterpiece, they'll have a hard time believing it's light!

SOUPS & STEWS

When you crave a satisfying, no-fuss meal that will nourish both body and soul, simmer up a hearty bowlful of Chicken Stew with Gnocchi (page 64), which serves up ladles of home-cooked comfort.

GARDEN-FRESH FAVORITES

Summer's bounty never tasted so good! Savor Corn Soup with Pico de Gallo (page 69) and other garden-fresh favorites to make the most of your homegrown harvest.

EXCEPTIONAL EGGS

Wake up taste buds with the bright, eye-opening delights our panel of judges considered top-notch, including first-place Apple-Bacon Egg Bake (page 80).

WARM & WELCOMING CASSEROLES

Sunday dinner will be something special when the bubbly, oven-baked goodness of a casserole or potpie is set on the table. Cozy up with one-dish wonders such as Zucchini Crescent Pie (page 85) for a meal you won't forget.

FLAVORS OF ITALY

Take your taste buds on a trip to Italy with our Grand Prize-winning Pepperoni Spinach Quiche (page 88), perfect for breakfast or any time of day.

HEARTY SOUPS

When the temperature takes a tumble, warm up with steamy spoonfuls of Wintertime Braised Beef Stew (page 94). Pair it with a fresh-baked loaf of bread or a crisp salad and dinner is served!

ONIONS & GARLIC GALORE

Take one bite into Roasted Chicken with Garlic-Sherry Sauce (page 98) and you'll agree...it's "clove" at first sight! Taste test more flavor-filled specialties that feature onion or garlic as their star ingredient.

PIZZA GOES LIGHT

For fantastic flavor without all the fat and calories, treat yourself to Chicken Pesto Pizza (page 104). We think you'll find it's a slice of oven-baked perfection.

ALL FIRED UP

Backyard barbecuing is a fast and fun way to beat the heat during the dog days of summer. Grilled Asian Flank Steak (page 109) is a surefire winner that will keep the kitchen cool and hungry tummies satisfied.

LET'S TALK TURKEY

Got Thanksgiving Day leftovers? Make use of every inch of that holiday bird with creamy, veggie-filled Next Day Turkey Primavera (page 112) and other tasty turkey choices.

SLOW-COOKED FAVORITES

An effortless, all-in-one meal is yours for the taking when you try Sunday Chicken Stew (page 117) or any one of our prized slow-simmered sensations.

CASSEROLE MAKEOVER

Craving the warmth and comfort of a casserole but only cooking for two? Then you'll love perfectly portioned recipes like Southwest Turkey Casserole (page 120) and other gotta-try, two-serving recipes.

BEAT-THE-CLOCK

Time-crunched cooks rejoice! Save time on busy weeknights with surprisingly easy, fast-to-table entrees like Shrimp 'n' Noodle Bowls (page 131), ready in just 30 minutes.

HOOKED ON FLAVOR

Get ready to reel in compliments when you serve up saucy, tender Southwestern Scallops (page 136) or any one of our judges' catch-of-the-day selections.

PASTA PERFECT

Enjoy oodles of noodles with our judges' top picks in pasta pleasers, including the Grand Prize-winning Four-Cheese Baked Ziti (page 142) that bakes up warm, bubbly and oh-so cheesy.

TENDERLOIN FOR 2

When a smaller yield will suffice, turn to Spicy Pork with Ginger-Maple Sauce (page 150) for a downsized dinner perfect for a twosome.

PUMPKIN PATCH SPECIALTIES

Pumpkins aren't only for pies. It's time to think outside the pie plate and put the wonderful flavor of pumpkin into a variety of dishes, including Grand Prize winner Pumpkin Scones with Berry Butter (page 162).

IT'S ALL ABOUT THE DOUGH

The versatility and deliciousness of refrigerated bread dough make easy work of homemade golden goodies. Pull-Apart Caramel Coffee Cake (page 169) rose to the occasion as our Grand Prize winner.

EASY FREEZER DESSERTS

Feeling too rushed to make a sweet treat? Keep your cool by preparing Winning Coffee Ice Cream Pie (page 201) ahead of time.

LEMON LOVERS

When life throws you lemons, make Lemon Chiffon Cake (page 208)! This luscious lemon dessert is just one of many that will have you sweet on citrus.

TREETOP TRIO

Ripe for the picking came Peaches and Cream Torte (page 216), a luscious dessert you'll want to serve all summer long.

HALLOWEEN SPOOKTACULAR

Scare up frightful fun for friends and family this Halloween. Spine-tingling Yummy Mummy with Veggie Dip (page 20) is the perfect ghoulish grub for a spooky celebration.

SANTA'S FAVORITE COOKIES

Double-Drizzle Pecan Cookies (page 188) snatched up the Grand Prize in this recipe contest packed with St. Nick's favorite cookie-tray delights.

GREATEST GIFT

Escape overcrowded shopping malls during the holiday season. Pecan Toffee Fudge (page 185) and other homemade gifts are as close as your kitchen...and guaranteed to warm hearts!

When you choose from the celebrated favorites in *Contest Winning Annual Recipes*, your meals just can't miss. So go ahead and select any scrumptious specialties you like to put on your own menus. One thing's for certain—every delectable dish you make for every occasion will be a true, honest-to-goodness winner!

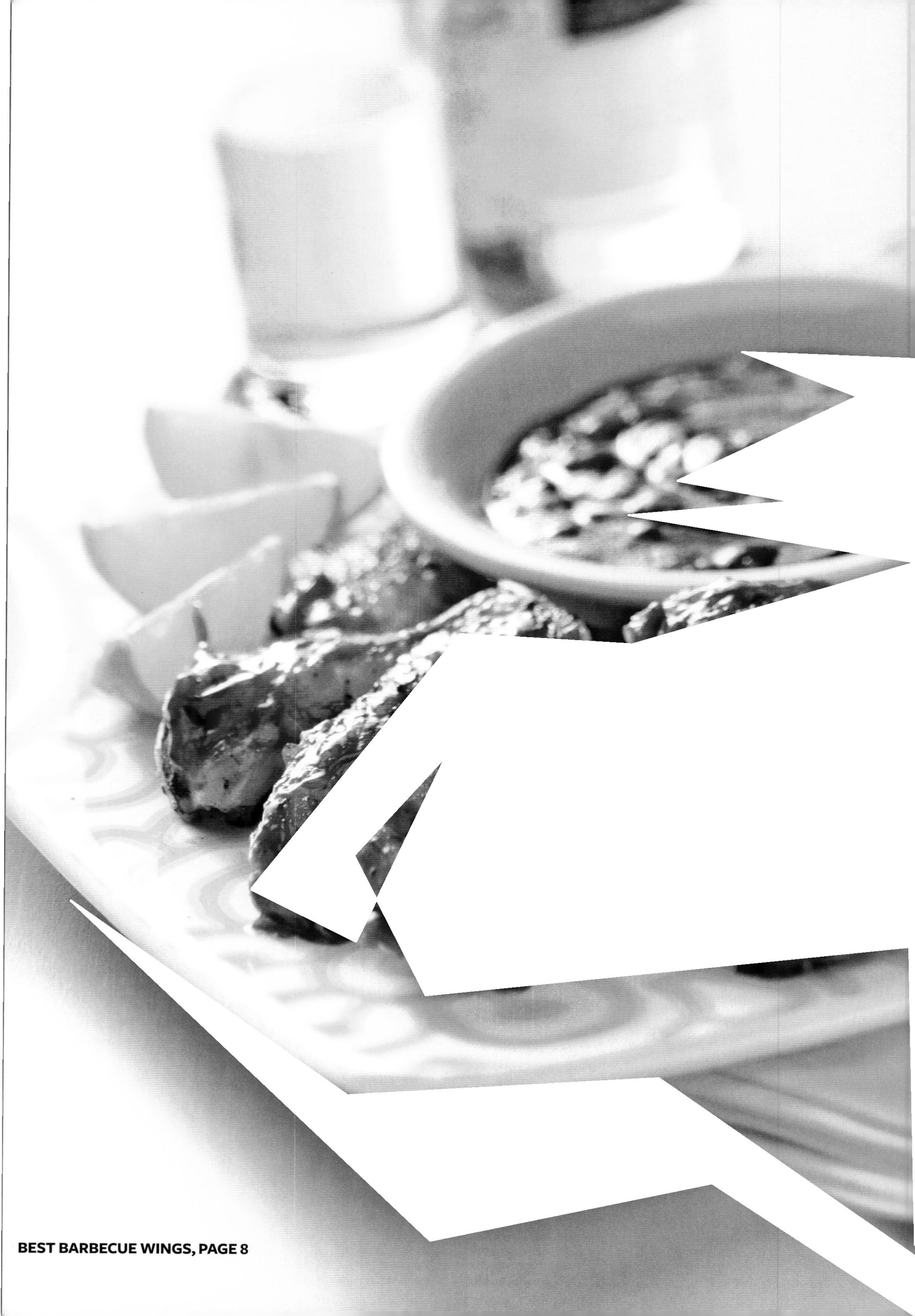

BEST BARBECUE WINGS, PAGE 8

Snacks & Appetizers

Look no further to **find all the best** in hot bites, finger foods, dips and spreads, munchies, beverages and more. These savory pop-in-your-mouth noshes are **quick, versatile and guaranteed** to be the hit of the party!

Best Barbecue Wings

My husband always calls this recipe finger lickin' good! The sweet-and-spicy flavor makes these wings stand apart from others. The sauce is also great on chicken breasts or burgers.

—LINDA GARDNER RICHMOND, VIRGINIA

PREP: 20 MIN. **GRILL:** 20 MIN. **MAKES:** 2½ DOZEN

- **½ cup finely chopped onion**
- **¼ cup canola oil**
- **3 teaspoons minced garlic**
- **1½ cups ketchup**
- **½ cup cider vinegar**
- **⅓ cup packed brown sugar**
- **⅓ cup Worcestershire sauce**
- **2 teaspoons chili powder**
- **½ teaspoon cayenne pepper**
- **½ teaspoon ground cumin**
- **⅛ teaspoon hot pepper sauce**

WINGS

- **¼ cup cider vinegar**
- **¼ cup olive oil**
- **⅛ teaspoon salt**
- **⅛ teaspoon pepper**
- **30 frozen chicken wingettes, thawed**

1. For barbecue sauce, in large saucepan, saute onion in oil until tender. Add garlic; cook 1 minute longer. Stir in the ketchup, vinegar, brown sugar, Worcestershire sauce, chili powder, cayenne and cumin. Simmer, uncovered, for 8-10 minutes, stirring often. Remove from the heat; stir in pepper sauce. Set aside ⅔ cup for serving.
2. In a large resealable plastic bag, combine vinegar, olive oil, salt and pepper; add chicken wings in batches and turn to coat.
3. Moisten a paper towel with cooking oil; using long-handled tongs, lightly coat the grill rack. Grill wings, covered, over medium heat or broil 4 in. from the heat for 12-16 minutes, turning occasionally. Brush with some of the barbecue sauce.
4. Grill, uncovered, 8-10 minutes longer or until juices run clear, basting and turning several times. Serve with reserved barbecue sauce.

Asian Turkey Lettuce Wraps

PREP/TOTAL TIME: 20 MIN. **MAKES:** 5 SERVINGS

- **1¼ pounds extra-lean ground turkey**
- **1 package (16 ounces) frozen stir-fry vegetable blend, thawed**
- **⅓ cup reduced-sodium teriyaki sauce**
- **¼ cup hoisin sauce**
- **3 tablespoons reduced-fat creamy peanut butter**
- **2 tablespoons minced fresh gingerroot**
- **1 tablespoon rice vinegar**
- **1 tablespoon sesame oil**
- **3 garlic cloves, minced**
- **4 green onions, chopped**
- **10 Boston lettuce leaves**
- **Additional hoisin sauce, optional**

1. In a large nonstick skillet coated with cooking spray, cook turkey over medium heat until no longer pink.
2. Coarsely chop stir-fry vegetables; add to the pan. Stir in the teriyaki sauce, hoisin sauce, peanut butter, ginger, vinegar and oil. Stir-fry over medium-high heat for 5 minutes. Add garlic; cook 1 minute longer.
3. Remove from the heat; stir in onions. Place a scant ½ cup turkey mixture on each lettuce leaf; fold lettuce over filling. Serve with additional hoisin sauce if desired.

Nutrition Facts: *2 wraps (calculated without additional hoisin sauce) equals 275 calories, 8 g fat (1 g saturated fat), 45 mg cholesterol, 686 mg sodium, 19 g carbohydrate, 4 g fiber, 34 g protein.*
Diabetic Exchanges: *3 lean meat, 1½ fat, 1 starch, 1 vegetable.*

"Chopped frozen veggies make these wraps a snap. Add some Asian chili sauce if you want to kick the spice level up a notch."

—SUSAN RILEY ALLEN, TEXAS

Corn Fritters with Caramelized Onion Jam

A friend's husband, who's a chef, came up with these light and fluffy fritters accompanied perfectly by a sweet-tart jam. I would never ask a chef to divulge his secrets, so I created my own version.
—KIM CUPO ALBANY, GEORGIA

PREP: 30 MIN. **COOK:** 15 MIN. **MAKES:** 2 DOZEN (¾ CUP JAM)

- **1 large sweet onion, halved and thinly sliced**
- **1 tablespoon olive oil**
- **2 teaspoons balsamic vinegar**
- **⅓ cup apple jelly**
- **⅓ cup canned diced tomatoes**
- **1 tablespoon tomato paste**
- **⅛ teaspoon curry powder**
- **⅛ teaspoon ground cinnamon**
- **Dash salt and pepper**

FRITTERS

- **2 cups biscuit/baking mix**
- **1 can (11 ounces) gold and white corn, drained**
- **2 eggs, lightly beaten**
- **½ cup 2% milk**
- **½ cup sour cream**
- **½ teaspoon salt**
- **Oil for frying**

1. In a small skillet, saute onion in oil until golden brown. Add vinegar; cook and stir for 2-3 minutes. Set aside.
2. In a small saucepan, combine the jelly, tomatoes, tomato paste, curry powder, cinnamon, salt and pepper. Cook over medium heat for 5-7 minutes or until heated through. Add onion mixture. Cook and stir for 3 minutes; set mixture aside and keep warm.
3. In a small bowl, combine the baking mix, corn, eggs, milk, sour cream and salt just until combined.
4. In a deep-fat fryer or electric skillet, heat oil to 375°. Drop batter by heaping tablespoonfuls, a few at a time, into hot oil; fry for 1½ minutes on each side or until golden brown. Drain on paper towels. Serve warm with jam.

Fruit Salsa with Cinnamon Tortilla Chips

If you are serious about getting your daily dose of fruit, then you'll love my deliciously fun—and addictive—way to do it! Paired with sweet homemade cinnamon tortilla chips, this bright red fruit salsa will be quickly gobbled up by your friends and family members. It's great not only as a delightful snack, but also as part of a brunch buffet. It is best eaten the day it is made.
—NANCY LEAVITT LOGANDALE, NEVADA

PREP: 20 MIN. + CHILLING **COOK:** 5 MIN./BATCH
MAKES: 6 CUPS SALSA AND 16 DOZEN TORTILLA STRIPS

- **1 pound fresh strawberries, finely chopped**
- **2 medium apples, peeled and finely chopped**
- **1 package (12 ounces) frozen unsweetened raspberries, thawed and well drained**
- **2 medium kiwifruit, peeled and finely chopped**
- **3 tablespoons peach or apricot preserves**
- **2 tablespoons sugar**
- **1 tablespoon brown sugar**

CINNAMON TORTILLA CHIPS

- **Oil for deep-fat frying**
- **10 flour tortillas (10 inches)**
- **½ cup sugar**
- **2 teaspoons ground cinnamon**

In a large bowl, combine the first seven ingredients; cover and chill for 20 minutes or until serving. In an electric skillet or deep-fat fryer, heat oil to 375°. Cut each tortilla in half; cut each half into 10 strips. Fry strips, a few at a time, until light golden brown on both sides. Drain on paper towels. Combine sugar and cinnamon; sprinkle over strips and toss to coat. Serve with salsa.

Nutrition Facts: *¼ cup salsa with 8 chips equals 166 calories, 4 g fat (1 g saturated fat), 0 cholesterol, 165 mg sodium, 28 g carbohydrate, 4 g fiber, 3 g protein.*

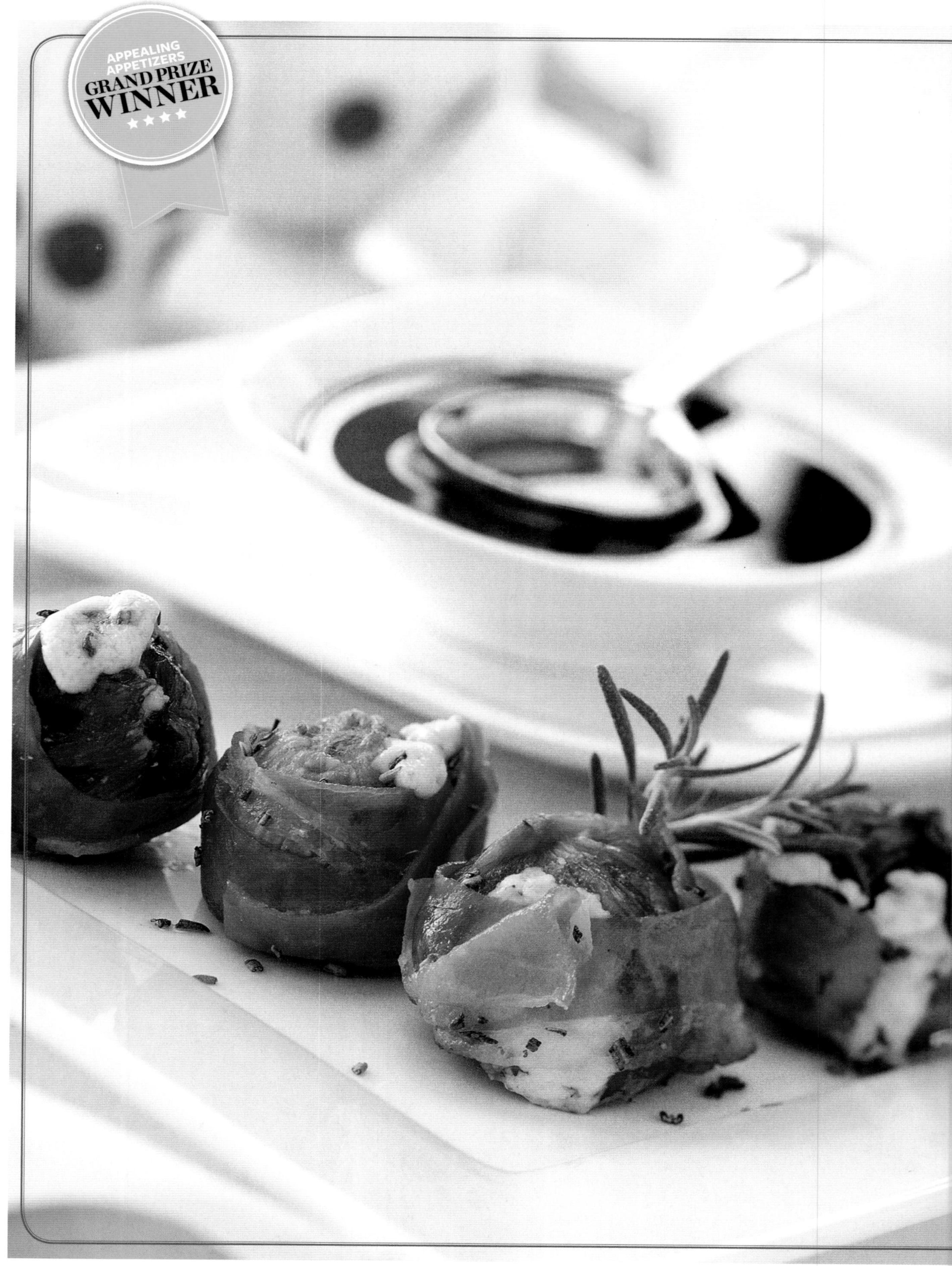
APPEALING APPETIZERS
GRAND PRIZE
WINNER

GRAND PRIZE

Gorgonzola Figs with Balsamic Glaze

For a fancy, eye-catching appetizer, try these delightful stuffed figs wrapped with prosciutto.

—SARAH VASQUES MILFORD, NEW HAMPSHIRE

PREP: 30 MIN. **BAKE:** 10 MIN. **MAKES:** 16 APPETIZERS

- **1 cup balsamic vinegar**
- **16 dried figs**
- **½ cup crumbled Gorgonzola cheese**
- **8 thin slices prosciutto, halved widthwise**
- **2 teaspoons minced fresh rosemary**
- **¼ teaspoon pepper**

1. For glaze, in a small saucepan, bring vinegar to a boil over medium heat; cook until reduced to about 1/4 cup.

2. Cut a lengthwise slit down the center of each fig; fill with 1 1/2 teaspoons cheese. Wrap each with a piece of prosciutto; place on a baking sheet. Sprinkle with rosemary and pepper.

3. Bake at 425° for 10-12 minutes or until prosciutto is crisp. Serve warm with glaze.

Editor's Note: *Amber-colored dried figs (labeled Turkish or Calimyrna) are recommended for this recipe. Mission figs, which are black, are smaller and hold less cheese. If large stems are present, remove them before stuffing figs.*

Nutrition Facts: *1 stuffed fig with 3/4 teaspoon glaze equals 90 calories, 2 g fat (1 g saturated fat), 9 mg cholesterol, 190 mg sodium, 15 g carbohydrate, 2 g fiber, 3 g protein.*

BALSAMIC VINEGAR

Balsamic vinegar is made from just-harvested sweet white grapes and aged in wooden barrels for at least 12 years, which is the main reason this ingredient carries a heavy price tag. Over the years, balsamic vinegar has gone from an exotic ingredient to a pantry staple. This Italian vinegar is a dark, thick, sweet-smelling liquid. When used in cooking, it adds a rich, dark color to the dish. When a dark color is undesirable, use white balsamic vinegar. Just like wine, the grapes, processing and aging method and aging time contribute to the cost of the vinegar. The higher-priced balsamic is best drizzled over cooked foods as a finishing touch. If you don't have balsamic vinegar on hand, you can substitute cider vinegar or a mild red wine vinegar. White wine vinegar can also be used, but it is much stronger and sharper and should be used sparingly if it's your only substitute.

Crab Crescent Loaf

Golden crescent roll slices are scrumptious filled with dilled cream cheese and tender crab. You're sure to appreciate the rich flavor and easy preparation.

—MAUREEN DONGOSKI PETERSBURG, WEST VIRGINIA

PREP: 20 MIN. **BAKE:** 20 MIN. **MAKES:** 1 LOAF (12 SLICES)

- **1 tube (8 ounces) refrigerated crescent rolls**
- **2 packages (3 ounces each) cream cheese, softened**
- **⅓ cup chopped onion**
- **½ teaspoon dill weed**
- **1 cup imitation crabmeat or 1 can (6 ounces) lump crabmeat, drained**
- **1 egg yolk, lightly beaten**

1. On a greased baking sheet, unroll crescent dough into one long rectangle; seal seams and perforations. In a small bowl, beat the cream cheese, onion and dill until blended. Spread mixture lengthwise over half of the dough to within 1/2 in. of edges. Top with crab.

2. Fold dough over filling; pinch seam to seal. Brush the top with egg yolk. Bake at 375° for 18-22 minutes or until golden brown. Cut into slices.

Smoked Salmon Cucumber Canapes

I make these tempting little canapes frequently for parties, showers, luncheons and family gatherings of all kinds. With their delicate smoked salmon flavor and refreshingly crisp cucumber crunch, the little bites disappear at an astonishing speed, so I usually double the recipe. This is one of those superstar recipes that is make-ahead convenient, but looks impressive.

—JUDY GREBETZ RACINE, WISCONSIN

PREP: 25 MIN. + CHILLING **MAKES:** ABOUT 3½ DOZEN

- **2 medium cucumbers, peeled**
- **4 ounces smoked salmon, flaked**
- **2 tablespoons lemon juice**
- **1 tablespoon finely chopped onion**
- **1 tablespoon capers, drained**
- **1 tablespoon minced fresh parsley**
- **½ teaspoon Dijon mustard**
- **⅛ teaspoon pepper**

1. Cut cucumbers in half lengthwise; remove and discard seeds. In a small bowl, combine the salmon, lemon juice, onion, capers, parsley, mustard and pepper. Spoon the filling into cucumber halves.

2. Wrap in plastic wrap. Refrigerate for 3-4 hours or until filling is firm. Cut into ½-in. slices.

Nutrition Facts: *1 each equals 6 calories, trace fat (trace saturated fat), 1 mg cholesterol, 27 mg sodium, 1 g carbohydrate, trace fiber, 1 g protein.* **Diabetic Exchanges:** *1 free food.*

Roasted Red Pepper Hummus

My son taught me how to make hummus, which is a great alternative to calorie-filled dips. This recipe is simply delicious. Fresh roasted red bell peppers make it really special.

—NANCY WATSON-PISTOLE SHAWNEE, KANSAS

PREP: 30 MIN. + STANDING **MAKES:** 3 CUPS

- **2 large sweet red peppers**
- **2 cans (15 ounces each) garbanzo beans or chickpeas, rinsed and drained**
- **⅓ cup lemon juice**
- **3 tablespoons tahini**
- **1 tablespoon olive oil**
- **2 garlic cloves, peeled**
- **1¼ teaspoons salt**
- **1 teaspoon curry powder**
- **½ teaspoon ground coriander**
- **½ teaspoon ground cumin**
- **½ teaspoon pepper**
- **Pita bread, warmed and cut into wedges, and reduced-fat wheat snack crackers**
- **Additional garbanzo beans or chickpeas, optional**

1. Broil red peppers 4 in. from the heat until skins blister, about 5 minutes. With tongs, rotate peppers a quarter turn. Broil and rotate until all sides are blistered and blackened. Immediately place peppers in a bowl; cover and let stand for 15-20 minutes.

2. Peel off and discard charred skin. Remove stems and seeds. Place the peppers in a food processor. Add the beans, lemon juice, tahini, oil, garlic and seasonings; cover and process until blended.

3. Transfer to a serving bowl. Serve with pita bread and crackers. Garnish with additional beans if desired.

Nutrition Facts: *¼ cup (calculated without pita bread, crackers or additional beans) equals 113 calories, 5 g fat (1 g saturated fat), 0 cholesterol, 339 mg sodium, 14 g carbohydrate, 4 g fiber, 4 g protein.* **Diabetic Exchanges:** *1 starch, 1 fat.*

Hot Chicken Swirls

I had some crescent rolls and leftover chicken breast I needed to use up, so I created this tasty appetizer. I use reduced- and fat-free ingredients to keep it light.

—EVELYN MCGINNIS BAY CITY, MICHIGAN

PREP: 25 MIN. **BAKE:** 10 MIN.
MAKES: 64 APPETIZERS

- **2 tubes (8 ounces each) refrigerated reduced-fat crescent rolls**
- **1 cup shredded cooked chicken breast**
- **4 ounces fat-free cream cheese**
- **¼ cup reduced-fat ranch salad dressing**
- **¼ cup shredded reduced-fat cheddar cheese**
- **¼ cup finely chopped sweet red pepper**
- **2 green onions, finely chopped**
- **2 tablespoons Louisiana-style hot sauce**

1. Separate each tube of crescent dough into four rectangles; gently press perforations to seal. In a small bowl, combine the remaining ingredients; spread evenly over rectangles. Roll up jelly-roll style, starting with a short side; pinch seams to seal.

2. Cut each into eight slices; place cut side down on ungreased baking sheets. Bake at 375° for 10-12 minutes or until golden brown. Refrigerate leftovers.

Nutrition Facts: *1 appetizer equals 34 calories, 2 g fat (trace saturated fat), 2 mg cholesterol, 82 mg sodium, 3 g carbohydrate, trace fiber, 2 g protein.* **Diabetic Exchange:** *1/2 starch.*

CHICKEN MADE EASY

If you don't have any leftover chicken breast on hand or just want to keep things simple, you can purchase fully-cooked refrigerated or frozen chicken breast strips and chop into pieces small enough for each chicken swirl. You can also use canned chicken or shred chicken from a deli rotisserie chicken. Leftover turkey also makes a great substitute for this hot and tasty appetizer.

Chesapeake Crab Dip

I rely on this mildly seasoned crab dip when hosting parties. It's a terrific time-saver when accompanied by celery sticks, crackers or your favorite raw veggies. It's so simple to prepare that it gives me time to get other appetizers ready or mingle with my guests.

—**CAROL BRZEZINSKI** MARRIOTTSVILLE, MARYLAND

PREP: 20 MIN. **BAKE:** 20 MIN. **MAKES:** 2¼ CUPS

- **1 package (8 ounces) cream cheese, softened**
- **1 cup (8 ounces) sour cream**
- **1 tablespoon lemon juice**
- **1 teaspoon ground mustard**
- **1 teaspoon seafood seasoning**
- **⅛ teaspoon garlic salt**
- **3 cans (6 ounces each) lump crabmeat, drained**
- **½ cup shredded cheddar cheese**
- **⅛ teaspoon paprika**
- **Assorted crackers**

1. In a large bowl, combine the cream cheese, sour cream, lemon juice, mustard, seafood seasoning and garlic salt. Fold in crab. Transfer to a greased 9-in. pie plate. Sprinkle with cheese and paprika.

2. Bake at 325° for 20-25 minutes or until bubbly. Serve warm with crackers. Refrigerate leftovers.

"Chill out with this delightful cooler, perfect for springtime bridal showers or hot summer days on the deck. It's a quick fix you'll stir up time after time."

—**JODI BLUBAUGH** EAGLE MOUNTAIN, UTAH

Sparkling Ginger Lemonade

PREP: 20 MIN. + COOLING **MAKES:** 5 SERVINGS

- **2 cups water**
- **1 cup honey**
- **2 tablespoons minced fresh gingerroot**
- **2 cups club soda, chilled**
- **1 cup lemon juice**

1. In a small saucepan, bring the water, honey and ginger to a boil. Remove from the heat; cover and steep for 10 minutes. Strain, discarding ginger. Cool.

2. Transfer to a pitcher; stir in soda and lemon juice. Serve immediately over ice.

Grilled Corn Salsa

Grilling the veggies gives this summery salsa notes of sweetness and smoke. As an option, make the salsa and refrigerate overnight for even more flavor.

—TERI KMAN LAPORTE, COLORADO

PREP: 30 MIN. **GRILL:** 30 MIN. + CHILLING **MAKES:** 7½ CUPS

- **8 medium ears sweet corn, husks removed**
- **2 small yellow summer squash, cut into ½-inch slices**
- **1 medium sweet red pepper, cut into four wedges**
- **1 medium red onion, cut into ½-inch rings**
- **1 medium tomato, seeded and chopped**

BASIL VINAIGRETTE

- **½ cup olive oil**
- **⅓ cup white balsamic or cider vinegar**
- **12 fresh basil leaves, chopped**
- **1 teaspoon salt**
- **1 teaspoon garlic powder**
- **1 teaspoon dried oregano**

1. Fill a soup kettle two-thirds full with water; bring to a boil. Add corn. Reduce heat; cover and simmer for 5 minutes or until crisp-tender. Remove corn; cool slightly.

2. Moisten a paper towel with cooking oil; using long-handled tongs, lightly coat the grill rack. Grill the corn, squash, red pepper and onion, covered, over medium heat for 8-10 minutes or until lightly browned, turning occasionally.

3. Cut corn from cobs; cut the squash, red pepper and onion into bite-size pieces. Place vegetables in a large bowl; add tomato.

4. In a small bowl, whisk the vinaigrette ingredients. Pour over vegetables; toss to coat. Cover and refrigerate until chilled. Serve with a slotted spoon.

Garlic-Onion Appetizer Rounds

This recipe is the perfect way to showcase our famous, local Maui sweet onions, which thrive in our balmy tropical climate and rich, volcanic soils. I know you'll love this appetizer, too.

—KRISTINE SNYDER KIHEI, HAWAII

PREP: 30 MIN. + COOLING **BAKE:** 15 MIN. **MAKES:** 16 APPETIZERS

- **2 large sweet onions, chopped (about 4 cups)**
- **2 tablespoons butter**
- **2 garlic cloves, minced**
- **1 sheet frozen puff pastry, thawed**
- **1 egg**
- **1 tablespoon water**
- **⅓ cup shredded Swiss cheese**
- **¼ cup grated Parmesan cheese**
- **2 tablespoons minced fresh basil**

1. In a large skillet over medium-low heat, cook onions in butter until golden brown, stirring frequently. Add garlic; cook 1 minute longer. Remove from the heat; cool to room temperature.

2. Unfold puff pastry. In a small bowl, whisk egg and water; brush over pastry. Spread onion mixture to within ½ in. of edges. Sprinkle with cheeses and basil; roll up jelly-roll style. Cut into 16 slices.

3. Place 2 in. apart on greased baking sheets. Bake at 425° for 12-14 minutes or until puffed and golden brown. Serve warm.

Crab Wonton Cups

These tasty little crab tarts make excellent appetizers served warm and crispy from the oven. You can add them to your list of holiday finger foods as well. They're true crowd-pleasers.

—CONNIE MCDOWELL
GREENWOOD, DELAWARE

PREP/TOTAL TIME: 30 MIN.
MAKES: 32 APPETIZERS

- **32 wonton wrappers**
- **Cooking spray**
- **1 package (8 ounces) cream cheese, softened**
- **½ cup heavy whipping cream**
- **1 egg**
- **1 tablespoon Dijon mustard**
- **1 teaspoon Worcestershire sauce**
- **5 drops hot pepper sauce**
- **1 cup lump crabmeat, drained**
- **¼ cup thinly sliced green onions**
- **¼ cup finely chopped sweet red pepper**
- **1 cup grated Parmesan cheese**

1. Press wonton wrappers into miniature muffin cups coated with cooking spray. Spritz wrappers with cooking spray. Bake at 350° for 8-9 minutes or until lightly browned.

2. Meanwhile, in a small bowl, beat the cream cheese, cream, egg, mustard, Worcestershire sauce and pepper sauce until smooth. Stir in the crab, green onions and red pepper; spoon into wonton cups. Sprinkle with Parmesan cheese.

3. Bake for 10-12 minutes or until filling is heated through. Serve warm. Refrigerate leftovers.

Nutrition Facts: *1 appetizer equals 77 calories, 5 g fat (3 g saturated fat), 26 mg cholesterol, 153 mg sodium, 5 g carbohydrate, trace fiber, 3 g protein.* **Diabetic Exchanges:** *1 fat, ½ starch.*

IMITATION CRAB

Substitute imitation crabmeat in this recipe if you like. Imitation crabmeat, also called surimi, is fish that is shaped, flavored and colored to resemble crab. It is typically made from Alaskan pollock, a lean firm fish with a delicate flavor. Both natural and artificial flavors are used as well as artificial coloring.

Grilled Corn Dip

Great for summer, this savory appetizer is a must-have on weekend family gatherings at our cottage on Sandusky Bay. It's well worth the time it takes to grill the corn and cut it from the cob.

—CATHY MYERS VICKERY, OHIO

PREP: 30 MIN. **BAKE:** 25 MIN. **MAKES:** 5 CUPS

- **6 medium ears sweet corn, husks removed**
- **1 large onion, chopped**
- **1 jalapeno pepper, finely chopped**
- **2 tablespoons butter**
- **2 garlic cloves, minced**
- **1 cup mayonnaise**
- **½ cup sour cream**
- **½ teaspoon chili powder**
- **2 cups (8 ounces) shredded Monterey Jack cheese**
- **1 can (2¼ ounces) sliced ripe olives, drained**
- **2 tablespoons sliced green onions**
- **Tortilla chips**

1. Grill corn, covered, over medium heat for 10-12 minutes or until tender, turning occasionally.

2. Cut corn from cobs. In a large skillet, saute the onion and jalapeno in butter for 2-3 minutes or until almost tender. Add corn and garlic; saute 1-2 minutes longer or until vegetables are tender. Remove from the heat.

3. In a large bowl, combine the mayonnaise, sour cream and chili powder. Stir in cheese and corn mixture. Transfer to a greased 2-qt. baking dish.

4. Bake, uncovered, at 400° for 25-30 minutes or until bubbly and golden brown. Sprinkle with olives and green onions; serve with chips.

Editor's Note: *Wear disposable gloves when cutting hot peppers; the oils can burn skin. Avoid touching your face.*

Brie Cherry Pastry Cups

Puff pastry from the freezer section hurries along these bite-size golden cups filled with creamy Brie and sweet cherry preserves. They look fancy and taste delicious but are a snap to put together for a special occasion. They also make a delightful mini dessert.

—MARILYN MCSWEEN MENTOR, OHIO

PREP/TOTAL TIME: 30 MIN. **MAKES:** 3 DOZEN

- **1 sheet frozen puff pastry, thawed**
- **½ cup cherry preserves**
- **4 ounces Brie cheese, cut into ½-inch cubes**
- **¼ cup chopped pecans or walnuts**
- **2 tablespoons minced chives**

1. Unfold puff pastry; cut into 36 squares. Gently press squares onto the bottoms of 36 greased miniature muffin cups.

2. Bake at 375° for 10 minutes. Using the end of a wooden spoon handle, make a ½-in.-deep indentation in the center of each. Bake 6-8 minutes longer or until golden brown. With spoon handle, press squares down again.

3. Spoon a rounded ½ teaspoonful of preserves into each cup. Top with cheese; sprinkle with nuts and chives. Bake for 3-5 minutes or until cheese is melted.

Nutrition Facts: *1 appetizer equals 61 calories, 3 g fat (1 g saturated fat), 3 mg cholesterol, 42 mg sodium, 7 g carbohydrate, 1 g fiber, 1 g protein.*

Santa Fe Deviled Eggs

My deviled eggs boast a zippy Southwestern flair. The smoky, spicy flavor is a hit with my husband, and the recipe is sized just right for a twosome, so it's one we indulge in often.

—**PATRICIA HARMON** BADEN, PENNSYLVANIA

PREP/TOTAL TIME: 15 MIN. **MAKES:** 2 SERVINGS

- **2 hard-cooked eggs**
- **1 tablespoon mayonnaise**
- **1 tablespoon canned chopped green chilies**
- **½ teaspoon chipotle pepper in adobo sauce**
- **⅛ teaspoon garlic salt**
- **4 teaspoons salsa**
- **1½ teaspoons thinly sliced green onion**
- **1 pitted ripe olive, quartered**

1. Cut eggs in half lengthwise. Remove yolks; set whites aside. In a small bowl, mash yolks. Stir in the mayonnaise, chilies, chipotle pepper and garlic salt. Stuff or pipe into egg whites.
2. Top with salsa, onion and an olive piece. Refrigerate eggs until serving.

FUSS-FREE DEVILED EGGS

To make easy work of filling a batch of deviled eggs, first prepare the yolk mixture and allow it to chill for several minutes in the refrigerator. Then use a small cookie scoop to fill the egg white halves. This simple, quick method yields attractive rounded tops on the deviled eggs and cleanup is a breeze.

Chicken Salad Caprese

This unique, flavorful salad and French baguette combo will earn you rave reviews—guaranteed!

—**FRANCES PIETSCH** FLOWER MOUND, TEXAS

PREP: 40 MIN. **BAKE:** 5 MIN.
MAKES: 8 CUPS SALAD (6-½ DOZEN CROSTINI)

- **2 cups shredded rotisserie chicken**
- **1 pound fresh mozzarella cheese, cubed**
- **2 cups grape tomatoes, halved**
- **1 can (14 ounces) water-packed artichoke hearts, rinsed, drained and coarsely chopped**
- **½ cup pitted Greek olives, thinly sliced**
- **¼ cup minced fresh basil**
- **¼ cup olive oil**
- **2 garlic cloves, minced**
- **½ teaspoon salt**
- **½ teaspoon coarsely ground pepper**

TOMATO CROSTINI:

- **2 French bread baguettes (10-½ ounces each)**
- **4 garlic cloves**
- **2 small tomatoes**
- **¼ cup olive oil**
- **1 teaspoon salt**

1. In a large bowl, combine the first six ingredients. In a small bowl, whisk the oil, garlic, salt and pepper; drizzle over chicken mixture and toss to coat. Refrigerate until serving.
2. Cut baguettes into ½-in. slices. Place on ungreased baking sheets. Bake at 425° for 2-4 minutes or until lightly browned. Cut garlic in half lengthwise; rub over bread. Cut tomatoes into quarters; rub over bread. Brush with oil and sprinkle with salt. Bake 2-3 minutes longer or until crisp. Serve crostini with chicken salad.

Nutrition Facts: *¼ cup salad with 2 or 3 crostini equals 179 calories, 10 g fat (3 g saturated fat), 19 mg cholesterol, 316 mg sodium, 16 g carbohydrate, 1 g fiber, 7 g protein.*

Stromboli Slices

PREP/TOTAL TIME: 25 MIN. **MAKES:** 1½ DOZEN

- **1 tube (11 ounces) refrigerated crusty French loaf**
- **2 tablespoons olive oil**
- **½ teaspoon dried basil**
- **1 package (3½ ounces) sliced pepperoni**
- **2 cups (8 ounces) shredded part-skim mozzarella cheese**
- **1 cup meatless spaghetti sauce, warmed**

1. Unroll loaf of dough at the seam into a square; cut in half. Combine oil and basil; brush lengthwise down half of each rectangle to within ½ in. of edges. Layer brushed side with pepperoni and cheese. Fold plain dough over filling and pinch edges to seal. Place on greased baking sheets.
2. Bake at 350° for 10-15 minutes or until golden brown. Cut into slices. Serve warm with spaghetti sauce.

"I've served this dish to teens, college students and a women's group. Everyone has loved it, and many people have asked for the recipe. Easy and delicious, it's sure to please your party guests!"

—**RACHEL JACKSON** PENNSVILLE, NEW JERSEY

Crab-Stuffed Jalapenos

These are always a hit when my husband and I bring them to parties. They're especially great for sporting events and always seem to complement the other food being served.

—**SUSAN DUGAT** ABILENE, TEXAS

PREP: 25 MIN. **BAKE:** 40 MIN. **MAKES:** 2 DOZEN

- **24 large jalapeno peppers**
- **6 ounces fat-free cream cheese**
- **2 teaspoons Worcestershire sauce**
- **¼ teaspoon garlic powder**
- **1 package (8 ounces) imitation crabmeat, chopped**
- **¼ cup shredded reduced-fat cheddar cheese**
- **12 turkey bacon strips, halved widthwise**

1. Cut stems off jalapenos; remove seeds and membranes; set aside. In a small bowl, beat the cream cheese, Worcestershire sauce and garlic powder until blended. Stir in crab and cheese.
2. Transfer to a resealable plastic bag; cut a small hole in a corner of the bag. Pipe filling into jalapenos. Wrap each with a piece of bacon; secure with toothpicks.
3. Place on an ungreased baking sheet. Bake at 350° for 40-50 minutes or until peppers are crisp-tender.

Editor's Note: *Wear disposable gloves when cutting hot peppers; the oils can burn skin. Avoid touching your face.*

Nutrition Facts: *1 stuffed pepper equals 41 calories, 2 g fat (1 g saturated fat), 9 mg cholesterol, 188 mg sodium, 3 g carbohydrate, trace fiber, 3 g protein.* **Diabetic Exchange:** *½ lean meat.*

Zucchini Salsa

I received this recipe through a friend at a weight-loss group. I like to serve it with bratwurst or other grilled meats. People love it!

—CHERYL JACOBSEN WARBURG, ALBERTA

PREP: 35 MIN. **COOK:** 45 MIN. + CHILLING **MAKES:** 7 CUPS

- **5 cups shredded zucchini (about 5 medium)**
- **4 medium tomatoes, peeled, seeded and chopped**
- **2 medium onions, chopped**
- **2 medium green peppers, chopped**
- **1 small sweet red pepper, chopped**
- **½ cup packed brown sugar**
- **1 jalapeno pepper, seeded and finely chopped**
- **1 cup white vinegar**
- **1 can (8 ounces) tomato sauce**
- **2 tablespoons tomato paste**
- **3 garlic cloves, minced**
- **3 teaspoons ground mustard**
- **2¼ teaspoons salt**
- **¾ teaspoon crushed red pepper flakes**
- **½ teaspoon garlic powder**
- **½ teaspoon each ground cumin, nutmeg and turmeric**
- **½ teaspoon pepper**

1. In a Dutch oven, combine all ingredients. Bring to a boil. Reduce heat; simmer, uncovered, for 40-50 minutes or until thickened, stirring occasionally.

2. Cool to room temperature. Cover and refrigerate until chilled. Serve with your favorite snack chips or grilled meats.

Editor's Note: *Wear disposable gloves when cutting hot peppers; the oils can burn skin. Avoid touching your face.*

Nutrition Facts: *¼ cup equals 35 calories, trace fat (trace saturated fat), 0 cholesterol, 233 mg sodium, 8 g carbohydrate, 1 g fiber, 1 g protein.* **Diabetic Exchange:** *½ starch.*

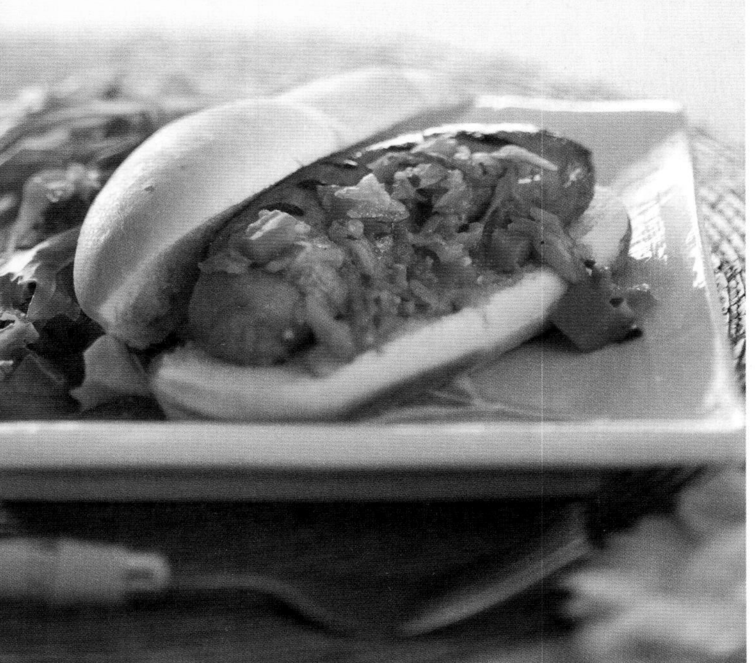

GRAND PRIZE

Yummy Mummy with Veggie Dip

While dressing up a veggie tray for our annual Halloween party, I came up with this idea—and everyone got "wrapped up" in it. Frozen bread dough and dip mix make it a simple and easy appetizer that's as much fun to display as it is to eat!

—HEATHER SNOW SALT LAKE CITY, UTAH

PREP: 25 MIN. **BAKE:** 20 MIN. + COOLING
MAKES: 16 SERVINGS (2 CUPS DIP)

- **1 loaf (1 pound) frozen bread dough, thawed**
- **3 pieces string cheese**
- **2 cups (16 ounces) sour cream**
- **1 envelope fiesta ranch dip mix**
- **1 pitted ripe olive**
- **Assorted crackers and fresh vegetables**

1. Let dough rise according to package directions. Place dough on a greased baking sheet. For mummy, roll out dough into a 12-in. oval that is narrower at the bottom. For the neck, make an indentation on each side, about 1 in. down from the top. Let rise in a warm place for 20 minutes.

2. Bake at 350° for 20-25 minutes or until golden brown. Arrange strips of string cheese over bread; bake 1-2 minutes longer or until cheese is melted. Remove from pan to a wire rack to cool.

3. Meanwhile, in a small bowl, combine sour cream and dip mix. Chill until serving.

4. Cut the mummy in half horizontally. Hollow out the bottom half, leaving a ¾-in. shell. Cut removed bread into cubes; set aside. Place bread bottom on a serving plate. Spoon dip into shell. Replace top. For eyes, cut olive and position on head. Serve with crackers, vegetables and reserved bread cubes.

FROZEN BREAD DOUGH

A fuss-free alternative to homemade dough, frozen bread dough will help you turn out eye-catching and creative breads in no time flat. Be sure the frozen dough is completely thawed before shaping the mummy and baking. It typically takes 4 to 5 hours for frozen bread dough to defrost to room temperature. Thawed bread dough should be soft, warm and pliable before it's rolled out. If the dough springs back when rolled, cover and let it rest 15 minutes longer. You can also hold the dough in place for a few seconds when rolling to help it retain the desired shape.

HALLOWEEN
SPOOKTACULAR
GRAND PRIZE
WINNER

Ghoul Punch

PREP: 10 MIN. + FREEZING **MAKES:** 32 SERVINGS (6 QUARTS)

- **12 gummy spiders**
- **1 vinyl glove**
- **1 gallon tropical fruit punch, chilled**
- **2 liters lemon-lime soda, chilled**
- **1 quart raspberry sherbet**

1. Pour water into an ice cube tray; add a gummy spider to each of 12 compartments. Freeze for at least 4 hours. Fill glove with water; tie or seal and freeze for at least 4 hours.
2. In a 7-qt. punch bowl, combine punch and soda. Add sherbet and ice cubes. Remove glove from hand-shaped ice; add to punch. Serve immediately.

Nutrition Facts: *3/4 cup equals 133 calories, trace fat (trace saturated fat), 0 cholesterol, 32 mg sodium, 33 g carbohydrate, 1 g fiber, trace protein.*

"My son's birthday falls close to Halloween, so I make this punch for his party every year. It's always a huge hit with the kids—especially the hand-shaped ice and gummy spiders!"

—**KATHERYN SIPOS** CANON CITY, COLORADO

Bloodshot Eyeballs

Keep your eyes peeled for fun with these deviled eggs full of flavor and crowd appeal. They make the perfect appetizer for a kids' party. For the best presentation, serve these little gems within 2 hours of preparing them.

—**BERNICE JANOWSKI** STEVENS POINT, WISCONSIN

PREP: 40 MIN. + STANDING **MAKES:** 1 DOZEN

- **6 eggs**
- **3 cups hot water**
- **2 tablespoons red food coloring**
- **1 tablespoon white vinegar**
- **1/3 cup mayonnaise**
- **1/4 cup chopped green onions**
- **2 tablespoons minced fresh cilantro**
- **2 teaspoons Dijon mustard**
- **12 sliced ripe olives**
- **1 teaspoon ketchup**

1. Place eggs in a single layer in a large saucepan; add enough cold water to cover by 1 in. Cover and bring to a boil over high heat. Remove from the heat; cover and let stand for 15 minutes. Place in ice water until completely cooled. Gently crack eggs (do not peel).
2. In a large bowl, combine 3 cups hot water, food coloring and vinegar. Add eggs. (If eggs are not completely covered by colored water, add more hot water.) Let stand for 30 minutes. Remove eggs with a slotted spoon; peel.
3. Cut eggs in half widthwise. Place yolks in a small bowl; set whites aside. Mash yolks with a fork; stir in the mayonnaise, onions, cilantro and mustard.
4. To level egg white halves, cut a small slice from the bottom of each; place on a serving platter. Pipe or stuff yolk mixture into center of whites. Place an olive slice on each; fill olives with ketchup. Refrigerate until serving. This recipe is best eaten the day it is prepared.

Nutrition Facts: *1 eyeball equals 83 calories, 7 g fat (1 g saturated fat), 108 mg cholesterol, 104 mg sodium, 1 g carbohydrate, trace fiber, 3 g protein.*

Ogre Eyes Hot Cocoa

Here's looking at you! Halloween guests of all ages will get a kick out of this eerie "vision" staring back at them. It couldn't be easier to make—thanks to the simple recipe.

—JEANNIE KLUGH LANCASTER, PENNSYLVANIA

PREP/TOTAL TIME: 25 MIN. **MAKES:** 8 SERVINGS

- **8 cups milk, divided**
- **1 cup mint chocolate chips**
- **1 cup instant hot cocoa mix**
- **16 large marshmallows**
- **16 Crows candies**
- **16 lollipop sticks**

1. In a large saucepan, combine 1 cup milk, chocolate chips and cocoa mix. Cook and stir over low heat until chips are melted. Stir in remaining milk; heat through.

2. Meanwhile, cut a slit in top of each marshmallow; insert a candy. Carefully insert a lollipop stick through the bottom of each marshmallow and into each candy.

3. Pour hot cocoa into mugs or cups; place two prepared marshmallows in each cup. Serve immediately.

Editor's Note: *If mint chocolate chips are not available, place 2 cups (12 ounces) semisweet chocolate chips and 1/4 teaspoon peppermint extract in a plastic bag; seal and toss to coat. Allow chips to stand for 24-48 hours.*

Nutrition Facts: *1 cup hot cocoa with 2 prepared marshmallows equals 396 calories, 17 g fat (10 g saturated fat), 24 mg cholesterol, 265 mg sodium, 57 g carbohydrate, 2 g fiber, 10 g protein.*

Crunchy Monster Claws

Cajun seasoning adds flavor, and a crunchy coating helps keep these chicken fingers moist and tender. This recipe makes a great appetizer to serve at any Halloween gathering. It'll "grab" the attention of party guests in a hurry!

—MARY ANN DELL PHOENIXVILLE, PENNSYLVANIA

PREP/TOTAL TIME: 30 MIN. **MAKES:** 15 APPETIZERS

- **1 small sweet yellow pepper**
- **2 tablespoons all-purpose flour**
- **2 teaspoons plus 1 tablespoon Cajun seasoning, divided**
- **3 eggs, lightly beaten**
- **1½ cups cornflake crumbs**
- **2 tablespoons chopped green onion**
- **1 pound boneless skinless chicken breasts, cut lengthwise into ¾-inch strips**
- **Barbecue sauce**

1. Cut yellow pepper into 15 triangles; set aside. In a large resealable plastic bag, combine flour and 2 teaspoons Cajun seasoning. Place eggs in a shallow bowl. In another shallow bowl, combine the cornflake crumbs, green onion and remaining Cajun seasoning.

2. Place a few pieces of chicken in bag; seal and shake to coat. Dip in eggs, then in crumb mixture. Place on a greased baking sheet. Repeat. Bake at 350° for 15-20 minutes or until juices run clear.

3. Cut a small slit into one end of each chicken strip; insert a pepper triangle into each. Serve with barbecue sauce.

Nutrition Facts: *1 claw (calculated without barbecue sauce) equals 58 calories, 1 g fat (trace saturated fat), 42 mg cholesterol, 150 mg sodium, 4 g carbohydrate, trace fiber, 7 g protein.* **Diabetic Exchanges:** *1 lean meat, 1 vegetable.*

Beef-Stuffed Crescents

These hand-held bundles are easy to make and require only six ingredients. I've made them for potlucks and family gatherings—and I never have leftovers!

—JENNIFER BUMGARNER TOPEKA, KANSAS

PREP: 25 MIN. **BAKE:** 15 MIN.
MAKES: 2 DOZEN

- **1 pound ground beef**
- **1 can (4 ounces) chopped green chilies**
- **1 package (8 ounces) cream cheese, cubed**
- **¼ teaspoon ground cumin**
- **¼ teaspoon chili powder**
- **3 tubes (8 ounces each) refrigerated crescent rolls**

1. In a large skillet, cook beef and chilies over medium heat until meat is no longer pink; drain. Add the cream cheese, cumin and chili powder. Cool slightly.

2. Separate crescent dough into 24 triangles. Place 1 tablespoon of beef mixture along the short end of each triangle; carefully roll up.

3. Place point side down 2 in. apart on ungreased baking sheets. Bake at 375° for 11-14 minutes or until golden brown. Serve warm.

GROUND BEEF

Ground beef is often labeled using the cut of meat that it is ground from, such as ground chuck or ground round. (Ground beef comes from a combination of beef cuts.) Ground beef can also be labeled according to the fat content of the ground mixture or the percentage of lean meat to fat, such as 85% or 90% lean. The higher the percentage, the leaner the meat. Select ground beef that is bright red in color and is in a tightly sealed package. Purchase all ground beef before the "sell by" date. Purchase the amount you need: 1 pound of ground beef serves 3 to 4. Handle the mixture as little as possible when shaping hamburgers, meat loaves or meatballs to keep the final product light in texture.

Cranberry Turkey Crostini

I wasn't quite sure what to expect when I made these, but they're fantastic! The jalapenos balance out the other ingredients perfectly. If you don't have shaved turkey, shaved chicken works just as well.

—BRIDGETTA EALY PONTIAC, MICHIGAN

PREP: 30 MIN. + CHILLING **MAKES:** 2½ DOZEN

- **1 package (12 ounces) fresh or frozen cranberries**
- **1 medium tangerine, peeled and seeded**
- **½ cup red wine vinegar**
- **¼ cup chopped shallots**
- **½ cup sugar**
- **¼ cup chopped seeded jalapeno peppers**
- **¼ teaspoon pepper**
- **30 slices French bread (¼ inch thick)**
- **Cooking spray**
- **1 package (8 ounces) reduced-fat cream cheese**
- **½ pound shaved deli smoked turkey**

1. Place cranberries and tangerine in a food processor; cover and process until coarsely chopped. Set aside.

2. In a small saucepan, bring vinegar and shallots to a boil. Reduce heat; simmer, uncovered, for 5 minutes or until mixture is reduced to 1/3 cup, stirring occasionally. Stir in the sugar, jalapenos, pepper and reserved cranberry mixture. Cook for 5 minutes over medium heat, stirring frequently. Transfer to a small bowl; refrigerate until chilled.

3. Place bread on ungreased baking sheets; lightly spray bread on both sides with cooking spray. Broil 3-4 in. from the heat for 1-2 minutes on each side or until lightly browned. Spread each slice with 1½ teaspoons cream cheese; top with turkey and 1 tablespoon cranberry mixture.

Editor's Note: *Wear disposable gloves when cutting hot peppers; the oils can burn skin. Avoid touching your face.*

Nutrition Facts: *1 appetizer equals 79 calories, 3 g fat (1 g saturated fat), 8 mg cholesterol, 131 mg sodium, 11 g carbohydrate, 1 g fiber, 3 g protein.* **Diabetic Exchanges:** *1 starch, ½ fat.*

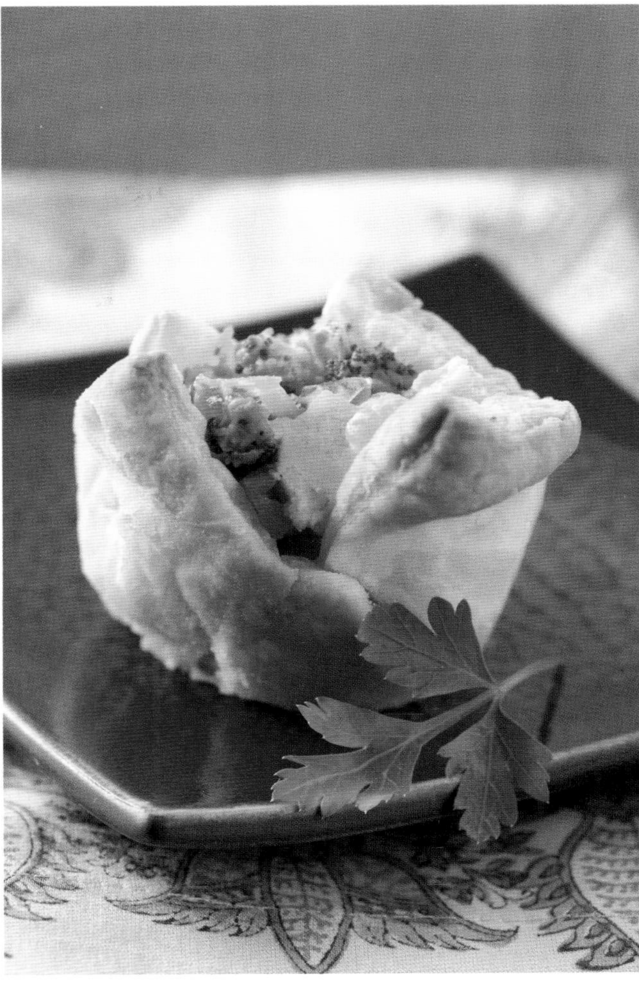

Broccoli Chicken Cups

Frozen puff pastry makes these rich and creamy appetizers a snap to prepare. Sometimes, instead of chopping the tomatoes, I put a slice on top of each cup before popping them in the oven.

—MARTY KINGERY POINT PLEASANT, WEST VIRGINIA

PREP: 15 MIN. **BAKE:** 25 MIN. **MAKES:** 1 DOZEN

- **2½ cups diced cooked chicken breast**
- **1 can (10¾ ounces) reduced-fat reduced-sodium condensed cream of chicken soup, undiluted**
- **1 cup frozen chopped broccoli, thawed and drained**
- **2 small plum tomatoes, seeded and chopped**
- **1 small carrot, grated**
- **1 tablespoon Dijon mustard**
- **1 garlic clove, minced**
- **¼ teaspoon pepper**
- **1 sheet frozen puff pastry, thawed**
- **¼ cup grated Parmesan cheese**

1. In a large bowl, combine the first eight ingredients; set aside. On a lightly floured surface, roll pastry into a 12-in. x 9-in. rectangle. Cut lengthwise into four strips and widthwise into three strips. Gently press puff pastry squares into muffin cups coated with cooking spray.

2. Spoon chicken mixture into pastry cups. Sprinkle with Parmesan. Bake at 375° for 25-30 minutes or until golden brown. Serve warm.

Southwest Spanakopita Bites

I'm a big fan of the Southwest-style egg rolls served at restaurants and wanted to re-create them without the fat of deep frying. Phyllo dough was the solution! If you want to try this for a main dish, simply fill small flour tortillas with the filling and bake.

—MARIANNE SHIRA OSCEOLA, WISCONSIN

PREP: 40 MIN. **BAKE:** 10 MIN.
MAKES: 2 DOZEN (½ CUP SAUCE)

- **2 tablespoons finely chopped sweet red pepper**
- **1 green onion, finely chopped**
- **1 teaspoon canola oil**
- **1 package (10 ounces) frozen chopped spinach, thawed and squeezed dry**
- **¾ cup shredded reduced-fat Monterey Jack cheese or Mexican cheese blend**
- **½ cup frozen corn, thawed**
- **½ cup canned black beans, rinsed and drained**
- **1 tablespoon chopped seeded jalapeno pepper**
- **½ teaspoon ground cumin**
- **½ teaspoon chili powder**
- **¼ teaspoon salt**
- **8 sheets phyllo dough (14 inches x 9 inches)**
- **Butter-flavored cooking spray**

SAUCE

- **⅓ cup cubed avocado**
- **¼ cup reduced-fat mayonnaise**
- **¼ cup reduced-fat sour cream**
- **1½ teaspoons white vinegar**

1. In a small skillet, saute red pepper and onion in oil until tender. Transfer to a large bowl; stir in ½ cup spinach (save the rest for another use). Stir in the cheese, corn, beans, jalapeno, cumin, chili powder and salt.

2. Place one sheet of phyllo dough on a work surface with a short end facing you. (Keep remaining phyllo covered with plastic wrap to prevent it from drying out.) Spray sheet with butter-flavored spray; cut into three 14-in. x 3-in. strips.

3. Place a scant tablespoon of filling on lower corner of each strip. Fold dough over filling, forming a triangle. Fold triangle up, then over, forming another triangle. Continue folding, like a flag, until you come to the end of the strip.

4. Spritz end of dough with spray and press onto triangle to seal. Turn triangle and spritz top with spray. Repeat with remaining phyllo and filling.

5. Place triangles on baking sheets coated with cooking spray. Bake at 375° for 10-12 minutes or until golden brown. Meanwhile, mash avocado with the mayonnaise, sour cream and vinegar. Serve with warm appetizers.

Editor's Note: *Wear disposable gloves when cutting hot peppers; the oils can burn skin. Avoid touching your face.*

Nutrition Facts: *1 appetizer with 1 teaspoon sauce equals 50 calories, 3 g fat (1 g saturated fat), 4 mg cholesterol, 103 mg sodium, 5 g carbohydrate, 1 g fiber, 2 g protein.* **Diabetic Exchanges:** *½ starch, ½ fat.*

Watermelon Salsa

This recipe took first place at a local fair. I'm especially proud of my fruity creation because all of the ingredients (except for the lime juice) came directly from my garden and bee hives.

—CAROLYN BUTTERFIELD LAKE STEVENS, WASHINGTON

PREP: 20 MIN. + CHILLING **MAKES:** 3 CUPS

- **2 cups seeded finely chopped watermelon**
- **½ cup finely chopped peeled cucumber**
- **¼ cup finely chopped red onion**
- **¼ cup finely chopped sweet red pepper**
- **1 jalapeno pepper, seeded and minced**
- **¼ cup minced fresh cilantro**
- **1 tablespoon minced fresh basil**
- **1 tablespoon minced fresh mint**
- **2 tablespoons honey**
- **1 teaspoon lime juice**
- **Baked tortilla chip scoops**

1. In a large bowl, combine the watermelon, cucumber, onion, peppers and herbs. Drizzle with honey and lime juice; gently toss to coat.

2. Refrigerate for at least 1 hour. Serve with chips.

Editor's Note: *Wear disposable gloves when cutting hot peppers; the oils can burn skin. Avoid touching your face.*

Nutrition Facts: *¼ cup equals 22 calories, trace fat (trace saturated fat), 0 cholesterol, 1 mg sodium, 6 g carbohydrate, trace fiber, trace protein.* **Diabetic Exchange:** *½ starch.*

Apple-Nut Blue Cheese Tartlets

These tasty appetizers look and taste gourmet, but they're a cinch to make. You'll love the tangy blue cheese flavor and the sweet crunch from walnuts sprinkled on top. The phyllo shells and filling can be made in advance—just fill the cups and warm them in the oven before serving.

—TRISHA KRUSE EAGLE, IDAHO

PREP: 25 MIN. **BAKE:** 10 MIN.
MAKES: 15 APPETIZERS

- **1 large apple, peeled and finely chopped**
- **1 medium onion, finely chopped**
- **2 teaspoons butter**
- **1 cup (4 ounces) crumbled blue cheese**
- **4 tablespoons finely chopped walnuts, toasted, divided**
- **½ teaspoon salt**
- **1 package (1.9 ounces) frozen miniature phyllo tart shells**

1. In a small nonstick skillet, saute apple and onion in butter until tender. Remove from the heat; stir in the blue cheese, 3 tablespoons walnuts and salt. Spoon a rounded tablespoonful into each tart shell.

2. Place on an ungreased baking sheet. Bake at 350° for 5 minutes. Sprinkle with remaining walnuts; bake 2-3 minutes longer or until lightly browned.

Nutrition Facts: *1 appetizer equals 76 calories, 5 g fat (2 g saturated fat), 7 mg cholesterol, 200 mg sodium, 5 g carbohydrate, trace fiber, 3 g protein.*
Diabetic Exchanges: *1 fat, ½ starch.*

SO APPLE-TIZING!

Looking for more ways to use up apples? Turn them into one of these "a-peeling" snacks. To make baked apples, core each apple and stuff with brown sugar, cinnamon and butter. Place in a baking dish with a little water and bake until the apples are tender. Another fun and easy idea is to blend a package of cream cheese with brown sugar and vanilla to taste. Serve as a dip with crisp apple slices. Or serve apple slices with a store-bought caramel dip.

SUMMER CORN SALAD, PAGE 32

Special Salads

Refreshing, packed with flavor and simple to toss together, a good salad is hard to beat. Get creative by topping your salad with sliced fruit, make it an entree with chicken or beef, or savor the **simplicity of a fresh medley** of colorful garden veggies.

"Here's a recipe that's perfect for that post-holiday meal. It makes use of cooked turkey and cranberry sauce in a light, interesting way. My guests love putting together their own salad cups."

—**JANICE ELDER** CHARLOTTE, NORTH CAROLINA

Colorful Turkey Salad Cups

PREP/TOTAL TIME: 30 MIN. **MAKES:** 6 SERVINGS

- **½ cup jellied cranberry sauce**
- **2 tablespoons orange marmalade**
- **2 tablespoons hoisin sauce**
- **½ teaspoon crushed red pepper flakes**
- **3 cups cubed cooked turkey**
- **1 small sweet red pepper, chopped**
- **1 small sweet onion, chopped**
- **½ cup chopped seeded peeled cucumber**
- **1 medium mango, peeled and chopped**
- **1 medium avocado, peeled and chopped**
- **¼ cup chopped pecans, toasted**
- **2 tablespoons finely chopped crystallized ginger**
- **12 Bibb lettuce leaves**
- **½ cup fresh mint leaves, thinly sliced**
- **½ cup fresh basil leaves, thinly sliced**

1. In a small saucepan, combine the cranberry sauce, marmalade, hoisin sauce and pepper flakes. Cook over medium heat for 2-3 minutes or until blended, stirring occasionally. Cool.

2. In a large bowl, combine the turkey, red pepper, onion, cucumber, mango, avocado, pecans, ginger and cranberry mixture. Spoon onto lettuce leaves; sprinkle with herbs. Refrigerate until serving.

Layered Tortellini Salad

My tempting tortellini salad combines layer upon layer of flavors and textures, and its colors are amazing. It's perfect for a salad luncheon. Feel free to mix it up by adding or substituting other cheeses such as Havarti, fontina or Monterey Jack.

—**NITA RAUSCH** DALLAS, TEXAS

PREP: 30 MIN. + CHILLING
MAKES: 12 SERVINGS (1½ CUPS DRESSING)

- **½ cup buttermilk**
- **½ cup plain yogurt**
- **¼ cup mayonnaise**
- **1 teaspoon sugar**
- **¼ teaspoon salt**
- **¼ teaspoon dill weed**
- **¼ teaspoon dried basil**
- **⅛ teaspoon white pepper**

SALAD

- **1 package (9 ounces) refrigerated cheese tortellini**
- **2 cups shredded red cabbage**
- **6 cups fresh baby spinach**
- **1 block (8 ounces) part-skim mozzarella cheese, cubed**
- **1 cup cherry tomatoes, halved**
- **1 small red onion, thinly sliced**
- **8 bacon strips, cooked and crumbled**
- **½ cup crumbled feta cheese**

1. For dressing, place the first eight ingredients in a blender. Cover and process until blended; process 1-2 minutes longer or until smooth.

2. Cook tortellini according to package directions. Drain and rinse in cold water.

3. In a large glass bowl, layer the cabbage, spinach and tortellini. Top with mozzarella cheese, tomatoes, onion, bacon and feta cheese. Cover and refrigerate for at least 3 hours. Drizzle with dressing; toss to coat.

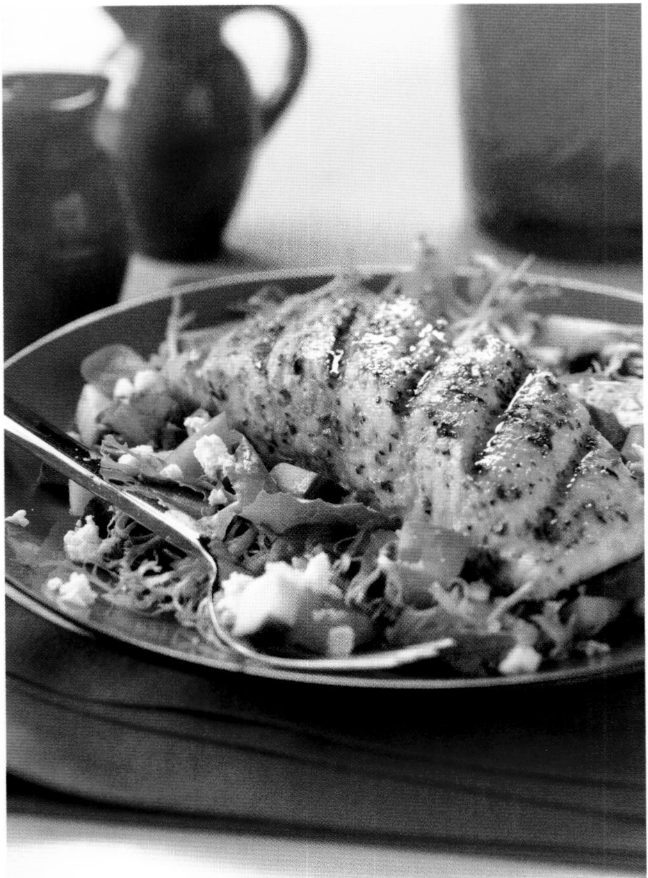

Ramen-Veggie Chicken Salad

Like a salad with plenty of crunch? Then this refreshing recipe is sure to please. Toasted noodles, almonds and sesame seeds provide the delightful topping. The chicken makes it a main dish.
—LINDA GEARHART GREENSBORO, NORTH CAROLINA

PREP: 30 MIN. **BAKE:** 10 MIN. **MAKES:** 2 SERVINGS

- **¼ cup sugar**
- **¼ cup canola oil**
- **2 tablespoons cider vinegar**
- **1 tablespoon reduced-sodium soy sauce**
- **1 package (3 ounces) ramen noodles**
- **1 tablespoon butter**
- **⅓ cup sliced almonds**
- **1 tablespoon sesame seeds**
- **1 boneless skinless chicken breast half (6 ounces)**
- **4 cups shredded Chinese or napa cabbage**
- **½ large sweet red pepper, thinly sliced**
- **3 green onions, thinly sliced**
- **1 medium carrot, julienned**

1. In a small saucepan, combine the sugar, oil, vinegar and soy sauce. Bring to a boil, cook and stir for 1 minute or until sugar is dissolved; set aside to cool.
2. Meanwhile, break noodles into small pieces (save seasoning packet for another use). In a small skillet, melt butter over medium heat. Add the noodles, almonds and sesame seeds; cook and stir for 1-2 minutes or until lightly toasted.
3. Grill chicken, covered, over medium heat for 4-6 minutes on each side or until a thermometer reads 170°.
4. Meanwhile, arrange the cabbage, red pepper, onions and carrot on two serving plates. Slice chicken; place on salad. Top with noodle mixture; drizzle with dressing.

Feta Salmon Salad

My son David always ordered the salmon sandwich at a local pub. In trying to replicate it, he came up with this salad. It's the only recipe he's ever made, and our entire family thinks it's great!
—SUSAN GRIFFITHS MT. PLEASANT, SOUTH CAROLINA

PREP/TOTAL TIME: 25 MIN. **MAKES:** 4 SERVINGS

- **¼ teaspoon salt**
- **¼ teaspoon garlic powder**
- **¼ teaspoon ground ginger**
- **¼ teaspoon dried parsley flakes**
- **¼ teaspoon pepper**
- **4 salmon fillets (6 ounces each)**
- **1 package (5 ounces) spring mix salad greens**
- **1 large cucumber, chopped**
- **1 large tomato, chopped**
- **½ cup crumbled feta cheese**
- **¼ cup red wine vinaigrette**

1. Combine the seasonings; sprinkle over salmon. Moisten a paper towel with cooking oil; using long-handled tongs, lightly coat the grill rack. Place salmon skin side down on grill rack.
2. Grill, covered, over medium heat or broil 4 in. from the heat for 10-12 minutes or until fish flakes easily with a fork.
3. In a large bowl, combine the salad greens, cucumber, tomato and feta cheese; divide among four plates. Top with salmon; drizzle with vinaigrette.
Nutrition Facts: *1 serving equals 416 calories, 25 g fat (6 g saturated fat), 108 mg cholesterol, 636 mg sodium, 7 g carbohydrate, 2 g fiber, 38 g protein.*

Turkey Tossed Salad

PREP/TOTAL TIME: 25 MIN. **MAKES:** 12 SERVINGS

- **1 snack-size cup (4 ounces) mandarin oranges**
- **1 package (10 ounces) ready-to-serve salad greens**
- **4 cups shredded cooked turkey**
- **1 cup (4 ounces) crumbled blue cheese**
- **½ cup sliced almonds**
- **½ cup dried cranberries**
- **¼ cup chopped celery**
- **¼ cup chopped red onion**
- **¼ cup orange juice**
- **2 tablespoons sugar**
- **2 tablespoons olive oil**
- **2 tablespoons cider vinegar**
- **Dash salt and pepper**

1. Drain oranges, reserving syrup. In a large bowl, combine the oranges, salad greens, turkey, blue cheese, almonds, cranberries, celery and onion.

2. In a small bowl, whisk remaining ingredients and reserved syrup. Pour over salad and toss to coat. Serve immediately.

Nutrition Facts: *1½ cups equals 199 calories, 10 g fat (3 g saturated fat), 44 mg cholesterol, 211 mg sodium, 11 g carbohydrate, 1 g fiber, 17 g protein.* **Diabetic Exchanges:** *2 lean meat, 2 fat, 1 vegetable.*

"I played around with my best friend's recipe for chicken salad until I had one that was perfect for Thanksgiving leftovers. This salad is light and refreshing... the perfect antidote for heavy holiday eating. Plus, it's easy to prepare."

—**KRISTY DILLS** FLINTSTONE, GEORGIA

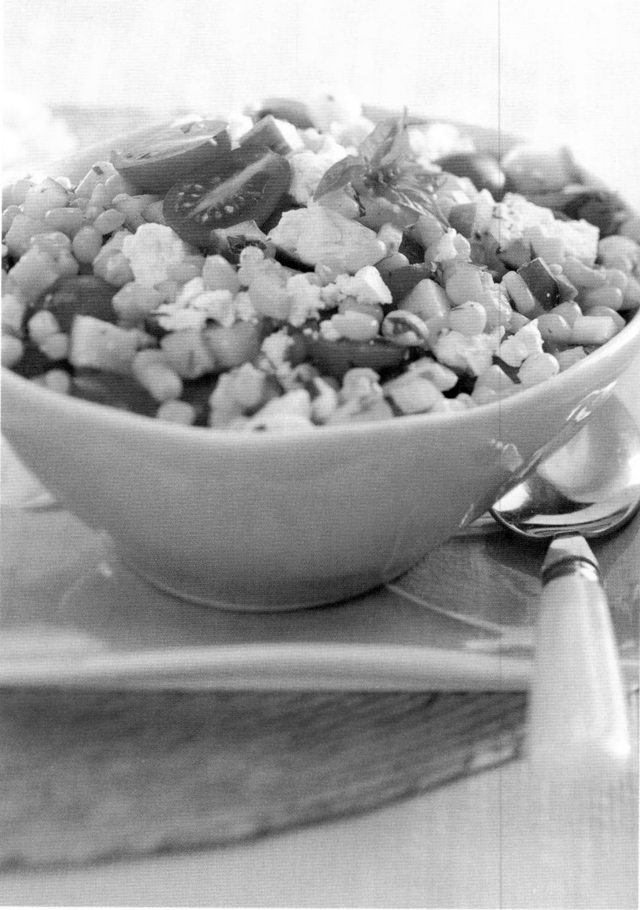

Summer Corn Salad

This beautiful salad truly captures the summer season. It's chock-full of fresh veggies and basil, and feta cheese gives it a rich, tangy flavor the whole family will love.

—**PRISCILLA YEE** CONCORD, CALIFORNIA

PREP: 20 MIN. + STANDING **MAKES:** 4 SERVINGS

- **5 teaspoons olive oil, divided**
- **1 tablespoon lime juice**
- **¼ teaspoon salt**
- **¼ teaspoon hot pepper sauce**
- **1½ cups fresh or frozen corn, thawed**
- **1½ cups cherry tomatoes, halved**
- **½ cup finely chopped cucumber**
- **¼ cup finely chopped red onion**
- **2 tablespoons minced fresh basil or 2 teaspoons dried basil**
- **¼ cup crumbled feta cheese**

1. In a small bowl, whisk 4 teaspoons oil, lime juice, salt and pepper sauce; set aside.

2. In a large skillet, cook and stir corn in remaining oil over medium-high heat until tender. Transfer to a salad bowl; cool slightly. Add the tomatoes, cucumber, onion and basil. Drizzle with dressing and toss to coat.

3. Let stand for 10 minutes before serving or refrigerate until chilled. Sprinkle with cheese just before serving.

Nutrition Facts: *¾ cup equals 136 calories, 8 g fat (2 g saturated fat), 4 mg cholesterol, 231 mg sodium, 16 g carbohydrate, 3 g fiber, 4 g protein.* **Diabetic Exchanges:** *1½ fat, 1 starch.*

Tex-Mex Chicken Salad

This refreshing recipe is totally flexible. You can use yellow onion instead of red, lemon juice instead of lime and Monterey Jack instead of cheddar cheese. Don't like hot sauce? Leave it out. Make it your own!

—**LILY JULOW** GAINESVILLE, FLORIDA

PREP: 25 MIN. + CHILLING
MAKES: 2 SERVINGS

- **4 cups water**
- **¾ pound chicken tenderloins**
- **¼ cup minced fresh cilantro**
- **¼ cup finely chopped red onion**
- **2 tablespoons lime juice**
- **2 tablespoons olive oil**
- **½ teaspoon hot pepper sauce**
- **¼ teaspoon grated lime peel**
- **¼ teaspoon taco seasoning**
- **2 cups chopped lettuce**
- **1 plum tomato, finely chopped**
- **½ cup shredded cheddar cheese**
- **2 tablespoons chopped dry roasted peanuts**

1. In a large nonstick skillet, bring water to a boil. Reduce heat; add chicken. Poach, uncovered, for 8-10 minutes or until no longer pink. Drain and cool slightly. Cut chicken into cubes.

2. In a small bowl, combine the cilantro, onion, lime juice, oil, pepper sauce, lime peel, taco seasoning and chicken. Cover and refrigerate for 1 hour.

3. Just before serving, toss the chicken mixture with the lettuce, tomato, cheese and peanuts.

Nutrition Facts: *1 serving (prepared with reduced-fat cheese) equals 438 calories, 25 g fat (6 g saturated fat), 120 mg cholesterol, 367 mg sodium, 10 g carbohydrate, 3 g fiber, 49 g protein.*

LETTUCE 101

Lettuce should be washed before storing. First, remove the core by grasping the head in your hand and hitting the core area against the countertop; lift out the core. Rinse the head under running water and drain core side down in a colander. Dry thoroughly with paper towels or in a salad spinner. Wrap lettuce in dry paper towels and place in a resealable plastic bag, removing as much air as possible. Store in the refrigerator.

SUPER SUPPER SALADS
GRAND PRIZE
WINNER

GRAND PRIZE

Shrimp 'n' Scallops Tropical Salad

A fruity dressing drapes this zippy salad. Served on a bed of greens, the scrumptious combo of grilled seafood, veggies and macadamia nuts is wonderful for a summer celebration.
—JACKIE PRESSINGER STUART, FLORIDA

PREP: 35 MIN. **COOK:** 5 MIN. **MAKES:** 2 SERVINGS

- **2 tablespoons diced peeled mango**
- **1 tablespoon diced fresh pineapple**
- **1½ teaspoons mango chutney**
- **1½ teaspoons olive oil**
- **1 teaspoon rice vinegar**
- **¾ teaspoon lime juice**
- **Dash salt**
- **Dash crushed red pepper flakes**
- **3 cups torn Bibb or Boston lettuce**
- **1 cup chopped peeled cucumber**
- **½ medium ripe avocado, peeled and sliced**
- **2 tablespoons coarsely chopped macadamia nuts, toasted**
- **1 tablespoon finely chopped red onion**
- **1 tablespoon minced fresh cilantro**
- **2 tablespoons canola oil**
- **1½ teaspoons Caribbean jerk seasoning**
- **6 uncooked large shrimp, peeled and deveined**
- **6 sea scallops, halved**

1. Place the first eight ingredients in a blender. Cover and process until blended; set aside. Divide the lettuce, cucumber, avocado, nuts, onion and cilantro between two serving plates.
2. In a small bowl, combine oil and jerk seasoning. Thread shrimp and scallops onto two metal or soaked wooden skewers; brush with oil mixture.
3. Grill, covered, over medium heat for 2-3 minutes on each side or until shrimp turn pink and scallops are firm and opaque. Place on salads; drizzle with dressing.

SHRIMP 'N' SCALLOPS

Shrimp are available fresh or frozen (raw or cooked, peeled or in the shell) or canned. Shrimp in the shell (fresh or frozen) are available in different sizes (medium, large, extra large or jumbo). Uncooked shrimp will have shells that range in color from gray or brown to pink or red. Fresh shrimp should have a firm texture with a mild odor.

Scallops are commonly found in two groups—the sea scallop, yielding 10-20 per pound, or the much smaller bay scallop, yielding 60-90 per pound. Scallops are usually available shucked, sold fresh or frozen and range in color from pale beige to creamy pink.

Spinach Citrus Salad

This tangy salad tastes as good as it looks. The homemade dressing is a cinch to prepare in a jar.
—MARLENE MOHR CINCINNATI, OHIO

PREP/TOTAL TIME: 20 MIN. **MAKES:** 6 SERVINGS

- **1 package (6 ounces) fresh baby spinach**
- **3 medium navel oranges, peeled and sectioned**
- **1 large grapefruit, peeled and sectioned**
- **6 slices red onion, separated into rings**

DRESSING

- **¼ cup ruby red grapefruit juice**
- **¼ cup olive oil**
- **¼ cup honey**
- **1 tablespoon Dijon mustard**
- **1 tablespoon grated onion**
- **2 teaspoons poppy seeds**
- **⅛ teaspoon salt**
- **Dash pepper**

1. In a large salad bowl, combine the spinach, oranges, grapefruit and onion.
2. In a jar with a tight-fitting lid, combine the dressing ingredients; shake well. Pour dressing over salad and toss to coat. Serve immediately.

Tomato-Cucumber Mozzarella Salad

I used fresh mozzarella for the first time last year and loved it. I wanted to incorporate it into as many dishes as possible and came up with this salad. It has quickly become a mainstay at my house.
—JENNIFER KLANN CORBETT, OREGON

PREP: 20 MIN. + CHILLING **MAKES:** 8 SERVINGS

- **3 medium tomatoes, chopped**
- **1 English cucumber, quartered and cut into ¼-inch slices**
- **1 small green pepper, chopped**
- **¼ cup thinly sliced onions**
- **12 pitted Greek olives, sliced**
- **2 tablespoons minced fresh parsley**
- **1 tablespoon minced fresh basil**
- **⅓ cup olive oil**
- **2 tablespoons red wine vinegar**
- **2 tablespoons balsamic vinegar**
- **1 teaspoon sugar**
- **½ teaspoon salt**
- **½ teaspoon dried oregano**
- **¼ teaspoon pepper**
- **4 ounces fresh mozzarella cheese, cubed**

1. In a large bowl, combine the tomatoes, cucumber, green pepper, onions, olives, parsley and basil.
2. For dressing, in a small bowl, whisk the oil, vinegars, sugar, salt, oregano and pepper. Pour over salad; toss to coat.
3. Cover and refrigerate for at least 15 minutes. Just before serving, stir in cheese. Serve with a slotted spoon.

Red-White-and-Blue Berry Delight

Loaded with fresh strawberries and blueberries, this luscious treat is just the thing for any Fourth of July celebration!
—CONSTANCE FENNELL GRAND JUNCTION, MICHIGAN

PREP: 25 MIN. + CHILLING **MAKES:** 8 SERVINGS

- **½ cup sugar**
- **2 envelopes unflavored gelatin**
- **4 cups white cranberry-peach juice drink, divided**
- **1 tablespoon lemon juice**
- **2 cups fresh strawberries, halved**
- **2 cups fresh blueberries**

CREAM

- **½ cup heavy whipping cream**
- **1 tablespoon sugar**
- **¼ teaspoon vanilla extract**

1. In a large saucepan, combine sugar and gelatin. Add 1 cup cranberry-peach juice; cook and stir over low heat until gelatin is completely dissolved, about 5 minutes. Remove from the heat; stir in lemon juice and remaining cranberry-peach juice.
2. Place strawberries in an 8-cup ring mold coated with cooking spray; add 2 cups gelatin mixture. Refrigerate until set but not firm, about 30 minutes. Set aside remaining gelatin mixture.
3. Stir blueberries into remaining gelatin mixture; spoon over strawberry layer. Refrigerate overnight. Unmold onto a serving platter.
4. In a small bowl, beat cream until it begins to thicken. Add the sugar and vanilla; beat until stiff peaks form. Serve with the gelatin.

Lime Chicken on Fruited Spring Greens

For a unique entree, serve this refreshing salad that pairs fresh fruit with chicken, greens and a tangy vinaigrette. This medley offers a powerhouse of nutrition.

—CHARLENE CHAMBERS
ORMOND BEACH, FLORIDA

PREP: 25 MIN. + MARINATING
COOK: 5 MIN. **MAKES:** 2 SERVINGS

- **7 teaspoons lime juice, divided**
- **3 teaspoons minced fresh thyme, divided**
- **½ teaspoon plus 4½ teaspoons olive oil, divided**
- **2 boneless skinless chicken breast halves (5 ounces each)**
- **¼ teaspoon salt, divided**
- **¼ teaspoon pepper, divided**
- **1 small garlic clove, minced**
- **3 cups spring mix salad greens**
- **1 medium nectarine, thinly sliced**
- **½ cup fresh raspberries**
- **½ cup fresh blackberries**
- **2 tablespoons pine nuts, toasted**
- **¼ cup goat cheese, optional**

1. In a large resealable plastic bag, combine 1½ teaspoons lime juice, 1½ teaspoons thyme and ½ teaspoon oil; add the chicken. Seal bag and turn to coat; refrigerate for 30 minutes.

2. Sprinkle chicken with ⅛ teaspoon each salt and pepper. Cook chicken on an indoor grill or panini maker for 4-6 minutes or until juices run clear. Remove and keep warm.

3. In a small bowl, whisk the garlic and remaining lime juice, thyme, oil, salt and pepper. In another bowl, toss salad greens and nectarine. Drizzle with dressing; toss to coat.

4. Divide salad mixture between two serving plates. Slice chicken; arrange over salad. Sprinkle with raspberries, blackberries, pine nuts and goat cheese if desired.

Mandarin Pork Salad

Try something different for dinner! This entree tosses together pork, mandarin oranges, beets and goat cheese. It's the perfect combination of flavors when you crave something with a little zing.

—**NANCI JENKINS** ANN ARBOR, MICHIGAN

PREP: 15 MIN. **GRILL:** 20 MIN. **MAKES:** 2 SERVINGS

- **1 pork tenderloin (½ pound)**
- **3 cups torn mixed salad greens**
- **1 snack-size cup (4 ounces) mandarin oranges, drained**
- **½ small red onion, thinly sliced**
- **¼ cup crumbled goat cheese**
- **¼ cup canned sliced beets, julienned**
- **2 tablespoons minced fresh cilantro**
- **1 teaspoon finely chopped seeded jalapeno pepper**
- **2 tablespoons balsamic vinegar**
- **2 teaspoons olive oil**
- **½ teaspoon salt**

1. Grill pork, covered, over medium heat or broil 4 in. from heat for 8-10 minutes on each side or until a thermometer reaches 160°.

2. Meanwhile, in a large bowl, combine the salad greens, oranges, onion, cheese, beets, cilantro and jalapeno. Transfer to a serving platter. Whisk the vinegar, oil and salt. Thinly slice pork; arrange over salad. Drizzle with dressing.

Editor's Note: *Wear disposable gloves when cutting hot peppers; the oils can burn skin. Avoid touching your face.*

Veggie Bow Tie Salad

Here's a healthy salad full of fresh vegetables, tender pasta and zippy, homemade vinaigrette dressing. It makes an ideal partner for lean meat or fish.

—**ELEKTRA HARRIS** VANCOUVER, BRITISH COLUMBIA

PREP/TOTAL TIME: 30 MIN. **MAKES:** 9 SERVINGS

- **2 cups uncooked bow tie pasta**
- **2 cups fresh broccoli florets**
- **1 cup fresh cauliflowerets**
- **1 medium sweet red pepper, chopped**
- **½ cup cherry tomatoes, halved**
- **½ cup chopped pitted green olives**
- **1 jar (4½ ounces) marinated artichoke hearts, drained**
- **¼ cup unsalted sunflower kernels**
- **¼ cup minced fresh basil**
- **¼ cup oil-packed sun-dried tomatoes, chopped, optional**

VINAIGRETTE

- **½ cup olive oil**
- **¼ cup balsamic vinegar**
- **2 tablespoons lemon juice**
- **1 teaspoon sugar**
- **½ teaspoon salt**
- **¼ teaspoon pepper**

1. Cook pasta according to package directions. Meanwhile, in a small saucepan, bring 1 in. of water to a boil. Add broccoli and cauliflower; cook for 2-3 minutes. Drain and immediately place vegetables in ice water; drain and pat dry. Drain pasta and rinse in cold water.

2. In a large salad bowl, combine the pasta, broccoli mixture, red pepper, cherry tomatoes, olives, artichokes, sunflower kernels, basil and sun-dried tomatoes if desired.

3. In a small bowl, whisk the vinaigrette ingredients. Pour over salad; toss to coat. Cover and refrigerate until serving.

Gourmet Garden Tomato Salad

PREP/TOTAL TIME: 15 MIN. **MAKES:** 6 SERVINGS

- **1½ pounds red, yellow and/or orange tomatoes, cut into ¼-inch slices**
- **⅓ cup olive oil**
- **⅓ cup balsamic vinegar**
- **1 tablespoon sugar**
- **¼ teaspoon salt**
- **¼ teaspoon pepper**
- **½ cup crumbled feta cheese**
- **⅓ cup fresh basil leaves, thinly sliced**

Arrange tomatoes on a serving platter. In a small bowl, whisk the oil, vinegar, sugar, salt and pepper. Drizzle over tomatoes. Sprinkle with cheese and basil.

"I came up with this invigorating salad for our weekly pool gatherings with friends. Each of us brings our own meat to grill and a side to share. This dish was definitely a hit."

—**STACY KIBLER** CENTERVILLE, OHIO

Lemony Mushroom Salad

Looking for a way to use up leftover mushrooms? This refreshing salad is topped with plenty of fresh mushrooms that have been marinated in a zesty lemon dressing.

—**MARIE HATTRUP** SPARKS, NEVADA

PREP: 15 MIN. + CHILLING **MAKES:** 12 SERVINGS

- **6 tablespoons lemon juice**
- **¼ cup olive oil**
- **¼ cup heavy whipping cream**
- **2 teaspoons sugar**
- **1 teaspoon salt**
- **¼ teaspoon white pepper**
- **2 pounds whole fresh mushrooms, stems removed**
- **1 cup chopped celery with leaves**
- **1 cup thinly sliced green onions**
- **4 cups torn Bibb or Boston lettuce**
- **¼ teaspoon paprika**
- **Parsley sprigs**

1. In a small bowl, whisk the first six ingredients until blended.

2. Place the mushrooms, celery and onions in a large bowl; drizzle with dressing and toss to coat. Cover and refrigerate until chilled.

3. Divide lettuce among 12 salad plates or arrange on a platter; top with mushroom mixture. Sprinkle with paprika and garnish with parsley.

Chickpea Crab Salad with Citrus Vinaigrette

Crab lovers will get a kick out of this salad that's as eye-appealing as it is appetizing. I like to add a little crumbled feta cheese, and sometimes I substitute chicken or turkey for the crab.

—SALLY SIBTHORPE
SHELBY TOWNSHIP, MICHIGAN

PREP/TOTAL TIME: 20 MIN.
MAKES: 2 SERVINGS

- **3 tablespoons orange juice**
- **3 tablespoons olive oil**
- **4½ teaspoons lime juice**
- **1 small garlic clove, minced**
- **¼ to ½ teaspoon ground cumin**
- **⅛ to ¼ teaspoon salt**
- **⅛ teaspoon cayenne pepper**
- **1 can (6 ounces) lump crabmeat, drained**
- **¾ cup garbanzo beans or chickpeas, rinsed and drained**
- **3 radishes, thinly sliced**
- **2 green onions, thinly sliced**
- **⅓ cup minced fresh parsley**
- **⅓ cup shredded carrot**
- **2 tablespoons pistachios, chopped**
- **3 cups spring mix salad greens**

1. In a small bowl, whisk the first seven ingredients. Set aside.
2. In a small bowl, combine the crab, garbanzo beans, radishes, onions, parsley, carrot and pistachios. Pour dressing over salad and toss to coat. Divide salad greens between two salad bowls; top with crab mixture.

Nutrition Facts: *1 serving equals 446 calories, 27 g fat (4 g saturated fat), 76 mg cholesterol, 635 mg sodium, 27 g carbohydrate, 8 g fiber, 25 g protein.*

FRESH CITRUS JUICE

Whenever lemons and limes are on sale, I purchase a bulk quantity of each and store in the freezer. Later, when I need fresh lemon or lime juice, I simply defrost a single lemon or lime in the microwave.

—JOAN F. TURAH, MONTANA

Tossed Salad with Peaches

Here's a colorful salad featuring a wide range of tastes and textures. There are sweet peaches, tart lemon, tangy vinegars and all kinds of yumminess from greens, bacon and nuts.
—**DENISE ELDER** HANOVER, ONTARIO

PREP/TOTAL TIME: 30 MIN. **MAKES:** 12 SERVINGS

- **4 medium ripe peaches, peeled**
- **2 tablespoons sugar**
- **2 tablespoons lemon juice**
- **2 tablespoons cider vinegar**
- **1 tablespoon rice vinegar**
- **¼ teaspoon salt**
- **⅓ cup canola oil**
- **6 cups spring mix salad greens**
- **4 cups torn romaine**
- **1 small red onion, halved and thinly sliced**
- **½ cup thinly sliced cucumber**
- **6 bacon strips, cooked and crumbled**
- **⅓ cup chopped pecans, toasted**

1. Slice three peaches; set aside. Cut the remaining peach in half; place in a blender. Add the sugar, lemon juice, vinegars and salt; cover and process until blended. While processing, gradually add oil in a steady stream.
2. In a large bowl, combine the salad greens, romaine, onion and cucumber. Pour about ⅔ cup dressing over salad and toss to coat.
3. Transfer to a serving platter; top with sliced peaches and bacon. Drizzle with remaining dressing; sprinkle with pecans.

Nutrition Facts: *1 serving equals 127 calories, 10 g fat (1 g saturated fat), 3 mg cholesterol, 131 mg sodium, 8 g carbohydrate, 2 g fiber, 3 g protein.*

Blue Cheese Orzo Salad

The crunch of walnuts and bacon is a pleasant contrast to the creamy rice-shaped pasta in this dish. Blue cheese and arugula lend a satisfying, savory quality.
—**HELEN CONWELL** PORTLAND, OREGON

PREP/TOTAL TIME: 30 MIN. **MAKES:** 5 SERVINGS

- **¾ cup uncooked orzo pasta**
- **3 cups fresh arugula, torn**
- **5 bacon strips, cooked and crumbled**
- **¾ cup crumbled blue cheese**
- **¼ cup sliced green onions**
- **¼ cup chopped walnuts, toasted**

WALNUT VINAIGRETTE

- **2 tablespoons red wine vinegar**
- **1 garlic clove, peeled**
- **1 teaspoon Creole or stone-ground mustard**
- **½ teaspoon salt**
- **½ teaspoon brown sugar**
- **¼ cup chopped walnuts, toasted**
- **¼ cup olive oil**

1. Cook orzo according to package directions; drain and place in a large bowl. Stir in the arugula, bacon, blue cheese, onions and walnuts.
2. In a blender, combine the first six vinaigrette ingredients; cover and process until smooth. While processing, gradually add oil in a steady stream. Pour over salad; toss to coat.

Nutrition Facts: *¾ cup equals 397 calories, 27 g fat (7 g saturated fat), 22 mg cholesterol, 692 mg sodium, 26 g carbohydrate, 2 g fiber, 14 g protein.*

Meatless Taco Salad

This colorful salad features all your favorite taco ingredients. You won't miss the ground beef because it packs plenty of protein with kidney beans. The guacamole dressing is extra-thick and creamy.
—KIMBERLY DRAY PFLUGERVILLE, TEXAS

PREP/TOTAL TIME: 20 MIN. **MAKES:** 2 SERVINGS

- **⅓ cup guacamole**
- **¼ cup sour cream**
- **2 tablespoons chopped green pepper**
- **1 tablespoon chopped green onions**
- **1 tablespoon prepared Italian salad dressing**
- **¼ teaspoon salt**
- **¼ teaspoon chili powder**
- **¼ teaspoon pepper**
- **3 cups shredded lettuce**
- **8 cherry tomatoes, halved**
- **½ cup canned kidney beans, rinsed and drained**
- **¼ cup sliced ripe olives**
- **½ cup crushed corn chips**
- **½ cup shredded cheddar cheese**

In a small bowl, combine the first eight ingredients; set aside. In a large bowl, combine the lettuce, tomatoes, beans and olives. Arrange lettuce mixture on a serving plate; top with guacamole mixture. Sprinkle with corn chips and cheese.

Mushroom Steak Salad with Walnut Vinaigrette

I fix this elegant yet easy salad when I want to serve a romantic dinner for just my husband and me. I round out the meal with crusty French bread, a special dessert and our favorite wine.
—CANDACE MCMENAMIN LEXINGTON, SOUTH CAROLINA

PREP/TOTAL TIME: 30 MIN. **MAKES:** 2 SERVINGS

- **8 ounces boneless beef sirloin steak (¾ inch thick)**
- **3 tablespoons olive oil, divided**
- **1 cup each sliced fresh baby portobello, shiitake and button mushrooms**
- **2 tablespoons balsamic vinegar**
- **1 tablespoon minced fresh thyme or 1 teaspoon dried thyme**
- **2 tablespoons walnut oil**
- **2 tablespoons finely chopped walnuts**
- **3 cups torn mixed salad greens**
- **1 shallot, sliced**
- **2 tablespoons crumbled goat cheese**

1. In a large skillet over medium heat, cook steak in 1 tablespoon olive oil for 4-6 minutes on each side or until meat reaches desired doneness (for medium-rare, a thermometer should read 145°; medium, 160°; well-done, 170°). Remove from the skillet; let stand for 5 minutes before slicing.
2. Meanwhile, in the same skillet, saute mushrooms until tender. In a small bowl, combine vinegar and thyme. Whisk in walnut oil and remaining olive oil. Stir in walnuts.
3. Divide salad greens and shallot between two serving bowls. Cut steak into slices. Top salads with steak and mushrooms. Drizzle with dressing; sprinkle with cheese.

Favorite Turkey Salad

Here's a fresh-tasting salad that's such a treat! I especially like to serve it in the summer when it's too hot to cook. You can also use it as a sandwich filling or stuffed into pita bread.

—TRISHA KRUSE EAGLE, IDAHO

PREP/TOTAL TIME: 20 MIN. **MAKES:** 8 SERVINGS

- **1 can (8 ounces) unsweetened pineapple chunks**
- **2 cups cubed cooked turkey**
- **1 medium apple, thinly sliced**
- **1 cup seedless red or green grapes, halved**
- **1 celery rib, thinly sliced**
- **4 green onions, thinly sliced**
- **⅓ cup chopped walnuts, toasted**
- **¾ cup mayonnaise**
- **1 tablespoon brown sugar**
- **1 teaspoon curry powder**
- **½ teaspoon salt**
- **16 radicchio or other lettuce leaves**
- **¼ cup flaked coconut, toasted**

1. Drain pineapple, reserving 2 tablespoons juice (save remaining juice for another use). In a large bowl, combine the pineapple, turkey, apple, grapes, celery, onions and walnuts.
2. In a small bowl, combine the mayonnaise, brown sugar, curry, salt and reserved pineapple juice. Fold into turkey mixture. Spoon onto lettuce leaves; sprinkle with coconut. Serve immediately.

Nutrition Facts: *3/4 cup equals 307 calories, 23 g fat (4 g saturated fat), 34 mg cholesterol, 305 mg sodium, 15 g carbohydrate, 2 g fiber, 12 g protein.*

ALL ABOUT APPLES

Select apples that are firm and have a smooth, unblemished skin that is free from bruises. Store unwashed apples in the refrigerator away from other vegetables with strong aromas. Apples can be refrigerated for up to 6 weeks. One pound (about 3 medium apples) yields 2¾ cups sliced.

Layered Salad with Walnuts

I love to cook and often fix this refreshing layered salad. It looks so pretty in a glass bowl, and our friends really enjoy it. Plus, I can make it ahead of time—at my convenience!

—VIRGINIA MIRACLE SARASOTA, FLORIDA

PREP: 25 MIN. + CHILLING **MAKES:** 8 SERVINGS

- **1 cup whole walnuts**
- **1 teaspoon canola oil**
- **¼ teaspoon garlic salt**
- **⅛ teaspoon dill weed**
- **5 cups shredded lettuce, divided**
- **8 cherry tomatoes, halved**
- **1 cup (4 ounces) shredded cheddar cheese**
- **1 package (10 ounces) frozen peas, thawed**

DRESSING

- **¾ cup mayonnaise**
- **½ cup sour cream**
- **2 tablespoons chopped green onion**
- **1 tablespoon lemon juice**
- **2 teaspoons chopped fresh parsley**
- **1 teaspoon prepared mustard**
- **¼ teaspoon salt**

1. In a small bowl, toss walnuts with the oil, garlic salt and dill. Spread in a single layer in an ungreased 15-in. x 10-in. x 1-in. baking pan. Bake at 350° for 8-10 minutes or until lightly browned, stirring once. Cool.
2. In a 2½-qt. bowl, layer 2 cups lettuce, tomatoes, cheese, peas, 3/4 cup walnuts and remaining lettuce.
3. In a small bowl, combine dressing ingredients. Spread dressing over top of salad (do not toss). Serve immediately or cover and refrigerate overnight.
4. Just before serving, top with remaining walnuts.

Turkey Spinach Salad with Maple Dressing

My husband and I love to hike in New England. The maple syrup in Vermont is wonderful, and we always bring some home to extend the vacation spirit. This recipe reminds us of those lovely days.

—JESSICA GERSCHITZ JERICHO, NEW YORK

PREP/TOTAL TIME: 15 MIN. **MAKES:** 2 SERVINGS

- **1 package (6 ounces) fresh baby spinach**
- **¼ pound sliced deli smoked turkey, cut into strips**
- **⅔ cup sliced baby portobello mushrooms**
- **1 hard-cooked egg, chopped**
- **⅓ cup sliced red onion**
- **¼ cup walnut halves**
- **¼ cup dried cranberries**
- **4½ teaspoons olive oil**
- **1 tablespoon maple syrup**
- **1½ teaspoons finely chopped shallot**
- **1½ teaspoons red wine vinegar**
- **1½ teaspoons Dijon mustard**
- **1 small garlic clove, minced**

In a large salad bowl, combine the first seven ingredients. In a small bowl, whisk the remaining ingredients. Drizzle over salad; toss to coat.

GRAND PRIZE

Tomato Corn Salad

Warm and colorful, this tantalizing side dish bursts with refreshing vegetable flavor. Fresh herbs and Dijon mustard add a little pizzazz.

—CARRIE COMPONILE ROSELLE PARK, NEW JERSEY

PREP/TOTAL TIME: 30 MIN. **MAKES:** 7 SERVINGS

- **3 large tomatoes, chopped**
- **1 small red onion, halved and thinly sliced**
- **⅓ cup chopped green onions**
- **¼ cup balsamic vinegar**
- **3 tablespoons minced fresh basil**
- **1 tablespoon minced fresh cilantro**
- **1 teaspoon salt**
- **½ teaspoon pepper**
- **4 cups fresh corn (about 9 ears of corn)**
- **2 tablespoons olive oil**
- **3 garlic cloves, peeled and thinly sliced**
- **1 tablespoon Dijon mustard**

In a large bowl, combine the first eight ingredients. In a large skillet, saute corn in oil until tender. Add garlic; cook 1 minute longer. Stir in mustard. Add to vegetable mixture; toss to coat. Serve with a slotted spoon.

KERNELS OF CORN FACTS

Fresh corn is at its peak May through September. Look for ears of corn with bright green tightly closed husks and golden brown silk. The kernels should be plump, milky and in closely spaced rows all the way to the tip. As soon as corn is picked, the sugar gradually begins to convert to starch, reducing its natural sweetness. So corn is best cooked and served the same day it's picked and purchased.

It's easy to cut kernels from fresh corncobs. Stand one end of the cob on a cutting board. Starting at the top, run a sharp knife down the cob, cutting deeply to remove whole kernels. One medium cob yields ⅓ to ½ cup kernels.

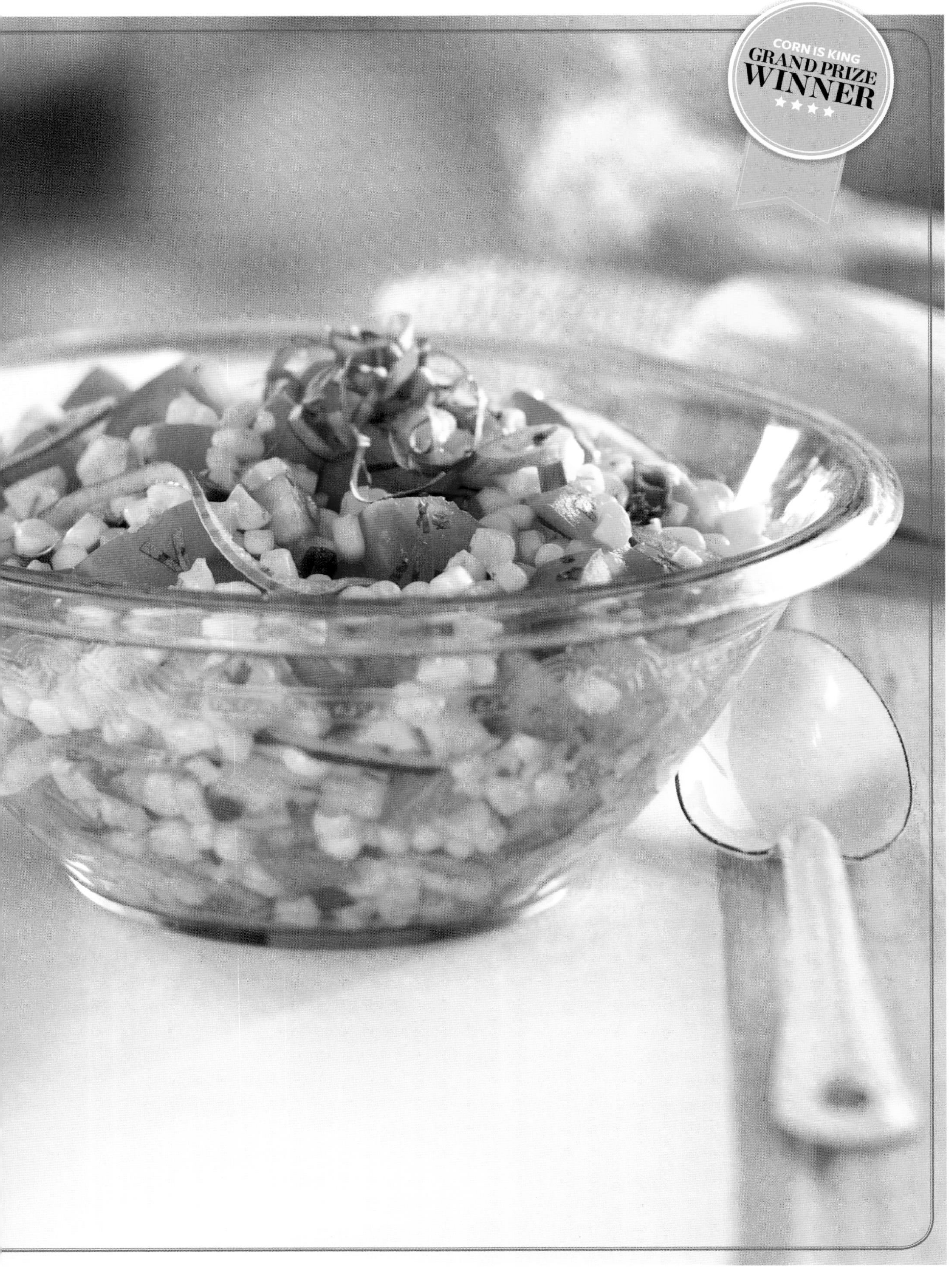
CORN IS KING
GRAND PRIZE
WINNER

Gorgonzola Pear Salad

This quick, easy recipe showcases sweet pears and tangy Gorgonzola cheese. I often add leftover cooked chicken to make this a satisfying main dish salad.

—CANDACE MCMENAMIN
LEXINGTON, SOUTH CAROLINA

PREP/TOTAL TIME: 25 MIN.
MAKES: 6 SERVINGS (1¼ CUPS DRESSING)

- **⅓ cup white wine vinegar**
- **1 can (15 ounces) pear halves, drained**
- **½ teaspoon salt**
- **⅓ cup olive oil**
- **6 cups torn mixed salad greens**
- **2 medium pears, chopped**
- **1 medium tomato, seeded and finely chopped**
- **¾ cup chopped walnuts**
- **¼ cup crumbled Gorgonzola cheese**
- **Coarsely ground pepper, optional**

1. For dressing, in a blender, combine the vinegar, pear halves and salt; cover and process until smooth. While processing, gradually add oil in a steady stream.

2. In a salad bowl, combine the greens, chopped pears, tomato, walnuts and cheese. Drizzle with desired amount of dressing; toss to coat. Serve salad with pepper if desired. Refrigerate any leftover dressing.

Gorgonzola is an Italian cheese from the blue cheese family that is cream-yellow in color with characteristic blue veins. Like blue cheese, it has a bold flavor and crumbles easily, making it a good addition to both salads and sauces.

Tossed Salad with Lemon Vinaigrette

I often take this dressed-up Caesar salad to church functions or family reunions, and I always come home with an empty bowl. It features an interesting blend of flavors that folks love.

—**TERESA OTTO** HARTWELL, GEORGIA

PREP/TOTAL TIME: 25 MIN. **MAKES:** 21 SERVINGS

- **1 bunch romaine, torn**
- **1 medium head iceberg lettuce, torn**
- **10 bacon strips, cooked and crumbled**
- **2 cups cherry tomatoes, halved**
- **1 cup slivered almonds**
- **1 cup shredded Parmesan cheese**
- **1 cup salad croutons**

VINAIGRETTE

- **3 tablespoons lemon juice**
- **3 tablespoons grated Parmesan cheese**
- **2 garlic cloves, minced**
- **½ teaspoon salt**
- **¼ teaspoon pepper**
- **⅔ cup olive oil**

In a large salad bowl, combine the first seven ingredients. In a small bowl, combine the lemon juice, grated Parmesan cheese, garlic, salt and pepper. Gradually whisk in oil. Pour over salad; toss to coat. Serve immediately.

Warm Roasted Beet Salad

Ruby-red beets will shine in their most tasty light in this hearty salad. It's beautiful on the plate, too. To add an extra punch of flavor, I sometimes use hazelnut oil in place of the olive oil.

—**JILL ANDERSON** SLEEPY EYE, MINNESOTA

PREP: 30 MIN. **BAKE:** 40 MIN.
MAKES: 6 SERVINGS

- **8 whole fresh beets**
- **Cooking spray**
- **1½ cups orange juice**
- **1 shallot, chopped**
- **2 tablespoons olive oil**
- **2 tablespoons balsamic vinegar**
- **1 teaspoon minced fresh thyme or ¼ teaspoon dried thyme**
- **½ teaspoon grated orange peel**
- **⅛ teaspoon salt**
- **⅛ teaspoon pepper**
- **6 cups fresh arugula or baby spinach**
- **3 tablespoons crumbled blue cheese**
- **3 tablespoons chopped hazelnuts, toasted**

1. Scrub beets and cut into wedges; place on a baking sheet coated with cooking spray. Lightly coat beets with additional cooking spray. Bake at 350° for 40-50 minutes or until tender, turning occasionally.

2. Meanwhile, for dressing, place orange juice in a small saucepan. Bring to a boil. Reduce heat; simmer, uncovered, until liquid is syrupy and reduced to about 1/3 cup. Remove from the heat. Whisk in the shallot, oil, vinegar, thyme, orange peel, salt and pepper. Set aside to cool.

3. Just before serving, place arugula in a large bowl. Drizzle with 1/4 cup dressing and toss to coat. Divide mixture among six salad plates. Place beets in the same bowl; add remaining dressing and toss to coat. Arrange on plates. Sprinkle salads with blue cheese and hazelnuts.

Nutrition Facts: *1 serving equals 147 calories, 8 g fat (2 g saturated fat), 3 mg cholesterol, 167 mg sodium, 17 g carbohydrate, 2 g fiber, 4 g protein.* **Diabetic Exchanges:** *2 vegetable, 1½ fat, ½ fruit.*

ROASTED VEGGIE AND MEATBALL SOUP, PAGE 60

Soups & Sandwiches

Be prepared for compliments when you choose a **soul-warming** soup, stew or chili or a hearty sandwich or burger from this chapter. Lunch and supper at your house will **never be ho-hum again!**

Tasty Tortilla Soup

Play with this recipe a bit to find ingredients that match your family's preferences. You can use packaged mesquite-flavored chicken, add more tomatoes and onions, or even get creative with the cheeses.

—JENNIFER GILES DES MOINES, IOWA

PREP: 20 MIN. **COOK:** 40 MIN. **MAKES:** 7 SERVINGS

- **1 large onion, chopped**
- **2 green onions, thinly sliced**
- **2 tablespoons butter**
- **4 garlic cloves, minced**
- **2 tablespoons all-purpose flour**
- **4½ cups reduced-sodium chicken broth**
- **2 cans (14½ ounces each) no-salt-added diced tomatoes, undrained**
- **1 can (8 ounces) no-salt-added tomato sauce**
- **1 can (4 ounces) chopped green chilies**
- **1 tablespoon minced fresh oregano or 1 teaspoon dried oregano**
- **2 teaspoons ground cumin**
- **¼ teaspoon pepper**
- **3 cups cubed cooked chicken breast**
- **2 tablespoons minced fresh cilantro**
- **1⅓ cups crushed baked tortilla chip scoops**
- **7 tablespoons shredded reduced-fat cheddar cheese**

1. In a Dutch oven, saute onion and green onions in butter until tender. Add garlic; cook 1 minute longer.
2. Stir in flour until blended; gradually add broth. Stir in the tomatoes, tomato sauce, chilies, oregano, cumin and pepper. Bring to a boil. Reduce heat; cover and simmer for 20 minutes. Add chicken and cilantro; heat through.
3. For each serving, place 2 tablespoons chips in a soup bowl. Top with 1½ cups soup. Garnish each serving with 1 tablespoon each of cheese and chips.

Nutrition Facts: *1 serving equals 256 calories, 8 g fat (4 g saturated fat), 60 mg cholesterol, 654 mg sodium, 23 g carbohydrate, 4 g fiber, 24 g protein.* **Diabetic Exchanges:** *3 lean meat, 2 vegetable, 1 starch, ½ fat.*

Curried Chicken Corn Chowder

Here's a recipe that's close to one my mom used to make for us kids whenever the weather turned cold. Hers called for heavy cream, but I came up with a slimmer version that I think is pretty true to the original!

—KENDRA DOSS KANSAS CITY, MISSOURI

PREP: 15 MIN. **COOK:** 30 MIN. **MAKES:** 9 SERVINGS (2¼ QUARTS)

- **2 medium onions, chopped**
- **2 celery ribs, chopped**
- **1 tablespoon butter**
- **3 cans (14½ ounces each) reduced-sodium chicken broth**
- **5 cups frozen corn**
- **2 teaspoons curry powder**
- **¼ teaspoon salt**
- **¼ teaspoon pepper**
- **Dash cayenne pepper**
- **½ cup all-purpose flour**
- **½ cup 2% milk**
- **3 cups cubed cooked chicken breast**
- **⅓ cup minced fresh cilantro**

1. In a Dutch oven, saute onions and celery in butter until tender. Stir in the broth, corn, curry powder, salt, pepper and cayenne. Bring to a boil. Reduce heat; cover and simmer for 15 minutes.
2. In a small bowl, whisk flour and milk until smooth. Whisk into the pan. Bring to a boil; cook and stir for 2 minutes or until thickened. Add chicken and cilantro; heat through.

Nutrition Facts: *1 cup equals 221 calories, 4 g fat (1 g saturated fat), 40 mg cholesterol, 517 mg sodium, 29 g carbohydrate, 3 g fiber, 20 g protein.* **Diabetic Exchanges:** *2 starch, 2 lean meat.*

Easy Beef Barley Soup

Look no further than this quick and easy soup on those days you're short on time. I like to serve it with homemade bread for supper. The next day, it makes a tasty and convenient leftover lunch.
—**CAROLE LANTHIER** COURTICE, ONTARIO

PREP: 15 MIN. **COOK:** 55 MIN. **MAKES:** 4 SERVINGS

- **½ pound lean ground beef (90% lean)**
- **2 large fresh mushrooms, sliced**
- **1 celery rib, chopped**
- **1 small onion, chopped**
- **2 teaspoons all-purpose flour**
- **3 cans (14½ ounces each) reduced-sodium beef broth**
- **2 medium carrots, sliced**
- **1 large potato, peeled and cubed**
- **½ teaspoon pepper**
- **⅛ teaspoon salt**
- **⅓ cup medium pearl barley**
- **1 can (5 ounces) evaporated milk**
- **2 tablespoons tomato paste**

1. In a Dutch oven over medium heat, cook and stir the beef, mushrooms, celery and onion until meat is no longer pink; drain. Stir in flour until blended; gradually add broth. Stir in the carrots, potato, pepper and salt. Bring to a boil. Stir in barley.
2. Reduce heat; cover and simmer for 45-50 minutes or until the barley is tender. Whisk in milk and tomato paste; heat through.

Nutrition Facts: *1¾ cups equals 317 calories, 7 g fat (3 g saturated fat), 45 mg cholesterol, 753 mg sodium, 42 g carbohydrate, 6 g fiber, 21 g protein.* **Diabetic Exchanges:** *2½ starch, 2 lean meat, 1 vegetable.*

Fully Loaded Chili

With lean ground beef, four types of beans and lots of seasonings and toppings, this chili is truly "fully loaded." But those features aren't the only heavyweights here—every serving provides a hefty 26 grams of protein and 11 grams of fiber.
—**CYNTHIA BACA** CRANBERRY TWP, PENNSYLVANIA

PREP: 20 MIN. **COOK:** 40 MIN. **MAKES:** 8 SERVINGS (2 QUARTS)

- **1 pound lean ground beef (90% lean)**
- **1 medium onion, chopped**
- **1 medium green pepper, chopped**
- **1¾ cups water**
- **2 cans (8 ounces each) tomato sauce**
- **1 can (16 ounces) kidney beans, rinsed and drained**
- **1 can (15½ ounces) great northern beans, rinsed and drained**
- **1 can (15 ounces) garbanzo beans or chickpeas, rinsed and drained**
- **1 can (15 ounces) black beans, rinsed and drained**
- **1 tablespoon baking cocoa**
- **2 teaspoons Louisiana-style hot sauce**
- **½ teaspoon pepper**
- **½ teaspoon chili powder**
- **¼ teaspoon garlic powder**
- **⅛ teaspoon cayenne pepper**

GARNISHES

- **½ cup reduced-fat sour cream**
- **½ cup crushed baked tortilla chip scoops**
- **½ cup shredded reduced-fat cheddar cheese**

1. In a Dutch oven over medium heat, cook the beef, onion and pepper until meat is no longer pink; drain.
2. Stir in the water, tomato sauce, beans, cocoa, hot sauce and seasonings. Bring to a boil. Reduce heat; cover and simmer for 30 minutes.
3. Garnish each serving with 1 tablespoon each of sour cream, crushed chips and cheese.

Nutrition Facts: *1 cup equals 351 calories, 9 g fat (4 g saturated fat), 38 mg cholesterol, 762 mg sodium, 42 g carbohydrate, 11 g fiber, 26 g protein.*

Black Bean Soup

This is a zippy meatless soup that will fill your tummy without expanding your waistline. A steaming loaf of fresh corn bread will complete a rustic weeknight menu.

—**ANGEE OWENS** LUFKIN, TEXAS

PREP: 20 MIN. **COOK:** 25 MIN. **MAKES:** 8 SERVINGS (2 QUARTS)

- **3 cans (15 ounces each) black beans, rinsed and drained, divided**
- **3 celery ribs with leaves, chopped**
- **1 large onion, chopped**
- **1 medium sweet red pepper, chopped**
- **1 jalapeno pepper, seeded and chopped**
- **2 tablespoons olive oil**
- **4 garlic cloves, minced**
- **2 cans (14½ ounces each) reduced-sodium chicken broth or vegetable broth**
- **1 can (14½ ounces) diced tomatoes with green peppers and onions, undrained**
- **3 teaspoons ground cumin**
- **1½ teaspoons ground coriander**
- **1 teaspoon Louisiana-style hot sauce**
- **¼ teaspoon pepper**
- **1 bay leaf**
- **1 teaspoon lime juice**
- **½ cup reduced-fat sour cream**
- **¼ cup chopped green onions**

1. In a small bowl, mash one can black beans; set aside. In a large saucepan, saute the celery, onion, red pepper and jalapeno in oil until tender. Add garlic; cook 1 minute longer.
2. Stir in the broth, tomatoes, cumin, coriander, hot sauce, pepper, bay leaf, remaining beans and reserved mashed beans. Bring to a boil. Reduce heat; cover and simmer for 15 minutes.
3. Discard bay leaf. Stir in lime juice. Garnish each serving with 1 tablespoon sour cream and 1½ teaspoons green onion.

Chicken Black Bean Soup: *Add 2 cups cubed cooked chicken with the broth.*

Editor's Note: *Wear disposable gloves when cutting hot peppers; the oils can burn skin. Avoid touching your face.*

Nutrition Facts: *1 cup equals 222 calories, 5 g fat (1 g saturated fat), 5 mg cholesterol, 779 mg sodium, 32 g carbohydrate, 9 g fiber, 11 g protein.* **Diabetic Exchanges:** *2 starch, 1 lean meat, 1 vegetable, 1 fat.*

Chili-Filled Coffin

Here's an easy main dish that's cute enough to double as a Halloween table centerpiece! The hearty meatless chili is spiced up with colorful serrano and red peppers and onion.

—**AGNES WARD** STRATFORD, ONTARIO

PREP: 45 MIN. + COOLING **COOK:** 10 MIN. **MAKES:** 6 SERVINGS

- **2 packages (8½ ounces each) corn bread/muffin mix**
- **⅔ cup milk**
- **2 eggs**
- **¼ teaspoon black paste food coloring**
- **1 medium sweet red pepper, sliced**
- **1 serrano pepper, seeded and finely chopped**
- **⅓ cup chopped onion**
- **1 tablespoon canola oil**
- **2 cans (15 ounces each) fat-free vegetarian chili**
- **1 tablespoon process cheese sauce**
- **1 tablespoon ketchup**

1. In a large bowl, combine the corn bread mix, milk, eggs and food coloring just until moistened. Pour into a greased 9-in. x 5-in. loaf pan. Bake at 400° for 30-35 minutes until a toothpick inserted near the center comes out clean. Cool for 10 minutes before removing from the pan to a wire rack to cool completely.
2. Cut top fourth off loaf of bread; carefully hollow out the bottom, leaving a 1-in. shell (discard removed bread or save for another use).
3. In a large skillet, saute peppers and onion in oil until tender. Set aside 1/4 cup pepper mixture. Stir chili into remaining pepper mixture; heat through. Spoon 2½ to 3 cups chili mixture into bread coffin; arrange reserved pepper mixture over chili. Replace the bread top. Transfer remaining chili to a serving bowl.
4. Place cheese sauce in a heavy-duty resealable plastic bag; cut a small hole in a corner of bag. Write "RIP" with cheese sauce, then repeat with ketchup. Serve immediately.

Editor's Note: *Wear disposable gloves when cutting hot peppers; the oils can burn skin. Avoid touching your face.*

Nutrition Facts: *1 serving equals 314 calories, 9 g fat (2 g saturated fat), 47 mg cholesterol, 613 mg sodium, 49 g carbohydrate, 8 g fiber, 12 g protein.*

Barbecued Burgers

I can't take all the credit for these winning burgers. My husband's uncle passed down the special barbecue sauce recipe. We love it on everything—so it seemed only natural to try it on—and in—burgers!

—**RHODA TROYER** GLENFORD, OHIO

PREP: 25 MIN. **GRILL:** 15 MIN.
MAKES: 6 SERVINGS

SAUCE

- **1 cup ketchup**
- **½ cup packed brown sugar**
- **⅓ cup sugar**
- **¼ cup honey**
- **¼ cup molasses**
- **2 teaspoons prepared mustard**
- **1½ teaspoons Worcestershire sauce**
- **¼ teaspoon salt**
- **¼ teaspoon Liquid Smoke**
- **⅛ teaspoon pepper**

BURGERS

- **1 egg, lightly beaten**
- **⅓ cup quick-cooking oats**
- **¼ teaspoon onion salt**
- **¼ teaspoon garlic salt**
- **¼ teaspoon pepper**
- **⅛ teaspoon salt**
- **1½ pounds ground beef**
- **6 hamburger buns, split**
- **Toppings of your choice**

1. In a small saucepan, combine the sauce ingredients. Bring to a boil. Remove from the heat. Set aside 1 cup barbecue sauce to serve with burgers.

2. In a large bowl, combine the egg, oats, 1/4 cup of the remaining barbecue sauce, onion salt, garlic salt, pepper and salt. Crumble beef over mixture and mix well. Shape into six patties.

3. Grill, covered, over medium heat for 6-8 minutes on each side or until a thermometer reads 160°, basting with 1/2 cup barbecue sauce during the last 5 minutes. Serve on buns with the toppings of your choice and reserved barbecue sauce.

SAUCE SHORTCUT

If you're pressed for time, skip making the barbecue sauce and use a sweet and tangy store-bought variety instead.

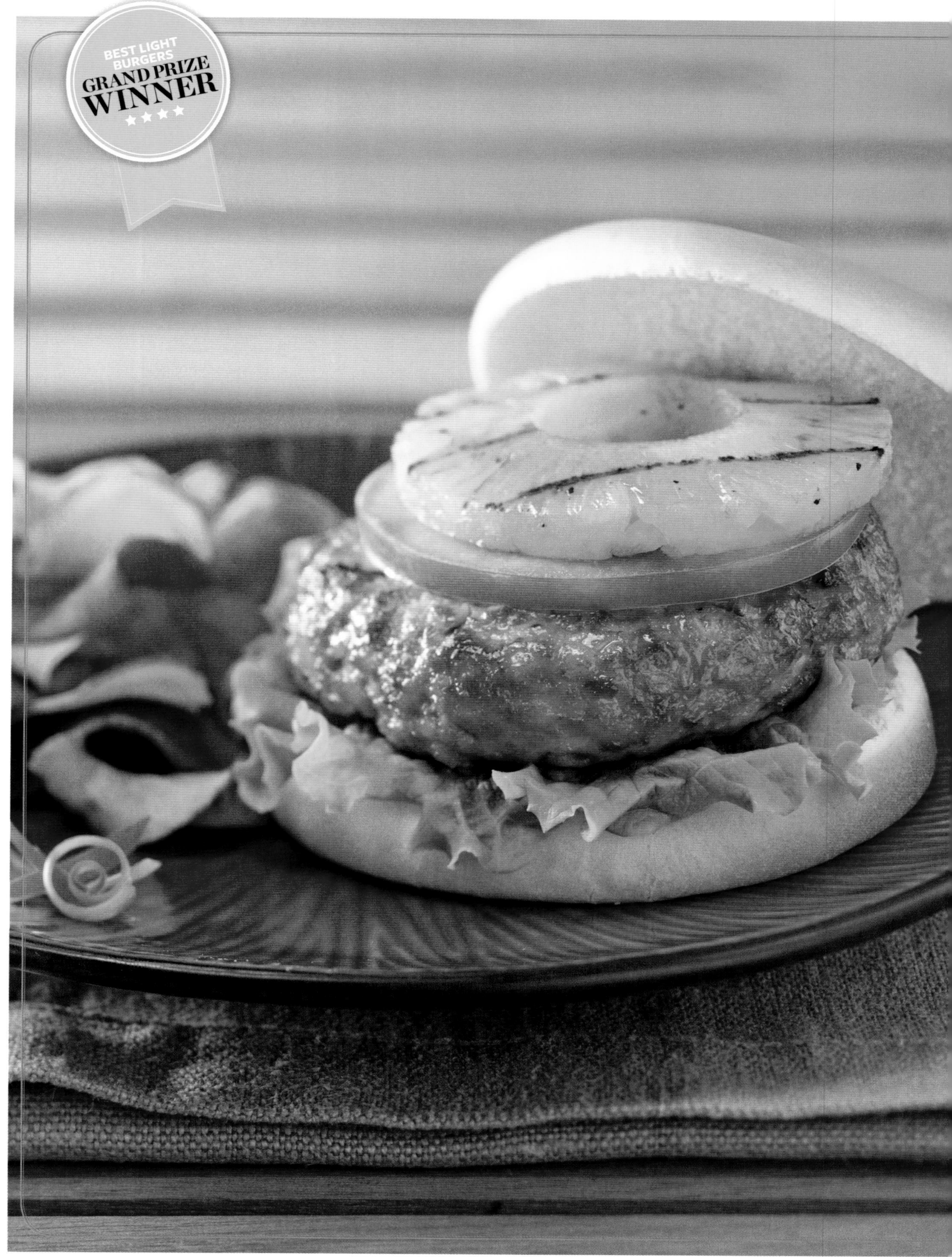
BEST LIGHT BURGERS
GRAND PRIZE
WINNER

GRAND PRIZE

Terrific Teriyaki Burgers

Golden flecks of pineapple give these beef and turkey burgers a touch of sweetness, while the gingerroot adds some spice. Ground chicken works well in this recipe, too.

—MARGARET WILSON SUN CITY, CALIFORNIA

PREP: 20 MIN. **GRILL:** 15 MIN. **MAKES:** 6 SERVINGS

- **¼ cup ketchup**
- **2 tablespoons reduced-sodium soy sauce**
- **1 tablespoon brown sugar**
- **1 tablespoon unsweetened crushed pineapple**
- **1½ teaspoons minced fresh gingerroot**
- **1 garlic clove, minced**
- **½ teaspoon sesame oil**

BURGERS

- **1 egg white, lightly beaten**
- **⅓ cup dry bread crumbs**
- **3 green onions, chopped**
- **2 tablespoons unsweetened crushed pineapple**
- **¾ pound ground beef**
- **¾ pound lean ground turkey**
- **6 slices unsweetened pineapple**
- **6 hamburger buns, split and toasted**
- **6 lettuce leaves**
- **6 slices tomato**

1. In a small bowl, combine the ketchup, soy sauce, brown sugar, pineapple, ginger, garlic and sesame oil; set aside.
2. In a large bowl, combine the egg white, bread crumbs, onions, crushed pineapple and 3 tablespoons reserved ketchup mixture. Crumble beef and turkey over mixture and mix well. Shape into six burgers.
3. Using long-handled tongs, moisten a paper towel with cooking oil and lightly coat the grill rack. Grill burgers, covered, over medium heat or broil 4 in. from the heat for 5-7 minutes on each side or until a thermometer reads 165° and juices run clear, brushing occasionally with remaining ketchup mixture.
4. Grill or broil pineapple slices for 2-3 minutes on each side or until heated through. Serve burgers and pineapple on buns with lettuce and tomato.

Nutrition Facts: *1 burger equals 386 calories, 12 g fat (4 g saturated fat), 79 mg cholesterol, 677 mg sodium, 41 g carbohydrate, 2 g fiber, 27 g protein.* **Diabetic Exchanges:** *3 lean meat, 2 starch, ½ fruit.*

BURGER BASICS

For winning burgers, chill the meat until immediately before seasoning and forming the patties. Next, be careful not to overblend the meat mixture. This will help ensure burgers are juicy and don't fall apart on the grill. Last, use a ¼ cup measure to get even portions.

Cream of Lentil Soup

Lentil lovers will want a second bowl of this nourishing soup with a subtle touch of curry. Fresh spinach adds appealing color—as does a little garnish of shredded cheese!

—KIM RUSSELL NORTH WALES, PENNSYLVANIA

PREP: 20 MIN. **COOK:** 35 MIN. **MAKES:** 9 SERVINGS (2¼ QUARTS)

- **6 cups reduced-sodium chicken broth or vegetable broth**
- **2 cups dried lentils, rinsed**
- **1 bay leaf**
- **1 whole clove**
- **1 medium red onion, chopped**
- **2 celery ribs, chopped**
- **2 tablespoons butter**
- **2 medium carrots, chopped**
- **1 teaspoon salt**
- **1 teaspoon sugar**
- **½ teaspoon curry powder**
- **⅛ teaspoon pepper**
- **2 garlic cloves, minced**
- **3 cups coarsely chopped fresh spinach**
- **1½ cups heavy whipping cream**
- **1 tablespoon lemon juice**
- **⅓ cup minced fresh parsley**

1. In a large saucepan, combine the broth, lentils, bay leaf and clove. Bring to a boil. Reduce heat; cover and simmer for 25-30 minutes or until lentils are tender.
2. Meanwhile, in a Dutch oven, saute onion and celery in butter until crisp-tender. Add the carrots, salt, sugar, curry powder and pepper; saute 2-3 minutes longer or until vegetables are tender. Add garlic; cook for 1 minute.
3. Drain lentils; discard bay leaf and clove. Add to vegetable mixture. Stir in the spinach, cream, lemon juice and parsley; cook over low heat until heated through and spinach is wilted.

Minestrone with Turkey

I remember my mom making this soup; now I make it as often as I can. It's a good way to use up leftover vegetables. Sometimes I add a can of rinsed and drained kidney or garbanzo beans.
—**ANGELA GOODMAN** KANEOHE, HAWAII

PREP/TOTAL TIME: 30 MIN. **MAKES:** 6 SERVINGS (2 QUARTS)

- **1 medium onion, chopped**
- **1 medium carrot, sliced**
- **1 celery rib, sliced**
- **1 tablespoon olive oil**
- **1 garlic clove, minced**
- **4 cups chicken broth or homemade turkey stock**
- **1 can (14½ ounces) diced tomatoes, undrained**
- **⅔ cup each frozen peas, corn and cut green beans, thawed**
- **½ cup uncooked elbow macaroni**
- **1 teaspoon salt**
- **¼ teaspoon dried basil**
- **¼ teaspoon dried oregano**
- **¼ teaspoon pepper**
- **1 bay leaf**
- **1 cup cubed cooked turkey**
- **1 small zucchini, halved lengthwise and cut into ¼-inch slices**
- **¼ cup grated Parmesan cheese, optional**

1. In a Dutch oven, saute the onion, carrot, celery in oil until tender. Add garlic; cook 1 minute longer. Add the broth, vegetables, macaroni and seasonings. Bring to a boil.
2. Reduce heat; simmer, uncovered, for 5 minutes. Add turkey and zucchini; cook until zucchini is crisp-tender. Discard bay leaf. Serve with grated cheese if desired.

Cream of Mussel Soup

Every New England home cook has a personal version of mussel soup, depending on the favored regional herbs and cooking customs. Feel free to start with my recipe to develop your own creative variation, or enjoy its comforting flavor just as it is.
—**DONNA NOEL** GRAY, MAINE

PREP: 35 MIN. **COOK:** 10 MIN. **MAKES:** 5 SERVINGS

- **3 pounds fresh mussels (about 5 dozen), scrubbed and beards removed**
- **2 medium onions, finely chopped**
- **2 celery ribs, finely chopped**
- **1 cup water**
- **1 cup white wine or chicken broth**
- **1 bottle (8 ounces) clam juice**
- **¼ cup minced fresh parsley**
- **2 garlic cloves, minced**
- **¼ teaspoon salt**
- **¼ teaspoon pepper**
- **1 cup half-and-half cream**

1. Tap mussels; discard any that do not close. Set aside. In a stockpot, combine the onions, celery, water, wine, clam juice, parsley, garlic, salt and pepper.
2. Bring to a boil. Reduce heat; add mussels. Cover and simmer for 5-6 minutes or until mussels have opened. Remove mussels with a slotted spoon, discarding any unopened mussels; set aside opened mussels and keep warm.
3. Cool cooking liquid slightly. In a blender, cover and process cooking liquid in batches until blended. Return all to pan. Add cream and reserved mussels; heat through (do not boil).

Nutrition Facts: *1 dozen mussels with ¾ cup cooking liquid equals 368 calories, 11 g fat (4 g saturated fat), 102 mg cholesterol, 1,043 mg sodium, 20 g carbohydrate, 2 g fiber, 35 g protein.*

Squirmy Wormy Sandwiches

PREP/TOTAL TIME: 20 MIN. **MAKES:** 6 SERVINGS

- **1 package (16 ounces) hot dogs**
- **1 tablespoon canola oil**
- **½ cup ketchup**
- **1 tablespoon brown sugar**
- **2 teaspoons Worcestershire sauce**
- **½ teaspoon spicy brown mustard**
- **Dash Liquid Smoke, optional**
- **6 hamburger buns, split**

1. Cut each hot dog into eight strips. In a large skillet, saute hot dogs in oil until golden brown.
2. Stir in the ketchup, brown sugar, Worcestershire sauce, mustard and Liquid Smoke if desired; heat through. Serve immediately on buns.

"My sister and I came up with this recipe while thinking of spooky, ghoulish foods for a Halloween party. You can also serve the worms as an appetizer on party picks alongside barbecue sauce for dipping. Either way, this dish is a hoot!"

—**DIANE EATON** CAMPBELL, CALIFORNIA

Southwestern Turkey Soup

This spicy soup is loaded with turkey, beans, corn and tomatoes. We like it hot, so I toss in all three tablespoons of jalapenos...and then some! It's sure to warm you up from the inside out on a cold, wintry day.

—**BRENDA KRUSE** AMES, IOWA

PREP: 20 MIN. **COOK:** 30 MIN. **MAKES:** 7 SERVINGS

- **1 medium onion, chopped**
- **1 tablespoon olive oil**
- **1 can (14½ ounces) chicken broth**
- **2 to 3 tablespoons diced jalapeno pepper**
- **3 teaspoons ground cumin**
- **1½ teaspoons chili powder**
- **¼ teaspoon salt**
- **¼ teaspoon cayenne pepper**
- **3 cups cubed cooked turkey**
- **1 can (15 ounces) black beans, rinsed and drained**
- **1 can (10 ounces) diced tomatoes and green chilies, undrained**
- **1½ cups frozen corn**
- **Sour cream, coarsely crushed tortilla chips, shredded cheddar cheese and sliced ripe olives, optional**

1. In a large saucepan, saute onion in oil until tender. Stir in the broth, jalapeno, cumin, chili powder, salt and cayenne. Add the turkey, beans, tomatoes and corn.
2. Bring to a boil. Reduce heat; cover and simmer for 20-30 minutes to allow flavors to blend. Garnish with sour cream, chips, cheese and olives if desired.

Editor's Note: *Wear disposable gloves when cutting hot peppers; the oils can burn skin. Avoid touching your face.*

Nutrition Facts: *1 cup (calculated without optional ingredients) equals 223 calories, 6 g fat (1 g saturated fat), 47 mg cholesterol, 680 mg sodium, 20 g carbohydrate, 5 g fiber, 23 g protein.*

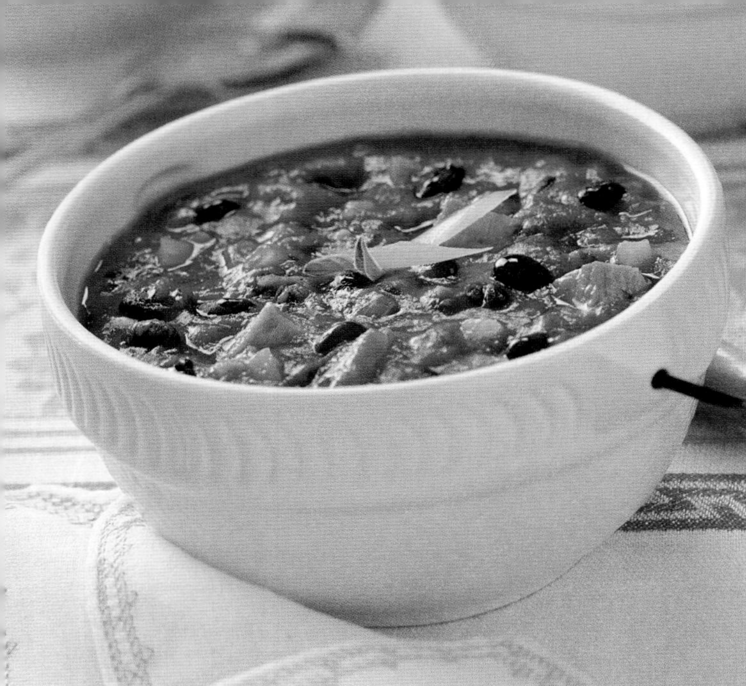

Black Bean 'n' Pumpkin Chili

Our family loves this slow-cooked recipe, especially when it's cold and rainy outside. It's a wonderful variation on standard chili that freezes well and tastes even better as leftovers.

—DEBORAH VLIET HOLLAND, MICHIGAN

PREP: 20 MIN. **COOK:** 4 HOURS
MAKES: 10 SERVINGS (2½ QUARTS)

- **1 medium onion, chopped**
- **1 medium sweet yellow pepper, chopped**
- **2 tablespoons olive oil**
- **3 garlic cloves, minced**
- **3 cups chicken broth**
- **2 cans (15 ounces each) black beans, rinsed and drained**
- **2½ cups cubed cooked turkey**
- **1 can (15 ounces) solid-pack pumpkin**
- **1 can (14½ ounces) diced tomatoes, undrained**
- **2 teaspoons dried parsley flakes**
- **2 teaspoons chili powder**
- **1½ teaspoons dried oregano**
- **1½ teaspoons ground cumin**
- **½ teaspoon salt**

In a large skillet, saute the onion and yellow pepper in oil until tender. Add garlic; cook 1 minute longer. Transfer to a 5-qt. slow cooker; stir in the remaining ingredients. Cover and cook on low for 4-5 hours or until heated through.

Nutrition Facts: *1 cup equals 192 calories, 5 g fat (1 g saturated fat), 28 mg cholesterol, 658 mg sodium, 21 g carbohydrate, 7 g fiber, 16 g protein.* **Diabetic Exchanges:** *2 lean meat, 1½ starch, ½ fat.*

Buffalo Chicken Burgers With Tangy Slaw

These burgers are my sneaky way of enjoying the flavors of barbecued chicken wings minus some of the fat and calories.

—JEANNE HOLT MENDOTA HEIGHTS, MINNESOTA

PREP: 25 MIN. **BROIL:** 10 MIN. **MAKES:** 4 SERVINGS

SLAW

- **¼ cup thinly sliced celery**
- **¼ cup shredded peeled apple**
- **2 tablespoons fat-free blue cheese salad dressing**
- **1 teaspoon finely chopped walnuts**

SAUCE

- **3 tablespoons Louisiana-style hot sauce**
- **2 teaspoons ketchup**
- **2 teaspoons reduced-fat butter, melted**

BURGERS

- **2 tablespoons chopped sweet red pepper**
- **2 tablespoons plus 4 teaspoons thinly sliced green onions, divided**
- **1 tablespoon unsweetened applesauce**
- **¼ teaspoon salt**
- **¼ teaspoon garlic salt**
- **¼ teaspoon pepper**
- **1 pound ground chicken**
- **4 lettuce leaves**
- **4 hamburger buns, split**

1. In a small bowl, combine the celery, apple, salad dressing and walnuts. In another small bowl, combine the hot sauce, ketchup and butter; set aside.
2. In a large bowl, combine the red pepper, 2 tablespoons green onions, applesauce, salt, garlic salt and pepper. Crumble chicken over mixture and mix well. Shape into four burgers.
3. Broil 6 in. from the heat for 5-7 minutes on each side or until a thermometer reads 165° and juices run clear, basting occasionally with reserved sauce.
4. Serve on lettuce-lined buns; top each with 2 tablespoons slaw and sprinkle with remaining green onions.

Editor's Note: *This recipe was tested with Land O'Lakes light stick butter.*

Nutrition Facts: *1 burger equals 312 calories, 12 g fat (4 g saturated fat), 78 mg cholesterol, 682 mg sodium, 29 g carbohydrate, 2 g fiber, 23 g protein.* **Diabetic Exchanges:** *3 lean meat, 2 starch.*

Special French Onion Soup

Combined with a salad, this rich soup is a meal for my husband and me. Brie, prosciutto and garlic make it extra tasty.

—LAURA MCALLISTER
MORGANTON, NORTH CAROLINA

PREP: 1½ HOURS **BAKE:** 10 MIN.
MAKES: 9 SERVINGS

- **¼ cup butter, cubed**
- **¼ cup plus 1 tablespoon olive oil, divided**
- **6 large sweet onions, thinly sliced (about 12 cups)**
- **1 whole garlic bulb**
- **¼ cup dry red wine or beef broth**
- **6 cups beef broth**
- **1½ teaspoons Worcestershire sauce**
- **1 bay leaf**
- **Dash cayenne pepper**
- **Pepper to taste**
- **9 slices French bread (1 inch thick)**
- **1 round (8 ounces) Brie cheese, rind removed, softened**
- **6 thin slices prosciutto or deli ham, chopped**
- **2 cups grated Parmesan cheese**

1. In a Dutch oven over medium heat, melt butter with 1/4 cup oil; add onions. Cook, stirring occasionally, for 15 minutes. Reduce heat to low. Cook 45 minutes longer or until onions are golden, stirring occasionally.
2. Meanwhile, remove papery outer skin from garlic (do not peel or separate cloves). Cut top off garlic bulb; brush with remaining oil. Wrap in heavy-duty foil.
3. Bake at 425° for 30-35 minutes or until softened. Cool 15 minutes. Squeeze garlic into a bowl; mash and set aside.
4. Add wine to the onion mixture; cook for 2 minutes. Stir in the broth, Worcestershire sauce, bay leaf, cayenne and pepper. Bring to a boil. Reduce heat; simmer, uncovered, for 15-20 minutes.
5. Place bread on a baking sheet. Bake at 425° for 3-5 minutes or until golden brown, turning once. Spread each slice with Brie and mashed garlic; sprinkle with prosciutto.
6. Discard bay leaf from soup; ladle 1 cup each into nine ovenproof bowls. Top with one slice of toast; sprinkle with Parmesan cheese. Place bowls on a baking sheet. Bake for 10 minutes or until cheese is melted.

Fiesta Ranch Burgers

Depending on how spicy you like your burgers, add more or less chipotle pepper, which also lends a nice smoky flavor.

—CAROL BREWER FAIRBORN, OHIO

PREP/TOTAL TIME: 30 MIN. **MAKES:** 5 SERVINGS

- **2 egg whites, lightly beaten**
- **½ cup canned diced tomatoes, drained**
- **½ cup canned black beans, rinsed and drained**
- **1 small onion, chopped**
- **1 tablespoon lime juice**
- **1 to 2 tablespoons chopped chipotle peppers in adobo sauce**
- **1 garlic clove, minced**
- **¼ teaspoon salt**
- **1¼ pounds lean ground turkey**
- **⅓ cup fat-free ranch salad dressing**
- **1 tablespoon minced fresh cilantro**
- **5 lettuce leaves**
- **5 hamburger buns, split**

1. In a large bowl, combine the first eight ingredients. Crumble ground turkey over the mixture and mix well. Shape into five burgers.
2. Broil 4 in. from the heat for 7-9 minutes on each side or until a thermometer reads 165° and juices run clear.
3. In a small bowl, combine the salad dressing and cilantro. Serve burgers with dressing on lettuce-lined buns.

Nutrition Facts: *1 burger equals 357 calories, 12 g fat (3 g saturated fat), 90 mg cholesterol, 745 mg sodium, 34 g carbohydrate, 3 g fiber, 27 g protein.* **Diabetic Exchanges:** *3 lean meat, 2 starch.*

CHIPOTLES 101

A Mexican kitchen staple, the chipotle pepper has hit American kitchens by storm. The somewhat spicy chili pepper is actually a dried or smoked jalapeno and is often accompanied by adobo sauce, made from tomatoes, vinegar and a variety of seasonings.

Roasted Veggie and Meatball Soup

I put together this appetizing soup almost every Sunday during our South Dakota winters. A variety of roasted vegetables and turkey meatballs perk up the broth. What a wonderful way to stay cozy!

—SANDY LUND BROOKINGS, SOUTH DAKOTA

PREP: 45 MIN. **COOK:** 50 MIN.
MAKES: 8 SERVINGS (3 QUARTS)

- **5 medium red potatoes, cubed**
- **4 large carrots, cut into ½-inch slices**
- **1 large red onion, halved and cut into wedges**
- **4 tablespoons canola oil, divided**
- **1¼ teaspoons salt, divided**
- **3 tablespoons minced fresh basil**
- **3 garlic cloves, crushed**
- **1 egg, lightly beaten**
- **½ cup seasoned bread crumbs**
- **¼ cup grated Parmesan cheese**
- **¼ cup minced fresh parsley**
- **½ teaspoon pepper**
- **1 pound ground turkey**
- **1 carton (32 ounces) reduced-sodium chicken broth**
- **2 cups water**
- **1 can (14½ ounces) diced tomatoes, undrained**

1. In a large bowl, combine the potatoes, carrots, onion, 2 tablespoons oil and ½ teaspoon salt. Place in a single layer in two greased 15-in. x 10-in. x 1-in. baking pans.
2. Bake at 425° for 20 minutes. Add basil and garlic; toss to coat. Bake 10-15 minutes longer or until vegetables are tender.
3. In a large bowl, combine the egg, bread crumbs, cheese, parsley, ½ teaspoon salt and pepper. Crumble turkey over mixture and mix well. Shape into 1-in. balls.
4. In a Dutch oven, brown meatballs in remaining oil in batches; drain and set aside.
5. In the same pan, combine the broth, water, tomatoes, roasted vegetables and remaining salt. Return meatballs to pan. Bring to a boil. Reduce heat; cover and simmer for 45-55 minutes or until meatballs are no longer pink.

Turkey Muffuletta

You'll want to dig into this impressive, multi-layered sandwich right after you assemble it, but it needs to chill in the refrigerator for at least 30 minutes to allow the flavors to meld. Once you take that first bite, you'll agree it's worth the wait!

—**GILDA LESTER** MILLSBORO, DELAWARE

PREP: 30 MIN. + CHILLING **MAKES:** 6 SERVINGS

- **1 loaf (1 pound) Italian bread**
- **⅓ cup olive oil**
- **3 tablespoons balsamic vinegar**
- **1 tablespoon minced fresh basil or 1 teaspoon dried basil**
- **1 garlic clove, minced**
- **½ teaspoon salt**
- **¼ teaspoon crushed red pepper flakes**
- **¾ pound sliced deli turkey**
- **6 ounces provolone cheese, thinly sliced**
- **1 jar (7 ounces) roasted sweet red peppers, drained and sliced**
- **½ cup sliced pimiento-stuffed olives**
- **1 large tomato, sliced**
- **3 tablespoons shredded Romano cheese**
- **1 tablespoon minced fresh oregano or 1 teaspoon dried oregano**
- **¼ teaspoon pepper**

1. Cut bread in half lengthwise; carefully hollow out top and bottom, leaving a 1-in. shell (discard removed bread or save for another use).
2. In a small bowl, combine the oil, vinegar, basil, garlic, salt and pepper flakes; brush over cut sides of bread.
3. In the bottom bread shell, layer with turkey, provolone cheese, red peppers, olives and tomato. Sprinkle with Romano cheese, oregano and pepper. Replace bread top.
4. Wrap in plastic wrap; refrigerate for 30 minutes. Cut sandwich into slices.

Pepperoni Cheese Soup

Children and adults will go for this creative soup that tastes like pizza in a bowl. It's just as fresh and flavorful, and you don't have to fuss with making a crust.

—**DEBBIE REID** CLEARWATER, FLORIDA

PREP: 45 MIN. **COOK:** 25 MIN.
MAKES: 10 SERVINGS (2½ QUARTS)

- **1 pint grape tomatoes**
- **2 tablespoons olive oil, divided**
- **½ teaspoon dried oregano**
- **½ teaspoon pepper, divided**
- **¾ cup chopped sweet onion**
- **¾ cup chopped carrots**
- **¾ cup chopped green pepper**
- **1 carton (32 ounces) reduced-sodium chicken broth**
- **1¼ cups cubed peeled potatoes**
- **3 cups (12 ounces) shredded part-skim mozzarella cheese, divided**
- **2 cups (8 ounces) shredded white cheddar cheese**
- **1 package (8 ounces) cream cheese, cubed**
- **1 cup milk**
- **2 teaspoons pizza or Italian seasoning**
- **¼ teaspoon crushed red pepper flakes**
- **2 packages (one 8 ounces, one 3½ ounces) sliced pepperoni, chopped, divided**

1. Place tomatoes in a greased 15-in. x 10-in. x 1-in. baking pan; drizzle with 1 tablespoon oil, oregano and 1/4 teaspoon pepper; toss gently. Bake at 400° for 10-15 minutes or until tender; set aside.
2. In a Dutch oven, saute onion in remaining oil until tender. Add the carrots, green pepper and remaining pepper; saute 4 minutes longer. Add broth and potatoes. Bring to a boil. Reduce heat; cover and cook 10-15 minutes or until potatoes are tender. Cool slightly.
3. In a blender, process soup in batches until smooth. Return all to the pan; heat through. Stir in 2 cups mozzarella cheese, cheddar cheese, cream cheese, milk, pizza seasoning and pepper flakes until cheeses are melted. Add 1⅓ cups pepperoni and reserved tomatoes; heat through. Serve with remaining mozzarella cheese and pepperoni.

Turkey Burgers with Avocado Sauce

I love burgers and I love Southwestern food, so why not combine the two in a light and juicy burger? I like to whip these up on a Friday, pop them in the fridge and cook them later for casual weekend entertaining or an exciting family treat!

—JAN WARREN-RUCKER CLEMMONS, NORTH CAROLINA

PREP: 30 MIN. + CHILLING **GRILL:** 10 MIN. **MAKES:** 4 SERVINGS

- **1 cup fresh or frozen corn, thawed**
- **½ cup chopped red onion**
- **1 small sweet red pepper, chopped**
- **2 jalapeno peppers, seeded and minced**
- **2 teaspoons olive oil**
- **2 tablespoons lime juice**
- **2 garlic cloves, minced**
- **½ teaspoon salt**
- **½ teaspoon ground cumin**
- **¼ teaspoon chili powder**
- **⅛ teaspoon dried oregano**
- **1 pound extra-lean ground turkey**

SAUCE

- **1 medium ripe avocado, peeled**
- **½ cup fat-free sour cream**
- **2 tablespoons minced fresh cilantro**
- **2 teaspoons lime juice**
- **1 garlic clove, minced**
- **⅛ teaspoon salt**

SERVING

- **4 whole wheat hamburger buns, split**
- **Shredded lettuce and reduced-fat Mexican cheese blend, optional**
- **Sliced tomato and red onion, optional**

1. In a large skillet, saute the corn, onion and peppers in oil until crisp-tender. Stir in the lime juice, garlic, salt, cumin, chili powder and oregano; cook 1 minute longer. Transfer to a large bowl and cool slightly. Crumble turkey over mixture and mix well. Shape into four burgers. Refrigerate for 30 minutes or more.

2. For sauce, in a small bowl, mash avocado with the sour cream, cilantro, lime juice, garlic and salt. Refrigerate until ready to serve.

3. Using long-handled tongs, moisten a paper towel with cooking oil and lightly coat the grill rack. Grill burgers, covered, over medium heat or broil 4 in. from the heat for 5-7 minutes on each side or until a thermometer reads 165° and juices run clear.

4. Place on buns; top each with about ¼ cup sauce. Serve with the lettuce, cheese, tomato and onion if desired.

Editor's Note: *Wear disposable gloves when cutting hot peppers; the oils can burn skin. Avoid touching your face.*

Nutrition Facts: *1 burger equals 413 calories, 13 g fat (2 g saturated fat), 50 mg cholesterol, 678 mg sodium, 43 g carbohydrate, 8 g fiber, 37 g protein.*

Moroccan Chickpea Stew

When I served this spicy stew to guests, including three vegetarians, they were thrilled with the abundance of winter squash, potatoes, tomatoes and zucchini.

—CINDY BEBERMAN ORLAND PARK, ILLINOIS

PREP: 20 MIN. **COOK:** 30 MIN.
MAKES: 9 SERVINGS (ABOUT 2 QUARTS)

- **1 large onion, finely chopped**
- **2 tablespoons olive oil**
- **1 tablespoon butter**
- **2 garlic cloves, minced**
- **2 teaspoons ground cumin**
- **1 cinnamon stick (3 inches)**
- **½ teaspoon chili powder**
- **4 cups vegetable broth**
- **2 cups cubed peeled butternut squash**
- **1 can (15 ounces) chickpeas or garbanzo beans, rinsed and drained**
- **1 can (14½ ounces) diced tomatoes, undrained**
- **1 medium red potato, cut into 1-inch cubes**
- **1 medium sweet potato, peeled and cut into 1-inch cubes**
- **1 medium lemon, thinly sliced**
- **¼ teaspoon salt**
- **2 small zucchini, cubed**
- **3 tablespoons minced fresh cilantro**

1. In a Dutch oven, saute onion in oil and butter until tender. Add the garlic, cumin, cinnamon stick and chili powder; saute 1 minute longer.

2. Stir in the broth, squash, chickpeas, tomatoes, potatoes, lemon and salt. Bring to a boil. Reduce heat; cover and simmer for 15-20 minutes or until the potatoes and butternut squash are almost tender.

3. Add zucchini; return to a boil. Reduce heat; cover and simmer for 5-8 minutes or until vegetables are tender. Discard cinnamon stick and lemon slices. Stir in cilantro.

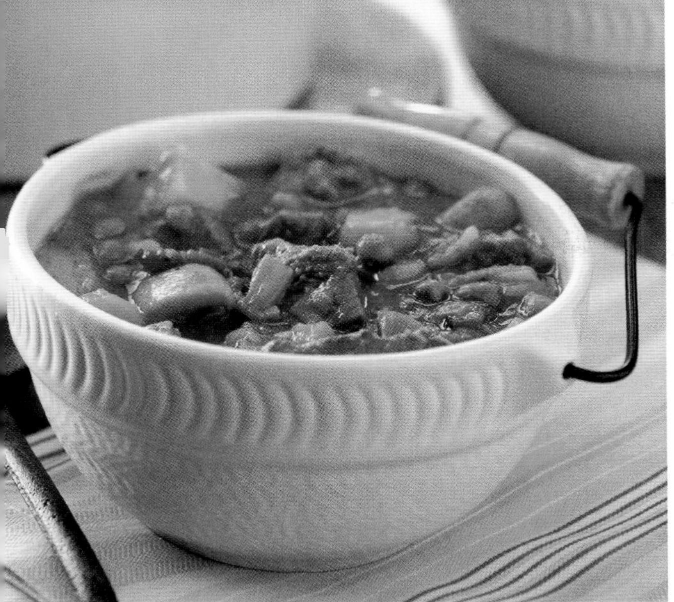

Irish Beef Stew

Rich and hearty, this stew is my husband's favorite. The beef is incredibly tender. Served with crusty bread, it's an ideal meal for cool weather and perfect for any Irish holiday.

—CARRIE KARLEEN ST. NICOLAS, QUEBEC

PREP: 40 MIN. **COOK:** 3¼ HOURS
MAKES: 15 SERVINGS (3¾ QUARTS)

- **8 bacon strips, diced**
- **⅓ cup all-purpose flour**
- **1 teaspoon salt**
- **½ teaspoon pepper**
- **3 pounds beef stew meat, cut into 1-inch cubes**
- **1 pound whole fresh mushrooms, quartered**
- **3 medium leeks (white portion only), chopped**
- **2 medium carrots, chopped**
- **¼ cup chopped celery**
- **1 tablespoon canola oil**
- **4 garlic cloves, minced**
- **1 tablespoon tomato paste**
- **4 cups reduced-sodium beef broth**
- **1 cup dark stout beer or additional reduced-sodium beef broth**
- **2 bay leaves**
- **1 teaspoon dried thyme**
- **1 teaspoon dried parsley flakes**
- **1 teaspoon dried rosemary, crushed**
- **2 pounds Yukon Gold potatoes, cut into 1-inch cubes**
- **2 tablespoons cornstarch**
- **2 tablespoons cold water**
- **1 cup frozen peas**

1. In a stockpot, cook bacon over medium heat until crisp. Using a slotted spoon, remove to paper towels. In a large resealable plastic bag, combine the flour, salt and pepper. Add beef, a few pieces at a time, and shake to coat. Brown beef in the bacon drippings. Remove and set aside.
2. In the same pan, saute the mushrooms, leeks, carrots and celery in oil until tender. Add garlic; cook 1 minute longer. Stir in tomato paste until blended. Add the broth, beer, bay leaves, thyme, parsley and rosemary. Return beef and bacon to pan. Bring to a boil. Reduce heat; cover and simmer for 2 hours or until beef is tender.
3. Add potatoes. Return to a boil. Reduce heat; cover and simmer 1 hour longer or until potatoes are tender. Combine cornstarch and water until smooth; stir into stew. Bring to a boil; cook and stir for 2 minutes or until thickened. Add peas; heat through. Discard bay leaves.

Nutrition Facts: *1 cup equals 301 calories, 13 g fat (4 g saturated fat), 66 mg cholesterol, 441 mg sodium, 21 g carbohydrate, 2 g fiber, 23 g protein.*

Asian Vegetable-Beef Soup

My husband is Korean-American, and I enjoy working Asian flavors into our menus. This tasty soup was something I put together one night with what I found in our fridge. Everyone loved it!

—MOLLIE LEE ROCKWALL, TEXAS

PREP: 30 MIN. **COOK:** 1¾ HOURS **MAKES:** 6 SERVINGS

- **1 pound beef stew meat, cut into 1-inch cubes**
- **1 tablespoon canola oil**
- **2 cups water**
- **1 cup beef broth**
- **¼ cup sherry or additional beef broth**
- **¼ cup reduced-sodium soy sauce**
- **6 green onions, chopped**
- **3 tablespoons brown sugar**
- **2 garlic cloves, minced**
- **1 tablespoon minced fresh gingerroot**
- **2 teaspoons sesame oil**
- **¼ teaspoon cayenne pepper**
- **1½ cups sliced fresh mushrooms**
- **1½ cups julienned carrots**
- **1 cup sliced bok choy**
- **1½ cups uncooked long grain rice**
- **Chive blossoms, optional**

1. In a large saucepan, brown meat in oil on all sides; drain. Add the water, broth, sherry, soy sauce, onions, brown sugar, garlic, ginger, sesame oil and cayenne. Bring to a boil. Reduce heat; cover and simmer for 1 hour.
2. Stir in the mushrooms, carrots and bok choy; cover and simmer 20-30 minutes longer or until vegetables are tender. Meanwhile, cook rice according to package directions.
3. Divide rice among six soup bowls, 3/4 cup in each; top each with 1 cup of soup. Garnish with chive blossoms if desired.

Sweet and Sassy Turkey Burgers

These burgers are simply scrumptious! I served them at our last family reunion and they were a huge hit. Cranberry sauce with turkey is a match made in heaven.

—MARLA CLARK MORIARTY, NEW MEXICO

PREP: 25 MIN. **GRILL:** 15 MIN. **MAKES:** 6 SERVINGS

- **6 turkey bacon strips, diced and cooked**
- **¼ cup dried cranberries**
- **1 tablespoon maple syrup**
- **1 teaspoon rubbed sage**
- **⅛ teaspoon pepper**
- **1¼ pounds extra-lean ground turkey**
- **1 Italian turkey sausage link (4 ounces), casing removed**
- **3 slices part-skim mozzarella cheese, cut in half**
- **6 onion rolls, split**
- **6 tablespoons jellied cranberry sauce**
- **6 tablespoons fat-free mayonnaise**
- **6 lettuce leaves**

1. In a large bowl, combine the first five ingredients. Crumble turkey and sausage over the mixture and mix well. Shape into six burgers.
2. Using long-handled tongs, moisten a paper towel with cooking oil and lightly coat the grill rack. Grill burgers, covered, over medium heat or broil 4 in. from the heat for 5-7 minutes on each side or until a thermometer reads 165° and juices run clear. Top with cheese; cook 1-2 minutes longer or until cheese is melted.
3. Toast the rolls; spread warm rolls with cranberry sauce and mayonnaise. Serve burgers on rolls with lettuce.

Nutrition Facts: *1 burger equals 418 calories, 12 g fat (4 g saturated fat), 73 mg cholesterol, 809 mg sodium, 41 g carbohydrate, 2 g fiber, 38 g protein.*

GRAND PRIZE

Chicken Stew with Gnocchi

My rustic chicken stew fills our house with a wonderful aroma as it gently simmers in the slow cooker. One whiff and my family heads to the kitchen to see if it's ready.

—MARGE DRAKE JUNIATA, NEBRASKA

PREP: 25 MIN. **COOK:** 6½ HOURS
MAKES: 8 SERVINGS (3 QUARTS)

- **3 medium parsnips, peeled and cut into ½-inch pieces**
- **2 large carrots, cut into ½-inch slices**
- **2 celery ribs, chopped**
- **1 large sweet potato, peeled and cut into 1-inch cubes**
- **4 green onions, chopped**
- **3 pounds bone-in chicken thighs, skin removed**
- **½ teaspoon dried sage leaves**
- **¼ teaspoon salt**
- **¼ teaspoon pepper**
- **4 cups chicken broth**
- **1 cup water**
- **3 tablespoons cornstarch**
- **¼ cup cold water**
- **1 package (16 ounces) potato gnocchi**
- **Hot pepper sauce, optional**

1. Place the parsnips, carrots, celery, sweet potato and onions in a 5-qt. slow cooker. Top with chicken; sprinkle with the sage, salt and pepper. Add broth and water. Cover and cook on low for 6-8 hours or until chicken is tender.
2. Remove chicken; when cool enough to handle, remove meat from bones and discard bones. Cut meat into bite-size pieces and return to the slow cooker.
3. Mix cornstarch and cold water until smooth; stir into stew. Add gnocchi. Cover and cook on high for 30 minutes or until thickened. Season with hot pepper sauce if desired.

GETTING TO KNOW GNOCCHI

Gnocchi (pronounced NO-key or NYO-key) seems to be one of those favorite old recipes that many creative cooks love to put a new twist or spin on. Gnocchi are Italian dumplings traditionally made with potatoes and flour or farina. Eggs and seasonings are added before the dough is shaped into long ropes, cut into small pieces and rolled into balls. The balls are usually rolled over the tines of a fork, cheese grater or a special gnocchi board to make small ridges in the dough. The indentations hold the sauce and help the gnocchi cook faster.

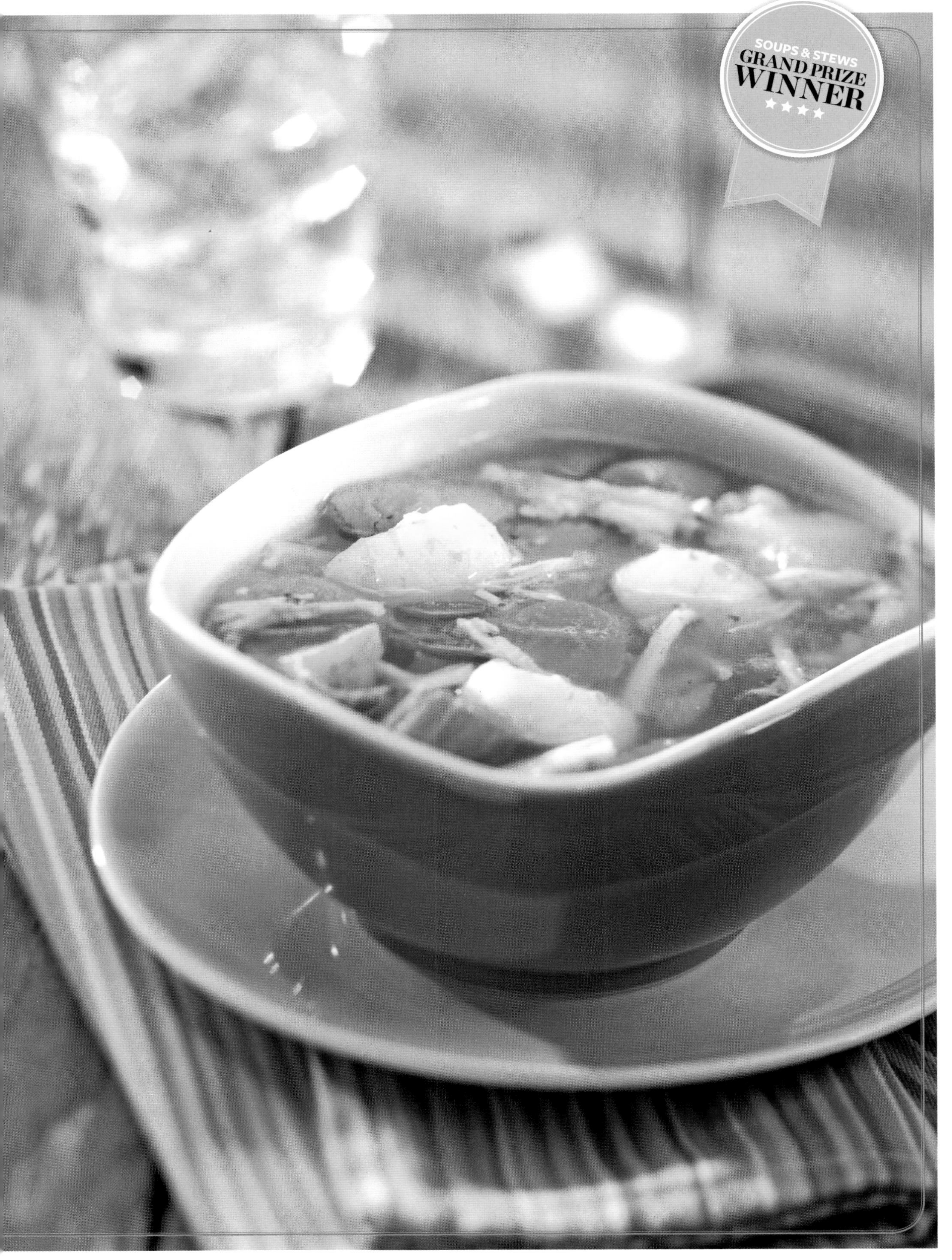
SOUPS & STEWS
GRAND PRIZE
WINNER

Turkey Apple Salad Wraps

PREP/TOTAL TIME: 25 MIN. **MAKES:** 2 SERVINGS

- **1½ teaspoons curry powder, divided**
- **¼ teaspoon salt**
- **½ pound turkey breast tenderloins, cut into ½-inch pieces**
- **1 teaspoon olive oil**
- **¼ cup unsweetened apple juice**
- **¼ cup sour cream**
- **¼ cup mayonnaise**
- **¼ teaspoon ground cinnamon**
- **1 cup diced peeled tart apple**
- **¼ cup raisins**
- **2 flour tortillas (8 inches), at room temperature**
- **2 lettuce leaves**

1. In a large resealable plastic bag, combine 1 teaspoon curry powder and salt. Add turkey, a few pieces at a time, and shake to coat. In a small skillet, cook turkey in oil over medium heat until no longer pink. Cool slightly.
2. In a blender, combine the apple juice, sour cream, mayonnaise, cinnamon, turkey and remaining curry powder; cover and process until blended. Stir in apple and raisins. Spread over tortillas; top with lettuce. Roll up tightly.

"Turkey, apple and raisins, with a touch of cinnamon and curry, make such a pleasing combination that you'll make these fun wraps often."

—**JESSIE APFEL** BERKELEY, CALIFORNIA

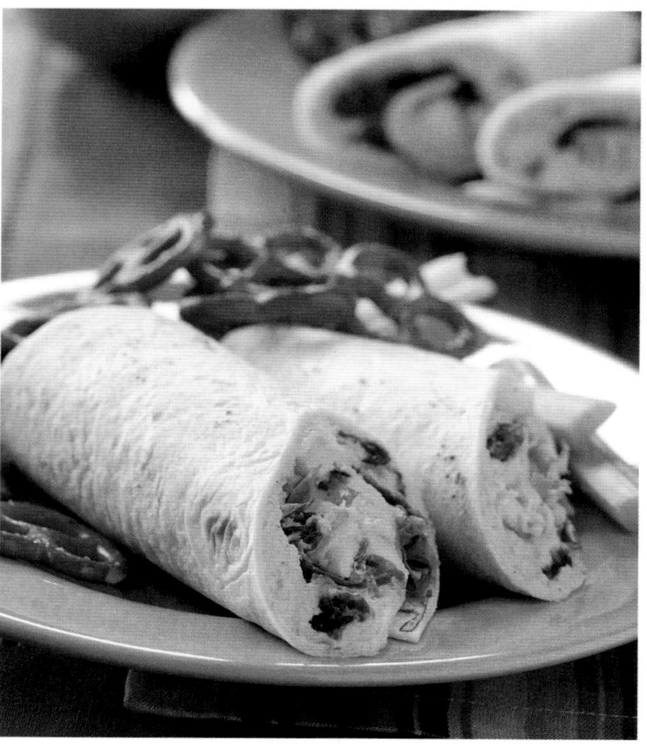

White Bean Chicken Chili

My sister shared this chili recipe with me. I usually double it and add one extra can of beans. The jalapeno offers just enough heat to notice but not too much for my children's palates.

—**KRISTINE BOWLES** RIO RANCHO, NEW MEXICO

PREP: 35 MIN. **COOK:** 3 HOURS **MAKES:** 6 SERVINGS

- **¾ pound boneless skinless chicken breasts, cubed**
- **½ teaspoon salt**
- **¼ teaspoon pepper**
- **2 tablespoons olive oil**
- **1 medium onion, chopped**
- **4 garlic cloves, minced**
- **1 jalapeno pepper, seeded and chopped**
- **2 teaspoons dried oregano**
- **1 teaspoon ground cumin**
- **2 cans (15 ounces each) white kidney or cannellini beans, rinsed and drained, divided**
- **3 cups chicken broth, divided**
- **1½ cups (6 ounces) shredded cheddar cheese**
- **Sour cream and minced fresh cilantro, optional**

1. Sprinkle chicken with salt and pepper. In a large skillet over medium heat, cook chicken in oil for 2 minutes.
2. Stir in the onion, garlic and jalapeno; cook 2 minutes longer. Sprinkle with oregano and cumin; cook 1 minute longer or until chicken is browned and vegetables are tender. Transfer to a 3-qt. slow cooker.
3. In a small bowl, mash 1 cup of beans; add ½ cup broth and stir until blended. Add to the slow cooker with the remaining beans and broth.
4. Cover and cook on low for 3 to 3½ hours or until chicken is tender. Stir before serving. Sprinkle with cheese. Garnish with sour cream and cilantro if desired.

Chicken Corn Chili: *Add 2 cups thawed frozen corn and ½ teaspoon ground coriander to the slow cooker along with the broth. Proceed as directed.*

Editor's Note: *Wear disposable gloves when cutting hot peppers; the oils can burn skin. Avoid touching your face.*

Nutrition Facts: *1 cup equals 334 calories, 15 g fat (7 g saturated fat), 64 mg cholesterol, 1,063 mg sodium, 25 g carbohydrate, 6 g fiber, 24 g protein.*

Rustic Tortellini Soup

This soup is quick to fix on a busy night and full of healthy, tasty ingredients. The recipe originally called for spicy sausage links, but I've found that turkey sausage, or even ground turkey breast, is just as good, but lower in fat.

—TRACY FASNACHT IRWIN, PENNSYLVANIA

PREP: 20 MIN. **COOK:** 20 MIN. **MAKES:** 6 SERVINGS (2 QUARTS)

- **3 Italian turkey sausage links (4 ounces each), casings removed**
- **1 medium onion, chopped**
- **6 garlic cloves, minced**
- **2 cans (14½ ounces each) reduced-sodium chicken broth**
- **1¾ cups water**
- **1 can (14½ ounces) diced tomatoes, undrained**
- **1 package (9 ounces) refrigerated cheese tortellini**
- **1 package (6 ounces) fresh baby spinach, coarsely chopped**
- **2¼ teaspoons minced fresh basil or ¾ teaspoon dried basil**
- **¼ teaspoon pepper**
- **Dash crushed red pepper flakes**
- **Shredded Parmesan cheese, optional**

1. Crumble sausage into a Dutch oven; add onion. Cook and stir over medium heat until meat is no longer pink. Add garlic; cook 1 minute longer. Stir in the broth, water and tomatoes. Bring to a boil.
2. Add tortellini; return to a boil. Cook for 7-9 minutes or until tender, stirring occasionally. Reduce heat; add the spinach, basil, pepper and pepper flakes. Cook 2-3 minutes longer or until spinach is wilted. Serve with cheese if desired.

Nutrition Facts: *1⅓ cups (calculated without cheese) equals 203 calories, 8 g fat (2 g saturated fat), 40 mg cholesterol, 878 mg sodium, 18 g carbohydrate, 3 g fiber, 16 g protein.*

Italian Peasant Soup

My father shared this recipe with me, and I use it when I need a hearty meal. It's my sons' favorite. Loaded with sausage, chicken, beans and spinach, the quick soup is nice for special occasions, too.

—KIM KNIGHT HAMBURG, PENNSYLVANIA

PREP/TOTAL TIME: 25 MIN. **MAKES:** 11 SERVINGS (2¾ QUARTS)

- **1 pound Italian sausage links, casings removed and cut into 1-inch slices**
- **2 medium onions, chopped**
- **6 garlic cloves, chopped**
- **1 pound boneless skinless chicken breasts, cut into 1-inch cubes**
- **2 cans (15 ounces each) white kidney or cannellini beans, rinsed and drained**
- **2 cans (14½ ounces each) chicken broth**
- **2 cans (14½ ounces each) diced tomatoes**
- **1 teaspoon dried basil**
- **1 teaspoon dried oregano**
- **6 cups fresh spinach leaves, chopped**
- **Shredded Parmesan cheese, optional**

1. In a Dutch oven, cook sausage and onions over medium heat until no longer pink. Add garlic; cook 1 minute longer. Drain. Add chicken; cook and stir until no longer pink.
2. Stir in the beans, broth, tomatoes, basil and oregano. Bring to a boil. Reduce heat; simmer, uncovered, for 10 minutes. Add the spinach and heat just until wilted. Serve with Parmesan cheese if desired.

Nutrition Facts: *1 cup equals 169 calories, 7 g fat (2 g saturated fat), 39 mg cholesterol, 471 mg sodium, 11 g carbohydrate, 3 g fiber, 16 g protein.*

PICKING PARMESAN

When a recipe calls for shredded Parmesan cheese, you can use preshredded cheese, or shred it from a block. Either way, the pieces are chunkier. Grated Parmesan, on the other hand, is finer. You can grate it from a block or use the pregrated type, sold in a shaker-type container.

GARDEN-FRESH FAVORITES
GRAND PRIZE
WINNER

GRAND PRIZE

Corn Soup with Pico de Gallo

The wonderful aroma of this summery, Southwestern soup lures my family to the dinner table. The blend of seasonings and succulent pico de gallo adds to its fabulous flavor.

—ELAINE SWEET DALLAS, TEXAS

PREP: 50 MIN. **COOK:** 20 MIN. **MAKES:** 6 SERVINGS

- **3 corn tortillas (6 inches), cut into 1-inch strips**
- **4 medium ears sweet corn, husks removed**
- **½ teaspoon canola oil**
- **½ teaspoon each salt, pepper and paprika**
- **1 medium red onion, chopped**
- **1 bacon strip, chopped**
- **6 garlic cloves, minced**
- **¼ cup all-purpose flour**
- **3 cups reduced-sodium chicken broth**
- **1 cup fat-free milk**
- **1 can (4 ounces) chopped green chilies**
- **1 teaspoon ground cumin**
- **1 teaspoon dried oregano**
- **½ cup minced fresh cilantro**
- **¼ cup lime juice**

PICO DE GALLO

- **2 plum tomatoes, chopped**
- **1 medium ripe avocado, peeled and chopped**
- **1 small serrano pepper, seeded and chopped**
- **1 garlic clove, minced**
- **¼ teaspoon salt**
- **¼ teaspoon pepper**

1. Place tortilla strips on a baking sheet coated with cooking spray; bake at 350° for 8-10 minutes or until crisp.
2. Rub corn with canola oil; sprinkle with seasonings. Moisten a paper towel with cooking oil; using long-handled tongs, lightly coat the grill rack.
3. Grill corn, covered, over medium heat for 10-12 minutes or until tender, turning frequently. Cool slightly; cut corn from cobs and set aside.
4. In a large saucepan, saute onion and bacon for 5 minutes; add garlic, cook 1 minute longer. Stir in flour until blended; gradually add broth. Bring to a boil; cook and stir for 2 minutes or until thickened. Add corn, milk, chilies, cumin and oregano; heat through. Remove from heat; stir in cilantro and lime juice.
5. Combine pico de gallo ingredients. Serve with soup and tortilla strips.

Editor's Note: *Wear disposable gloves when cutting hot peppers; the oils can burn skin. Avoid touching your face.*

Nutrition Facts: *¾ cup soup with ¼ cup pico de gallo and 3 tortilla strips equals 217 calories, 8 g fat (1 g saturated fat), 3 mg cholesterol, 740 mg sodium, 33 g carbohydrate, 6 g fiber, 8 g protein.* **Diabetic Exchanges:** *2 starch, 1½ fat.*

Grilled Italian Meatball Burgers

It's like taking a trip to Italy after the first bite into one my famous meatball burgers. They're a big hit with both adults and kids. I serve them with sliced green peppers, fresh tomato and onion slices and a jar of crushed red peppers on the side.

—PRISCILLA GILBERT INDIAN HARBOUR BEACH, FLORIDA

PREP: 25 MIN. **GRILL:** 15 MIN. **MAKES:** 8 SERVINGS

- **1 egg, lightly beaten**
- **⅓ cup seasoned bread crumbs**
- **3 garlic cloves, minced**
- **1 teaspoon dried oregano**
- **1 teaspoon dried basil**
- **¼ teaspoon salt**
- **¼ teaspoon dried thyme**
- **1½ pounds lean ground beef (90% lean)**
- **½ pound Italian turkey sausage links, casings removed**
- **¾ cup shredded part-skim mozzarella cheese**
- **8 kaiser rolls, split**
- **1 cup roasted garlic Parmesan spaghetti sauce, warmed**

1. In a large bowl, combine the first seven ingredients. Crumble beef and sausage over mixture and blend well. Shape into eight burgers.
2. Using long-handled tongs, moisten a paper towel with cooking oil and lightly coat the grill rack. Grill burgers, covered, over medium heat or broil 4 in. from the heat for 5-7 minutes on each side or until a thermometer reads 165° and juices run clear.
3. Sprinkle burgers with cheese; cook 2-3 minutes longer or until cheese is melted. Remove and keep warm.
4. Grill or broil rolls for 1-2 minutes or until toasted. Serve burgers on rolls with spaghetti sauce.

Flank Steak Sandwiches

My sister and I found this recipe 15 years ago and changed a few ingredients to make it our own. Now, when family and friends hear we're assembling these sandwiches, they come running!

—ELIZABETH HINER CHICO, CALIFORNIA

PREP: 25 MIN. + MARINATING **GRILL:** 25 MIN.
MAKES: 6 SERVINGS

- **1 cup chopped onion**
- **1 cup dry red wine or beef broth**
- **¾ cup reduced-sodium soy sauce**
- **½ cup olive oil, divided**
- **4½ teaspoons minced garlic, divided**
- **1½ teaspoons ground mustard**
- **1½ teaspoons ground ginger**
- **1 beef flank steak (1½ pounds)**
- **1 medium sweet red pepper, cut into 1-inch strips**
- **1 medium sweet yellow pepper, cut into 1-inch strips**
- **1 medium red onion, thickly sliced**
- **¼ teaspoon pepper**
- **6 French rolls, split**

1. In a small bowl, combine the onion, wine, soy sauce, 1/4 cup olive oil, 2½ teaspoons garlic, mustard and ginger. Pour 1¾ cups into a large resealable plastic bag; add steak. Pour remaining marinade into another resealable plastic bag; add the peppers and onion. Seal bags and turn to coat; refrigerate for 3 hours or overnight, turning occasionally.
2. Drain and discard marinade from steak. Using long-handled tongs, dip a paper towel in cooking oil and lightly coat the grill rack. Grill, covered, over medium heat for 6-7 minutes on each side or until meat reaches desired doneness (for medium-rare, a thermometer should read 145°; medium, 160°; well-done, 170°).
3. Drain and discard marinade from vegetables. Place in a grill basket. Grill, uncovered, over medium-hot heat for 9-11 minutes or until tender, stirring frequently.
4. In a small bowl, combine the pepper, and remaining oil and garlic; brush over cut sides of rolls. Place cut side down on grill for 2-3 minutes or until golden brown.
5. Thinly slice steak across the grain; place on bun bottoms. Top with vegetables and bun tops. Serve immediately.

Editor's Note: *If you do not have a grill wok or basket, use a disposable foil pan. Poke holes in the bottom of the pan with a meat fork to allow liquid to drain.*

New England Clam Chowder

Living in the Pacific Northwest, I have the pleasure of digging and grinding my own razor clams. Not everyone is as lucky to have this local treasure, so I recommend canned clams as a good substitute.

—SANDY LARSON PORT ANGELES, WASHINGTON

PREP: 20 MIN. **COOK:** 35 MIN. **MAKES:** 5 SERVINGS

- **4 center-cut bacon strips**
- **2 celery ribs, chopped**
- **1 large onion, chopped**
- **1 garlic clove, minced**
- **3 small potatoes, peeled and cubed**
- **1 cup water**
- **1 bottle (8 ounces) clam juice**
- **3 teaspoons reduced-sodium chicken bouillon granules**
- **¼ teaspoon white pepper**
- **¼ teaspoon dried thyme**
- **⅓ cup all-purpose flour**
- **2 cups fat-free half-and-half, divided**
- **2 cans (6½ ounces each) chopped clams, undrained**

1. In a Dutch oven, cook bacon over medium heat until crisp. Remove to paper towels to drain; set aside. Saute celery and onion in the drippings until tender. Add garlic; cook 1 minute longer. Stir in the potatoes, water, clam juice, bouillon, pepper and thyme. Bring to a boil. Reduce heat; simmer, uncovered, for 15-20 minutes or until potatoes are tender.
2. In a small bowl, combine flour and 1 cup half-and-half until smooth. Gradually stir into soup. Bring to a boil; cook and stir for 1-2 minutes or until thickened.
3. Stir in clams and remaining half-and-half; heat through (do not boil). Crumble the reserved bacon; sprinkle over each serving of chowder.

Nutrition Facts: *1⅓ cups equals 260 calories, 4 g fat (1 g saturated fat), 22 mg cholesterol, 788 mg sodium, 39 g carbohydrate, 3 g fiber, 13 g protein.* **Diabetic Exchanges:** *2½ starch, 1 lean meat.*

Grilled Veggie Sandwiches with Cilantro Pesto

I ordered this sandwich while vacationing in Sedona, Arizona, and fell in love with it. When I returned home, I developed this recipe that tastes just like the original.

—**CAROLYN PHENICIE** TITUSVILLE, PENNSYLVANIA

PREP: 20 MIN. + STANDING **GRILL:** 10 MIN. **MAKES:** 4 SERVINGS

- **2/3 cup packed fresh cilantro sprigs**
- **1/4 cup packed fresh parsley sprigs**
- **2 tablespoons grated Parmesan cheese**
- **2 garlic cloves, peeled**
- **2 tablespoons water**
- **1 tablespoon pine nuts**
- **1 tablespoon olive oil**
- **Cooking spray**
- **2 large sweet red peppers**
- **4 slices eggplant (1/2 inch thick)**
- **1/2 teaspoon salt**
- **1/4 teaspoon pepper**
- **1/2 cup shredded part-skim mozzarella cheese**
- **4 hard rolls, split**

1. For pesto, place the cilantro, parsley, Parmesan cheese and garlic in a small food processor; cover and pulse until chopped. Add water and pine nuts; cover and process until blended. While processing, gradually add oil in a steady stream. Set aside.
2. Using long-handled tongs, moisten a paper towel with cooking oil and lightly coat the grill rack. Grill peppers over medium heat for 10-15 minutes or until the skins blister, turning frequently.
3. Immediately place peppers in a large bowl; cover and let stand for 15-20 minutes. Peel off and discard charred skin. Halve and seed peppers; set aside.
4. Lightly coat eggplant on both sides with cooking spray; sprinkle with salt and pepper. Grill, covered, over medium heat for 3-5 minutes on each side or until tender.
5. Top each eggplant slice with a pepper half; sprinkle with mozzarella cheese. Grill, covered, for 2-3 minutes or until cheese is melted. Spread each roll with 1 tablespoon reserved pesto; top each with an eggplant stack. Replace roll tops.

Nutrition Facts: *1 sandwich equals 290 calories, 10 g fat (3 g saturated fat), 10 mg cholesterol, 717 mg sodium, 39 g carbohydrate, 5 g fiber, 12 g protein.* **Diabetic Exchanges:** *2 starch, 1 lean meat, 1 vegetable, 1 fat.*

Italian Sausage Bean Soup

Nothing beats putting on a big pot of this comforting soup when it's cold outside. I love that I can turn my attention to other tasks while it slowly simmers on the stovetop.

—**GLENNA REIMER** GIG HARBOR, WASHINGTON

PREP: 20 MIN. **COOK:** 1 1/2 HOURS
MAKES: 8 SERVINGS (3 QUARTS)

- **1 pound bulk Italian sausage**
- **1 medium onion, finely chopped**
- **3 garlic cloves, sliced**
- **4 cans (14 1/2 ounces each) reduced-sodium chicken broth**
- **2 cans (15 ounces each) pinto beans, rinsed and drained**
- **1 can (14 1/2 ounces) diced tomatoes, undrained**
- **1 cup medium pearl barley**
- **1 large carrot, sliced**
- **1 celery rib, sliced**
- **1 teaspoon minced fresh sage**
- **1/2 teaspoon minced fresh rosemary or 1/8 teaspoon dried rosemary, crushed**
- **6 cups chopped fresh kale**

1. In a Dutch oven, cook sausage and onion over medium heat until meat is no longer pink. Add the garlic; cook for 1 minute longer. Drain.
2. Stir in the broth, beans, tomatoes, barley, carrot, celery, sage and rosemary. Bring to a boil. Reduce heat; cover and simmer for 45 minutes.
3. Stir in the kale; return to a boil. Reduce heat; cover and simmer for 25-30 minutes or until vegetables are tender and kale is wilted.

Cheesy Corn Chowder

I've been making this chowder recipe for more than 30 years, and the whole family really enjoys its cheesy, corn-filled flavor. It makes a big pot—enough for seconds!

—LOLA COMER MARYSVILLE, WASHINGTON

PREP: 30 MIN. **COOK:** 30 MIN.
MAKES: 15 SERVINGS (3¾ QUARTS)

- **6 bacon strips, chopped**
- **¾ cup chopped sweet onion**
- **2½ cups water**
- **2½ cups cubed peeled potatoes**
- **2 cups sliced fresh carrots**
- **2 teaspoons chicken bouillon granules**
- **3 cans (11 ounces each) gold and white corn, drained**
- **½ teaspoon pepper**
- **7 tablespoons all-purpose flour**
- **5 cups 2% milk**
- **3 cups (12 ounces) shredded cheddar cheese**
- **1 cup cubed process cheese (Velveeta)**

1. In a Dutch oven, cook bacon and onion over medium heat until onion is tender. Add the water, potatoes, carrots and bouillon; bring to a boil. Reduce heat; cover and simmer for 15-20 minutes or until potatoes are tender.
2. Stir in corn and pepper. In a large bowl, whisk flour and milk until smooth; add to soup. Bring to a boil; cook and stir for 2 minutes or until thickened. Reduce heat. Add the cheeses; cook and stir until melted.

Nutrition Facts: *1 cup equals 282 calories, 16 g fat (9 g saturated fat), 44 mg cholesterol, 644 mg sodium, 25 g carbohydrate, 2 g fiber, 12 g protein.*

Floribbean Fish Burgers with Tropical Sauce

I make fish burgers because they're lower in saturated fat and cholesterol than other types of burgers. I like to garnish them with avocado for extra flavor.

—VIRGINIA ANTHONY JACKSONVILLE, FLORIDA

PREP: 35 MIN. **GRILL:** 10 MIN. **MAKES:** 6 SERVINGS

- **½ cup fat-free mayonnaise**
- **1 tablespoon minced fresh cilantro**
- **1 tablespoon minced chives**
- **1 tablespoon sweet pickle relish**
- **1 tablespoon lime juice**
- **1 teaspoon grated lime peel**
- **1½ teaspoons Caribbean jerk seasoning**
- **⅛ teaspoon hot pepper sauce**

BURGERS

- **1 egg white, lightly beaten**
- **4 green onions, chopped**
- **⅓ cup soft bread crumbs**
- **2 tablespoons minced fresh cilantro**
- **2 teaspoons Caribbean jerk seasoning**
- **1 garlic clove, minced**
- **⅛ teaspoon salt**
- **1½ pounds grouper or red snapper fillets**
- **6 kaiser rolls, split**
- **6 lettuce leaves**
- **1 medium ripe avocado, peeled and cut into 12 slices**

1. In a small bowl, combine the first eight ingredients; cover and refrigerate until serving.
2. In a large bowl, combine the egg white, onions, bread crumbs, cilantro, jerk seasoning, garlic and salt. Place fish in a food processor; cover and process until finely chopped. Add to egg white mixture and mix well. Shape into six burgers.
3. Spray both sides of burgers with cooking spray. Using long-handled tongs, moisten a paper towel with cooking oil and lightly coat the grill rack. Grill burgers, covered, over medium heat or broil 4 in. from the heat for 4-5 minutes on each side or until a thermometer reads 160°.
4. Serve each on a roll with lettuce, avocado and 5 teaspoons tropical sauce.

Nutrition Facts: *1 burger equals 353 calories, 9 g fat (1 g saturated fat), 44 mg cholesterol, 797 mg sodium, 39 g carbohydrate, 4 g fiber, 29 g protein.* **Diabetic Exchanges:** *3 lean meat, 2½ starch, 1 fat.*

Grilled Vegetable Sandwich

Wow! Meat lovers won't even miss the meat, but they'll rave about the simply fabulous flavor of this hearty grilled veggie sandwich. It's wonderful paired with the ciabatta bread's crispy crust and light, airy texture.

—DIANA TSEPERKAS HAMDEN, CONNECTICUT

PREP: 20 MIN. + MARINATING **GRILL:** 10 MIN.
MAKES: 4 SERVINGS

- **1 medium zucchini, thinly sliced lengthwise**
- **1 medium sweet red pepper, quartered**
- **1 small red onion, cut into ½-inch slices**
- **¼ cup prepared Italian salad dressing**
- **1 loaf ciabatta bread (14 ounces), halved lengthwise**
- **2 tablespoons olive oil**
- **¼ cup reduced-fat mayonnaise**
- **1 tablespoon lemon juice**
- **2 teaspoons grated lemon peel**
- **1 teaspoon minced garlic**
- **½ cup crumbled feta cheese**

1. In a large resealable plastic bag, combine the zucchini, pepper, onion and salad dressing. Seal bag and turn to coat; refrigerate for at least 1 hour. Drain and discard marinade.
2. Brush cut sides of bread with oil; set aside. Place vegetables on grill rack. Grill, covered, over medium heat for 4-5 minutes on each side or until crisp-tender. Remove and keep warm. Grill bread, oil side down, over medium heat for 30-60 seconds or until toasted.
3. In a small bowl, combine the mayonnaise, lemon juice, peel and garlic. Spread over bread bottom; sprinkle with cheese. Top with vegetables and remaining bread. Cut into four slices.

Greek-Style Chicken Burgers

The original recipe for these burgers called for lamb or beef, but I decided to try ground chicken to slim it down. The sauce easily doubles as a delicious dip for veggies and toasted pita chips.

—JUDY PUSKAS WALLACEBURG, ONTARIO

PREP: 25 MIN. + CHILLING **GRILL:** 10 MIN. **MAKES:** 4 SERVINGS

- **½ cup fat-free plain yogurt**
- **¼ cup chopped peeled cucumber**
- **¼ cup crumbled reduced-fat feta cheese**
- **1½ teaspoons snipped fresh dill**
- **1½ teaspoons lemon juice**
- **1 small garlic clove, minced**

BURGERS

- **1 medium onion, finely chopped**
- **¼ cup dry bread crumbs**
- **1 tablespoon dried oregano**
- **1 tablespoon lemon juice**
- **2 garlic cloves, minced**
- **½ teaspoon salt**
- **¼ teaspoon pepper**
- **1 pound ground chicken**
- **4 hamburger buns, split**
- **4 lettuce leaves**
- **4 tomato slices**

1. Line a strainer with four layers of cheesecloth or one coffee filter and place over a bowl. Place yogurt in prepared strainer; cover yogurt with edges of cheesecloth. Refrigerate for 8 hours or overnight.
2. Remove yogurt from cheesecloth and discard liquid from bowl. Stir in the cucumber, feta cheese, dill, lemon juice and garlic; set aside.
3. In a small bowl, combine the onion, bread crumbs, oregano, lemon juice, garlic, salt and pepper. Crumble chicken over mixture and mix well. Shape into four burgers.
4. Using long-handled tongs, moisten a paper towel with cooking oil and lightly coat the grill rack. Grill burgers, covered, over medium heat or broil 4 in. from the heat for 5-7 minutes on each side or until a thermometer reads 165° and juices run clear.
5. Serve each on a bun with lettuce, tomato and 2 tablespoons yogurt sauce.

Nutrition Facts: *1 burger equals 350 calories, 12 g fat (4 g saturated fat), 78 mg cholesterol, 732 mg sodium, 35 g carbohydrate, 3 g fiber, 27 g protein.* **Diabetic Exchanges:** *3 lean meat, 2 starch, 1 vegetable.*

I'M STUFFED FRENCH TOAST, PAGE 86

76
85
80

Breakfast & Brunch

No matter how cozy their beds, everyone will be up and at ’em, ready to tuck into the **hearty breakfasts** here. Hosting morning guests? Our satisfying brunch dishes are **certain to impress.**

Omelet Paninis

When you're in a hurry to get out the door, this speedy breakfast recipe does the trick, keeping you energized until lunchtime.

—DOROTHY MCCLINTON NORTH CHICAGO, ILLINOIS

PREP/TOTAL TIME: 20 MIN. **MAKES:** 2 SERVINGS

- **4 slices sourdough bread (½ inch thick)**
- **2 teaspoons stone-ground mustard**
- **2 slices Havarti cheese (1 ounce each)**
- **4 thin slices prosciutto or deli ham**
- **5 teaspoons butter, softened, divided**
- **2 eggs**
- **1 tablespoon finely chopped onion**
- **2 teaspoons grated Parmesan cheese**
- **1 teaspoon minced chives**
- **1 teaspoon 2% milk**

1. Spread two slices of bread with mustard. Top with Havarti cheese and prosciutto; set aside.

2. In a small nonstick skillet, melt 1 teaspoon butter over medium-high heat. In a small bowl, whisk the eggs, onion, Parmesan cheese, chives and milk. Pour into skillet (mixture should set immediately at edges). As eggs set, push cooked edges toward the center, letting uncooked portion flow underneath.

3. Invert omelet onto a plate; cut in half. Place over prosciutto; top with remaining bread. Lightly spread remaining butter over outsides of sandwiches.

4. Cook on a panini maker or indoor grill for 1-2 minutes or until bread is browned and cheese is melted.

Breakfast Pizza

Pizza for breakfast? Yes, please! I used to make this for my morning drivers when I worked at a pizza delivery place. It's a quick and easy eye-opener that appeals to all.

—CATHY SHORTALL EASTON, MARYLAND

PREP/TOTAL TIME: 25 MIN. **MAKES:** 8 SLICES

- **1 tube (13.8 ounces) refrigerated pizza crust**
- **2 tablespoons olive oil, divided**
- **6 eggs**
- **2 tablespoons water**
- **1 package (3 ounces) real bacon bits**
- **1 cup (4 ounces) shredded Monterey Jack cheese**
- **1 cup (4 ounces) shredded cheddar cheese**

1. Unroll crust into a greased 15-in. x 10-in. x 1-in. baking pan; flatten dough and build up edges slightly. Brush with 1 tablespoon oil. Prick dough thoroughly with a fork. Bake at 400° for 7-8 minutes or until lightly browned.

2. Meanwhile, in a small bowl, whisk eggs and water. In a small skillet, heat remaining oil until hot. Add eggs; cook and stir over medium heat until completely set.

3. Spoon eggs over crust. Sprinkle with bacon and cheeses. Bake 5-7 minutes longer or until cheese is melted.

Canadian Bacon Onion Quiche

For more than 20 years, we sold our homegrown specialty onions at the farmers market. I handed out this classic quiche recipe to all our customers.

—JANICE REDFORD CAMBRIDGE, WISCONSIN

PREP: 30 MIN. **BAKE:** 40 MIN.
MAKES: 6-8 SERVINGS

- **1 cup all-purpose flour**
- **¾ teaspoon salt, divided**
- **½ cup plus 3 tablespoons cold butter, divided**
- **½ cup 4% small-curd cottage cheese**
- **3 large sweet onions, sliced (about 6 cups)**
- **4 ounces Canadian bacon, diced**
- **¼ teaspoon pepper**
- **3 eggs, lightly beaten**
- **1 cup (4 ounces) shredded cheddar cheese**

1. In a small bowl, combine flour and 1/4 teaspoon salt; cut in 1/2 cup butter until crumbly. Gradually add cottage cheese, tossing with a fork until dough forms a ball.

2. Roll out pastry to fit a 9-in. pie plate. Transfer pastry to pie plate. Trim pastry to 1/2 in. beyond edge of plate; flute edges.

3. In a large skillet, saute onions in remaining butter until golden brown. Stir in the Canadian bacon, pepper and remaining salt. Remove from the heat; add eggs and cheddar cheese. Pour into pastry shell.

4. Bake at 350° for 40-45 minutes or until a knife inserted near the center comes out clean.

STORING SWEET ONIONS

When storing sweet onions, keep them cool, dry and separate. Place in a single layer, wrapped individually in foil or paper towels, in the vegetable bin of the refrigerator. If it's not possible to keep them chilled, store sweet onions in the coolest area of your home that also has good air circulation.

Italian Garden Frittata

I like to whip up this pretty frittata for a delicious, nutritious breakfast or brunch. Melon wedges are a sweet complement.

—**SALLY MALONEY** DALLAS, GEORGIA

PREP/TOTAL TIME: 30 MIN. **MAKES:** 4 SERVINGS

- **6 egg whites**
- **4 eggs**
- **½ cup grated Romano cheese, divided**
- **1 tablespoon minced fresh sage**
- **½ teaspoon salt**
- **¼ teaspoon pepper**
- **1 small zucchini, sliced**
- **2 green onions, sliced**
- **1 teaspoon olive oil**
- **2 plum tomatoes, thinly sliced**

1. In a large bowl, whisk the egg whites, eggs, 1/4 cup Romano cheese, sage, salt and pepper; set aside.

2. In a 10-in. ovenproof skillet coated with cooking spray, saute zucchini and onions in oil for 2 minutes. Add egg mixture; cover and cook for 4-6 minutes or until eggs are nearly set.

3. Uncover; top with tomato slices and remaining cheese. Broil 3-4 in. from the heat for 2-3 minutes or until eggs are completely set. Let stand for 5 minutes. Cut into wedges.

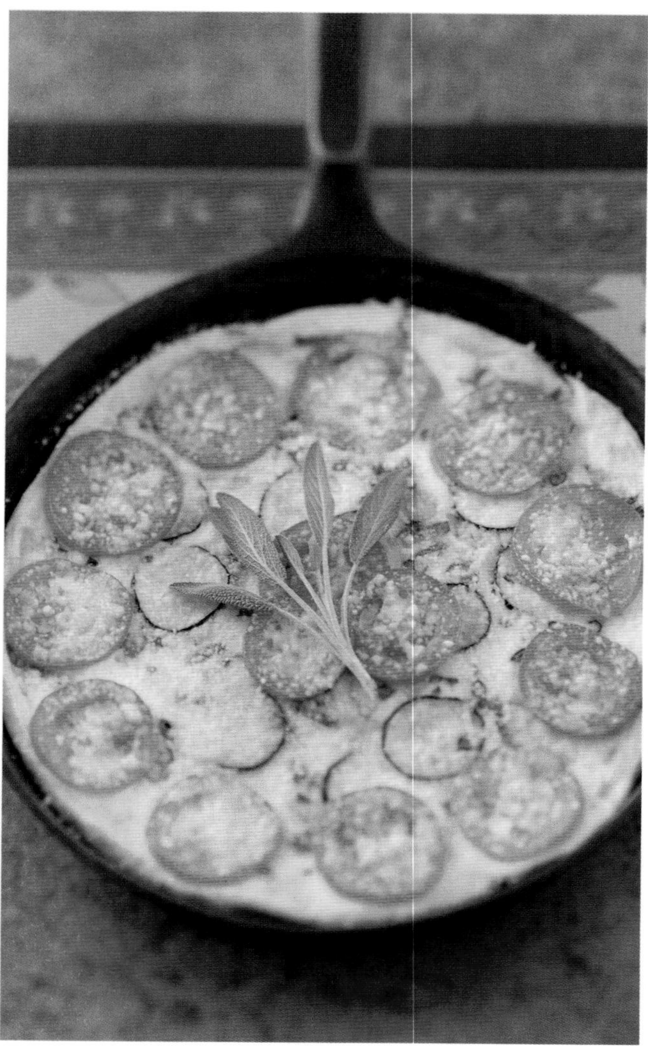

"A friend often makes these scones and shares them with me. Flecks of cheese, ham and green onions are sure signs that your taste buds are in for a treat."

—**FELICITY LA RUE** PALMDALE, CALIFORNIA

Ham and Cheddar Scones

PREP: 25 MIN. **BAKE:** 20 MIN. **MAKES:** 1 DOZEN

- **3 cups all-purpose flour**
- **½ cup sugar**
- **2 tablespoons baking powder**
- **½ teaspoon salt**
- **2 cups heavy whipping cream**
- **1 cup diced fully cooked ham**
- **½ cup diced cheddar cheese**
- **4 green onions, thinly sliced**

1. In a large bowl, combine the flour, sugar, baking powder and salt. Stir in cream just until moistened. Stir in the ham, cheese and onions. Turn onto a floured surface; knead 10 times.

2. Transfer dough to a greased baking sheet. Pat into a 9-in. circle. Cut into 12 wedges, but do not separate. Bake at 400° for 20-25 minutes or until golden brown. Serve warm.

Toasty Pumpkin Waffles

Whenever I want to set something on the table that is guaranteed to impress folks, I serve these waffles. They're beautiful with a fresh sprig of mint atop the sweet butter. This was my most requested recipe when I owned a bed-and-breakfast.

—BRENDA RYAN MARSHALL, MISSOURI

PREP/TOTAL TIME: 30 MIN. **MAKES:** 4 SERVINGS (1 CUP BUTTER)

- **1 cup all-purpose flour**
- **1 tablespoon brown sugar**
- **1 teaspoon baking powder**
- **¼ teaspoon salt**
- **1 egg, lightly beaten**
- **1¼ cups milk**
- **⅔ cup canned pumpkin**
- **4½ teaspoons butter, melted**
- **⅓ cup chopped pecans**

MAPLE CRANBERRY BUTTER

- **½ cup fresh or frozen cranberries**
- **¼ cup maple syrup**
- **1 cup butter, softened**
- **Additional maple syrup, optional**

1. In a large bowl, combine the flour, brown sugar, baking powder and salt. Whisk the egg, milk, pumpkin and butter; stir into dry ingredients until blended. Fold in pecans.

2. Bake in a preheated waffle iron according to manufacturer's directions until golden brown.

3. Meanwhile, in a small saucepan, combine cranberries and syrup. Cook over medium heat until berries pop, about 10 minutes. Transfer to a small bowl; cool slightly. Beat in butter until blended.

4. Serve waffles with maple cranberry butter and syrup if desired. Refrigerate or freeze leftover butter.

Hearty Shrimp Omelet

I've been cooking for many years and enjoy making quick, easy and tasty meals. This coastal-inspired omelet is a breeze to prepare. Your dining partner is sure to exclaim, "Wow, what a meal!"

—GREG PARSONS CANDOR, NORTH CAROLINA

PREP/TOTAL TIME: 25 MIN. **MAKES:** 2 SERVINGS

- **10 uncooked small shrimp, peeled and deveined**
- **¼ cup chopped sweet red pepper**
- **1 bacon strip, cooked and crumbled**
- **1 green onion, finely chopped**
- **1 tablespoon lemon juice**
- **2 teaspoons diced seeded jalapeno pepper**
- **¼ teaspoon dried basil**
- **¼ teaspoon Greek seasoning**
- **¼ teaspoon pepper**
- **⅛ teaspoon garlic powder**
- **1 tablespoon olive oil**
- **2 tablespoons butter, divided**
- **4 eggs, lightly beaten**
- **½ cup shredded Monterey Jack cheese**
- **1 teaspoon minced fresh parsley**

1. In a large nonstick skillet, saute the shrimp, red pepper, bacon, onion, lemon juice, jalapeno and seasonings in oil and 1 tablespoon butter for 2-3 minutes or until shrimp turn pink and vegetables are tender. Remove and keep warm.

2. In the same skillet, melt remaining butter over medium-high heat; add eggs (mixture should set immediately at edges). As eggs set, push cooked edges toward the center, letting uncooked portion flow underneath.

3. When the eggs are set, spoon shrimp mixture on one side and sprinkle with cheese; fold other side over the filling. Invert omelet onto a plate; cut in half. Sprinkle with parsley.

Editor's Note: *Wear disposable gloves when cutting hot peppers; the oils can burn skin. Avoid touching your face.*

Warm 'n' Fruity Breakfast Cereal

Overnight guests will love the heartiness of this healthful slow-cooked cereal that is spiced with cinnamon and loaded with fruit and nuts. We enjoy it with yogurt and banana or berries.

—JOHN VALE HARDIN, MONTANA

PREP: 10 MIN. **COOK:** 6 HOURS **MAKES:** 10 CUPS

- **5 cups water**
- **2 cups seven-grain cereal**
- **1 medium apple, peeled and chopped**
- **1 cup unsweetened apple juice**
- **¼ cup dried apricots, chopped**
- **¼ cup dried cranberries**
- **¼ cup raisins**
- **¼ cup chopped dates**
- **¼ cup maple syrup**
- **1 teaspoon ground cinnamon**
- **½ teaspoon salt**
- **Chopped walnuts, optional**

In a 5-qt. slow cooker, combine the first 11 ingredients. Cover and cook on low for 6-7 hours or until fruits are softened. Sprinkle individual servings with walnuts if desired.

GRAND PRIZE

Apple-Bacon Egg Bake

PREP: 15 MIN. **BAKE:** 30 MIN. **MAKES:** 2 SERVINGS

- **3 eggs**
- **1 small apple, diced**
- **¾ cup frozen O'Brien potatoes, thawed**
- **⅓ cup 2% milk**
- **⅓ cup sour cream**
- **⅓ cup shredded cheddar cheese, divided**
- **3 bacon strips, cooked and crumbled, divided**
- **Dash salt and pepper**

1. In a small bowl, beat the eggs. Stir in apple, hash browns, milk, sour cream, 3 tablespoons cheese, 1 tablespoon bacon, salt and pepper.

2. Pour into two 2-cup baking dishes coated with cooking spray. Sprinkle with remaining cheese and bacon.

3. Bake, uncovered, at 350° for 30-35 minutes or until a knife inserted near the center comes out clean.

"I wanted a healthy, inexpensive egg dish for Sunday brunch, so I came up with this recipe. It's hearty and delicious, and the apples give it a slight sweetness."

—NANCY MILLER BETTENDORF, IOWA

FRESH EGGS

Properly refrigerated, eggs will keep for about 3 weeks after you bring them home without a significant reduction in quality. You can easily check the freshness of an uncooked egg by placing it in a glass of cold water. If the egg is fresh, it will remain on the bottom of the glass. If the egg floats to the surface of the water, it is not fresh and should not be used. If the egg stands upright and bobs on the bottom of the glass, it is less than fresh but still alright to use. This type of egg is good when you need to prepare hard-cooked eggs because it's easier to peel.

EXCEPTIONAL EGGS
GRAND PRIZE
WINNER

Pretty Pumpkin Cinnamon Buns

My husband loves sticky buns and cinnamon rolls, so I make them often. One day, I had some fresh pumpkin on hand and decided to use it in cinnamon buns. We loved the results!

—**GLENDA JOSEPH** CHAMBERSBURG, PENNSYLVANIA

PREP: 45 MIN. + RISING **BAKE:** 25 MIN. **MAKES:** 2 DOZEN

- **2 tablespoons active dry yeast**
- **½ cup warm water (110° to 115°)**
- **4 eggs**
- **1 cup shortening**
- **1 cup canned pumpkin**
- **1 cup warm milk (110° to 115°)**
- **½ cup sugar**
- **½ cup packed brown sugar**
- **⅓ cup instant vanilla pudding mix**
- **⅓ cup instant butterscotch pudding mix**
- **1 teaspoon salt**
- **7 to 8 cups all-purpose flour, divided**

FILLING

- **¼ cup butter, melted**
- **1 cup packed brown sugar**
- **2 teaspoons ground cinnamon**

ICING

- **3 tablespoons water**
- **2 tablespoons butter, softened**
- **1 teaspoon ground cinnamon**
- **2 cups confectioners' sugar**
- **1½ teaspoons vanilla extract**

1. In a large bowl, dissolve yeast in warm water. Add the eggs, shortening, pumpkin, milk, sugars, pudding mixes, salt and 6 cups flour. Beat until smooth. Stir in enough remaining flour to form a soft dough (dough will be sticky).

2. Turn onto a floured surface; knead until smooth and elastic, about 6-8 minutes. Place in a greased bowl, turning once to grease the top. Cover and let rise in a warm place until doubled in size, about 1 hour.

3. Punch dough down; divide in half. Roll each portion into a 12-in. x 8-in. rectangle; brush with butter. Combine the brown sugar and cinnamon; sprinkle over the dough to within ½ in. of edges.

4. Roll up jelly-roll style, starting with a long side; pinch the seams to seal. Cut each into 12 slices. Place cut side down in two greased 13-in. x 9-in. baking pans. Cover and let rise until doubled, about 30 minutes.

5. Bake at 350° for 22-28 minutes or until golden brown. In a small bowl, combine the water, butter and cinnamon. Add confectioners' sugar and vanilla; beat until smooth. Spread over buns. Serve warm.

Crisp 'n' Tender Corn Waffles

I serve these crisp, golden-brown waffles with drizzled honey and a side of applesauce. For a savory change of pace, top them with a generous scoop of creamed chicken.

—**MAXINE REESE** CANDLER, NORTH CAROLINA

PREP: 15 MIN. + STANDING **COOK:** 20 MIN. **MAKES:** 16 WAFFLES

- **2 eggs, separated**
- **2 cups all-purpose flour**
- **2½ teaspoons baking powder**
- **½ teaspoon salt**
- **1½ cups milk**
- **1 can (8¼ ounces) cream-style corn**
- **½ cup canola oil**

1. Place egg whites in a small bowl; let stand at room temperature for 30 minutes.

2. In a large bowl, combine the flour, baking powder and salt. Combine the milk, corn, egg yolks and oil; stir into dry ingredients just until combined.

3. Beat reserved egg whites until stiff peaks form; fold into batter. Pour batter by ¼-cupfuls into a preheated waffle iron; bake according to manufacturer's directions until golden brown.

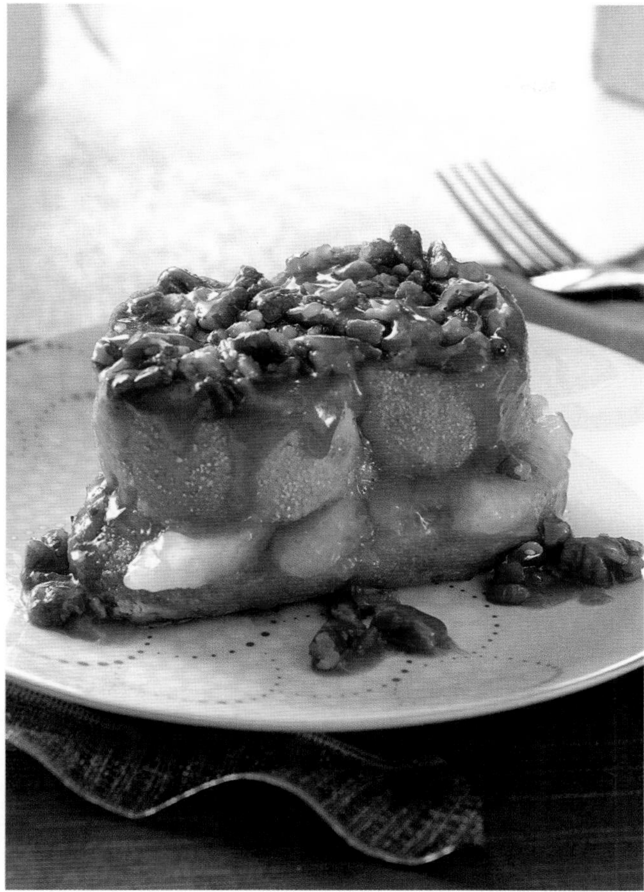

Baked Apple French Toast

This special prep-ahead brunch recipe will have everyone around the table asking for seconds. I frequently serve it with whipped cream, maple syrup and additional nuts.

—BEVERLY JOHNSTON RUBICON, WISCONSIN

PREP: 20 MIN. + CHILLING **BAKE:** 35 MIN. **MAKES:** 10 SERVINGS

- **20 slices French bread (1 inch thick)**
- **1 can (21 ounces) apple pie filling**
- **8 eggs, lightly beaten**
- **2 cups 2% milk**
- **2 teaspoons vanilla extract**
- **½ teaspoon ground cinnamon**
- **½ teaspoon ground nutmeg**

TOPPING

- **1 cup packed brown sugar**
- **½ cup cold butter, cubed**
- **1 cup chopped pecans**
- **2 tablespoons corn syrup**

1. Arrange 10 slices of bread in a greased 13-in. x 9-in. baking dish. Spread with pie filling; top with remaining bread. In a large bowl, whisk the eggs, milk, vanilla, cinnamon and nutmeg. Pour over bread. Cover and refrigerate overnight.

2. Remove from the refrigerator 30 minutes before baking. Meanwhile, place brown sugar in a small bowl. Cut in butter until mixture resembles coarse crumbs. Stir in pecans and corn syrup. Sprinkle over French toast.

3. Bake, uncovered, at 350° for 35-40 minutes or until a knife inserted near the center comes out clean.

Sausage and Egg Pizza

I use turkey sausage, fat-free cheddar cheese, egg substitute and reduced-fat crescent rolls to help cut calories and fat in this flavor-packed pizza. It's still a slice of breakfast heaven.

—VICKI MEYERS CASTALIA, OHIO

PREP/TOTAL TIME: 30 MIN. **MAKES:** 6 SLICES

- **1 tube (8 ounces) refrigerated reduced-fat crescent rolls**
- **½ pound Italian turkey sausage links, casings removed**
- **1¾ cups sliced fresh mushrooms**
- **1¼ cups frozen shredded hash brown potatoes**
- **¼ teaspoon garlic salt**
- **¼ teaspoon pepper**
- **2 green onions, chopped**
- **2 tablespoons finely chopped sweet red pepper**
- **½ cup shredded fat-free cheddar cheese**
- **¾ cup egg substitute**

1. Separate crescent dough into eight triangles; place on an ungreased 12-in. pizza pan with points toward the center. Press onto the bottom and up the sides of pan to form a crust; seal perforations. Bake at 375° for 8 minutes.

2. Meanwhile, crumble sausage into a large nonstick skillet coated with cooking spray. Add mushrooms; cook and stir over medium heat until meat is no longer pink. Drain and set aside. In the same skillet, cook the potatoes, garlic salt and pepper over medium heat until browned.

3. Sprinkle sausage mixture over the crust. Layer with potatoes, onions, red pepper and cheese; pour egg substitute over the top. Bake for 10-12 minutes or until egg is set and cheese is melted.

Nutrition Facts: *1 slice equals 241 calories, 10 g fat (2 g saturated fat), 24 mg cholesterol, 744 mg sodium, 22 g carbohydrate, 1 g fiber, 16 g protein.* **Diabetic Exchanges:** *2 lean meat, 1½ starch, ½ fat.*

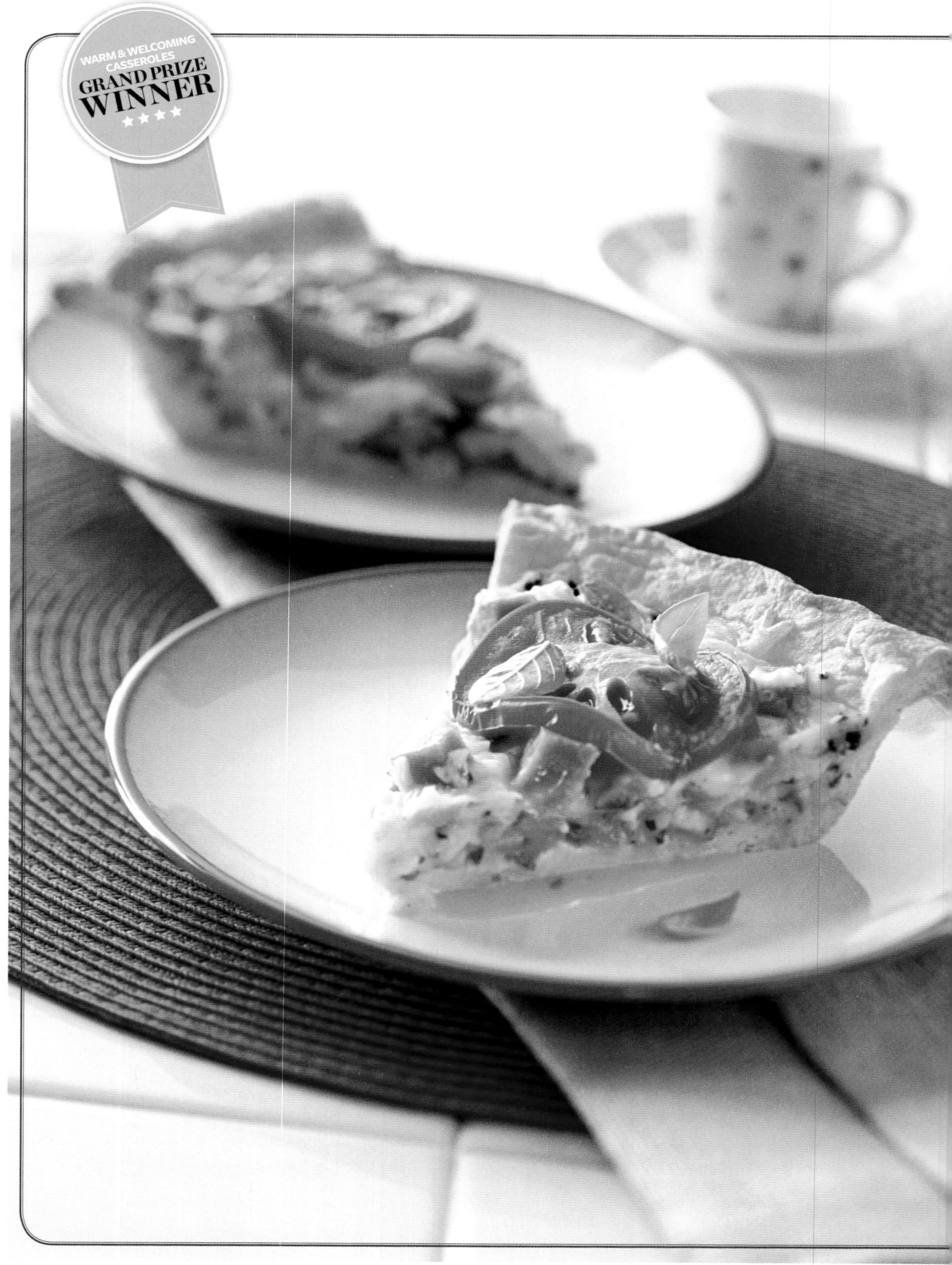
WARM & WELCOMING CASSEROLES
GRAND PRIZE
WINNER

GRAND PRIZE

Zucchini Crescent Pie

This is one of my mother's many recipes designed to take advantage of a bountiful zucchini crop. Refrigerated crescent rolls and cooked ham cut prep time but not taste!

—**SUSAN DAVIS** ANN ARBOR, MICHIGAN

PREP: 25 MIN. **BAKE:** 20 MIN. **MAKES:** 6 SERVINGS

- **1 package (8 ounces) refrigerated crescent rolls**
- **2 medium zucchini, sliced lengthwise and quartered**
- **½ cup chopped onion**
- **¼ cup butter, cubed**
- **2 teaspoons minced fresh parsley**
- **½ teaspoon salt**
- **½ teaspoon garlic powder**
- **½ teaspoon pepper**
- **¼ teaspoon dried basil**
- **¼ teaspoon dried oregano**
- **2 eggs, lightly beaten**
- **2 cups (8 ounces) shredded part-skim mozzarella cheese**
- **¾ cup cubed fully cooked ham**
- **1 medium plum tomato, thinly sliced**

1. Separate crescent dough into eight triangles; place in a greased 9-in. pie plate with points toward the center. Press onto the bottom and up the sides to form a crust; seal seams and perforations. Bake at 375° for 5-8 minutes or until lightly browned.

2. Meanwhile, in a large skillet, saute zucchini and onion in butter until tender; stir in seasonings. Spoon into crust. Combine the eggs, cheese and ham; pour over zucchini mixture. Top with tomato slices.

3. Bake at 375° for 20-25 minutes or until a knife inserted near the center comes out clean. Let stand for 5 minutes before cutting.

ALL ABOUT ZUCCHINI

Handle zucchini carefully; they're thin-skinned and easily damaged. To pick the freshest zucchini, look for a firm heavy squash with a moist stem end and a shiny skin. Smaller squash are generally sweeter and more tender than larger ones. One medium (⅓ pound) zucchini yields about 2 cups sliced or 1½ cups shredded zucchini. Store zucchini in a plastic bag in the refrigerator crisper for 4 to 5 days. Do not wash until ready to use. When grating zucchini, leave the stem on to give you a grip as you work. There are about 15 calories in ½ cup of cooked sliced zucchini. This nutrient-rich veggie provides beta carotene, B vitamins, folic acid, vitamin C and calcium, plus a healthy amount of potassium.

Southwest Brunch Casserole

My husband used to take this casserole, doubled, to office potlucks, and it was always a favorite. I serve it at home as a special-occasion breakfast or even dinner for the two of us. Any leftovers taste just as good, reheated in the microwave.

—**LINDA HINKLEY** FLORENCE, OREGON

PREP: 15 MIN. + CHILLING **BAKE:** 20 MIN. **MAKES:** 4 SERVINGS

- **4 teaspoons butter, softened**
- **2 English muffins, split**
- **½ pound bulk pork sausage**
- **4 eggs**
- **¼ cup sour cream**
- **½ cup shredded sharp cheddar cheese**
- **¼ cup canned chopped green chilies**

1. Spread butter over cut sides of each muffin half. Place buttered side up in an 8-in. square baking dish coated with cooking spray; set aside.

2. In a small skillet, cook sausage over medium heat until no longer pink; drain. Spoon sausage over muffin halves. In a small bowl, whisk eggs and sour cream; pour over sausage. Sprinkle with cheese and chilies. Cover and refrigerate for 3 hours or overnight.

3. Remove from the refrigerator 30 minutes before baking. Bake at 350° for 20-25 minutes or until a knife inserted near the center of the casserole comes out clean. Let stand for 5 minutes before cutting.

Nutrition Facts: *1 slice (prepared with reduced-fat butter, reduced-fat pork sausage, reduced-fat sour cream and reduced-fat cheese) equals 350 calories, 22 g fat (9 g saturated fat), 271 mg cholesterol, 717 mg sodium, 16 g carbohydrate, 1 g fiber, 23 g protein.*

I'm Stuffed French Toast

I re-created this decadent dish I enjoyed while eating at a favorite restaurant. The fruit adds a special touch.

—MELISSA KERRICK AUBURN, NEW YORK

PREP: 30 MIN. **COOK:** 5 MIN. **MAKES:** 4 SERVINGS

- **2 medium ripe bananas, sliced**
- **2 tablespoons brown sugar**
- **1 teaspoon banana or vanilla extract**
- **1 package (8 ounces) reduced-fat cream cheese**
- **8 slices oat bread (½ inch thick)**
- **2 eggs**
- **⅔ cup evaporated milk**
- **1¼ teaspoons ground cinnamon**
- **1¼ teaspoons vanilla extract**
- **1 tablespoon butter**
- **1 cup sliced fresh strawberries or frozen unsweetened sliced strawberries, thawed**
- **½ cup fresh blueberries or frozen unsweetened blueberries**
- **1 tablespoon sugar**
- **Confectioners' sugar**

1. In a large skillet coated with cooking spray, saute bananas with brown sugar. Stir in banana extract. In a small bowl, beat cream cheese until smooth. Add banana mixture; beat well. Spread on four slices of bread; top with remaining bread.

2. In a shallow bowl, whisk the eggs, milk, cinnamon and vanilla. Dip both sides of sandwiches in the egg mixture.

3. In a large skillet, toast sandwiches in butter for 2-3 minutes on each side or until golden brown.

4. Meanwhile, in a small saucepan, combine the strawberries, blueberries and sugar; heat through. Serve with French toast; sprinkle with confectioners' sugar.

Nutrition Facts: *1 stuffed French toast with ¼ cup berries (calculated without confectioners' sugar) equals 496 calories, 22 g fat (13 g saturated fat), 167 mg cholesterol, 659 mg sodium, 58 g carbohydrate, 5 g fiber, 17 g protein.*

Scrambled Eggs with Chorizo

This scrambled-egg breakfast can also be served for lunch or dinner with a tossed salad or green vegetable such as steamed spinach. You can replace the tortillas with taco chips, if you like.

—DONNA MARIE RYAN TOPSFIELD, MASSACHUSETTS

PREP/TOTAL TIME: 15 MIN. **MAKES:** 2 SERVINGS

- **3 flour tortillas (6 inches)**
- **2 tablespoons butter, divided**
- **3 ounces uncooked chorizo or bulk spicy pork sausage**
- **1 tablespoon diced seeded jalapeno pepper**
- **2 garlic cloves, minced**
- **2 plum tomatoes, seeded and chopped**
- **½ teaspoon Cajun seasoning**
- **4 eggs, lightly beaten**
- **3 tablespoons picante sauce**

1. Cut tortillas into quarters; place on a baking sheet coated with cooking spray. Bake at 400° for 3-5 minutes or until crisp.

2. Meanwhile, in a small skillet, heat 1 tablespoon butter. Crumble chorizo into the pan; add jalapeno and garlic. Cook and stir over medium heat until meat is fully cooked; drain. Stir in tomatoes and Cajun seasoning.

3. In another skillet, heat remaining butter until hot. Add eggs; cook and stir over medium heat until completely set. Divide scrambled eggs between two plates. Serve with chorizo mixture, tortillas and picante sauce.

Editor's Note: *Wear disposable gloves when cutting hot peppers; the oils can burn skin. Avoid touching your face.*

Ham 'n' Cheese Omelet Roll

I'd always had trouble making omelets until a friend gave me this recipe. It's so simple and versatile. You can use any combination of meats, veggies and cheeses you wish.

—**CHRISTA LEE** OMAHA, NEBRASKA

PREP/TOTAL TIME: 30 MIN. **MAKES:** 2 SERVINGS

- **3 eggs**
- **1/2 cup 2% milk**
- **1/4 cup all-purpose flour**
- **1/8 teaspoon salt**
- **1/8 teaspoon pepper**
- **1/2 cup diced fully cooked ham**
- **3/4 cup shredded Colby-Monterey Jack cheese, divided**
- **2 bacon strips, cooked and crumbled**

1. In a small bowl, whisk the eggs, milk, flour, salt and pepper. Pour into an 8-in. square baking dish coated with cooking spray.

2. Bake, uncovered, at 450° for 7-9 minutes or until eggs are set. Sprinkle with ham and 1/2 cup cheese. Bake 3-5 minutes longer or until cheese is melted.

3. Loosen edges of omelet from baking dish with a knife. Using two small spatulas, carefully roll up tightly, jelly-roll style, leaving it in the dish. Sprinkle bacon and remaining cheese over omelet roll. Bake for 3-4 minutes or until cheese is melted.

OMELETS DONE LIGHT

To cut some of the fat and calories in omelets, use egg substitute and reduced-fat cheese in place of their higher-fat counterparts. Bake the bacon in parchment paper-lined baking pans at 350° until crispy and drain thoroughly on paper towels.

"This comforting quiche makes a tasty meatless entree at any time of day. A slice or two of ham satisfies meat-and-potatoes folks, and a side of fresh fruit nicely rounds out the meal."

—**DONNA GONDA** NORTH CANTON, OHIO

Golden Corn Quiche

PREP: 20 MIN. **BAKE:** 35 MIN. + STANDING **MAKES:** 8 SERVINGS

- **1 unbaked pastry shell (9 inches)**
- **1 1/3 cups half-and-half cream**
- **3 eggs**
- **3 tablespoons butter, melted**
- **1/2 small onion, cut into wedges**
- **1 tablespoon all-purpose flour**
- **1 tablespoon sugar**
- **1 teaspoon salt**
- **2 cups frozen corn, thawed**

1. Let pastry shell stand at room temperature for 10 minutes. Line unpricked pastry shell with a double thickness of heavy-duty foil. Bake at 375° for 5 minutes. Remove foil; bake for 5 minutes longer.

2. In a blender, combine the cream, eggs, butter, onion, flour, sugar and salt; cover and process until blended. Stir in corn; pour into crust.

3. Bake for 35-40 minutes or until a knife inserted near the center comes out clean. Allow quiche to stand for 10 minutes before cutting.

Banana Mocha-Chip Muffins

These moist muffins combine my two favorite things—chocolate and coffee. The banana is just an additional flavor bonus.

—MELISSA WILLIAMS TAYLORVILLE, ILLINOIS

PREP: 20 MIN. **BAKE:** 20 MIN. **MAKES:** 2 DOZEN

- **5 teaspoons instant coffee granules**
- **5 teaspoons hot water**
- **¾ cup butter, softened**
- **1¼ cups sugar**
- **1 egg**
- **1⅓ cups mashed ripe bananas**
- **1 teaspoon vanilla extract**
- **2¼ cups all-purpose flour**
- **1½ teaspoons baking powder**
- **½ teaspoon baking soda**
- **½ teaspoon salt**
- **1½ cups semisweet chocolate chips**

1. In a small bowl, dissolve coffee granules in hot water. In a large bowl, cream butter and sugar until light and fluffy. Add egg; beat well. Beat in the bananas, vanilla and coffee mixture. Combine the flour, baking powder, baking soda and salt; add to creamed mixture just until moistened. Fold in chocolate chips.

2. Fill paper-lined muffin cups two-thirds full. Bake at 350° for 18-20 minutes or until a toothpick inserted in muffin comes out clean. Cool for 5 minutes before removing from pans to wire racks. Serve warm.

GRAND PRIZE

Pepperoni Spinach Quiche

Several years ago, I had to come up with a dish to serve at a pool party, and this colorful quiche was a hit. Cut into wedges, it also becomes the star of an antipasto tray.

—ELLY TOWNSEND SUMMERFIELD, FLORIDA

PREP: 25 MIN. **BAKE:** 25 MIN. **MAKES:** 8 SERVINGS

- **1 tube (8 ounces) refrigerated crescent rolls**
- **1 large sweet red pepper, chopped**
- **1 tablespoon olive oil**
- **1 garlic clove, minced**
- **5 eggs, lightly beaten**
- **½ cup shredded part-skim mozzarella cheese**
- **½ cup frozen chopped spinach, thawed and squeezed dry**
- **¼ cup sliced pepperoni, cut into strips**
- **¼ cup half-and-half cream**
- **2 tablespoons grated Parmesan cheese**
- **1 tablespoon minced fresh parsley**
- **1 tablespoon minced fresh basil or 1 teaspoon dried basil**
- **Dash pepper**

1. Separate crescent dough into eight triangles; place in an ungreased 9-in. fluted tart pan with removable bottom with points toward the center. Press onto the bottom and up the sides to form a crust; seal seams. Set aside.

2. In a small skillet, saute red pepper in oil until tender. Add garlic; cook 1 minute longer. Remove from the heat. In another small bowl, combine the remaining ingredients; stir in red pepper mixture. Pour into crust.

3. Bake at 375° for 25-30 minutes or until a knife inserted near the center comes out clean. Let stand for 5 minutes before cutting.

PEPPERONI, DEGREASED

I love cooking with pepperoni, but it's greasy. So I place the pepperoni on a microwave-safe paper towel-lined plate, then cover it with another paper towel. I microwave the pepperoni for about 30 seconds on high, remove it and blot out the grease. The pepperoni tastes much better and has less fat.

—TRACY C. SIOUX CITY, IOWA

FLAVORS OF ITALY
GRAND PRIZE
WINNER

SNEAKY LASAGNA, PAGE 92

Beef & Poultry Entrees

Whether you're looking for a **family-pleasing casserole** or an impressive entree for a dinner party with friends, you can't go wrong with any of the **classic beef and poultry choices** in this extra-big chapter!

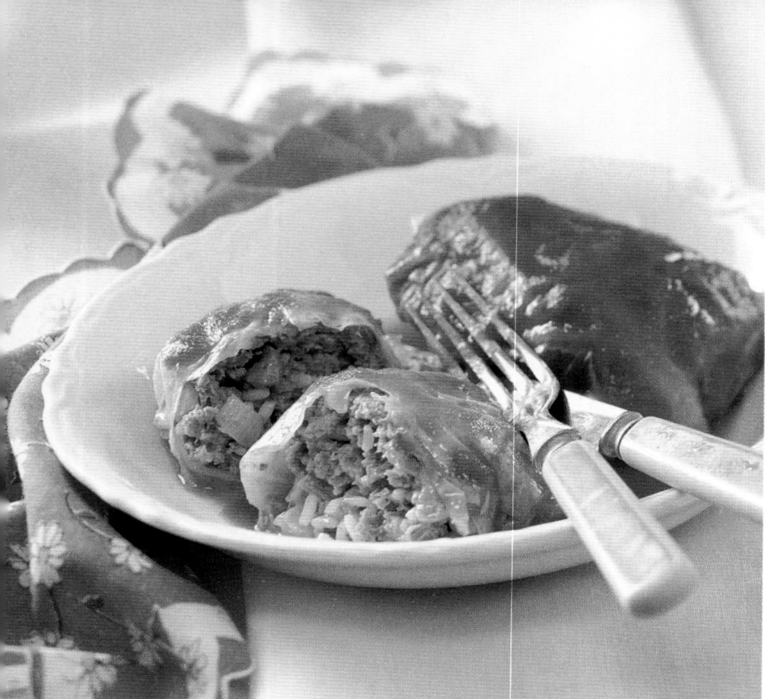

Sweet 'n' Tender Cabbage Rolls

I've used this recipe for more than 30 years, and the extra time it takes to assemble the rolls is well worth the effort. I always make two batches because they go so fast. You can assemble the night before and cook the next day.

—SONJA BENZ CARMEL, INDIANA

PREP: 40 MIN. **COOK:** 7 HOURS **MAKES:** 7 SERVINGS

- **1 large head cabbage**
- **2 eggs, lightly beaten**
- **½ cup 2% milk**
- **2 cups cooked long grain rice**
- **2 jars (4½ ounces each) sliced mushrooms, well drained**
- **1 small onion, chopped**
- **2 teaspoons salt**
- **1 teaspoon dried parsley flakes**
- **1 teaspoon dried oregano**
- **1 teaspoon dried basil**
- **½ teaspoon pepper**
- **2 pounds lean ground beef (90% lean)**

SAUCE

- **2 cans (8 ounces each) tomato sauce**
- **½ cup packed brown sugar**
- **2 tablespoons lemon juice**
- **2 teaspoons Worcestershire sauce**

1. Cook cabbage in boiling water just until leaves fall off head. Set aside 14 large leaves for rolls. (Refrigerate remaining cabbage for another use.) Cut out the thick vein from the bottom of each reserved leaf, making a V-shaped cut.

2. In a large bowl, combine the eggs, milk, rice, mushrooms, onion and seasonings. Crumble beef over mixture and mix well. Place about ½ cup on each cabbage leaf; overlap cut ends and fold in sides, beginning from the cut end. Roll up completely to enclose filling.

3. Place seven rolls, seam side down, in a 5-qt. slow cooker. Combine sauce ingredients; pour half over cabbage rolls. Top with remaining rolls and sauce. Cover and cook on low for 7-8 hours or until a thermometer reads 160°.

Stovetop Sweet & Tender Cabbage Rolls: *Prepare recipe as directed in steps 1 and 2. Place rolls in a Dutch oven. Combine tomato sauce, brown sugar, lemon juice and Worcestershire sauce; pour over cabbage rolls. Bring to a boil. Reduce heat; cover and simmer for 60-70 minutes, spooning sauce over rolls occasionally during cooking.*

Nutrition Facts: *2 cabbage rolls equals 389 calories, 12 g fat (5 g saturated fat), 141 mg cholesterol, 1,243 mg sodium, 39 g carbohydrate, 3 g fiber, 31 g protein.*

Sneaky Lasagna

Lasagna's always been a family favorite. But since my children and husband aren't very fond of veggies, I started sneaking them into this classic dish. They hardly notice! It feeds a crowd and is great for potlucks or family reunions.

—CATHERINE YODER NEW PARIS, INDIANA

PREP: 25 MIN. **BAKE:** 55 MIN. + STANDING
MAKES: 10-12 SERVINGS

- **2 pounds ground beef**
- **1 package (16 ounces) frozen California-blend vegetables**
- **2 eggs, beaten**
- **3 cups (24 ounces) 2% cottage cheese**
- **2 jars (26 ounces each) spaghetti sauce**
- **12 no-cook lasagna noodles**
- **2 cups (8 ounces) shredded part-skim mozzarella cheese**

1. In a Dutch oven, cook beef over medium heat until no longer pink. Meanwhile, cook vegetables according to package directions; drain. Finely chop the vegetables; place in a bowl. Stir in eggs and cottage cheese; set aside.

2. Drain beef; stir in spaghetti sauce. Spread 2 cups meat mixture into a greased 13-in. x 9-in. baking dish. Top with four noodles. Spread half of the vegetable mixture to edges of noodles. Layer with 2 cups meat mixture and 1 cup mozzarella cheese. Top with four noodles, remaining vegetable mixture and 2 cups meat mixture. Layer with remaining noodles, meat mixture and mozzarella cheese.

3. Cover and bake at 375° for 50 minutes or until a thermometer reads 160°. Uncover; bake 5-10 minutes longer or until bubbly and cheese is melted. Let stand for 15 minutes before cutting.

Tastes Like Thanksgiving Casserole

This hearty, rich-tasting dish is sure to be a hit with your family. It's a delicious way to use up Thanksgiving turkey, and you can substitute 5½ cups leftover mashed potatoes for the 6 potatoes.

—**MARY LOU TIMPSON** COLORADO CITY, ARIZONA

PREP: 30 MIN. **BAKE:** 30 MIN. **MAKES:** 8 SERVINGS

- **6 medium potatoes, peeled and cut into chunks**
- **1¼ cups chopped celery**
- **¾ cup chopped onion**
- **½ cup butter, cubed**
- **6 cups unseasoned stuffing cubes**
- **1 teaspoon poultry seasoning**
- **¼ teaspoon rubbed sage**
- **1 cup chicken broth**
- **4 cups cubed cooked turkey**
- **2 cans (10¾ ounces each) condensed cream of chicken soup, undiluted**
- **1 teaspoon garlic powder**
- **¾ cup sour cream, divided**
- **4 ounces cream cheese, softened**
- **½ teaspoon pepper**
- **¼ teaspoon salt**
- **1½ cups (6 ounces) shredded cheddar cheese**

1. Place potatoes in a Dutch oven and cover with water. Bring to a boil. Reduce heat; cover and cook for 10-15 minutes or until potatoes are tender.
2. Meanwhile, in a large skillet, saute celery and onion in butter until tender. Remove from the heat.
3. In a large bowl, combine the stuffing cubes, poultry seasoning and sage. Stir in broth and celery mixture. Transfer to a greased 13-in. x 9-in. baking dish.
4. In another large bowl, combine the turkey, soup, garlic powder and ¼ cup sour cream; spoon over stuffing mixture. Drain potatoes; mash in a large bowl. Beat in the cream cheese, pepper, salt and remaining sour cream; spread over turkey mixture. Sprinkle with cheese.
5. Bake casserole, uncovered, at 350° for 30-35 minutes or until heated through.

Orange Chicken with Sweet Potatoes

Orange peel and pineapple juice lend a fruity flavor to this super chicken and sweet potato combo. Served over rice, the appealing entree is bound to win you accolades.

—**VICKI SMITH** OKEECHOBEE, FLORIDA

PREP: 25 MIN. **COOK:** 3½ HOURS **MAKES:** 4 SERVINGS

- **3 medium sweet potatoes, peeled and sliced**
- **⅔ cup plus 3 tablespoons all-purpose flour, divided**
- **1 teaspoon salt**
- **1 teaspoon onion powder**
- **1 teaspoon ground nutmeg**
- **1 teaspoon ground cinnamon**
- **1 teaspoon pepper**
- **4 boneless skinless chicken breast halves (5 ounces each)**
- **2 tablespoons butter**
- **1 can (10¾ ounces) condensed cream of chicken soup, undiluted**
- **¾ cup unsweetened pineapple juice**
- **2 teaspoons brown sugar**
- **1 teaspoon grated orange peel**
- **½ pound sliced fresh mushrooms**
- **Hot cooked rice**

1. Layer sweet potatoes in a 3-qt. slow cooker. In a large resealable plastic bag, combine ⅔ cup flour and seasonings; add chicken, one piece at a time, and shake to coat.
2. In a large skillet over medium heat, cook chicken in butter for 3 minutes on each side or until lightly browned. Arrange chicken over sweet potatoes.
3. Place remaining flour in a small bowl. Stir in the soup, pineapple juice, brown sugar and orange peel until blended. Add the mushrooms; pour over chicken. Cover and cook on low for 3-4 hours or until the meat and potatoes are tender. Serve with rice.

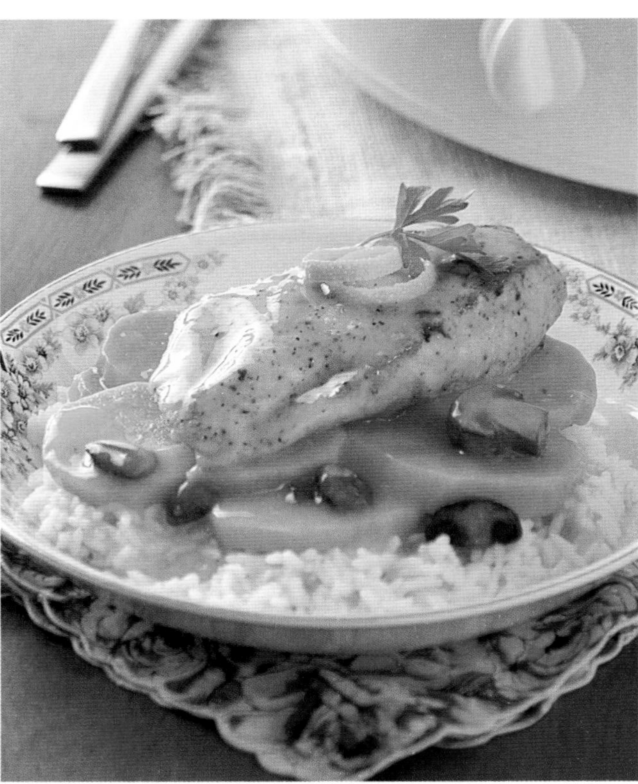

Thai Chicken Pizzas

I found a recipe like this in a cookbook and modified it by cutting down on the peanut butter and adding cilantro for more flavor.

—LYNETTE RANDLEMAN BUFFALO, WYOMING

PREP/TOTAL TIME: 20 MIN. **MAKES:** 4 SERVINGS

- **4 whole wheat tortillas (8 inches)**
- **¼ cup reduced-fat creamy peanut butter**
- **2 tablespoons reduced-sodium soy sauce**
- **4½ teaspoons honey**
- **2¼ teaspoons rice vinegar**
- **2 cups shredded cooked chicken breast**
- **2 small carrots, shredded**
- **½ cup minced fresh cilantro**
- **1 cup (4 ounces) shredded part-skim mozzarella cheese**

1. Coat both sides of tortillas with cooking spray; place on ungreased baking sheets. In a small bowl, combine the peanut butter, soy sauce, honey and vinegar. Stir in chicken until blended. Spread over tortillas. Top with carrots, cilantro and cheese.

2. Bake at 400° for 10-12 minutes or until cheese is melted.

GRAND PRIZE

Wintertime Braised Beef Stew

This easy beef stew has a deep, rich taste. Since it's even better a day or two later, you may want to make a double batch.

—MICHAELA ROSENTHAL WOODLAND HILLS, CALIFORNIA

PREP: 40 MIN. **BAKE:** 2 HOURS
MAKES: 8 SERVINGS (2 QUARTS)

- **2 tablespoons all-purpose flour**
- **2 teaspoons Montreal steak seasoning**
- **2 pounds boneless beef sirloin steak, cut into 1-inch cubes**
- **2 tablespoons olive oil, divided**
- **1 large onion, chopped**
- **2 celery ribs, chopped**
- **2 medium parsnips, peeled and cut into 1½-inch pieces**
- **2 medium carrots, peeled and cut into 1½-inch pieces**
- **2 garlic cloves, minced**
- **1 can (14½ ounces) diced tomatoes, undrained**
- **1 cup dry red wine or reduced-sodium beef broth**
- **2 tablespoons red currant jelly**
- **2 bay leaves**
- **2 fresh oregano sprigs**
- **1 can (15 ounces) white kidney or cannellini beans, rinsed and drained**

1. In a large resealable plastic bag, combine flour and steak seasoning. Add beef, a few pieces at a time, and shake to coat. Heat 1 tablespoon oil in an ovenproof Dutch oven; brown beef in batches on all sides. Remove and keep warm.

2. In the same pan, saute the onion, celery, parsnips and carrots in remaining oil until crisp-tender. Add garlic; cook 1 minute longer. Add the tomatoes, wine, jelly, bay leaves, oregano and beef; bring to a boil.

3. Cover and bake at 350° for 1½ hours. Stir in beans; cover and bake 30-40 minutes longer or until the beef and vegetables are tender. Discard bay leaves and oregano.

4. Serve immediately or cool and freeze in a freezer container for up to 3 months.

To use frozen stew: *Thaw in the refrigerator overnight. Transfer to a saucepan; add water to thin if necessary. Cover and cook over medium heat until hot and bubbly, stirring occasionally.*

Nutrition Facts: *1 cup equals 310 calories, 9 g fat (3 g saturated fat), 64 mg cholesterol, 373 mg sodium, 26 g carbohydrate, 5 g fiber, 25 g protein.* **Diabetic Exchanges:** *3 lean meat, 1 starch, 1 vegetable, 1 fat.*

LIVELY LEFTOVERS

Have leftover beef stew on hand? One tasty idea is to reheat any leftovers in the oven with a pastry crust on top for a down-home beef pot pie. Another twist on this comforting favorite is to add beef broth to the leftover beef stew and puree in a blender to make a thick soup.

HEARTY SOUPS
GRAND PRIZE
WINNER

Crescent-Topped Turkey Amandine

Featuring a comforting turkey flavor and nice crunch from celery and water chestnuts, my tasty dish is bound to become a favorite!
—**BECKY LARSON** MALLARD, IOWA

PREP: 20 MIN. **BAKE:** 30 MIN. **MAKES:** 4 SERVINGS

- **3 cups cubed cooked turkey**
- **1 can (10¾ ounces) condensed cream of mushroom soup, undiluted**
- **1 can (8 ounces) sliced water chestnuts, drained**
- **⅔ cup mayonnaise**
- **½ cup chopped celery**
- **½ cup chopped onion**
- **1 tube (4 ounces) refrigerated crescent rolls**
- **⅔ cup shredded Swiss cheese**
- **½ cup sliced almonds**
- **¼ cup butter, melted**

1. In a large saucepan, combine the first six ingredients; heat through. Transfer to a greased 2-qt. baking dish. Unroll crescent dough and place over turkey mixture.
2. In a small bowl, combine the cheese, almonds and butter. Spoon over dough. Bake, uncovered, at 375° for 30-35 minutes or until crust is golden brown and filling is bubbly.

MINCING & CHOPPING

To mince or chop, hold handle of a chef's knife with one hand, and rest the fingers of your other hand on top of the blade near tip. Using the handle to guide and apply pressure, move knife in an arc across food with a rocking motion until pieces of food are desired size. Mincing results in pieces no larger than ⅛ in., while chopping can produce ¼-in. to ½-in. pieces.

Hearty Pizza Casserole

Here's a cheesy, meaty meal that's easy to make and can be prepared ahead of time. We love this unique twist on pizza!
—**BARBARA WALKER** BROOKVILLE, KANSAS

PREP: 20 MIN. **BAKE:** 20 MIN. **MAKES:** 4 SERVINGS

- **1 cup uncooked elbow macaroni**
- **½ pound lean ground beef (90% lean)**
- **6 small fresh mushrooms, halved**
- **⅓ cup chopped onion**
- **1 can (8 ounces) tomato sauce**
- **1 package (3½ ounces) sliced pepperoni**
- **2 tablespoons sliced ripe olives**
- **1 teaspoon sugar**
- **¾ teaspoon Italian seasoning**
- **¼ teaspoon pepper**
- **¼ cup shredded cheddar cheese**
- **¼ cup shredded part-skim mozzarella cheese**

1. Cook macaroni according to package directions. Meanwhile, in a large skillet, cook the beef, mushrooms and onion over medium heat until meat is no longer pink; drain. Stir in the tomato sauce, pepperoni, olives, sugar, Italian seasoning and pepper.
2. Drain macaroni; add to meat mixture. Transfer to a 1½-qt. baking dish coated with cooking spray. Sprinkle with cheeses.
3. Bake, uncovered, at 350° for 20-25 minutes or until heated through. Or before baking, cover and freeze casserole for up to 3 months.
To use frozen casserole: *Thaw in the refrigerator overnight. Remove from the refrigerator 30 minutes before baking. Bake according to directions.*
Nutrition Facts: *1 serving (prepared with reduced-fat cheese) equals 340 calories, 19 g fat (8 g saturated fat), 58 mg cholesterol, 871 mg sodium, 20 g carbohydrate, 2 g fiber, 23 g protein.*

Spicy Chicken Bundles

A friend introduced me to these popovers, and I enhanced the recipe a bit by adding jalapeno peppers. My family has savored these for over 18 years. I hope yours does, too!

—VICKI BLUEMNER COLLINSVILLE, ILLINOIS

PREP: 25 MIN. **BAKE:** 15 MIN. **MAKES:** 8 SERVINGS

- **1 package (3 ounces) cream cheese, softened**
- **2 tablespoons 2% milk**
- **1 tablespoon pickled jalapeno slices, chopped**
- **¼ teaspoon pepper**
- **2 cups cubed cooked chicken**
- **½ cup chopped onion**
- **2 tubes (8 ounces each) refrigerated crescent rolls**
- **1 tablespoon butter, melted**
- **4 teaspoons seasoned bread crumbs**

MUSHROOM SAUCE

- **1 can (10¾ ounces) condensed cream of mushroom soup, undiluted**
- **½ cup 2% milk**

1. In a large bowl, beat the cream cheese, milk, jalapenos and pepper until blended. Stir in chicken and onion.

2. Separate crescent dough into eight rectangles; seal perforations. Spoon 1/4 cup chicken mixture onto the center of each rectangle; bring corners up to the center and pinch edges to seal.

3. Place on an ungreased baking sheet. Brush with butter; sprinkle with bread crumbs. Bake at 375° for 15-20 minutes or until golden brown.

4. In a small saucepan, combine soup and milk. Cook and stir over medium heat until heated through. Serve with bundles.

Editor's Note: *Wear disposable gloves when cutting hot peppers; the oils can burn skin. Avoid touching your face.*

Nutrition Facts: *1 bundle with 3 tablespoons gravy equals 391 calories, 22 g fat (8 g saturated fat), 51 mg cholesterol, 841 mg sodium, 28 g carbohydrate, 1 g fiber, 17 g protein.*

Winning Creamy Chicken Casserole

French onion dip lends a tangy accent to this cheesy rice bake. Short prep time means you can eat a scrumptious dinner without spending hours in the kitchen.

—JAKY BROUSSARD GREENSBORO, ALABAMA

PREP: 20 MIN. **BAKE:** 25 MIN. **MAKES:** 2 SERVINGS

- **⅔ cup uncooked instant rice**
- **¼ cup chopped onion**
- **2 teaspoons butter**
- **½ cup 4% cottage cheese**
- **⅓ cup French onion dip**
- **3 tablespoons sour cream**
- **¼ teaspoon salt**
- **Dash white pepper**
- **½ cup cubed cooked chicken**
- **½ cup shredded cheddar cheese**
- **2 tablespoons chopped green chilies**

1. Cook rice according to package directions. Meanwhile, in a small skillet, saute onion in butter until tender; set aside. In a small bowl, combine the cottage cheese, onion dip, sour cream, salt and pepper. Stir in rice and onion.

2. Spread half of the rice mixture into a 3-cup baking dish coated with cooking spray. Layer with chicken, 1/4 cup cheddar cheese and green chilies. Top with remaining rice mixture; sprinkle with remaining cheese.

3. Bake, uncovered, at 350° for 25-30 minutes or until bubbly.

Nutrition Facts: *1½ cups (prepared with reduced-fat butter, 1% cottage cheese and reduced-fat cheddar cheese) equals 454 calories, 20 g fat (12 g saturated fat), 69 mg cholesterol, 1,085 mg sodium, 38 g carbohydrate, 1 g fiber, 29 g protein.*

ONIONS & GARLIC GALORE
GRAND PRIZE
WINNER

GRAND PRIZE

Roasted Chicken with Garlic-Sherry Sauce

This garlic-kissed chicken is delicious, plain or fancy. It's an elegant entree for guests, and my husband and I love the leftovers in rice casseroles and hot, open-face sandwiches.

—SHERI SIDWELL ALTON, ILLINOIS

PREP: 30 MIN. + MARINATING **BAKE:** 20 MIN.
MAKES: 4 SERVINGS

- **2 quarts water**
- **½ cup salt**
- **4 bone-in chicken breast halves (12 ounces each)**
- **¾ teaspoon pepper, divided**
- **2 teaspoons canola oil**
- **8 garlic cloves, peeled and thinly sliced**
- **1 cup reduced-sodium chicken broth**
- **½ cup sherry or additional reduced-sodium chicken broth**
- **3 fresh thyme sprigs**
- **¼ cup butter, cubed**
- **1 teaspoon lemon juice**

1. For brine, in a large saucepan, bring water and salt to a boil. Cook and stir until salt is dissolved. Remove from the heat; cool to room temperature.
2. Place a large heavy-duty resealable plastic bag inside a second large resealable plastic bag; add chicken. Carefully pour cooled brine into bag. Squeeze out as much air as possible; seal bags and turn to coat. Refrigerate for 1-2 hours, turning several times.
3. Drain and discard brine. Rinse chicken with cold water; pat dry. Sprinkle with ½ teaspoon pepper. In a large ovenproof skillet, brown chicken in oil over medium heat.
4. Bake, uncovered, at 400° for 20-25 minutes or until a thermometer reads 170°. Remove chicken and keep warm. Drain drippings, reserving 1 tablespoon.
5. In the drippings, saute garlic for 1 minute. Add the broth, sherry or additional broth and thyme. Bring to a boil; cook until liquid is reduced to 1 cup. Discard thyme. Stir in the butter, lemon juice and remaining pepper. Serve sauce with the chicken.

BRINING, DEFINED

Brining means to soak meat in a solution of water and salt. A brine can be flavored with sugars, juices or seasonings. Kosher salt, table salt or even sea salt can be used in the brining solution. Brining is a way to help tenderize lean meats such as poultry—or fish or seafood—because lean meats can easily dry out when cooked.

Pronto Penne Pasta

I have four boys and have to trick them into eating healthy. It's not an easy task, but this veggie-filled recipe works like a charm!

—TOMISSA HUART UNION, ILLINOIS

PREP/TOTAL TIME: 30 MIN. **MAKES:** 6 SERVINGS

- **2¼ cups uncooked whole wheat penne pasta**
- **1 pound Italian turkey sausage links, casings removed**
- **1 medium red onion, chopped**
- **1 medium green pepper, chopped**
- **1 can (14½ ounces) no-salt-added diced tomatoes, undrained**
- **1 can (14½ ounces) reduced-sodium chicken broth**
- **2 garlic cloves, minced**
- **2 teaspoons dried tarragon**
- **2 teaspoons dried basil**
- **¼ teaspoon cayenne pepper**
- **¼ cup all-purpose flour**
- **½ cup fat-free milk**
- **½ cup shredded reduced-fat cheddar cheese**
- **¼ cup grated Parmesan cheese**

1. Cook pasta according to package directions. Meanwhile, crumble sausage into a large nonstick skillet coated with cooking spray. Add onion and green pepper; cook and stir over medium heat until meat is no longer pink. Drain. Stir in the tomatoes, broth, garlic, tarragon, basil and cayenne.
2. In a small bowl, combine flour and milk until smooth; stir into sausage mixture. Bring to a boil; cook and stir for 2 minutes or until thickened.
3. Remove from the heat. Stir in cheddar cheese until melted. Drain pasta; toss with sausage mixture. Sprinkle each serving with 2 teaspoons Parmesan cheese.

Nutrition Facts: *1 cup equals 373 calories, 11 g fat (3 g saturated fat), 55 mg cholesterol, 800 mg sodium, 45 g carbohydrate, 4 g fiber, 24 g protein.* **Diabetic Exchanges:** *2½ starch, 2 medium-fat meat, 1 vegetable.*

Easy Beef Stroganoff

I lightened my mother-in-law's wonderful Stroganoff and came up with this one. We call it "special noodles" in our house.

—**JENNIFER RIORDAN** ST. LOUIS, MISSOURI

PREP/TOTAL TIME: 30 MIN. **MAKES:** 6 SERVINGS

- **4½ cups uncooked yolk-free noodles**
- **1 pound lean ground beef (90% lean)**
- **½ pound sliced fresh mushrooms**
- **1 large onion, halved and sliced**
- **3 garlic cloves, minced**
- **1 tablespoon reduced-fat butter**
- **2 tablespoons all-purpose flour**
- **1 can (14½ ounces) reduced-sodium beef broth**
- **2 tablespoons tomato paste**
- **1 cup (8 ounces) fat-free sour cream**
- **¼ teaspoon salt**
- **¼ teaspoon pepper**

1. Cook noodles according to package directions. Meanwhile, in a large saucepan, cook the beef, mushrooms and onion over medium heat until meat is no longer pink. Add garlic; cook 1 minute longer. Drain. Remove and keep warm.

2. In the same pan, melt butter. Stir in flour until smooth; gradually add broth and tomato paste. Bring to a boil; cook and stir for 2 minutes or until thickened.

3. Carefully return beef mixture to the pan. Add the sour cream, salt and pepper; cook and stir until heated through (do not boil). Drain noodles; serve with beef mixture.

Editor's Note: *This recipe was tested with Land O'Lakes light stick butter.*

Nutrition Facts: *2/3 cup beef mixture with 3/4 cup noodles equals 326 calories, 7 g fat (3 g saturated fat), 48 mg cholesterol, 342 mg sodium, 39 g carbohydrate, 3 g fiber, 24 g protein.* **Diabetic Exchanges:** *2 starch, 2 lean meat, 1 vegetable.*

Greek Lemon Chicken

This is one of my family's summertime specials, and it's so easy and delicious. Five simple ingredients combine to create the enticing Mediterranean flavor!

—**DAWN ELLEN** BISHOPVILLE, SOUTH CAROLINA

PREP: 10 MIN. + MARINATING **GRILL:** 10 MIN.
MAKES: 4 SERVINGS

- **1¼ cups Greek vinaigrette, divided**
- **4 boneless skinless chicken breast halves (5 ounces each)**
- **1 medium lemon, quartered**
- **3 tablespoons sliced oil-packed sun-dried tomatoes**
- **¼ cup crumbled feta cheese**

1. Pour 3/4 cup vinaigrette into a large resealable plastic bag; add chicken breasts. Seal bag and turn to coat; refrigerate for up to 4 hours. Cover and refrigerate the remaining vinaigrette for basting.

2. Drain and discard marinade. Grill chicken, covered, over medium heat or broil 4 in. from the heat for 4 minutes. Turn and baste with some of the reserved vinaigrette. Grill or broil 4-5 minutes longer or until a thermometer reads 170°, basting occasionally.

3. Squeeze lemon wedges over chicken. Sprinkle with tomatoes and cheese.

Nutrition Facts: *1 chicken breast half equals 366 calories, 23 g fat (4 g saturated fat), 82 mg cholesterol, 679 mg sodium, 6 g carbohydrate, 1 g fiber, 30 g protein.*

Turkey Potpies

With their golden brown crust and scrumptious filling, these comforting potpies will warm you down to your toes. Because the recipe makes two, you can eat one now and freeze the other for later. They bake and cut beautifully.

—**LAURIE JENSEN** CADILLAC, MICHIGAN

PREP: 40 MIN.
BAKE: 40 MIN. + STANDING
MAKES: 2 PIES (6 SERVINGS EACH)

- **2 medium potatoes, peeled and cut into 1-inch pieces**
- **3 medium carrots, cut into 1-inch slices**
- **1 medium onion, chopped**
- **1 celery rib, diced**
- **2 tablespoons butter**
- **1 tablespoon olive oil**
- **6 tablespoons all-purpose flour**
- **3 cups chicken broth**
- **4 cups cubed cooked turkey**
- **⅔ cup frozen peas**
- **½ cup plus 1 tablespoon heavy whipping cream, divided**
- **1 tablespoon minced fresh parsley**
- **1 teaspoon garlic salt**
- **¼ teaspoon pepper**
- **1 package (15 ounces) refrigerated pie pastry**
- **1 egg**

1. In a Dutch oven, saute the potatoes, carrots, onion and celery in butter and oil until tender. Stir in flour until blended; gradually add broth. Bring to a boil; cook and stir for 2 minutes or until thickened. Stir in the turkey, peas, ½ cup cream, parsley, garlic salt and pepper.

2. Spoon into two ungreased 9-in. pie plates. Roll out pastry to fit top of each pie; place over filling. Trim, seal and flute edges. Cut out a decorative center or cut slits in pastry. In a small bowl, whisk egg and remaining cream; brush over pastry.

3. Cover and freeze one potpie for up to 3 months. Bake the remaining potpie at 375° for 40-45 minutes or until golden brown. Let stand for 10 minutes before cutting.

To use frozen potpie: *Remove from the freezer 30 minutes before baking. Cover edges of crust loosely with foil; place on a baking sheet. Bake at 425° for 30 minutes. Reduce heat to 350°; remove foil. Bake 55-60 minutes longer or until golden brown.*

Nutrition Facts: *1 piece equals 287 calories, 15 g fat (7 g saturated fat), 78 mg cholesterol, 542 mg sodium, 21 g carbohydrate, 2 g fiber, 17 g protein.*

Pizza Loaf

My hungry clan can't get enough of my grandmother's famous braided stromboli.

—**AMANDA WIERSEMA** ARCHER, IOWA

PREP: 25 MIN. **BAKE:** 20 MIN.
MAKES: 6 SERVINGS

- **1 pound ground beef**
- **½ cup chopped onion**
- **½ cup chopped green pepper**
- **1 cup Italian tomato sauce**
- **1 can (4 ounces) mushroom stems and pieces, drained**
- **1 teaspoon paprika**
- **½ teaspoon garlic salt**
- **½ teaspoon dried oregano**
- **⅛ teaspoon pepper**
- **1 tube (13.8 ounces) refrigerated pizza crust**
- **½ cup shredded part-skim mozzarella cheese**
- **½ cup shredded cheddar cheese**

1. In a large skillet, cook the beef, onion and green pepper over medium heat until meat is no longer pink; drain. Stir in the tomato sauce, mushrooms, paprika, garlic salt, oregano and pepper.
2. Unroll pizza dough onto a greased baking sheet; roll into a 15-in. x 12-in. rectangle. Spoon meat mixture down the center; sprinkle with cheeses.
3. On each long side, cut 1-in.-wide strips about 2½ in. into center. Starting at one end, fold alternating strips at an angle across filling. Pinch ends to seal. Bake the loaf at 350° for 20-25 minutes or until golden brown.

Nutrition Facts: *1 serving equals 372 calories, 13 g fat (6 g saturated fat), 52 mg cholesterol, 1,020 mg sodium, 37 g carbohydrate, 2 g fiber, 25 g protein.*

TRY BREAD DOUGH

To shake things up, try using frozen bread dough in place of the pizza dough in this recipe. On a greased baking sheet, roll out thawed bread dough into a 15-in. x 12-in. rectangle. Add beef mixture and cheese and roll up, jelly-roll style, starting with a long side; pinch seam to seal and tuck ends under. Place seam side down and brush with egg whites for a pretty shine. Do not let rise. Bake at 350° for 35-40 minutes or until golden brown.

Chicken Fingers with Lemon Sauce

PREP: 20 MIN. **COOK:** 5 MIN./BATCH
MAKES: 4 SERVINGS (1¼ CUPS SAUCE)

- **1 jar (10 ounces) lemon curd**
- **¼ cup chicken broth**
- **½ teaspoon soy sauce**
- **¼ teaspoon ground ginger**
- **1 cup buttermilk**
- **1 tablespoon grated lemon peel**
- **1 cup all-purpose flour**
- **½ cup cornstarch**
- **1¼ pounds boneless skinless chicken breasts, cut into strips**
- **Oil for frying**

1. In a small saucepan, combine the lemon curd, broth, soy sauce and ginger. Cook and stir until combined and heated through; keep warm.
2. In a shallow bowl, combine buttermilk and lemon peel. In another bowl, combine flour and cornstarch. Dip chicken in buttermilk mixture, then coat with flour mixture.
3. In an electric skillet, heat oil to 375°. Fry chicken, a few strips at a time, for 2-3 minutes on each side or until no longer pink. Drain on paper towels. Serve with lemon sauce.

“My husband turned up his nose when he saw me making this the first time, but he absolutely flipped when he tasted it. I like to serve the chicken with an apple rice pilaf salad.”

—**AMANDA DONNELLY** FAIRBORN, OHIO

Curry Chicken Tenderloin with Sweet Potatoes

What I love about this recipe is the luscious, fragrant sauce and the addition of sweet potatoes, which are a favorite of mine.

—**GLORIA BRADLEY** NAPERVILLE, ILLINOIS

PREP: 15 MIN. **COOK:** 25 MIN. **MAKES:** 3 SERVINGS

- **¾ pound chicken tenderloins, cut into 1-inch cubes**
- **1 small green pepper, cut into thin strips**
- **2 shallots, thinly sliced**
- **2 teaspoons minced fresh gingerroot**
- **1 teaspoon curry powder**
- **1 garlic clove, minced**
- **1 tablespoon canola oil**
- **1⅓ cups chicken broth**
- **1 tablespoon lime juice**
- **½ teaspoon sugar**
- **¼ teaspoon crushed red pepper flakes**
- **1 medium sweet potato, peeled and cut into 1-inch pieces**
- **¾ cup light coconut milk**
- **Chopped peanuts and flaked coconut, optional**
- **Hot cooked rice, optional**

1. In a large skillet, saute the chicken, green pepper, shallots, ginger, curry and garlic in oil until chicken is no longer pink. Stir in the broth, lime juice, sugar and pepper flakes. Bring to a boil. Reduce heat; simmer, uncovered, for 10 minutes or until thickened.
2. Add sweet potato and coconut milk; bring to a boil. Reduce heat; cover and simmer for 8-10 minutes or until potato is tender. If desired, sprinkle with peanuts and coconut and serve with rice.

Nutrition Facts: *1⅓ cups (prepared with reduced-sodium broth; calculated without peanuts, coconut and rice) equals 317 calories, 13 g fat (6 g saturated fat), 67 mg cholesterol, 355 mg sodium, 20 g carbohydrate, 2 g fiber, 29 g protein.*

Butternut Turkey Bake

Butternut squash adds a little sweetness to this satisfying turkey entree. You can use leftover meat and even replace the croutons with leftover stuffing, if you wish. It's sure to have your family asking for seconds.

—MARY ANN DELL PHOENIXVILLE, PENNSYLVANIA

PREP: 70 MIN. **BAKE:** 25 MIN. **MAKES:** 4 SERVINGS

- **1 medium butternut squash (about 2½ pounds)**
- **¾ cup finely chopped onion**
- **2 tablespoons butter**
- **2 cups seasoned salad croutons**
- **½ teaspoon salt**
- **½ teaspoon poultry seasoning**
- **½ teaspoon pepper**
- **2 cups cubed cooked turkey**
- **1 cup chicken broth**
- **½ cup shredded cheddar cheese**

1. Cut squash in half; discard seeds. Place cut side down in a 15-in. x 10-in. x 1-in. baking pan; add ½ in. of hot water. Bake, uncovered, at 350° for 45 minutes.

2. Drain water from pan; turn squash cut side up. Bake 10-15 minutes longer or until tender. Scoop out pulp; mash and set aside.

3. In a large skillet, saute onion in butter until tender. Stir in the croutons, salt, poultry seasoning and pepper. Cook 2-3 minutes longer or until croutons are toasted. Stir in the squash, turkey and broth; heat through.

4. Transfer to a greased 1½-qt. baking dish. Bake, uncovered, at 350° for 20 minutes. Sprinkle with cheese. Bake 5-10 minutes longer or until edges are bubbly and cheese is melted.

Nutrition Facts: *1¼ cup equals 383 calories, 15 g fat (8 g saturated fat), 85 mg cholesterol, 828 mg sodium, 37 g carbohydrate, 8 g fiber, 28 g protein.*

GRAND PRIZE

Chicken Pesto Pizza

Keeping the spices simple helps the flavor of the chicken and vegetables to come through in this good-for-you pizza.

—HEATHER THOMPSON WOODLAND HILLS, CALIFORNIA

PREP: 35 MIN. + RISING **BAKE:** 20 MIN. **MAKES:** 8 SLICES

- **2 teaspoons active dry yeast**
- **1 cup warm water (110° to 115°)**
- **2¾ cups bread flour, divided**
- **1 tablespoon plus 2 teaspoons olive oil, divided**
- **1 tablespoon sugar**
- **1½ teaspoons salt, divided**
- **½ pound boneless skinless chicken breasts, cut into ½-inch pieces**
- **1 small onion, halved and thinly sliced**
- **½ each small green, sweet red and yellow peppers, julienned**
- **½ cup sliced fresh mushrooms**
- **3 tablespoons prepared pesto**
- **1½ cups (6 ounces) shredded part-skim mozzarella cheese**
- **¼ teaspoon pepper**

1. In a bowl, dissolve yeast in warm water. Beat in 1 cup flour, 1 tablespoon oil, sugar and 1 teaspoon salt. Add the remaining flour; beat until combined.

2. Turn onto a lightly floured surface; knead until smooth and elastic, about 6-8 minutes. Place in a bowl coated with cooking spray, turning once to coat top. Cover and let rise in a warm place until doubled, about 1 hour.

3. In a large nonstick skillet over medium heat, cook the chicken, onion, peppers and mushrooms in remaining oil until chicken is no longer pink and vegetables are tender. Remove from the heat; set aside.

4. Punch dough down; roll into a 15-in. circle. Transfer to a 14-in. pizza pan. Build up edges slightly. Spread with pesto. Top with chicken mixture and cheese. Sprinkle with pepper and remaining salt.

5. Bake at 400° for 18-20 minutes or until lightly browned.

Nutrition Facts: *1 slice equals 293 calories, 10 g fat (3 g saturated fat), 30 mg cholesterol, 601 mg sodium, 35 g carbohydrate, 2 g fiber, 18 g protein.* **Diabetic Exchanges:** *2 starch, 1 lean meat, 1 fat.*

PERFECT PIZZA CRUST

It's easy as pie to achieve a pizza crust that is crispy on the outside yet chewy on the inside. Make the dough ahead and store in the refrigerator for at least 2 hours. This allows the dough to relax, making it easier to handle.

Use a pizza stone for a crispier crust and better browning. Before preheating the oven, place the stone on an oven rack in the lower third of the oven. A preheated baking sheet will also work.

PIZZA GOES LIGHT
GRAND PRIZE
WINNER

Pineapple Beef Kabobs

I saw a similar recipe for beef kabobs in a magazine but wanted to put my own unique twist on it. These succulent skewers are easy, colorful, and the basting helps keep them juicy and tender.

—MARGUERITE SHAEFFER SEWELL, NEW JERSEY

PREP: 20 MIN. + MARINATING **GRILL:** 10 MIN.
MAKES: 6 SERVINGS

- **1 can (6 ounces) unsweetened pineapple juice**
- **⅓ cup honey**
- **⅓ cup soy sauce**
- **3 tablespoons cider vinegar**
- **1½ teaspoons minced garlic**
- **1½ teaspoons ground ginger**
- **1½ pounds beef top sirloin steak, cut into 1-inch pieces**
- **1 fresh pineapple, peeled and cut into 1-inch chunks**
- **12 large fresh mushrooms**
- **1 medium sweet red pepper, cut into 1-inch pieces**
- **1 medium sweet yellow pepper, cut into 1-inch pieces**
- **1 medium red onion, cut into 1-inch pieces**
- **2½ cups uncooked instant rice**

1. In a small bowl, combine the first six ingredients. Pour ¾ cup into a large resealable plastic bag; add beef. Seal bag and turn to coat; refrigerate for 1-4 hours. Cover and refrigerate remaining marinade for basting.

2. Drain and discard marinade. On 12 metal or soaked wooden skewers, alternately thread the beef, pineapple, mushrooms, peppers and onion. Using long-handled tongs, moisten a paper towel with cooking oil and lightly coat the grill rack.

3. Grill, covered, over medium-hot heat for 8-10 minutes or until meat reaches desired doneness, turning occasionally and basting frequently with reserved marinade.

4. Cook rice according to package directions; serve with kabobs.

"I love combining fruits and chilies to make flavorful glazes. This recipe has evolved over the years. It uses ancho chili powder, which lends a nice smokey flavor. I like to serve the juicy filets over rice, potatoes or cheesy grits."

—ANNA GINSBERG AUSTIN, TEXAS

Peach-Glazed Beef Filets

PREP/TOTAL TIME: 30 MIN. **MAKES:** 2 SERVINGS

- **2 beef tenderloin steaks (5 ounces each)**
- **¼ teaspoon salt**
- **⅛ teaspoon pepper**
- **1 teaspoon canola oil**
- **¼ cup peach preserves**
- **2 tablespoons chicken broth**
- **1 tablespoon balsamic vinegar**
- **2 teaspoons minced fresh cilantro**
- **¾ teaspoon ground ancho chili pepper**
- **1 garlic clove, minced**

1. Sprinkle beef with salt and pepper. In a large skillet, cook steaks in oil over medium heat for 5-8 minutes on each side or until meat reaches desired doneness (for medium-rare, a thermometer should read 145°; medium, 160°; well-done, 170°).

2. In a small bowl, combine the remaining ingredients; pour over steaks. Cook for 1-2 minutes or until glaze is heated through.

Nutrition Facts: *1 filet with 3½ teaspoons glaze equals 350 calories, 12 g fat (4 g saturated fat), 89 mg cholesterol, 422 mg sodium, 28 g carbohydrate, trace fiber, 30 g protein.*
Diabetic Exchanges: *4 lean meat, 2 fruit, ½ fat.*

Jalapeno Chicken Pizza

This is one of our favorite pizza recipes. It calls for a pre-made crust, so it's really quick and easy on busy weeknights.

—LINDA EWANKOWICH RALEIGH, NORTH CAROLINA

PREP/TOTAL TIME: 25 MIN. **MAKES:** 12 PIECES

- **2 plum tomatoes, quartered**
- **½ cup fresh cilantro leaves**
- **1 tablespoon tomato paste**
- **1 teaspoon chopped chipotle peppers in adobo sauce**
- **1 garlic clove, peeled and quartered**
- **½ teaspoon salt**
- **1 prebaked 12-inch thin pizza crust**
- **2 cups shredded cooked chicken breast**
- **¾ cup shredded reduced-fat Monterey Jack cheese or Mexican cheese blend**
- **2 jalapeno peppers, seeded and sliced into rings**

1. Place the first six ingredients in a food processor; cover and process until blended. Place the crust on an ungreased 12-in. pizza pan; spread with tomato mixture. Top with chicken, cheese and jalapenos.

2. Bake at 450° for 10-12 minutes or until heated through and cheese is melted.

Editor's Note: *Wear disposable gloves when cutting hot peppers; the oils can burn skin. Avoid touching your face.*

Nutrition Facts: *2 pieces equals 262 calories, 8 g fat (2 g saturated fat), 46 mg cholesterol, 613 mg sodium, 26 g carbohydrate, 1 g fiber, 23 g protein.* **Diabetic Exchanges:** *3 lean meat, 1½ starch.*

Chicken Penne Casserole

I make this delicious casserole at least once every week or two, and we never tire of it. I like that I can clean my kitchen and then relax while it bakes. It won't disappoint...I promise!

—CARMEN VANOSCH VERNON, BRITISH COLUMBIA

PREP: 35 MIN. **BAKE:** 45 MIN. **MAKES:** 4 SERVINGS

- **1 pound boneless skinless chicken thighs, cut into 1-inch pieces**
- **½ cup each chopped onion, green pepper and sweet red pepper**
- **1 teaspoon each dried basil, oregano and parsley flakes**
- **½ teaspoon salt**
- **½ teaspoon crushed red pepper flakes**
- **1 tablespoon canola oil**
- **3 garlic cloves, minced**
- **1½ cups uncooked penne pasta**
- **1 can (14½ ounces) diced tomatoes, undrained**
- **3 tablespoons tomato paste**
- **¾ cup chicken broth**
- **2 cups (8 ounces) shredded part-skim mozzarella cheese**
- **½ cup grated Romano cheese**

1. In a large saucepan, saute the chicken, onion, peppers and seasonings in oil until chicken is no longer pink. Add garlic; cook 1 minute longer.

2. Cook pasta according to package directions. Meanwhile, process tomatoes and tomato paste in a blender; add to chicken mixture. Stir in broth. Bring to a boil. Reduce heat; cover and simmer for 10-15 minutes or until slightly thickened.

3. Drain pasta; toss with chicken mixture. Spoon half of the mixture into a greased 2-qt. baking dish. Sprinkle with half of the cheeses. Repeat layers.

4. Cover and bake at 350° for 30 minutes. Uncover; bake 15-20 minutes longer or until heated through.

Chicken Pasta Casserole: *Substitute chicken breast for the chicken thighs, spiral pasta for the penne and shredded provolone for the mozzarella. Proceed as directed. Serve immediately or before baking, cover and freeze for up to 3 months.*

To use frozen casserole: *Thaw in the refrigerator overnight. Remove from the refrigerator 30 minutes before baking. Cover and bake at 350° for 50-60 minutes.*

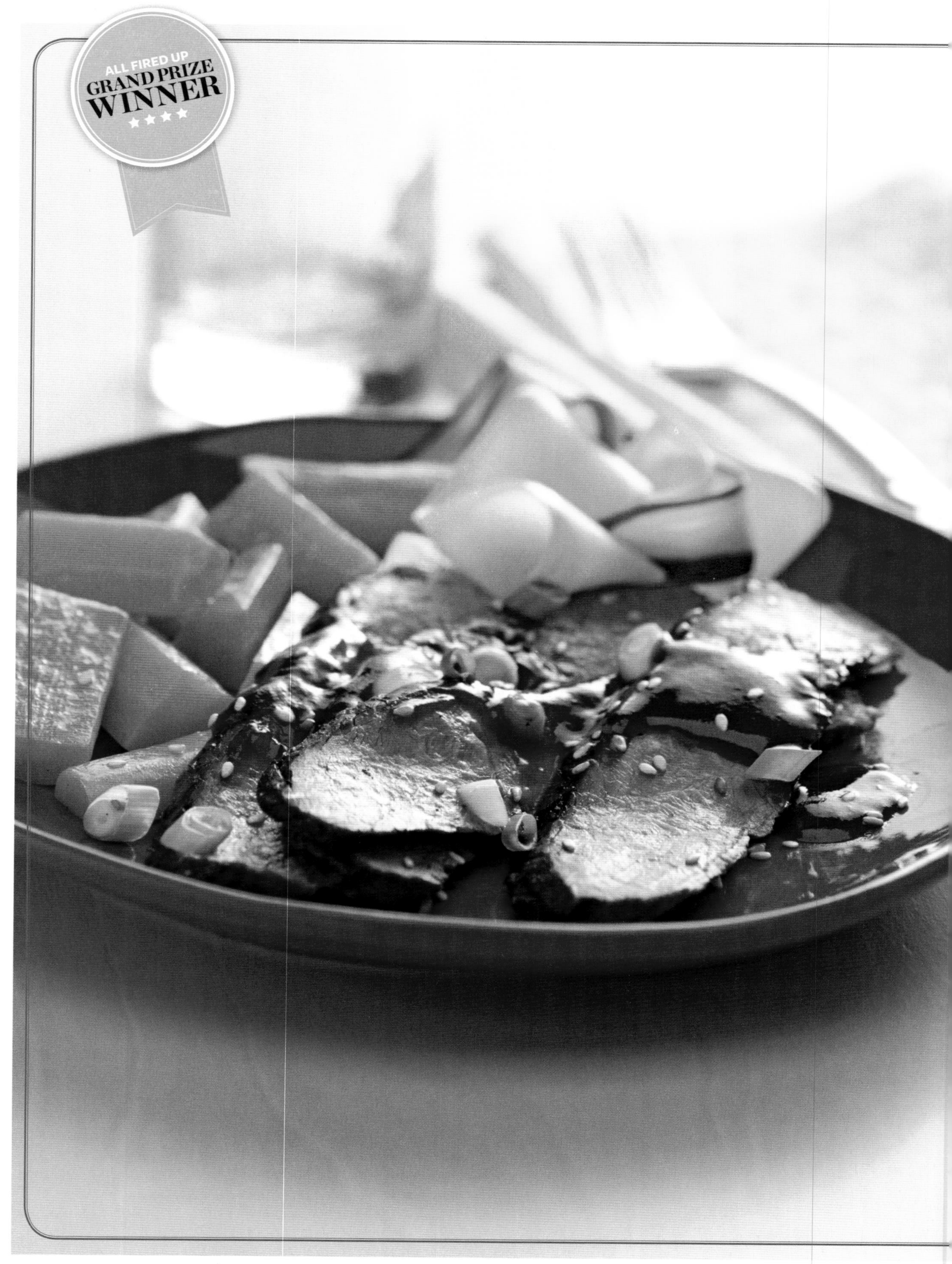
ALL FIRED UP
GRAND PRIZE
WINNER

GRAND PRIZE

Grilled Asian Flank Steak

This recipe is a variation of one my mother used to make. It was so good. So is the wonderful flavor and aroma of this incredibly tender but lighter version. You'll want to try this one!

—**SHAWN SOLLEY** MORGANTOWN, WEST VIRGINIA

PREP: 15 MIN. + MARINATING **GRILL:** 15 MIN.
MAKES: 6 SERVINGS

- **¼ cup Worcestershire sauce**
- **¼ cup reduced-sodium soy sauce**
- **3 tablespoons honey**
- **1 tablespoon sesame oil**
- **1 teaspoon Chinese five-spice powder**
- **1 teaspoon minced garlic**
- **½ teaspoon minced fresh gingerroot**
- **1 beef flank steak (1½ pounds)**
- **2 tablespoons hoisin sauce, warmed**
- **3 green onions, thinly sliced**
- **1 tablespoon sesame seeds, toasted, optional**

1. In a large resealable plastic bag, combine the first seven ingredients; add steak. Seal bag and turn to coat; refrigerate overnight.

2. Drain and discard marinade. Grill steak, covered, over medium heat for 6-7 minutes on each side or until meat reaches desired doneness (for medium-rare, a thermometer should read 145°; medium, 160°; well-done, 170°). Let stand for 5 minutes.

3. Thinly slice steak across the grain. Drizzle with hoisin sauce; garnish with onions. Sprinkle with sesame seeds if desired.

Nutrition Facts: *3 ounces cooked beef (calculated without sesame seeds) equals 193 calories, 9 g fat (4 g saturated fat), 54 mg cholesterol, 241 mg sodium, 5 g carbohydrate, trace fiber, 22 g protein.* **Diabetic Exchange:** *3 lean meat.*

SCORE FLANK STEAK

To prevent the edges of beef flank steak from curling when broiling or grilling, score the surface with shallow diagonal cuts, making diamond shapes. This helps to tenderize the meat as well.

—**LOIS M.** OCEANSIDE, CALIFORNIA

Turkey Enchiladas

My family likes these enchiladas so much, they request a turkey dinner several times a year just so I'll make this dish with the leftovers! I usually double the recipe.

—**BEVERLY MATTHEWS** PASCO, WASHINGTON

PREP: 40 MIN. **BAKE:** 40 MIN. **MAKES:** 8 SERVINGS

- **3 cups cubed cooked turkey**
- **1 cup chicken broth**
- **1 cup cooked long grain rice**
- **2 plum tomatoes, chopped**
- **1 medium onion, chopped**
- **½ cup canned chopped green chilies**
- **½ cup sour cream**
- **¼ cup sliced ripe or green olives with pimientos**
- **¼ cup minced fresh cilantro**
- **1 teaspoon ground cumin**
- **8 flour tortillas (10 inches)**
- **1 can (28 ounces) green enchilada sauce, divided**
- **2 cups (8 ounces) shredded Mexican cheese blend, divided**

1. In a large saucepan, combine the first 10 ingredients. Bring to a boil. Reduce heat; simmer, uncovered, for 20 minutes. Remove from the heat.

2. Place ½ cup turkey mixture down the center of each tortilla; top each with 1 teaspoon enchilada sauce and 1 tablespoon cheese. Roll up and place seam side down in a greased 13-in. x 9-in. baking dish. Pour remaining enchilada sauce over top; sprinkle with remaining cheese.

3. Cover and bake at 350° for 30 minutes. Uncover; bake 8-10 minutes longer or until bubbly.

Steak and Rice Roll-Ups

This has been a favorite family recipe since I started making it in the 1960s. It makes a meal no one ever wants to miss.
—**ELAINE SELANDER** LITTLETON, COLORADO

PREP: 25 MIN. **COOK:** 1¼ HOURS **MAKES:** 6 SERVINGS

- **1 cup finely chopped fresh mushrooms**
- **2 green onions, finely chopped**
- **¼ cup finely chopped green pepper**
- **2 tablespoons butter**
- **1½ cups cooked long grain rice**
- **2 tablespoons diced pimientos**
- **¼ teaspoon dried thyme**
- **¼ teaspoon dried marjoram**
- **2 pounds beef top round steak (½ inch thick)**
- **2 tablespoons canola oil**
- **2 tablespoons plus 1 teaspoon onion soup mix**
- **1 cup water**

1. In a large skillet, saute the mushrooms, onions and pepper in butter until tender. Transfer to a small bowl; stir in the rice, pimientos, thyme and marjoram.
2. Cut steak into six pieces; flatten to 1/2-in. thickness. Spread evenly with mushroom mixture; roll up and secure with toothpicks.
3. In the same skillet, brown roll-ups in oil on all sides. Add soup mix and water; cover and simmer for 1 to 1¼ hours or until meat is tender, occasionally spooning cooking liquid over roll-ups.
4. Thicken cooking juices if desired; serve with roll-ups. Discard toothpicks.

Wild West Wellingtons

This zippy twist on traditional beef Wellington is perfect for a special occasion or when you want to treat your sweetheart to a romantic meal with Western flair. If you like extra-spicy food, choose a hot salsa rather than a mild or medium one.
—**JENNI DISE** PHOENIX, ARIZONA

PREP: 15 MIN. **BAKE:** 20 MIN. **MAKES:** 2 SERVINGS

- **2 beef tenderloin steaks (6 ounces each)**
- **¼ teaspoon salt**
- **¼ teaspoon ground cumin**
- **¼ teaspoon pepper**
- **2 ounces cream cheese, softened**
- **¼ cup canned chopped green chilies**
- **½ sheet frozen puff pastry, thawed**
- **2 teaspoons beaten egg**
- **½ teaspoon water**
- **Salsa, optional**

1. Sprinkle steaks with salt, cumin and pepper. In a large nonstick skillet coated with cooking spray, brown steaks on both sides; remove and keep warm. In a small bowl, combine cream cheese and chilies; set aside.
2. On a lightly floured surface, roll pastry into a 16-in. x 12-in. rectangle. Cut into two 12-in. x 8-in. rectangles. Place a steak on one side of each rectangle; top with cream cheese mixture. Fold pastry over meat; seal seams. Place seam side down on a rack in a shallow baking pan.
3. Combine egg and water; brush over pastry. Bake at 400° for 18-22 minutes or until meat reaches desired doneness (for medium-rare, a thermometer should read 145°; medium, 160°; well-done, 170°). Let stand for 5 minutes. Serve with salsa if desired.

Nutrition Facts: *1 serving (prepared with reduced-fat cream cheese; calculated without salsa) equals 644 calories, 35 g fat (12 g saturated fat), 148 mg cholesterol, 773 mg sodium, 37 g carbohydrate, 5 g fiber, 44 g protein.*

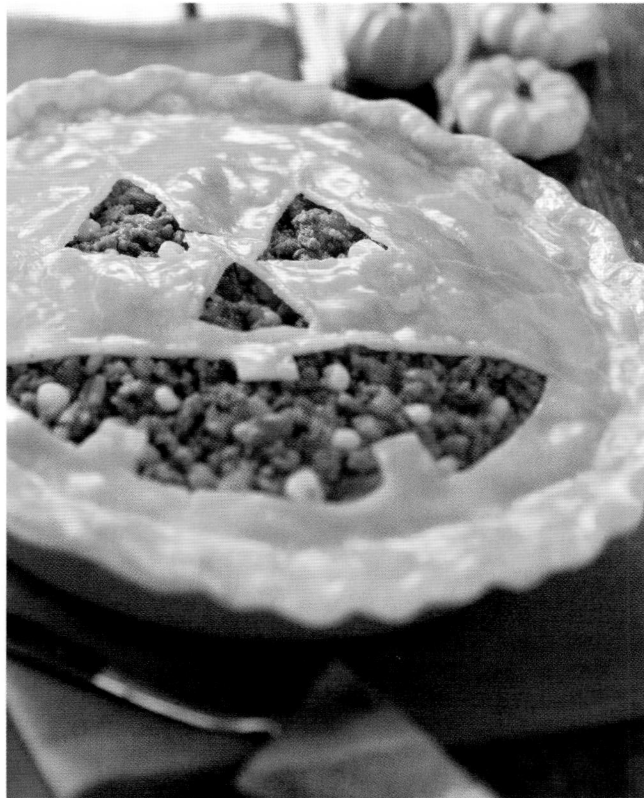

Jack-o'-Lantern Sloppy Joe Pie

This is so much fun to fix, and kids love it! You will never have to worry about leftovers. It's even good for adult Halloween parties, but you might want to increase the heat level with a hotter salsa or seasonings.

—BONNIE HAWKINS ELKHORN, WISCONSIN

PREP/TOTAL TIME: 30 MIN. **MAKES:** 6 SERVINGS

1½ pounds lean ground beef (90% lean)
½ cup chopped onion
2 teaspoons all-purpose flour
1 cup salsa
½ cup chili sauce
1 cup frozen corn
1 can (4 ounces) chopped green chilies
2 tablespoons brown sugar
1 sheet refrigerated pie pastry
1 egg
Orange paste food coloring

1. In a large skillet, cook beef and onion over medium heat until meat is no longer pink; drain. In a small bowl, combine the flour, salsa and chili sauce until blended; stir into skillet. Add the corn, chilies and brown sugar.
2. Transfer to a deep-dish 9-in. pie plate. Unroll pastry; place over filling. With a sharp knife, cut out a face to resemble a jack-o'-lantern; flute edges. Beat egg and food coloring; brush over pastry.
3. Bake at 450° for 9-11 minutes or until crust is golden brown and filling is bubbly.

Nutrition Facts: *1 serving equals 428 calories, 19 g fat (8 g saturated fat), 97 mg cholesterol, 764 mg sodium, 38 g carbohydrate, 1 g fiber, 25 g protein.*

Chipotle Chicken Fajitas

I've had this recipe in my collection for years, and my husband and I both love it. I changed it up a little to fit our taste. Be careful with the chipotle peppers as they can be hot. You may want to adjust the amount to suit your own preference.

—MELISSA THOMECZEK HANNIBAL, MISSOURI

PREP: 30 MIN. + MARINATING **GRILL:** 10 MIN.
MAKES: 5 SERVINGS

1 bottle (12 ounces) chili sauce
¼ cup lime juice
4 chipotle peppers in adobo sauce
1 pound boneless skinless chicken breasts, cut into strips
½ cup cider vinegar
⅓ cup packed brown sugar
⅓ cup molasses
4 medium green peppers, cut into 1-inch pieces
1 large onion, cut into 1-inch pieces
1 tablespoon olive oil
⅛ teaspoon salt
⅛ teaspoon pepper
10 flour tortillas (8 inches)
1½ cups chopped tomatoes
1 cup (4 ounces) shredded Mexican cheese blend

1. Place the chili sauce, lime juice and chipotle peppers in a food processor; cover and process until blended. Transfer ½ cup to a large resealable plastic bag; add chicken. Seal bag and turn to coat; refrigerate for 1-4 hours.
2. Pour remaining marinade into a small bowl; add the vinegar, brown sugar and molasses. Cover and refrigerate.
3. On six metal or soaked wooden skewers, alternately thread chicken and vegetables. Brush with oil; sprinkle with salt and pepper. Grill, covered, over medium heat for 10-16 minutes or until a thermometer reads 170°, turning occasionally.
4. Unskewer chicken and veggies into a large bowl; add ½ cup chipotle-molasses mixture and toss to coat. Keep warm.
5. Grill the tortillas, uncovered, over medium heat for 45-55 seconds on each side or until warmed. Top with the chicken mixture, tomatoes, cheese and remaining chipotle-molasses mixture.

Grilled Chicken with Chutney

My husband never liked plums until he tasted them cooked with peaches, dried cranberries and spices in this robust chutney. It wakes up just about any kind of meat—from tender chicken breasts to savory pork tenderloin.

—**GILDA LESTER** MILLSBORO, DELAWARE

PREP: 30 MIN. + COOLING **GRILL:** 10 MIN. **MAKES:** 6 SERVINGS

- **3 medium plums, chopped**
- **⅔ cup sugar**
- **½ cup white wine vinegar**
- **3 tablespoons balsamic vinegar**
- **2 tablespoons dried cranberries**
- **1 garlic clove, minced**
- **1 teaspoon minced fresh gingerroot**
- **¼ teaspoon ground allspice**
- **¼ teaspoon crushed red pepper flakes**
- **2 cups chopped peeled peaches**
- **¼ cup finely chopped red onion**
- **1 teaspoon Dijon mustard**
- **½ teaspoon minced seeded jalapeno pepper**
- **6 boneless skinless chicken breast halves (5 ounces each)**
- **2 tablespoons olive oil**
- **1 tablespoon Tex-Mex chili seasoning mix**
- **Red leaf lettuce**
- **Additional chopped jalapenos, optional**

1. For chutney, in a large saucepan, combine the first nine ingredients. Bring to a boil; cook and stir for 6-8 minutes or until thickened. Stir in the peaches, onion, mustard and jalapeno. Cool to room temperature.

2. Brush chicken with oil; sprinkle with chili seasoning mix. Grill chicken, covered, over medium heat for 5-6 minutes on each side or until a thermometer reads 170°. Slice chicken; serve on lettuce leaves with chutney. Sprinkle with additional jalapenos if desired.

Editor's Note: *Wear disposable gloves when cutting hot peppers; the oils can burn skin. Avoid touching your face.*

Nutrition Facts: *1 chicken breast half with 1⁄3 cup chutney equals 346 calories, 8 g fat (2 g saturated fat), 78 mg cholesterol, 178 mg sodium, 38 g carbohydrate, 2 g fiber, 30 g protein.* **Diabetic Exchanges:** *4 lean meat, 1½ starch, 1 fruit, 1 fat.*

GRAND PRIZE

Next Day Turkey Primavera

I make this recipe often around the holidays. It's a wonderful way to use up leftover turkey without feeling like it's a "repeat" meal. I love pasta, and the creamy sauce in this primavera is so easy to make.

—**ROBYN HARDISTY** LAKEWOOD, CALIFORNIA

PREP/TOTAL TIME: 30 MIN. **MAKES:** 4 SERVINGS

- **1 cup uncooked penne pasta**
- **8 fresh asparagus spears, trimmed and cut into 1-inch pieces**
- **⅔ cup julienned carrot**
- **3 tablespoons butter**
- **4 large fresh mushrooms, sliced**
- **½ cup chopped yellow summer squash**
- **½ cup chopped zucchini**
- **1½ cups shredded cooked turkey**
- **1 medium tomato, chopped**
- **1 envelope Italian salad dressing mix**
- **1 cup heavy whipping cream**
- **¼ cup grated Parmesan cheese**

1. Cook pasta according to package directions. Meanwhile, in a large skillet, saute asparagus and carrot in butter for 3 minutes. Add the mushrooms, yellow squash and zucchini; saute until crisp-tender.

2. Stir in the turkey, tomato, dressing mix and cream. Bring to a boil; cook and stir for 2 minutes.

3. Drain pasta; add to vegetable mixture and toss to combine. Sprinkle with cheese and toss again.

ALL ABOUT ASPARAGUS

The peak months for buying asparagus are April and May. When buying, look for firm, straight, uniform-size spears. The tips should be closed with crisp stalks. It's best to use asparagus within a few days of purchase. For a little longer storage, place bundled stalks upright in a bowl filled with 1 inch of water; refrigerate. Or wrap the cut ends in moist paper towels. Cover the towel with plastic wrap; refrigerate. To clean, soak asparagus in cold water. Cut or snap off the tough white portion.

LET'S TALK TURKEY
GRAND PRIZE
WINNER

Turkey Cabbage Bake

I revised this old recipe by using ground turkey instead of ground beef (to make it healthier), by finely chopping the cabbage to improve texture and by adding thyme to take the flavor up a notch. Crescent rolls help it go together in a snap.

—IRENE GUTZ FORT DODGE, IOWA

PREP: 30 MIN. **BAKE:** 15 MIN. **MAKES:** 6 SERVINGS

- **2 tubes (8 ounces each) refrigerated crescent rolls**
- **1½ pounds ground turkey**
- **½ cup chopped onion**
- **½ cup finely chopped carrot**
- **1 teaspoon minced garlic**
- **2 cups finely chopped cabbage**
- **1 can (10¾ ounces) condensed cream of mushroom soup, undiluted**
- **½ teaspoon dried thyme**
- **1 cup (4 ounces) shredded part-skim mozzarella cheese**

1. Unroll one tube of crescent dough into one long rectangle; seal seams and perforations. Press onto the bottom of a greased 13-in. x 9-in. baking dish. Bake at 425° for 6-8 minutes or until golden brown.

2. Meanwhile, in a large skillet, cook the turkey, onion and carrot over medium heat until meat is no longer pink. Add garlic; cook 1 minute longer. Drain. Add the cabbage, soup and thyme. Pour over crust; sprinkle with cheese.

3. On a lightly floured surface, press second tube of crescent dough into a 13-in. x 9-in. rectangle, sealing seams and perforations. Place over casserole.

4. Bake, uncovered, at 375° for 14-16 minutes or until crust is golden brown.

"My family loves this tangy, slow-cooked beef roast with gravy. If there are any leftovers, we enjoy tasty sandwiches the next day."

—DEBORAH DAILEY VANCOUVER, WASHINGTON

Pot Roast with Gravy

PREP: 30 MIN. **COOK:** 7½ HOURS **MAKES:** 10 SERVINGS

- **1 beef rump roast or bottom round roast (5 pounds)**
- **6 tablespoons balsamic vinegar, divided**
- **1 teaspoon salt**
- **½ teaspoon garlic powder**
- **¼ teaspoon pepper**
- **2 tablespoons canola oil**
- **3 garlic cloves, minced**
- **4 bay leaves**
- **1 large onion, thinly sliced**
- **3 teaspoons beef bouillon granules**
- **½ cup boiling water**
- **1 can (10¾ ounces) condensed cream of mushroom soup, undiluted**
- **4 to 5 tablespoons cornstarch**
- **¼ cup cold water**

1. Cut roast in half; rub with 2 tablespoons vinegar. Combine the salt, garlic powder and pepper; rub over meat. In a large skillet, brown roast in oil on all sides. Transfer to a 5-qt. slow cooker.

2. Add the garlic, bay leaves and onion over roast. In a small bowl, dissolve bouillon in boiling water; stir in soup and remaining vinegar. Slowly pour over roast. Cover and cook on low for 6-8 hours or until meat is tender.

3. Remove roast; keep warm. Discard bay leaves. Whisk cornstarch and cold water until smooth; stir into cooking juices. Cover and cook on high for 30 minutes or until gravy is thickened. Slice roast; return to slow cooker and heat through.

Cordon Bleu Lasagna

Five different cheeses and a jar of prepared Alfredo sauce enhance this terrific lasagna recipe. It's effortless to prepare, serves a crowd, and kids really love it, too.

—**KARLENE BURTON** JACKSON, TENNESSEE

PREP: 25 MIN. **BAKE:** 50 MIN. + STANDING **MAKES:** 12 SERVINGS

- **2 eggs, lightly beaten**
- **1 carton (15 ounces) ricotta cheese**
- **1 cup (8 ounces) 4% cottage cheese**
- **½ cup grated Parmesan cheese**
- **¼ cup plus 2 tablespoons minced fresh parsley, divided**
- **1 jar (15 ounces) roasted garlic Alfredo sauce**
- **2 cups cubed cooked chicken**
- **2 cups cubed cooked ham**
- **¼ teaspoon garlic powder**
- **6 lasagna noodles, cooked and drained**
- **2 cups (8 ounces) shredded part-skim mozzarella cheese**
- **1 cup (4 ounces) shredded Swiss cheese**

1. In a large bowl, combine the eggs, ricotta, cottage cheese, Parmesan and 1/4 cup parsley; set aside. In another bowl, combine the Alfredo sauce, chicken, ham and garlic powder.
2. Spread 1/2 cup of the chicken mixture in the bottom of a greased 13-in. x 9-in. baking dish. Layer with half of the noodles and ricotta mixture. Top with half of the remaining chicken mixture and half of the mozzarella and Swiss cheeses. Repeat layers.
3. Cover and bake at 350° for 40 minutes. Uncover; bake 10 minutes longer or a meat thermometer reads 160°. Let stand for 15 minutes before serving. Sprinkle with remaining parsley. Serve immediately. Or, if saving lasagna for future use, cover and freeze for up to 3 months.
To use frozen lasagna: *Thaw in the refrigerator overnight. Remove from the refrigerator 30 minutes before baking. Cover and bake according to directions.*

Mayonnaise Lover's Chicken

My father-in-law was looking for a good chicken marinade when a friend suggested mayonnaise with Italian dressing. He added the ham and cheese on his own, and we can't get enough of it!

—**JENNIFER RYTTING** WEST JORDAN, UTAH

PREP: 15 MIN. + MARINATING **GRILL:** 10 MIN.
MAKES: 6 SERVINGS

- **½ cup Italian salad dressing**
- **1¼ cups mayonnaise, divided**
- **6 boneless skinless chicken breast halves (4 ounces each)**
- **6 slices deli ham**
- **6 slices Swiss cheese**
- **1½ teaspoons prepared mustard**
- **1½ teaspoons honey**

1. In a small bowl, combine salad dressing and 1/2 cup mayonnaise. Pour 3/4 cup into a large resealable plastic bag; add chicken. Seal bag and turn to coat; refrigerate for at least 30 minutes. Cover and refrigerate the remaining marinade for basting.
2. Drain and discard marinade. Grill chicken, covered, over medium heat or broil 4 in. from the heat for 4-6 minutes on each side or until a thermometer reads 170°, basting frequently with reserved marinade.
3. Top each piece of chicken with a slice of ham and cheese. Grill, covered, 1-2 minutes longer or until cheese is melted.
4. In a small bowl, combine the mustard, honey and remaining mayonnaise. Serve with chicken.

SLOW-COOKED FAVORITES
GRAND PRIZE
WINNER

GRAND PRIZE

Sunday Chicken Stew

I love this recipe because I can prep the veggies Saturday night. In the morning, I brown the chicken and assemble everything in the slow cooker before we leave for church. Then I'm free to spend all day Sunday with my family while dinner slowly cooks.

—DIANE HALFERTY CORPUS CHRISTI, TEXAS

PREP: 30 MIN. **COOK:** 6½ HOURS **MAKES:** 6 SERVINGS

- **½ cup all-purpose flour**
- **1 teaspoon salt**
- **½ teaspoon white pepper**
- **1 broiler/fryer chicken (3 pounds), cut up and skin removed**
- **2 tablespoons canola oil**
- **3 cups chicken broth**
- **6 large carrots, cut into 1-inch pieces**
- **2 celery ribs, cut into ½-inch pieces**
- **1 large sweet onion, thinly sliced**
- **1 teaspoon dried rosemary, crushed**
- **1½ cups frozen peas**

DUMPLINGS

- **1 cup all-purpose flour**
- **2 teaspoons baking powder**
- **½ teaspoon salt**
- **½ teaspoon dried rosemary, crushed**
- **1 egg, lightly beaten**
- **½ cup 2% milk**

1. In a large resealable plastic bag, combine the flour, salt and pepper; add chicken, a few pieces at a time, and shake to coat. In a large skillet, brown chicken in oil; remove and keep warm. Gradually add broth to the skillet; bring to a boil.

2. In a 5-qt. slow cooker, layer the carrots, celery and onion; sprinkle with rosemary. Add the chicken and hot broth. Cover and cook on low for 6-8 hours or until chicken and vegetables are tender and stew is bubbling.

3. Remove chicken; when cool enough to handle, remove meat from the bones and discard bones. Cut meat into bite-size pieces and return to the slow cooker. Stir in peas.

4. For dumplings, in a small bowl, combine the flour, baking powder, salt and rosemary. Combine the egg and milk; stir into dry ingredients. Drop by heaping teaspoonfuls onto simmering chicken mixture. Cover and cook on high for 25-30 minutes or until a toothpick inserted in a dumpling comes out clean (do not lift the cover while simmering).

SNIP IN A SNAP

To save time and effort when cutting up a broiler/fryer chicken, use kitchen scissors instead of a knife.

—SARAH T. MOUTH OF WILSON, VIRGINIA

Sicilian Supper

Ground beef, tomato and a tasty cream cheese sauce come together in this hot, hearty casserole. I recently took it to a banquet, and recipe requests came from every table!

—GLORIA WARCZAK CEDARBURG, WISCONSIN

PREP: 30 MIN. **BAKE:** 20 MIN. **MAKES:** 4 SERVINGS

- **2 cups uncooked egg noodles**
- **1 pound ground beef**
- **½ cup chopped onion**
- **¼ cup chopped green pepper**
- **1 can (6 ounces) tomato paste**
- **¾ cup water**
- **1½ teaspoons sugar, divided**
- **½ teaspoon salt**
- **½ teaspoon dried basil**
- **¼ teaspoon garlic powder**
- **¼ teaspoon chili powder**
- **¼ teaspoon pepper, divided**
- **1 tablespoon finely chopped green onion**
- **1 tablespoon olive oil**
- **1 package (8 ounces) cream cheese, cubed**
- **¾ cup milk**
- **⅓ cup plus 2 tablespoons grated Parmesan cheese, divided**

1. Cook noodles according to package directions. Meanwhile, in a large skillet, cook the beef, onion and green pepper over medium heat until meat is no longer pink; drain. Stir in the tomato paste, water, 1 teaspoon sugar, salt, basil, garlic powder, chili powder and ⅛ teaspoon pepper.

2. In a large saucepan, saute green onion in oil until tender. Add cream cheese and milk; stir until blended. Stir in ⅓ cup cheese, and remaining sugar and pepper. Drain noodles; stir into cheese mixture.

3. In a greased 8-in. square baking dish, arrange alternate rows of beef and noodle mixtures. Sprinkle with remaining cheese. Cover and bake casserole at 350° for 20-25 minutes or until bubbly.

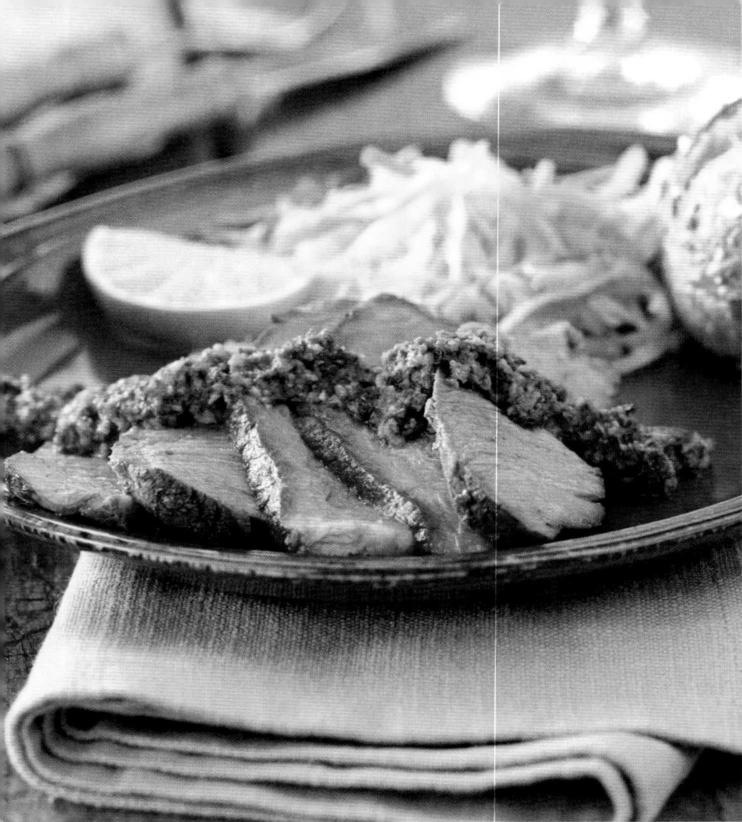

Chicken & Tomato Risotto

Store-bought spaghetti sauce cuts down on prep time for this creamy dish. You'll enjoy every mouthwatering bite!

—LORRAINE CALAND SHUNIAH, ONTARIO

PREP: 25 MIN. **COOK:** 25 MIN. **MAKES:** 4 SERVINGS

- **3 cups chicken broth**
- **1 pound boneless skinless chicken breasts, cut into 1-inch cubes**
- **1 tablespoon olive oil**
- **1½ cups sliced fresh mushrooms**
- **1 medium onion, chopped**
- **2 tablespoons butter**
- **1 garlic clove, minced**
- **1 cup uncooked arborio rice**
- **1 cup meatless spaghetti sauce**
- **¼ cup grated Parmesan cheese**

1. In a small saucepan, heat broth and keep warm. In a large skillet, saute chicken in oil until no longer pink. Remove and keep warm.

2. In the same skillet, saute mushrooms and onion in butter until crisp-tender. Add garlic; cook 1 minute longer. Add rice; cook and stir for 3 minutes. Carefully stir in 1 cup warm broth. Cook and stir until all of the liquid is absorbed.

3. Add remaining broth, ½ cup at a time, stirring constantly. Allow the liquid to absorb between additions. Cook until risotto is creamy and rice is almost tender. (Cooking time is about 20 minutes.)

4. Stir in the spaghetti sauce, cheese and reserved chicken; cook and stir until thickened.

Nutrition Facts: *1¼ cups equals 462 calories, 14 g fat (6 g saturated fat), 86 mg cholesterol, 1,186 mg sodium, 51 g carbohydrate, 3 g fiber, 31 g protein.*

Steak with Chipotle-Lime Chimichurri

Steak gets a flavor kick from chimichurri, a piquant all-purpose herb sauce that is so versatile, it complements almost any grilled meat, poultry or fish.

—LAUREEN PITTMAN RIVERSIDE, CALIFORNIA

PREP/TOTAL TIME: 30 MIN. **MAKES:** 8 SERVINGS

- **2 cups chopped fresh parsley**
- **1½ cups chopped fresh cilantro**
- **1 small red onion, quartered**
- **5 garlic cloves, quartered**
- **2 chipotle peppers in adobo sauce**
- **½ cup plus 1 tablespoon olive oil, divided**
- **¼ cup white wine vinegar**
- **¼ cup lime juice**
- **1 tablespoon dried oregano**
- **1 teaspoon grated lime peel**
- **1¼ teaspoons salt, divided**
- **¾ teaspoon pepper, divided**
- **2 beef flat iron steaks or top sirloin steaks (1 pound each)**

1. For chimichurri, place the parsley, cilantro, onion, garlic and chipotle peppers in a food processor; cover and pulse until minced. Add ½ cup oil, vinegar, lime juice, oregano, lime peel, ½ teaspoon salt and ¼ teaspoon pepper; cover and process until blended. Cover and refrigerate until serving.

2. Drizzle steaks with remaining oil; sprinkle with remaining salt and pepper. Grill, covered, over medium heat for 8-10 minutes on each side or until meat reaches desired doneness (for medium-rare, a thermometer should read 145°; medium, 160°; well-done, 170°). Thinly slice across the grain; serve with chimichurri.

Nutrition Facts: *1 each equals 297 calories, 21 g fat (6 g saturated fat), 73 mg cholesterol, 475 mg sodium, 5 g carbohydrate, 1 g fiber, 23 g protein.*

Meaty Pasta Casseroles

I love this recipe because it makes two hearty casseroles. Every time I fix it I add something different, such as extra garlic, for a little extra flavor punch.

—DEBRA BUTCHER DECATUR, INDIANA

PREP: 45 MIN. **BAKE:** 35 MIN.
MAKES: 2 CASSEROLES (6 SERVINGS EACH)

- **1 package (16 ounces) penne pasta**
- **1 pound ground beef**
- **1 pound bulk Italian pork sausage**
- **1¾ cups sliced fresh mushrooms**
- **1 medium onion, chopped**
- **1 medium green pepper, chopped**
- **2 cans (14½ ounces each) Italian diced tomatoes**
- **1 jar (23½ ounces) Italian sausage and garlic spaghetti sauce**
- **1 jar (16 ounces) chunky mild salsa**
- **1 package (8 ounces) sliced pepperoni, chopped**
- **1 cup (4 ounces) shredded Swiss cheese, divided**
- **4 cups (16 ounces) shredded part-skim mozzarella cheese, divided**
- **1½ cups shredded Parmesan cheese, divided**
- **1 jar (24 ounces) three-cheese spaghetti sauce**

1. Cook pasta according to package directions. Meanwhile, in a Dutch oven, cook the beef, sausage, mushrooms, onion and green pepper over medium heat until the meat is no longer pink; drain.
2. Drain pasta; add to the meat mixture. Stir in the tomatoes, sausage and garlic spaghetti sauce, salsa and pepperoni.
3. Divide half of pasta mixture between two greased 13-in. x 9-in. baking dishes. Sprinkle each with ¼ cup Swiss cheese, 1 cup mozzarella cheese and ⅓ cup Parmesan cheese. Spread ¾ cup of three-cheese spaghetti sauce over each. Top with remaining pasta mixture and three-cheese spaghetti sauce. Sprinkle with remaining cheeses.
4. Cover and freeze one casserole for up to 3 months. Cover and bake remaining casserole at 350° for 25 minutes. Uncover; bake 10 minutes longer or until cheese is melted.

To use frozen casserole: *Thaw in the refrigerator overnight. Remove from the refrigerator 30 minutes before baking. Cover and bake at 350° for 45 minutes. Uncover; bake 10 minutes longer or until cheese is melted.*

Chicken Lasagna

This lasagna is quick, easy and so delicious! I serve it with a green salad and warm rolls. Also, it can be frozen and saved for a busy weeknight sometime in the future.

—JANELLE RUTROUGH ROCKY MOUNT, VIRGINIA

PREP: 25 MIN. **BAKE:** 30 MIN. + STANDING **MAKES:** 8 SERVINGS

- **2 cups (16 ounces) 2% cottage cheese**
- **1 package (3 ounces) cream cheese, softened**
- **4 cups cubed cooked chicken**
- **1 can (10¾ ounces) condensed cream of chicken soup, undiluted**
- **1 can (10¾ ounces) condensed cream of celery soup, undiluted**
- **⅔ cup 2% milk**
- **½ cup chopped onion**
- **½ teaspoon salt**
- **6 lasagna noodles, cooked and drained**
- **1 package (6 ounces) stuffing mix**
- **½ cup butter, melted**

1. In a small bowl, combine cottage cheese and cream cheese. In a large bowl, combine chicken, soups, milk, onion and salt.
2. Spread half of the chicken mixture into a greased 13-in. x 9-in. baking dish. Top with three noodles. Spread with half of the cheese mixture. Repeat layers. Toss stuffing mix with butter; sprinkle over casserole.
3. Bake, uncovered, at 350° for 30-40 minutes or until bubbly and golden brown. Let stand for 10 minutes before cutting.

Tortilla Lasagna

I found a similar recipe online and experimented with the ingredients to create this delicious lasagna. It was an instant hit with my family! They love spicy food, and this simple dish has become a new favorite.

—LYNN SMITH WARRENSBURG, MISSOURI

PREP: 25 MIN. **BAKE:** 50 MIN. + STANDING **MAKES:** 8 SERVINGS

- **1 pound ground beef**
- **1 cup water**
- **1 envelope taco seasoning**
- **½ teaspoon garlic powder**
- **¼ teaspoon cayenne pepper**
- **1½ cups (12 ounces) sour cream**
- **1½ teaspoons chili powder**
- **2 cups (8 ounces) shredded Monterey Jack cheese**
- **2 cups (8 ounces) shredded cheddar cheese**
- **1 tablespoon cornmeal**
- **10 flour tortillas (6 inches)**
- **1 cup salsa**
- **1 small onion, sliced**

1. In a large skillet, cook beef over medium heat until no longer pink; drain. Stir in the water, taco seasoning, garlic powder and cayenne. Bring to a boil. Reduce heat; simmer, uncovered, for 10 minutes.
2. Meanwhile, in a small bowl, combine sour cream and chili powder. In a large bowl, combine cheeses; set aside. Sprinkle cornmeal into a greased 13-in. x 9-in. baking dish.
3. Arrange five tortillas, overlapping, in the bottom of prepared dish; spread with ½ cup salsa. Layer with half of the meat mixture, onion and sour cream mixture. Sprinkle with 1½ cups cheese mixture. Repeat layers.
4. Bake, uncovered, at 375° for 40 minutes. Sprinkle with remaining cheese mixture. Bake 10 minutes longer or until cheese is melted. Let stand for 10 minutes before cutting.

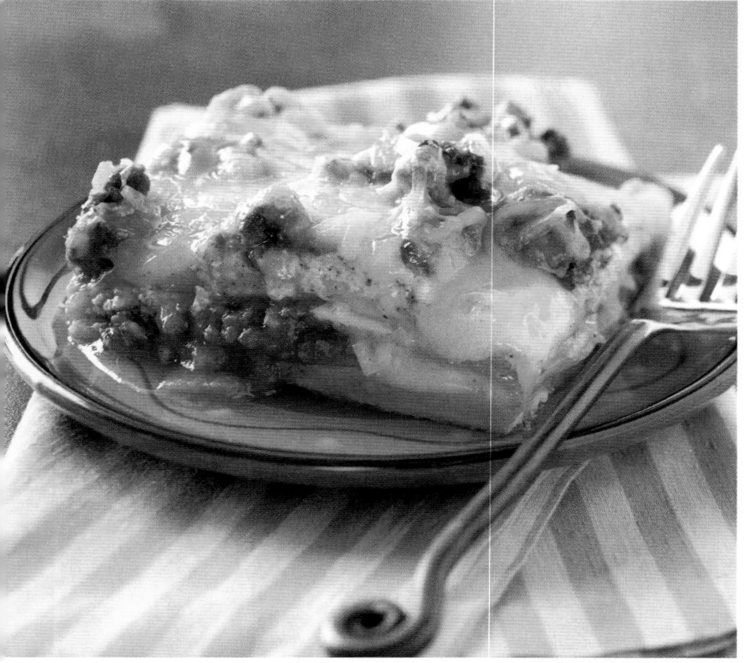

GRAND PRIZE

Southwest Turkey Casserole

PREP: 20 MIN. **BAKE:** 20 MIN. **MAKES:** 2 SERVINGS

- **½ cup uncooked elbow macaroni**
- **¼ cup chopped onion**
- **¼ cup chopped sweet red pepper**
- **4½ teaspoons butter**
- **1 tablespoon canola oil**
- **1 tablespoon all-purpose flour**
- **½ teaspoon salt**
- **½ teaspoon ground cumin**
- **Dash pepper**
- **1 cup 2% milk**
- **1 cup (4 ounces) shredded cheddar cheese**
- **1 cup cubed cooked turkey**
- **⅔ cup canned diced tomatoes and green chilies**
- **⅓ cup frozen corn**
- **⅓ cup frozen peas**

1. Cook macaroni according to package directions. Meanwhile, in a large skillet, saute onion and red pepper in butter and oil until tender. Stir in the flour, salt, cumin and pepper until blended; gradually add milk. Bring to a boil; cook and stir for 1-2 minutes or until thickened. Stir in cheese until melted.
2. Drain macaroni; add to cheese mixture. Stir in the turkey, tomatoes, corn and peas. Transfer to a 1-qt. baking dish coated with cooking spray. Bake, uncovered, at 350° for 20-25 minutes or until bubbly.

“When I was small, my mother and stepfather—who was a professional cook—joined efforts in the kitchen to make this colorful dinner. Whenever I make it, it brings back fond memories.”

—MARIA LUISA REYES BASTROP, TEXAS

CASSEROLE
MAKEOVER
GRAND PRIZE
WINNER

Spinach-Stuffed Chicken Breasts

Here's a savory entree that's easy to make but elegant enough for company. I often double the recipe and then freeze individual size portions for those long, busy days when I work late and don't have time to cook.

—SANDY FRIEDE
NEWBURYPORT, MASSACHUSETTS

PREP: 30 MIN. **BAKE:** 40 MIN.
MAKES: 6 SERVINGS

- **¼ cup chopped onion**
- **4½ teaspoons plus ¼ cup butter, divided**
- **1 garlic clove, minced**
- **1 package (10 ounces) frozen chopped spinach, thawed and squeezed dry**
- **6 ounces cream cheese, cubed**
- **¼ cup seasoned bread crumbs**
- **6 boneless skinless chicken breast halves (6 ounces each)**
- **½ teaspoon salt**
- **½ teaspoon pepper**
- **¼ cup honey**
- **2 tablespoons stone-ground mustard**
- **1 tablespoon lemon juice**

1. In a large skillet, saute onion in 4½ teaspoons butter until tender. Add garlic; saute 1 minute longer. Add spinach and cream cheese; cook and stir over low heat until blended. Remove from the heat; stir in bread crumbs.

2. Flatten chicken to ¼-in. thickness; sprinkle both sides with salt and pepper. Place about ¼ cup spinach mixture down the center of each chicken breast half. Fold chicken over filling and secure with toothpicks.

3. Place seam side down in a greased 11-in. x 7-in. baking dish. Melt remaining butter; stir in the honey, mustard and lemon juice. Pour over chicken.

4. Bake, uncovered, at 350° for 40-50 minutes or until meat is no longer pink, basting every 15 minutes with pan juices. Discard toothpicks.

Creamy Chicken Angel Hair

Our pasta-loving family often requests this recipe featuring chicken and vegetables. Lemon adds a light touch to the sauce, which is nicely seasoned with garlic and herbs.

—VANESSA SORENSON ISANTI, MINNESOTA

PREP: 15 MIN. **COOK:** 20 MIN. **MAKES:** 6 SERVINGS

- **1 package (16 ounces) angel hair pasta**
- **1¼ pounds boneless skinless chicken breasts, cut into 1-inch cubes**
- **½ teaspoon salt**
- **¼ teaspoon pepper**
- **3 tablespoons olive oil, divided**
- **1 large carrot, diced**
- **2 tablespoons butter**
- **1 medium onion, chopped**
- **1 celery rib, diced**
- **3 large garlic cloves, minced**
- **2 cups heavy whipping cream**
- **5 bacon strips, cooked and crumbled**
- **3 tablespoons lemon juice**
- **1 teaspoon Italian seasoning**
- **1 cup shredded Parmesan cheese**

1. Cook pasta according to package directions. Meanwhile, in a large skillet, saute the chicken, salt and pepper in 2 tablespoons oil until no longer pink. Remove and keep warm.
2. In the same skillet, saute carrot in butter and remaining oil for 1 minute. Add onion and celery; saute 3-4 minutes longer or until tender. Add garlic; cook for 1 minute.
3. Stir in the cream, bacon, lemon juice and Italian seasoning. Bring to a boil. Reduce heat; simmer, uncovered, for 2-3 minutes or until slightly thickened, stirring constantly. Return chicken to the pan.
4. Drain the pasta; toss with chicken mixture. Garnish with Parmesan cheese.

Nutrition Facts: *1½ cup equals 859 calories, 50 g fat (26 g saturated fat), 187 mg cholesterol, 666 mg sodium, 64 g carbohydrate, 3 g fiber, 39 g protein.*

Crunchy Baked Chicken

I've fixed this dish many times for company, and I've never had anyone fail to ask for the recipe. The leftovers—if there are any—are delicious heated up in the microwave.

—ELVA JEAN CRISWELL CHARLESTON, MISSISSIPPI

PREP: 10 MIN. **BAKE:** 50 MIN. **MAKES:** 4-6 SERVINGS

- **1 egg**
- **1 tablespoon milk**
- **1 can (2.8 ounces) French-fried onions, crushed**
- **¾ cup grated Parmesan cheese**
- **¼ cup dry bread crumbs**
- **1 teaspoon paprika**
- **½ teaspoon salt**
- **Dash pepper**
- **1 broiler/fryer chicken (3 to 4 pounds), cut up**
- **¼ cup butter, melted**

1. In a shallow bowl, whisk egg and milk. In another shallow bowl, combine the onions, cheese, bread crumbs, paprika, salt and pepper. Dip chicken in egg mixture, then roll in onion mixture.
2. Place in a greased 13-in. x 9-in. baking dish. Drizzle with butter. Bake, uncovered, at 350° for 50-60 minutes or until juices run clear.

POTLUCK HAM AND PASTA, PAGE 132

Pork & More Entrees

Whether your family is partial to **succulent cuts** of pork or ham, barbecued chops, classic pizzas, fresh fish and seafood fare or sensational meatless mainstays—each of these **enticing entrees** is guaranteed to have them running to the table!

Pepperoni 'n' Tomato Pasta

A casual dinner turns into a bow-tie affair when I toss pasta, mushrooms, pepperoni and tomato sauce together. This recipe is my version of a favorite restaurant dish.

—DAWN ONUFFER CRESTVIEW, FLORIDA

PREP: 25 MIN. **COOK:** 20 MIN. **MAKES:** 8 SERVINGS

- **1 medium onion, chopped**
- **1 large green pepper, chopped**
- **1 cup sliced fresh mushrooms**
- **1 tablespoon olive oil**
- **2 cans (15 ounces each) tomato sauce**
- **2 cans (14½ ounces each) stewed tomatoes, chopped**
- **2 bay leaves**
- **1 tablespoon sugar**
- **½ teaspoon dried basil**
- **½ teaspoon dried oregano**
- **½ teaspoon fennel seed, crushed**
- **½ teaspoon crushed red pepper flakes**
- **¼ teaspoon pepper**
- **1 package (8 ounces) sliced pepperoni, quartered**
- **4 cups uncooked ziti or bow tie pasta**
- **½ cup grated Parmesan cheese**
- **1½ cups (6 ounces) shredded part-skim mozzarella cheese**

1. In a large saucepan, saute the onion, green pepper and mushrooms in oil until tender.

2. Stir in the tomato sauce, tomatoes, bay leaves, sugar and seasonings. Bring to a boil. Stir in pepperoni. Reduce heat; simmer, uncovered, for 15 minutes.

3. Meanwhile, cook pasta according to package directions. Drain and place in a large serving bowl. Discard bay leaves from sauce; stir in Parmesan cheese. Pour over pasta; toss to coat. Sprinkle with mozzarella cheese.

Reuben Casserole

I've had this recipe in my file for quite some time, and you can tell from the stains on it that it's been well used. Sauerkraut, kielbasa and Swiss cheese combine for a creamy, Reuben-style entree.

—SALLY MANGEL BRADFORD, PENNSYLVANIA

PREP/TOTAL TIME: 30 MIN. **MAKES:** 2 SERVINGS

- **1½ cups uncooked egg noodles**
- **⅔ cup condensed cream of mushroom soup, undiluted**
- **⅓ cup 2% milk**
- **2 tablespoons chopped onion**
- **¾ teaspoon prepared mustard**
- **1 can (8 ounces) sauerkraut, rinsed and well drained**
- **⅓ pound smoked kielbasa or Polish sausage, cut into ½-inch slices**
- **½ cup shredded Swiss cheese**
- **3 tablespoons soft whole wheat bread crumbs**
- **1½ teaspoons butter, melted**

1. Cook noodles according to package directions. Meanwhile, in a small bowl, combine the soup, milk, onion and mustard; set aside.

2. Spread sauerkraut into a 1-qt. baking dish coated with cooking spray. Drain noodles; place over sauerkraut. Layer with soup mixture and kielbasa; sprinkle with cheese.

3. In a small bowl, combine bread crumbs and butter; sprinkle over casserole. Bake, uncovered, at 350° for 15-20 minutes or until bubbly.

Nutrition Facts: *2 cups (prepared with reduced-fat butter) equals 587 calories, 37 g fat (15 g saturated fat), 109 mg cholesterol, 2,315 mg sodium, 40 g carbohydrate, 5 g fiber, 26 g protein.*

Loaded Mexican Pizza

My husband is a picky eater, but this healthy pizza has lots of flavor, and he actually looks forward to it. Leftovers are no problem because this is one of those rare meals that's even better the next day!

—MARY BARKER KNOXVILLE, TENNESSEE

PREP/TOTAL TIME: 30 MIN.
MAKES: 6 SLICES

- **1 can (15 ounces) black beans, rinsed and drained**
- **1 medium red onion, chopped**
- **1 small sweet yellow pepper, chopped**
- **3 teaspoons chili powder**
- **¾ teaspoon ground cumin**
- **3 medium tomatoes, chopped**
- **1 jalapeno pepper, seeded and finely chopped**
- **1 garlic clove, minced**
- **1 prebaked 12-inch thin pizza crust**
- **2 cups chopped fresh spinach**
- **2 tablespoons minced fresh cilantro**
- **Hot pepper sauce to taste**
- **½ cup shredded reduced-fat cheddar cheese**
- **½ cup shredded pepper jack cheese**

1. In a small bowl, mash black beans. Stir in the onion, yellow pepper, chili powder and cumin. In another bowl, combine the tomatoes, jalapeno and garlic.

2. Place crust on an ungreased 12-in. pizza pan; spread with bean mixture. Top with tomato mixture and spinach. Sprinkle with the cilantro, pepper sauce and cheeses.

3. Bake at 400° for 12-15 minutes or until cheese is melted.

Editor's Note: *Wear disposable gloves when cutting hot peppers; the oils can burn skin. Avoid touching your face.*

Nutrition Facts: *1 slice equals 297 calories, 9 g fat (4 g saturated fat), 17 mg cholesterol, 566 mg sodium, 41 g carbohydrate, 6 g fiber, 15 g protein.* **Diabetic Exchanges:** *2½ starch, 1 lean meat, 1 vegetable.*

Tortellini with Salmon-Ricotta Sauce

I like to serve this with a colorful vegetable, such as a tomato salad or peas and carrots. It's equally good with canned salmon or tuna.
—BETH DAUENHAUER PUEBLO, COLORADO

PREP/TOTAL TIME: 30 MIN. **MAKES:** 4 SERVINGS

- **1 package (9 ounces) refrigerated cheese tortellini**
- **2 green onions, sliced**
- **1 teaspoon butter**
- **2 garlic cloves, minced**
- **1 teaspoon cornstarch**
- **1 cup fat-free milk**
- **½ cup shredded part-skim mozzarella cheese**
- **1 cup fat-free ricotta cheese**
- **1 pouch (7.1 ounces) boneless skinless pink salmon**
- **2 tablespoons snipped fresh dill or 2 teaspoons dill weed**
- **1½ teaspoons grated lemon peel**
- **1½ teaspoons lemon juice**
- **¼ teaspoon salt**

1. Cook tortellini according to package directions. Meanwhile, in a large saucepan, saute onions in butter until tender. Add garlic; cook 1 minute longer. Combine cornstarch and milk until smooth; gradually stir into the pan. Bring to a boil; cook and stir for 2 minutes or until slightly thickened.
2. Stir in mozzarella cheese until melted. Stir in the ricotta cheese, salmon, dill, lemon peel, lemon juice and salt.
3. Drain tortellini; add to ricotta sauce. Cook and stir until heated through.

Nutrition Facts: *1 cup equals 373 calories, 11 g fat (6 g saturated fat), 67 mg cholesterol, 797 mg sodium, 40 g carbohydrate, 2 g fiber, 28 g protein.* **Diabetic Exchanges:** *3 medium-fat meat, 2½ starch.*

Comforting Tuna Casserole

This is my mother's delicious twist on classic tuna casserole. I sometimes use sliced stuffed olives instead of pimientos.
—DOROTHY COLEMAN HOBE SOUND, FLORIDA

PREP: 15 MIN. **BAKE:** 20 MIN. **MAKES:** 2 SERVINGS

- **1¾ cups uncooked wide egg noodles**
- **6 teaspoons butter, divided**
- **4 teaspoons all-purpose flour**
- **¼ teaspoon salt**
- **Dash pepper**
- **¾ cup 2% milk**
- **1 package (3 ounces) cream cheese, softened**
- **1 pouch (2½ ounces) albacore white tuna in water**
- **2 tablespoons diced pimientos**
- **2 teaspoons minced chives**
- **2 slices Muenster cheese (¾ ounce each)**
- **2 tablespoons soft bread crumbs**

1. Cook noodles according to package directions. Meanwhile, in a small saucepan, melt 5 teaspoons butter. Stir in the flour, salt and pepper until blended; gradually add milk. Bring to a boil; cook and stir for 1-2 minutes or until thickened. Reduce heat; add the cream cheese, tuna, pimientos and chives. Cook and stir until cream cheese is melted.
2. Drain noodles. Spread 1/4 cup tuna mixture into a 3-cup baking dish coated with cooking spray. Layer with half of the noodles, 1/2 cup tuna mixture and one slice of cheese. Repeat layers.
3. In a small microwave-safe bowl, melt remaining butter; stir in bread crumbs. Sprinkle over top of casserole. Bake, uncovered, at 350° for 20-25 minutes or until bubbly.

Nutrition Facts: *1½ cup equals 493 calories, 26 g fat (15 g saturated fat), 118 mg cholesterol, 941 mg sodium, 37 g carbohydrate, 2 g fiber, 28 g protein.*

Salmon with Polenta

My husband was of Italian-Swiss descent, and one of his favorite dishes was salmon or bass with tomato sauce served over polenta. I still prepare this recipe for my son and his family.

—RENA PILOTTI RIPON, CALIFORNIA

PREP: 20 MIN. + SIMMERING **COOK:** 25 MIN. **MAKES:** 6 SERVINGS

- **2 celery ribs, chopped**
- **1 medium onion, chopped**
- **2 tablespoons olive oil, divided**
- **1 can (28 ounces) diced tomatoes, undrained**
- **1 can (8 ounces) tomato sauce**
- **¼ cup minced fresh parsley**
- **1½ teaspoons salt, divided**
- **1 teaspoon Italian seasoning**
- **½ teaspoon dried thyme**
- **½ teaspoon dried basil**
- **½ teaspoon pepper**
- **6 cups water**
- **2 cups cornmeal**
- **¼ cup all-purpose flour**
- **6 salmon fillets (6 ounces each)**

1. In a Dutch oven, saute celery and onion in 1 tablespoon oil until tender. Add the tomatoes, tomato sauce, parsley, ½ teaspoon salt, Italian seasoning, thyme, basil and pepper. Cover and simmer for 1 hour, stirring occasionally.

2. In a large heavy saucepan, bring water and remaining salt to a boil. Reduce heat to a gentle boil; slowly whisk in cornmeal. Cook and stir with a wooden spoon for 15-20 minutes or until polenta is thickened and pulls away cleanly from the sides of the pan.

3. Place flour in a large shallow bowl; coat salmon on both sides. In a large skillet, brown salmon in remaining oil. Transfer salmon to tomato mixture; cook, uncovered, for 3-5 minutes or until fish flakes easily with a fork. Serve salmon and sauce with polenta.

Nutrition Facts: *1 salmon fillet with 1 cup polenta and ⅔ cup sauce equals 583 calories, 24 g fat (4 g saturated fat), 100 mg cholesterol, 1,068 mg sodium, 50 g carbohydrate, 7 g fiber, 40 g protein.*

Vegetarian Stuffed Peppers

These filling and flavorful peppers are an updated version of my mom's stuffed peppers, a favorite when I was growing up in upstate New York. Whenever I make them, I'm reminded of home.

—MELISSA MCCABE LONG BEACH, CALIFORNIA

PREP: 30 MIN. **COOK:** 3½ HOURS **MAKES:** 6 SERVINGS

- **6 large sweet peppers**
- **2 cups cooked brown rice**
- **3 small tomatoes, chopped**
- **1 cup frozen corn, thawed**
- **1 small sweet onion, chopped**
- **⅓ cup canned red beans, rinsed and drained**
- **⅓ cup canned black beans, rinsed and drained**
- **¾ cup cubed Monterey Jack cheese**
- **1 can (4¼ ounces) chopped ripe olives**
- **4 fresh basil leaves, thinly sliced**
- **3 garlic cloves, minced**
- **1 teaspoon salt**
- **½ teaspoon pepper**
- **¾ cup meatless spaghetti sauce**
- **½ cup water**
- **4 tablespoons grated Parmesan cheese, divided**

1. Cut tops off peppers and remove seeds; set aside. In a large bowl, combine the rice, tomatoes, corn, onion and beans. Stir in the Monterey Jack cheese, olives, basil, garlic, salt and pepper. Spoon into peppers.

2. Combine spaghetti sauce and water; pour half into an oval 5-qt. slow cooker. Add the stuffed peppers. Top with remaining sauce. Sprinkle with 2 tablespoons Parmesan cheese.

3. Cover and cook on low for 3½ to 4 hours or until peppers are tender and filling is heated through. Sprinkle with remaining Parmesan cheese.

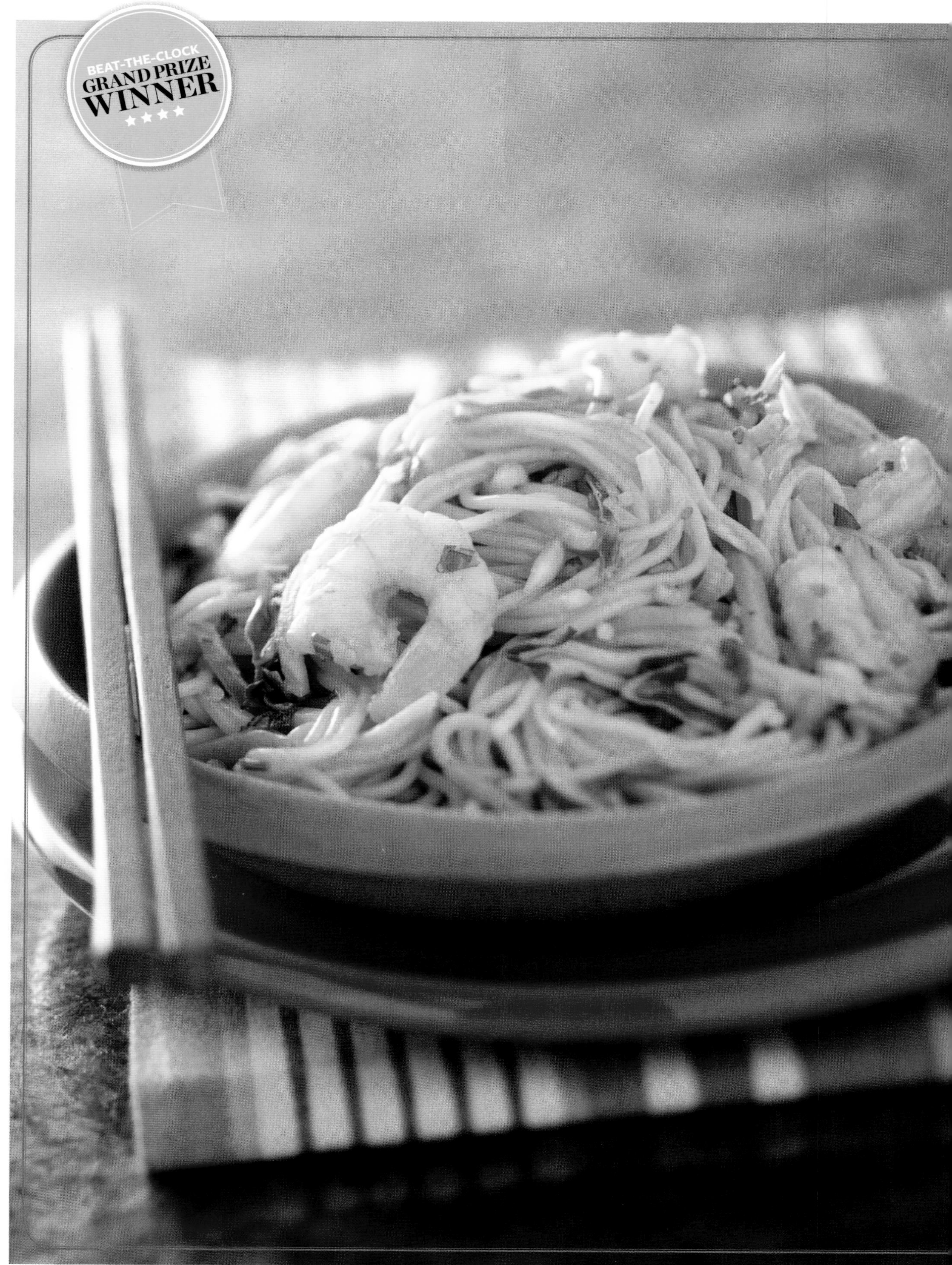
BEAT-THE-CLOCK
GRAND PRIZE
WINNER

GRAND PRIZE

Shrimp 'n' Noodle Bowls

PREP/TOTAL TIME: 25 MIN. **MAKES:** 6 SERVINGS

- **8 ounces uncooked angel hair pasta**
- **1 pound cooked small shrimp**
- **2 cups broccoli coleslaw mix**
- **6 green onions, thinly sliced**
- **½ cup minced fresh cilantro**
- **⅔ cup reduced-fat sesame ginger salad dressing**

Cook pasta according to package directions; drain and rinse in cold water. Transfer to a large bowl. Add the shrimp, coleslaw mix, onions and cilantro. Drizzle with dressing; toss to coat. Cover and refrigerate until serving.

Nutrition Facts: *1⅓ cups equals 260 calories, 3 g fat (trace saturated fat), 147 mg cholesterol, 523 mg sodium, 36 g carbohydrate, 2 g fiber, 22 g protein.*
Diabetic Exchanges: *2 starch, 2 lean meat, 1 vegetable.*

"Here's a quick meal that tastes like it came from a restaurant. Prepackaged coleslaw mix and bottled dressing reduce prep time, leaving you more time to savor this tasty delight."

—**MARY BERGFELD** EUGENE, OREGON

HOW TO COOK SHRIMP

To cook raw shrimp in water, add 1 pound shrimp (with or without shells) and 1 teaspoon salt to 3 quarts boiling water. Reduce heat and simmer, uncovered, for 1 to 3 minutes or until the shrimp turns pink. Watch closely to avoid overcooking. The meat of uncooked shrimp will turn from translucent, when raw, to pink and opaque when cooked. Drain immediately.

Tasty Pork Ribs

I like to serve these tender, country-style ribs over rice. The tantalizing aroma and zippy Cajun barbecue sauce are sure to make this dish a favorite at your house.

—**MICHELLE ROMINGER** ALBIA, IOWA

PREP: 10 MIN. **COOK:** 6 HOURS **MAKES:** 8 SERVINGS

- **8 bone-in country-style pork ribs (8 ounces each)**
- **1 cup ketchup**
- **1 cup barbecue sauce**
- **¼ cup packed brown sugar**
- **¼ cup Worcestershire sauce**
- **1 tablespoon balsamic vinegar**
- **1 tablespoon molasses**
- **1 garlic clove, minced**
- **2 tablespoons dried minced onion**
- **1 teaspoon Cajun seasoning**
- **1 teaspoon ground mustard**
- **½ teaspoon salt**
- **¼ teaspoon pepper**

Place ribs in a 5-qt. slow cooker. Combine the remaining ingredients; pour over ribs. Cover and cook on low for 6-7 hours or until meat is tender.

Potluck Ham and Pasta

Looking for an easy supper that's a real crowd-pleaser on chilly nights? Because this dish bakes in two pans, you could freeze one for later, depending on your needs. It's nice and creamy and has a wonderful ham-and-cheese flavor.

—**NANCY FOUST** STONEBORO, PENNSYLVANIA

PREP: 40 MIN. **BAKE:** 25 MIN. **MAKES:** 12 SERVINGS

- **1 package (16 ounces) elbow macaroni**
- **4 cups fresh broccoli florets**
- **½ cup finely chopped onion**
- **½ cup butter, cubed**
- **½ cup all-purpose flour**
- **1 teaspoon ground mustard**
- **1 teaspoon salt**
- **¼ teaspoon pepper**
- **6 cups 2% milk**
- **1 jar (15 ounces) process cheese sauce**
- **2 cups (8 ounces) shredded cheddar cheese, divided**
- **4 cups cubed fully cooked ham**

1. Cook macaroni according to package directions, adding broccoli during the last 3-4 minutes; drain.
2. In a large Dutch oven, saute onion in butter for 2 minutes. Stir in the flour, mustard, salt and pepper until blended. Gradually stir in milk. Bring to a boil; cook and stir for 2 minutes or until thickened. Stir in cheese sauce and 1 cup cheddar cheese until blended.
3. Remove from the heat; stir in the ham, macaroni and broccoli. Divide between a greased 13-in. x 9-in. baking dish and a greased 8-in. square baking dish. Sprinkle with remaining cheese.
4. Bake, uncovered, at 350° for 25-35 minutes or until bubbly and heated through.
5. Serve immediately or before baking, cover and freeze casseroles for up to 3 months.

To use frozen casseroles: *Thaw in the refrigerator overnight. Remove from the refrigerator 30 minutes before baking. Cover and bake at 350° for 50-60 minutes or until bubbly.*

Nutrition Facts: *1¼ cup equals 532 calories, 28 g fat (17 g saturated fat), 95 mg cholesterol, 1,610 mg sodium, 44 g carbohydrate, 2 g fiber, 27 g protein.*

Chipotle Pork Tenderloins

Here's a pork tenderloin that beats all at a cookout! The recipe came from a family member and is such a treat. Fresh strawberries and avocado in the salsa help cool the spicy heat of the pork.

—**PRISCILLA GILBERT** INDIAN HARBOUR BEACH, FLORIDA

PREP: 20 MIN. + MARINATING **GRILL:** 20 MIN.
MAKES: 9 SERVINGS (5 CUPS SALSA)

- **1 cup sliced onion**
- **½ cup chipotle peppers in adobo sauce, chopped**
- **¼ cup lime juice**
- **1½ teaspoons minced garlic**
- **3 pork tenderloins (1 pound each)**

STRAWBERRY SALSA

- **5 cups sliced fresh strawberries**
- **¼ cup thinly sliced green onions**
- **¼ cup minced fresh cilantro**
- **¼ cup lime juice**
- **¼ teaspoon salt**
- **1 medium ripe avocado, peeled and chopped**

1. In a large resealable plastic bag, combine the onion, chipotle peppers, lime juice and garlic; add pork. Seal bag and turn to coat; refrigerate for at least 1 hour.
2. Prepare grill for indirect heat. Drain and discard marinade. Grill pork, covered, over indirect medium-hot heat for 20-27 minutes or until a thermometer reads 145°. Let stand for 5 minutes before slicing.
3. For salsa, in a large bowl, combine the strawberries, green onions, cilantro, lime juice and salt. Gently stir in avocado. Serve with pork.

Roasted Chipotle Pork Tenderloins: *Drain and discard marinade from pork. Place tenderloins on a rack in a shallow roasting pan. Bake, uncovered, at 425° for 25-30 minutes or until a thermometer reads 160°. Serve as directed.*

Nutrition Facts: *4 ounces cooked pork with ½ cup salsa equals 246 calories, 9 g fat (2 g saturated fat), 84 mg cholesterol, 173 mg sodium, 11 g carbohydrate, 3 g fiber, 31 g protein.*

Grilled Stuffed Salmon

My husband worked with the U.S. Fish and Wildlife Service, so I've prepared fish all kinds of different ways. This variation of stuffed salmon gets high marks from my whole family.

—CATHIE BEARD PHILOMATH, OREGON

PREP: 30 MIN. **GRILL:** 40 MIN. **MAKES:** 12 SERVINGS

- **1 whole salmon (8 pounds)**
- **2 teaspoons salt, divided**
- **1¼ teaspoons pepper, divided**
- **2 cups unseasoned stuffing cubes**
- **1 cup shredded carrots**
- **1 cup sliced mushrooms**
- **1 large onion, finely chopped**
- **½ cup minced fresh parsley**
- **¾ cup butter, melted, divided**
- **¼ cup egg substitute**
- **4½ teaspoons plus ¼ cup lemon juice, divided**
- **1 garlic clove, minced**
- **2 tablespoons canola oil**

1. Remove head and tail from salmon if desired. Sprinkle the cavity with 1 teaspoon each salt and pepper.

2. In a large bowl, combine the stuffing cubes, carrots, mushrooms, onion, parsley, 1/4 cup butter, egg substitute, 4 1/2 teaspoons lemon juice, garlic and remaining salt and pepper; stuff cavity. Secure with metal skewers. Drizzle salmon with oil. Moisten a paper towel with cooking oil; using long-handled tongs, lightly coat the grill rack.

3. Prepare grill for indirect heat using a drip pan. Place salmon over drip pan and grill, covered, over indirect medium heat for 40-50 minutes or until fish flakes easily with a fork and a thermometer reads 165° for stuffing.

4. In a small bowl, combine remaining butter and lemon juice. Serve with salmon.

Nutrition Facts: *9 ounces cooked salmon with 1/2 cup stuffing equals 723 calories, 47 g fat (14 g saturated fat), 209 mg cholesterol, 795 mg sodium, 10 g carbohydrate, 1 g fiber, 63 g protein.*

Ham and Cheese Loaf

This golden loaf relies on the convenience of refrigerated pizza dough. I created the recipe by experimenting with a few simple ingredients. It makes a delicious sandwich perfect for a Sunday football party or anytime you want something hot and satisfying.

—GLORIA LINDELL WELCOME, MINNESOTA

PREP: 15 MIN. **BAKE:** 30 MIN. **MAKES:** 6 SERVINGS

- **1 tube (13.8 ounces) refrigerated pizza crust**
- **10 slices deli ham**
- **¼ cup sliced green onions**
- **1 cup (4 ounces) shredded part-skim mozzarella cheese**
- **1 cup (4 ounces) shredded cheddar cheese**
- **4 slices provolone cheese**
- **1 tablespoon butter, melted**

1. Unroll dough onto a greased baking sheet; top with the ham, onions and cheeses. Roll up tightly jelly-roll style, starting with a long side; pinch seam to seal and tuck ends under. Brush with butter.

2. Bake at 350° for 30-35 minutes or until golden brown. Let stand for 5 minutes; cut into 1-in. slices.

3. If desired, cool loaf on a wire rack; wrap in foil and freeze for up to 3 months.

To use frozen loaf: *Thaw at room temperature for 2 hours. Unwrap and place on a greased baking sheet. Bake at 350° for 15-20 minutes or until heated through. Let stand for 5 minutes; cut into 1-in. slices.*

Nutrition Facts: *2 slices equals 406 calories, 18 g fat (10 g saturated fat), 65 mg cholesterol, 1,151 mg sodium, 34 g carbohydrate, 1 g fiber, 26 g protein.*

Tomato-Basil Shrimp Skewers

I promise you that these are the best, most perfectly seasoned shrimp you will ever eat. My husband doesn't normally care for shrimp, but he raves over these!

—JENNIFER FULK
MORENO VALLEY, CALIFORNIA

PREP: 30 MIN. + MARINATING
GRILL: 10 MIN. **MAKES:** 6 SERVINGS

- **1/3 cup olive oil**
- **1/4 cup tomato sauce**
- **2 tablespoons minced fresh basil**
- **2 tablespoons red wine vinegar**
- **1 1/2 teaspoons minced garlic**
- **1/4 teaspoon cayenne pepper**
- **2 pounds uncooked jumbo shrimp, peeled and deveined**

1. In a large resealable plastic bag, combine the first six ingredients; add shrimp. Seal bag and turn to coat; refrigerate for up to 30 minutes.
2. Drain and discard marinade. Thread shrimp onto six metal or soaked wooden skewers. Grill, covered, over medium heat for 3-5 minutes on each side or until shrimp turn pink, turning once.

Nutrition Facts: *1 skewer equals 218 calories, 13 g fat (2 g saturated fat), 224 mg cholesterol, 302 mg sodium, 1 g carbohydrate, trace fiber, 24 g protein.*

BASIL CHIFFONADE

Homegrown basil is a wonderful addition to recipes and makes a pretty garnish, too. But chopping one leaf at a time can be tedious. To quickly chop a lot of basil and end up with attractive results, create basil chiffonade, which is just a fancy term for thin-shredded strips. Before cutting basil chiffonade, sprinkle a few drops of vegetable oil on the leaves and gently rub to evenly coat the leaves. This will prevent them from darkening. Stack several basil leaves and roll them into a tight tube. Slice the leaves widthwise into narrow pieces to create long thin strips. This cutting method also works well with other leafy herbs, such as sage.

Pork Tenderloin with Spiced Plum Sauce

This is one of my most requested dishes. I have prepared it for at least 20 years. Folks love the unique spiced plum sauce drizzled over the succulent pork tenderloin.

—RUTH LEE TROY, ONTARIO

PREP: 30 MIN. **BAKE:** 40 MIN. **MAKES:** 8 SERVINGS

- **2 pounds medium plums, halved and pitted**
- **⅔ cup cider vinegar**
- **1 cup packed brown sugar**
- **1 teaspoon ground cinnamon**
- **½ teaspoon salt**
- **¼ teaspoon cayenne pepper**
- **⅛ teaspoon each ground cloves, cardamom and allspice**
- **2 pork tenderloins (1 pound each)**
- **½ teaspoon pepper**

1. In a large saucepan, bring plums and vinegar to a boil. Reduce heat; cover and simmer 10-15 minutes or until tender. Cool slightly; transfer to a food processor. Cover and process for 1-2 minutes or until blended; strain.

2. Return plum mixture to the pan; stir in the brown sugar and seasonings. Bring to a boil. Reduce heat; simmer, uncovered, for 8-10 minutes or until thickened, stirring occasionally.

3. Place pork on a rack in a roasting pan; sprinkle with pepper. Set aside ½ cup plum sauce for serving. Spoon half of the remaining sauce over pork.

4. Bake at 350° for 40-50 minutes or until a thermometer reads 160°, basting occasionally with remaining sauce. Serve with reserved sauce.

Greek Pizza

Every year my sisters and I have a "Sisters Day," which includes a special lunch. This fast-and-easy pizza is one of our favorites. Served with a garden salad, it makes a light and nutritious meal.

—DEBORAH PREVOST BARNET, VERMONT

PREP/TOTAL TIME: 20 MIN. **MAKES:** 12 PIECES

- **1 prebaked 12-inch thin whole wheat pizza crust**
- **3 tablespoons prepared pesto**
- **2 medium tomatoes, thinly sliced**
- **¾ cup water-packed artichoke hearts, rinsed, drained and chopped**
- **½ cup crumbled reduced-fat feta cheese**
- **¼ cup sliced ripe olives**

1. Place the crust on an ungreased 12-in. pizza pan; spread with pesto. Top with tomatoes, artichokes, cheese and olives.

2. Bake at 450° for 10-12 minutes or until heated through.

Nutrition Facts: *2 pieces equals 206 calories, 8 g fat (3 g saturated fat), 6 mg cholesterol, 547 mg sodium, 27 g carbohydrate, 4 g fiber, 10 g protein.* **Diabetic Exchanges:** *2 starch, 1½ fat.*

Pork Tenderloin with Glazed Onions

My husband and I love pork, especially when it's dressed up like this. Sweet apricots and glazed onions go beautifully with the juicy meat.

—JANICE CHRISTOFFERSON EAGLE RIVER, WISCONSIN

PREP: 20 MIN. **BAKE:** 20 MIN. **MAKES:** 8 SERVINGS

- **4 large sweet onions, sliced (about 8 cups)**
- **¼ cup butter, cubed**
- **1 cup chopped dried apricots or golden raisins**
- **¼ cup packed brown sugar**
- **¼ cup balsamic vinegar**
- **½ teaspoon salt**
- **½ teaspoon pepper**
- **2 pork tenderloins (1 pound each)**

1. In large skillet, saute onions in butter for 2 minutes. Stir in the apricots, brown sugar, vinegar, salt and pepper; cook until onions are tender.

2. Place pork tenderloins on a rack coated with cooking spray in a shallow roasting pan; top with onion mixture.

3. Bake, uncovered, at 425° for 20-27 minutes or until a thermometer reads 145°. Let stand for 5 minutes before slicing. Serve with onion mixture.

Nutrition Facts: *4 ounces cooked pork with 1/4 cup onion mixture equals 284 calories, 10 g fat (5 g saturated fat), 78 mg cholesterol, 252 mg sodium, 26 g carbohydrate, 2 g fiber, 24 g protein.* **Diabetic Exchanges:** *3 lean meat, 1 vegetable, 1 fruit, 1 fat, 1/2 starch.*

GRAND PRIZE

Southwestern Scallops

PREP/TOTAL TIME: 20 MIN. **MAKES:** 4 SERVINGS

- **2 teaspoons chili powder**
- **½ teaspoon ground cumin**
- **¼ teaspoon salt**
- **⅛ teaspoon pepper**
- **1 pound sea scallops (about 12)**
- **2 tablespoons butter, divided**
- **½ cup white wine or chicken broth**

1. In a small bowl, combine the chili powder, cumin, salt and pepper. Pat scallops dry with paper towels. Rub seasoning mixture over scallops.

2. In a large heavy skillet over medium heat, melt 1 tablespoon butter. Cook scallops for 2 minutes on each side or until opaque and golden brown. Remove from the skillet; keep warm.

3. Add wine to skillet, stirring to loosen any browned bits from pan. Bring to a boil; cook until liquid is reduced by half. Stir in remaining butter until melted. Serve with scallops.

Nutrition Facts: *3 scallops with 1 tablespoon sauce equals 180 calories, 7 g fat (4 g saturated fat), 52 mg cholesterol, 386 mg sodium, 4 g carbohydrate, 1 g fiber, 19 g protein.* **Diabetic Exchanges:** *3 lean meat, 1 fat.*

"My saucy sea scallops are so tender, they practically melt in your mouth. The seasoning gives the sweet shellfish a pleasant kick you're sure to love. I serve these alongside rice pilaf, a tossed green salad and a bottle of white wine."

—MAGGIE FONTENOT THE WOODLANDS, TEXAS

SEA SCALLOPS

Sea scallops can range from ½ to 1 inch thick. To cook thicker scallops more quickly, cut them in half horizontally.

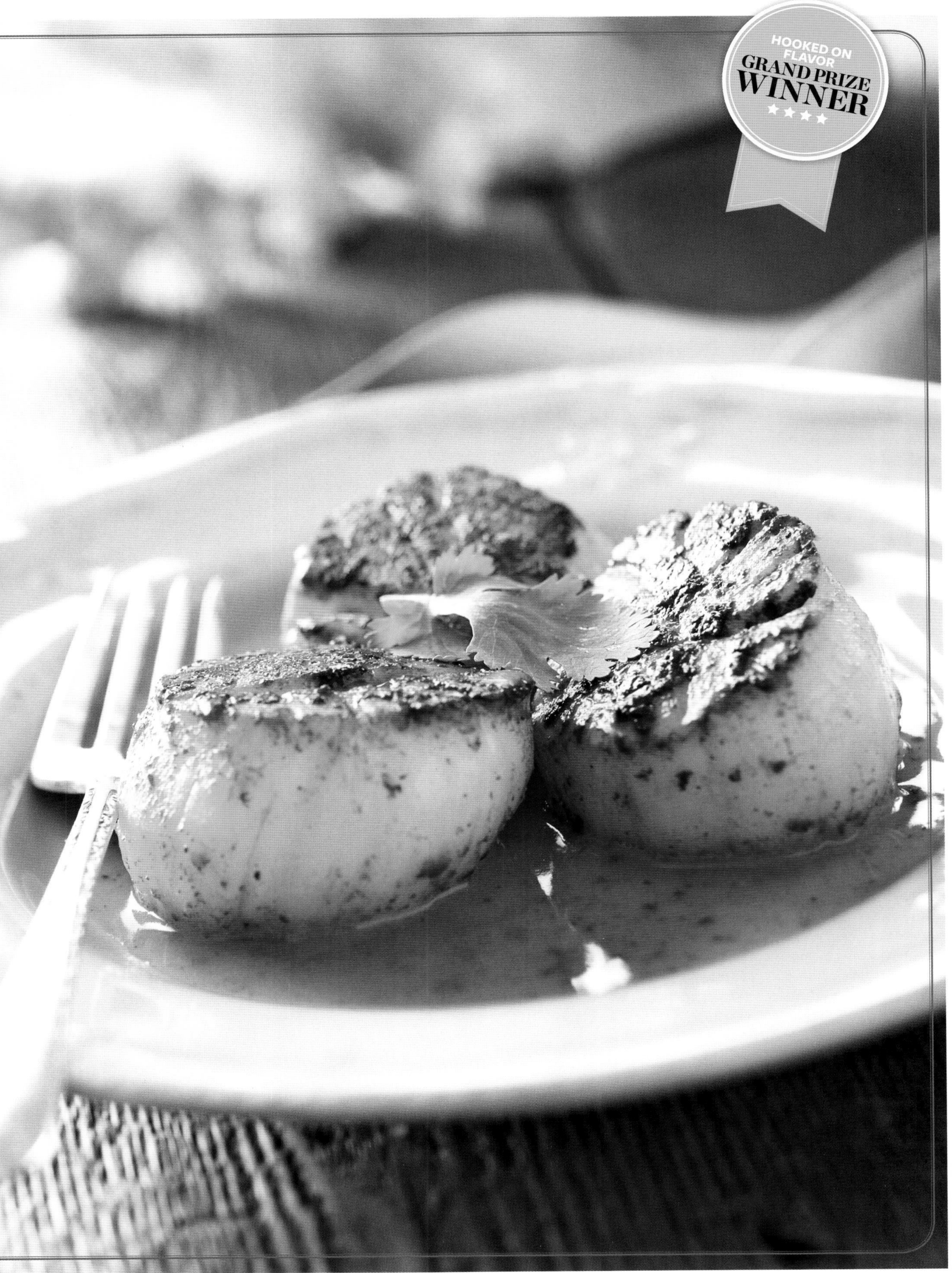
HOOKED ON FLAVOR
GRAND PRIZE
WINNER

Baked Potato Pizza

I re-created a lighter version of the restaurant pizza my friends and I enjoyed in college. Now I can enjoy the same great flavor without all the calories!

—CHARLOTTE GEHLE
BROWNSTOWN, MICHIGAN

PREP: 25 MIN. **BAKE:** 25 MIN.
MAKES: 12 PIECES

- **3 medium potatoes, peeled and cut into ⅛-inch slices**
- **1 loaf (1 pound) frozen pizza dough, thawed**
- **3 tablespoons reduced-fat butter**
- **4 garlic cloves, minced**
- **¼ teaspoon salt**
- **¼ teaspoon pepper**
- **1 cup (4 ounces) shredded part-skim mozzarella cheese**
- **¼ cup shredded Parmigiano-Reggiano cheese**
- **6 turkey bacon strips, cooked and crumbled**
- **2 green onions, chopped**
- **2 tablespoons minced chives**
- **Reduced-fat sour cream, optional**

1. Place potatoes in a small saucepan and cover with water. Bring to a boil. Reduce heat; cover and simmer for 15 minutes or until tender. Drain and pat dry.

2. Unroll dough onto a 14-in. pizza pan coated with cooking spray; flatten dough and build up edges slightly. In a microwave-safe bowl, melt butter with garlic; brush over dough.

3. Arrange potato slices in a single layer over dough; sprinkle with salt and pepper. Top with cheeses. Bake at 400° for 22-28 minutes or until crust is golden and cheese is melted.

4. Sprinkle with bacon, onions and chives. Serve with sour cream if desired.

Editor's Note: *This recipe was tested with Land O'Lakes light stick butter.*

Nutrition Facts: *2 pieces (calculated without sour cream) equals 359 calories, 11 g fat (5 g saturated fat), 36 mg cholesterol, 799 mg sodium, 48 g carbohydrate, 1 g fiber, 14 g protein.*

Vegetarian Pasta Sauce

Loaded with fresh vegetables and herbs, this hefty, meatless sauce is a perfect way for gardeners to make delicious use of their harvest. You can add some of your favorite red wine to the sauce during the cooking process, if you wish.

—JERRY TAMBURINO SACRAMENTO, CALIFORNIA

PREP: 35 MIN. **COOK:** 2 HOURS
MAKES: 14 SERVINGS (3½ QUARTS)

- **3 medium onions, chopped**
- **1 medium green pepper, chopped**
- **1 medium sweet red pepper, chopped**
- **2 tablespoons olive oil**
- **5 garlic cloves, minced**
- **3 medium zucchini, chopped**
- **3 medium yellow summer squash, chopped**
- **3 medium tomatoes, chopped**
- **1 medium eggplant, peeled and cubed**
- **½ pound sliced fresh mushrooms**
- **2 cans (28 ounces each) Italian crushed tomatoes**
- **1 can (6 ounces) tomato paste**
- **2 cans (2¼ ounces each) sliced ripe olives, drained**
- **¼ cup minced fresh basil**
- **3 tablespoons minced fresh oregano**
- **2 tablespoons minced fresh rosemary**
- **2 teaspoons Italian seasoning**
- **1½ teaspoons salt**
- **½ teaspoon pepper**

1. In a Dutch oven, saute the onions and peppers in oil until tender. Add garlic; cook 1 minute longer. Add the zucchini, summer squash, tomatoes, eggplant and mushrooms; cook and stir for 5 minutes.

2. Stir in the remaining ingredients. Bring to a boil. Reduce heat; simmer, uncovered, for 1½ to 2 hours or until sauce is thickened.

Nutrition Facts: *1 cup equals 131 calories, 3 g fat (trace saturated fat), 0 cholesterol, 705 mg sodium, 23 g carbohydrate, 6 g fiber, 5 g protein.*

"Hearty and so tasty, this potato salad is an old family recipe that was updated using cream of potato soup to ease preparation. The sausage and sauerkraut give it a special zip."

—TERESA MCGILL TROTWOOD, OHIO

German Potato Salad with Sausage

PREP: 30 MIN. **COOK:** 6 HOURS **MAKES:** 5 SERVINGS

- **8 bacon strips, diced**
- **1 large onion, chopped**
- **1 pound smoked kielbasa or Polish sausage, halved and cut into ½-inch slices**
- **2 pounds medium red potatoes, cut into chunks**
- **1 can (10¾ ounces) condensed cream of potato soup, undiluted**
- **1 cup sauerkraut, rinsed and well drained**
- **½ cup water**
- **¼ cup cider vinegar**
- **1 tablespoon sugar**
- **½ teaspoon salt**
- **½ teaspoon coarsely ground pepper**

1. In a large skillet, cook bacon over medium heat until crisp. Remove to paper towels with a slotted spoon to drain. Saute onion in drippings for 1 minute. Add sausage; cook until lightly browned. Add potatoes; cook 2 minutes longer. Drain.

2. Transfer sausage mixture to a 3-qt. slow cooker. In a small bowl, combine the soup, sauerkraut, water, vinegar, sugar, salt and pepper. Pour over sausage mixture. Sprinkle with bacon. Cover and cook on low for 6-7 hours or until potatoes are tender.

Savory Pumpkin Ravioli

This recipe may look complicated, but if you follow the simple steps, it really isn't. The result will be pure pumpkin heaven! I like to sprinkle the ravioli with Parmesan as well. You can also add salt and pepper to the rich sage sauce to suit your taste.

—CHRISTOPHER PRESUTTI JACKSONVILLE, FLORIDA

PREP: 2 HOURS **COOK:** 10 MIN. **MAKES:** 6 SERVINGS

- **2½ to 3 cups all-purpose flour**
- **5 eggs**
- **1 tablespoon olive oil**

FILLING

- **1 small pie pumpkin (about 2¼ pounds), peeled and cut into 1-inch cubes**
- **4 teaspoons chopped shallot**
- **⅓ cup butter, cubed**
- **2 teaspoons minced fresh sage**
- **¾ teaspoon minced fresh thyme**
- **¼ teaspoon salt**
- **¼ teaspoon pepper**
- **⅔ cup heavy whipping cream**
- **1 small bay leaf**
- **1 egg, lightly beaten**

SAUCE

- **1 cup heavy whipping cream**
- **3 tablespoons butter**
- **2 teaspoons minced fresh sage**

1. Place 2½ cups flour in a large bowl; make a well in the center. Beat eggs and oil; pour into well. Stir together, forming a ball. Turn onto a floured surface; knead until smooth and elastic, about 8-10 minutes, adding remaining flour if necessary to keep dough from sticking. Cover and let rest for 30 minutes.

2. Meanwhile, in a large skillet, saute pumpkin and shallot in butter until tender. Add the sage, thyme, salt and pepper. Transfer to a food processor; cover and process until blended. Return to the pan; stir in cream and bay leaf. Bring to a boil, stirring constantly. Reduce heat; simmer, uncovered, for 15-20 minutes or until thickened. Discard bay leaf.

3. Divide pasta dough into fourths; roll one portion to 1/16-in. thickness. (Keep remaining dough covered until ready to use.) Working quickly, place rounded teaspoonfuls of filling 1 in. apart over half of pasta sheet. Brush around filling with egg. Fold sheet over; press down to seal. Cut into squares with a pastry wheel. Repeat with remaining dough and filling.

4. Bring a stock pot of salted water to a boil. Add ravioli. Reduce heat to a gentle simmer; cook for 1-2 minutes or until ravioli float to the top and are tender. Drain and keep warm.

5. In a small saucepan, bring cream to a boil; cook, uncovered, until reduced by half. Stir in butter and sage. Serve with ravioli.

Editor's Note: *If pumpkin is not available, use butternut squash.*

Sausage Zucchini Skillet

I began serving a version of this dish as a side with grilled salmon. I added sausage and rice or noodles to make it a complete meal.

—DEBBY ABEL FLAT ROCK, NORTH CAROLINA

PREP/TOTAL TIME: 25 MIN. **MAKES:** 4 SERVINGS

- **1 pound Italian turkey sausage links, casings removed**
- **2 large zucchini, chopped**
- **1 large sweet onion, chopped**
- **2 garlic cloves, minced**
- **1 can (14½ ounces) no-salt-added diced tomatoes, undrained**
- **¼ teaspoon pepper**
- **2 cups hot cooked rice**

1. In a large nonstick skillet coated with cooking spray, combine the sausage, zucchini and onion; cook and stir over medium heat until meat is no longer pink. Add garlic; cook 1 minute longer. Drain.

2. Stir in tomatoes and pepper; bring to a boil. Reduce heat; simmer, uncovered, for 4-5 minutes or until liquid is evaporated. Serve with rice.

Nutrition Facts: *1¼ cups sausage mixture with ½ cup rice equals 329 calories, 11 g fat (2 g saturated fat), 68 mg cholesterol, 724 mg sodium, 36 g carbohydrate, 5 g fiber, 23 g protein.* **Diabetic Exchanges:** *3 lean meat, 2 vegetable, 1½ starch.*

Pizza Margherita

My classic pie starts with a chewy homemade crust topped with tomatoes, mozzarella, oregano and fresh basil. It's so scrumptious that you'll be glad the recipe makes not one but two 13-inch pizzas!
—LORETTA LAWRENCE MYRTLE BEACH, SOUTH CAROLINA

PREP: 30 MIN. + RISING **BAKE:** 15 MIN.
MAKES: 2 PIZZAS (8 SLICES EACH)

- **3 teaspoons active dry yeast**
- **1 cup warm water (110° to 115°)**
- **2 tablespoons olive oil**
- **1 teaspoon sugar**
- **1 teaspoon salt**
- **3 cups bread flour**

TOPPINGS

- **2 cans (14½ ounces each) diced tomatoes, drained**
- **20 fresh basil leaves, thinly sliced**
- **2 tablespoons minced fresh oregano or 2 teaspoons dried oregano**
- **8 cups (2 pounds) shredded part-skim mozzarella cheese**
- **½ teaspoon crushed red pepper flakes**
- **⅛ teaspoon salt**
- **⅛ teaspoon pepper**
- **2 tablespoons olive oil**

1. In a small bowl, dissolve yeast in warm water. In a large bowl, combine the oil, sugar, salt and 1 cup flour; beat until smooth. Stir in enough remaining flour to form a soft dough.
2. Turn onto a floured surface; knead until smooth and elastic, about 6-8 minutes. Place in a greased bowl, turning once to grease the top. Cover with plastic wrap and let rise in a warm place until doubled, about 1 hour.
3. Punch dough down; divide in half. Roll each portion into a 13-in. circle. Transfer to two greased 14-in. pizza pans; build up edges slightly. Cover with a clean kitchen towel; let rest for 10 minutes.
4. Spoon tomatoes over dough. Top with basil, oregano, cheese, pepper flakes, salt and pepper. Drizzle with oil. Bake at 450° for 15-20 minutes or until crust is golden brown.
Nutrition Facts: *1 slice equals 263 calories, 12 g fat (6 g saturated fat), 33 mg cholesterol, 523 mg sodium, 21 g carbohydrate, 1 g fiber, 17 g protein.* **Diabetic Exchanges:** *2 lean meat, 1½ starch, 1 fat.*

Giant Calzone

Here's an impressive calzone that's the champion of all sandwiches. Fill it to the brim with your favorite ingredients or pizza toppings. We use the extra sauce for dipping. If desired, you can make two smaller calzones instead of one large one.
—RONNA ANDERSON PRAGUE, OKLAHOMA

PREP: 25 MIN. + RISING **BAKE:** 40 MIN. **MAKES:** 6 SERVINGS

- **1½ cups water (70° to 80°)**
- **2 tablespoons olive oil**
- **2 teaspoons sugar**
- **2 teaspoons salt**
- **4½ cups all-purpose flour**
- **2 teaspoons active dry yeast**
- **1 pound bulk Italian sausage**
- **1 can (26 ounces) garlic and herb spaghetti sauce, divided**
- **3 tablespoons grated Parmesan cheese**
- **1 jar (4½ ounces) sliced mushrooms, drained**
- **½ cup finely chopped green pepper**
- **¼ cup finely chopped onion**
- **1½ cups (6 ounces) shredded part-skim mozzarella cheese**
- **1 egg, lightly beaten**

1. In bread machine pan, place the first six ingredients in order suggested by manufacturer. Select dough setting (check dough after 5 minutes of mixing; add 1 to 2 tablespoons of water or flour if needed).
2. Meanwhile, in a large skillet, cook sausage over medium heat until no longer pink; drain and cool. When bread machine cycle is completed, turn dough onto a lightly floured surface. Roll out to a 15-in. circle. Transfer dough to a lightly greased baking sheet.
3. Spread ½ cup spaghetti sauce over half of circle to within ¼ in. of edges. Layer with Parmesan cheese, sausage, mushrooms, green pepper, onion and mozzarella cheese. Fold dough over filling and pinch edges to seal.
4. With a sharp knife, make two slashes in dough; brush with egg. Bake at 350° for 40-45 minutes or until golden brown. Let stand for 5 minutes before cutting into six wedges. Warm remaining spaghetti sauce; serve with calzone.
Nutrition Facts: *1 wedge with ⅓ cup sauce equals 719 calories, 26 g fat (9 g saturated fat), 87 mg cholesterol, 2,032 mg sodium, 89 g carbohydrate, 6 g fiber, 30 g protein.*

PASTA PERFECT
GRAND PRIZE
WINNER

GRAND PRIZE

Four-Cheese Baked Ziti

This pasta dish, made with Alfredo sauce, is delightfully different from typical tomato-based recipes. Extra cheesy, it goes together quickly and is really popular at potlucks.

—LISA VARNER EL PASO, TEXAS

PREP: 20 MIN. **BAKE:** 30 MIN. **MAKES:** 8 SERVINGS

- **1 package (16 ounces) ziti or small tube pasta**
- **2 cartons (10 ounces each) refrigerated Alfredo sauce**
- **1 cup (8 ounces) sour cream**
- **2 eggs, lightly beaten**
- **1 carton (15 ounces) ricotta cheese**
- **½ cup grated Parmesan cheese, divided**
- **¼ cup grated Romano cheese**
- **¼ cup minced fresh parsley**
- **1¾ cups shredded part-skim mozzarella cheese**

1. Cook ziti according to package directions; drain and return to the pan. Stir in Alfredo sauce and sour cream. Spoon half into a lightly greased 3-qt. baking dish.

2. In a small bowl, combine the eggs, ricotta cheese, 1/4 cup Parmesan cheese, Romano cheese and parsley; spread over pasta. Top with remaining pasta mixture; sprinkle with mozzarella and remaining Parmesan.

3. Cover and bake at 350° for 25 minutes or until a thermometer reads 160°. Uncover; bake 5-10 minutes longer or until bubbly.

PASTA POINTERS

To cook pasta more evenly, prevent it from sticking together and avoid boil-overs, always cook it in a large kettle or Dutch oven. Unless you have a very large kettle, don't cook more than 2 pounds of pasta at a time. For every 8 ounces of pasta, bring 3 quarts of water to a full rolling boil.

To flavor, add 1 tablespoon salt if desired. Stir in the pasta all at once. Return to a boil; boil, uncovered, stirring occasionally. Cooking times vary with the size and variety of pasta. Dried pasta can take from 5 to 15 minutes to cook; fresh pasta can cook in as little as 2 to 3 minutes. Follow recommended cooking directions on packaged pasta. As soon as the pasta is firm yet tender, pour into a large colander to drain, being careful of the steam as you pour. If using pasta in a salad or at a later time, rinse it with cold water to stop cooking and to remove excess starch.

Barbecued Pork Chops

Sherry, honey, barbecue and steak sauces combine to give these chops a beautiful glaze and dressed-up flavor. The sauce works well on chicken breasts and other grilled meats, too, and couldn't be much easier to put together.

—LAJUANA KAY HOLLAND AMARILLO, TEXAS

PREP/TOTAL TIME: 20 MIN. **MAKES:** 6 SERVINGS

- **½ cup hickory smoke-flavored barbecue sauce**
- **½ cup A.1. steak sauce**
- **½ cup sherry or unsweetened apple juice**
- **3 tablespoons honey**
- **6 bone-in pork loin chops (¾ inch thick and 8 ounces each)**
- **¾ teaspoon salt**
- **½ teaspoon pepper**

1. In a small bowl, combine the barbecue sauce, steak sauce, sherry or apple juice and honey. Transfer 1/3 cup sauce to another bowl; set aside for serving.

2. Sprinkle pork chops with salt and pepper. Moisten a paper towel with cooking oil; using long-handled tongs, lightly coat the grill rack. Grill pork chops, covered, over medium heat or broil 4-5 in. from the heat for 4-5 minutes on each side or until a thermometer reads 145°, basting frequently with remaining sauce. Let meat stand for 5 minutes before serving. Serve with reserved sauce.

Bavarian Pork Loin

I received the recipe for this tender pork roast from my aunt. With sauerkraut, carrots, onions and apples, it's a delicious taste sensation that can't be beat!

—EDIE DESPAIN LOGAN, UTAH

PREP: 25 MIN. **COOK:** 6 HOURS **MAKES:** 10 SERVINGS

- **1 boneless whole pork loin roast (3 to 4 pounds)**
- **1 can (14 ounces) Bavarian sauerkraut, rinsed and drained**
- **1¾ cups chopped carrots**
- **1 large onion, finely chopped**
- **½ cup unsweetened apple juice**
- **2 teaspoons dried parsley flakes**
- **3 large tart apples, peeled and quartered**

1. Cut roast in half; place in a 5-qt. slow cooker. In a small bowl, combine the sauerkraut, carrots, onion, apple juice and parsley; spoon over roast. Cover and cook on low for 4 hours.
2. Add apples to slow cooker. Cover and cook 2-3 hours longer or until meat is tender. Remove roast. Serve with sauerkraut mixture.

Stovetop Bavarian Pork Loin: *Cut roast in half. In a Dutch oven coated with cooking spray, brown roast on all sides. Combine the sauerkraut, carrots, onion, 3/4 cup apple juice and parsley; spoon over roast. Bring to a boil. Reduce heat; cover and simmer for 1 hour. Stir in apples. Cover and simmer 20-25 minutes longer or until apples are tender and a thermometer reads 160°.*

Nutrition Facts: *1 serving equals 235 calories, 6 g fat (2 g saturated fat), 68 mg cholesterol, 294 mg sodium, 17 g carbohydrate, 2 g fiber, 27 g protein.*

Baked Ham Tetrazzini

Rich, creamy pasta and cubed ham blend perfectly in this hearty meal for two. It's a great way to use up leftover holiday ham.

—ELVI KAUKINEN HORSEHEADS, NEW YORK

PREP: 20 MIN. **BAKE:** 20 MIN. **MAKES:** 2 SERVINGS

- **4 ounces uncooked spaghetti, broken into 2-inch pieces**
- **1 cup (4 ounces) shredded sharp cheddar cheese**
- **⅔ cup condensed cream of mushroom soup, undiluted**
- **½ cup 2% milk**
- **1 tablespoon minced fresh parsley**
- **2 teaspoons diced pimientos, drained**
- **1 teaspoon finely chopped onion**
- **½ teaspoon Worcestershire sauce**
- **Dash pepper**
- **¾ cup cubed fully cooked ham**

1. Cook spaghetti according to package directions. Meanwhile, in a small bowl, combine the cheese, soup, milk, parsley, pimientos, onion, Worcestershire sauce and pepper.
2. Drain spaghetti; add to soup mixture. Spread half into a 1½-qt. baking dish coated with cooking spray. Layer with ham and remaining spaghetti mixture.
3. Bake, uncovered, at 375° for 20-25 minutes or until bubbly.

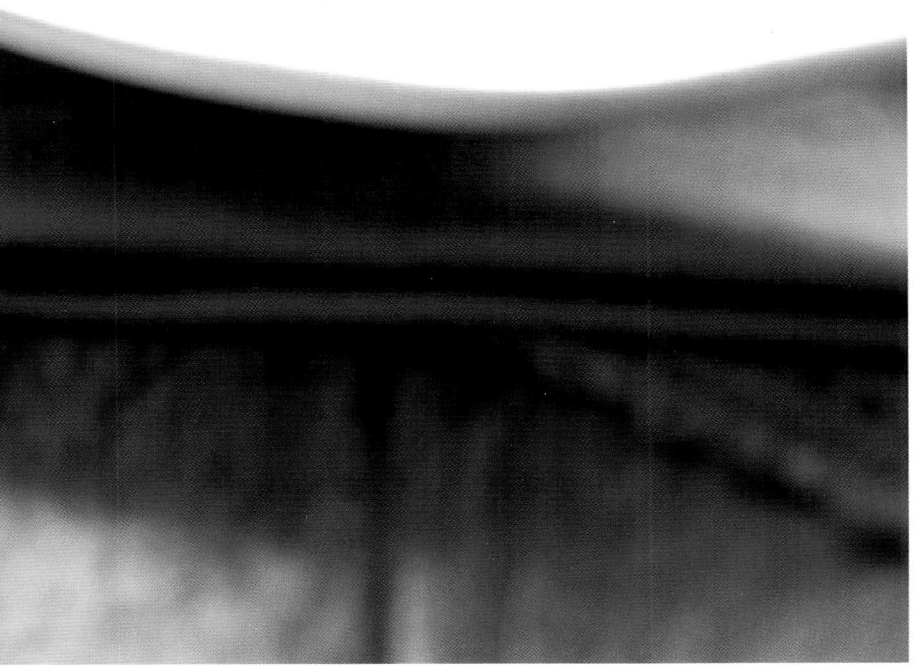

Fiesta Bean Casserole

I don't recall the origin of this recipe, but it doesn't matter because it is a definite keeper! Triscuit crackers make a unique crust for the meatless pleaser.

—KAREN TJELMELAND ELY, IOWA

PREP: 20 MIN. **BAKE:** 20 MIN.
MAKES: 2 SERVINGS

- **¾ cup kidney beans, rinsed and drained**
- **¼ cup chopped onion**
- **¼ cup chopped green chilies, drained**
- **¼ teaspoon ground cumin**
- **16 Triscuits or other crackers**
- **¾ cup shredded cheddar cheese**
- **½ cup 2% milk**
- **⅓ cup mayonnaise**
- **2 tablespoons beaten egg**
- **Sour cream and sliced ripe olives, optional**

1. In a small bowl, combine the beans, onion, green chilies and cumin. Place eight crackers in an 8-in. x 4-in. loaf pan coated with cooking spray. Top with half of the bean mixture; layer with remaining crackers and bean mixture. Sprinkle with cheese.

2. In a small bowl, combine the milk, mayonnaise and egg; pour over the cheese. Bake, uncovered, at 350° for 20-25 minutes or until a thermometer reads 160°. Serve with sour cream and olives if desired.

EASY CHOPPED ONIONS

Looking for a speedy way to chop onions without a lot of tears? Consider your blender! Quarter the onions, place them in the blender and cover with water. Put the top back on the blender and process on high speed for a second or two or until chopped. Pour into a colander to drain and you're all done. The chopped onions don't lose their flavor—and they freeze beautifully.

—SHIRLEY M. ALVIN, TEXAS

Forgotten Jambalaya

During chilly months, I fix this jambalaya at least once a month. It's so easy—just chop the vegetables, toss everything in the slow cooker and forget it! Even my sons, who are picky about spicy foods, devour this dish.

—**CINDI COSS** COPPELL, TEXAS

PREP: 35 MIN. **COOK:** 4¼ HOURS **MAKES:** 11 SERVINGS

- **1 can (14½ ounces) diced tomatoes, undrained**
- **1 can (14½ ounces) beef or chicken broth**
- **1 can (6 ounces) tomato paste**
- **2 medium green peppers, chopped**
- **1 medium onion, chopped**
- **3 celery ribs, chopped**
- **5 garlic cloves, minced**
- **3 teaspoons dried parsley flakes**
- **2 teaspoons dried basil**
- **1½ teaspoons dried oregano**
- **1¼ teaspoons salt**
- **½ teaspoon cayenne pepper**
- **½ teaspoon hot pepper sauce**
- **1 pound boneless skinless chicken breasts, cut into 1-inch cubes**
- **1 pound smoked sausage, halved and cut into ¼-inch slices**
- **½ pound uncooked medium shrimp, peeled and deveined**
- **Hot cooked rice**

1. In a 5-qt. slow cooker, combine the tomatoes, broth and tomato paste. Stir in the green peppers, onion, celery, garlic and seasonings. Stir in chicken and sausage.

2. Cover and cook on low for 4-6 hours or until chicken is no longer pink. Stir in shrimp. Cover and cook 15-30 minutes longer or until shrimp turn pink. Serve with rice.

Nutrition Facts: *1 cup calculated without rice equals 230 calories, 13 g fat (5 g saturated fat), 75 mg cholesterol, 1,016 mg sodium, 9 g carbohydrate, 2 g fiber, 20 g protein.*

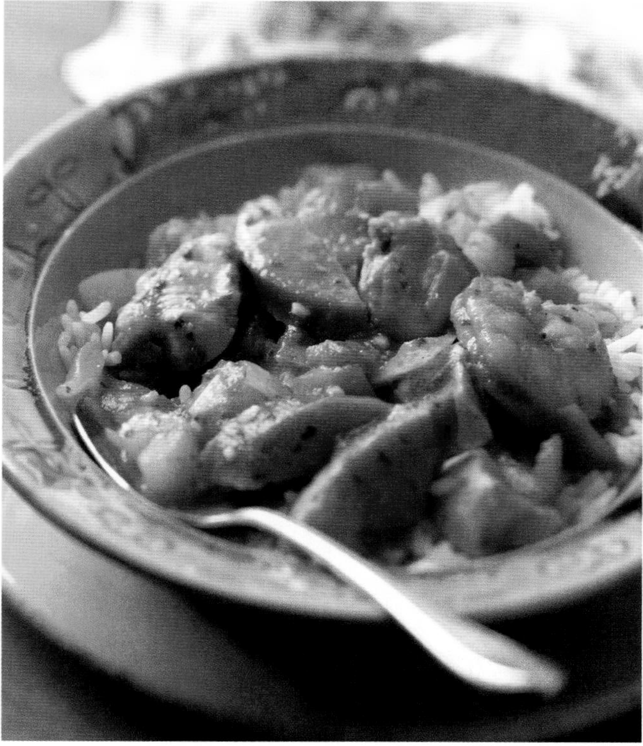

Gnocchi with Thyme Butter

If you've never attempted homemade gnocchi, this recipe is the one to try. The gnocchi are tender, with a delicate butter and thyme flavor. They're absolutely delicious as a side dish with your favorite meat or seafood.

—**ANNETTE LEAR** SANBORNVILLE, NEW HAMPSHIRE

PREP: 70 MIN. **COOK:** 10 MIN. **MAKES:** 5 SERVINGS

- **1½ pounds russet potatoes, peeled and quartered**
- **1 cup all-purpose flour**
- **1 egg**
- **1 teaspoon salt**
- **½ teaspoon pepper**
- **4 quarts water**
- **½ cup butter, cubed**
- **4 teaspoons fresh thyme leaves**
- **Grated Parmesan cheese, optional**

1. Place potatoes in a large saucepan and cover with water. Bring to a boil. Reduce heat; cover and simmer for 15-20 minutes or until tender. Drain; return potatoes to the pan.

2. Over very low heat, stir potatoes for 1-2 minutes or until steam has evaporated. Press through a potato ricer or strainer into a small bowl; cool slightly.

3. Using a fork, make a well in the potatoes; sprinkle with flour. Whisk the egg, salt and pepper; pour into well. Stir until blended. On a lightly floured surface, knead 10-12 times, forming a soft dough.

4. Divide dough into four portions. On a floured surface, roll each portion into ½-in.-thick ropes; cut into ¾-in. pieces. Press and roll each piece with a lightly floured fork.

5. In a Dutch oven, bring water to a boil. Cook gnocchi in batches for 30-60 seconds or until they float. Remove with a slotted spoon; keep warm.

6. In a large heavy saucepan, melt butter over medium heat. Add thyme and gnocchi; stir gently to coat. Sprinkle with cheese if desired.

Nutrition Facts: *¾ cup equals 375 calories, 20 g fat (12 g saturated fat), 90 mg cholesterol, 624 mg sodium, 44 g carbohydrate, 3 g fiber, 7 g protein.*

Seafood Medley with Linguine

Who can resist a savory blend of seafood and pasta? This dish of steaming scallops and shrimp with linguine and tomatoes is nutritious and rich in flavor.

—**CHARLENE CHAMBERS** ORMOND BEACH, FLORIDA

PREP: 35 MIN. **COOK:** 5 MIN. **MAKES:** 8 SERVINGS

- **1 large onion, chopped**
- **2 tablespoons butter**
- **1 tablespoon olive oil**
- **3 garlic cloves, minced**
- **1 cup white wine or chicken broth**
- **1 can (28 ounces) diced fire-roasted tomatoes**
- **1 tablespoon minced fresh rosemary or 1 teaspoon dried rosemary, crushed**
- **1 teaspoon sugar**
- **1 teaspoon minced fresh oregano or 1/4 teaspoon dried oregano**
- **1/4 teaspoon salt**
- **1/4 teaspoon pepper**
- **1 package (16 ounces) linguine**
- **1 pound sea scallops**
- **9 ounces uncooked large shrimp, peeled and deveined**
- **2 tablespoons minced fresh parsley**
- **Shredded Parmesan cheese, optional**

1. In a large skillet, saute onion in butter and oil until tender. Add garlic; cook 1 minute longer. Add wine. Bring to a boil; cook until liquid is reduced to 1/2 cup. Add the tomatoes, rosemary, sugar, oregano, salt and pepper. Bring to a boil over medium heat. Reduce heat; simmer, uncovered, for 15 minutes.
2. Meanwhile, cook linguine according to package directions. Add scallops and shrimp to tomato mixture; cook for 4-5 minutes or until shrimp turn pink and scallops are opaque. Stir in parsley.
3. Drain linguine. Serve seafood mixture with linguine; garnish with cheese if desired.

Nutrition Facts: *3/4 cup seafood mixture with 1 1/4 cups linguine (calculated without Parmesan cheese) equals 374 calories, 7 g fat (2 g saturated fat), 74 mg cholesterol, 372 mg sodium, 51 g carbohydrate, 4 g fiber, 23 g protein.*

Rustic Roasted Vegetable Tart

No one will miss the meat in this appealing tart. The flaky, rustic-style crust holds an assortment of flavorful veggies simply seasoned with garlic and olive oil. It's guaranteed to make a grand impression on your dinner guests.

—**MARIE RIZZIO** INTERLOCHEN, MICHIGAN

PREP: 45 MIN. **BAKE:** 20 MIN. **MAKES:** 8 SERVINGS

- **1 small eggplant, cut into 1-inch pieces**
- **1 large zucchini, cut into 1/4-inch slices**
- **4 plum tomatoes, chopped**
- **1 medium sweet red pepper, cut into 1-inch pieces**
- **4 tablespoons olive oil, divided**
- **4 garlic cloves, minced**
- **1/2 teaspoon salt**
- **1/8 teaspoon pepper**
- **1 sheet refrigerated pie pastry**
- **1 tablespoon cornmeal**
- **2 tablespoons shredded Parmesan cheese**
- **Minced fresh basil, optional**

1. In a large bowl, combine the vegetables, 3 tablespoons oil, garlic, salt and pepper. Transfer to an ungreased 15-in. x 10-in. x 1-in. baking pan. Bake at 450° for 25-30 minutes or until vegetables are tender and moisture has evaporated, stirring every 10 minutes.
2. On a lightly floured surface, roll pastry into a 13-in. circle. Sprinkle cornmeal over a greased 14-in. pizza pan; place pastry on prepared pan. Spoon vegetable mixture over pastry to within 1 1/2 in. of edges. Fold up edges of pastry over filling, leaving center uncovered. Brush pastry with remaining oil.
3. Bake at 450° for 20-25 minutes or until crust is golden brown. Sprinkle with cheese. Cut into wedges. Garnish with basil if desired.

Nutrition Facts: *1 wedge equals 219 calories, 14 g fat (4 g saturated fat), 6 mg cholesterol, 277 mg sodium, 21 g carbohydrate, 2 g fiber, 3 g protein.*

Jalapeno-Apricot Pork Tenderloin

The perfect blend of spices is what sets this dish apart. I like to double the recipe and freeze the second tenderloin for later. The sweet-spicy glaze would also taste delicious over chicken.

—AMBER SHEA FORD
OVERLAND PARK, KANSAS

PREP: 15 MIN. + MARINATING
BAKE: 20 MIN. **MAKES:** 2 SERVINGS

- **2 teaspoons olive oil**
- **1 garlic clove, minced**
- **1 teaspoon dried oregano**
- **½ teaspoon salt**
- **½ teaspoon ground cumin**
- **¼ teaspoon ground coriander**
- **1 pork tenderloin (¾ pound)**

GLAZE

- **⅓ cup apricot preserves**
- **1 tablespoon lime juice**
- **1 tablespoon diced seeded jalapeno pepper**
- **¼ teaspoon ground cumin**
- **⅛ teaspoon garlic salt**

1. In a large resealable plastic bag, combine the first six ingredients; add the pork. Seal bag and turn to coat; refrigerate for up to 2 hours. Drain and discard marinade.
2. Place pork in an 11-in. x 7-in. baking dish coated with cooking spray. Bake, uncovered, at 400° for 15 minutes.
3. In a small bowl, combine the glaze ingredients; spoon 1/4 cup over pork. Bake 5-10 minutes longer or until a thermometer reads 160°. Let stand for 5 minutes before slicing. Serve with remaining glaze.

Editor's Note: *Wear disposable gloves when cutting hot peppers; the oils can burn skin. Avoid touching your face.*

Nutrition Facts: *5 ounces cooked pork with 1/4 cup glaze equals 378 calories, 11 g fat (3 g saturated fat), 95 mg cholesterol, 818 mg sodium, 37 g carbohydrate, 1 g fiber, 35 g protein.*

Peanutty Pork Stir-Fry

Here's an easy, colorful stir-fry with an Asian flavor that's likely to become a popular mainstay at your house. It even tastes delicious eaten cold as leftovers.

—**GINA BERRY** CHANHASSEN, MINNESOTA

PREP/TOTAL TIME: 25 MIN. **MAKES:** 2 SERVINGS

1 can (8 ounces) pineapple chunks
½ pound pork tenderloin, cut into ½-inch strips
1 tablespoon sesame oil
¾ cup julienned sweet red pepper
¾ cup chopped carrot
2 green onions, chopped
3 tablespoons reduced-sodium soy sauce
3 tablespoons reduced-sodium teriyaki sauce
1 tablespoon creamy peanut butter
¼ cup unsalted dry roasted peanuts, finely chopped
Hot cooked rice, optional

1. Drain pineapple, reserving juice; set aside. In a large skillet, stir-fry pork in oil until no longer pink. Add the red pepper, carrot and onions; cook and stir for 2-3 minutes or until crisp-tender.

2. Stir in the soy sauce, teriyaki sauce, peanut butter and reserved pineapple juice. Bring to a boil; cook and stir for 1-2 minutes or until thickened. Stir in peanuts and pineapple. Serve with rice if desired.

Tomato Cheese Pizza

I've been making this recipe for several years, and it's a favorite with family and friends. It can be used either as an appetizer or as a quick and easy main dish that goes well with a fresh salad or pasta.

—**GRETA SAWYERS** MOUNT AIRY, NORTH CAROLINA

PREP/TOTAL TIME: 30 MIN. **MAKES:** 8 SLICES

1 tube (13.8 ounces) refrigerated pizza crust
1 teaspoon minced garlic
2 cups (8 ounces) shredded part-skim mozzarella cheese
⅔ cup grated Romano cheese
2 teaspoons dried oregano
2 plum tomatoes, thinly sliced

1. Unroll pizza dough onto a greased 12-in. pizza pan; flatten dough and build up edges slightly. Spread garlic over crust. Bake at 375° for 7 minutes.

2. Sprinkle half of the cheeses and oregano over crust. Arrange tomatoes on top. Sprinkle with remaining cheeses and oregano. Bake for 15-17 minutes or until crust is golden brown and cheese is melted.

Nutrition Facts: *1 slice equals 246 calories, 9 g fat (5 g saturated fat), 26 mg cholesterol, 599 mg sodium, 25 g carbohydrate, 1 g fiber, 15 g protein.*

Hickory Barbecued Salmon with Tartar Sauce

Guests of all ages love this succulent seafood dish. The idea of using hickory chips came from my dad. He always prepared his salmon in this unique way.

—LINDA CHEVALIER BATTLE GROUND, WASHINGTON

PREP/TOTAL TIME: 30 MIN. **MAKES:** 8 SERVINGS (1 CUP SAUCE)

- **½ cup butter, cubed**
- **2 garlic cloves, minced**
- **1 salmon fillet (3 pounds)**
- **2 medium lemons, thinly sliced**
- **2 cups soaked hickory chips**

TARTAR SAUCE

- **1 cup mayonnaise**
- **¼ cup chopped sweet pickles**
- **1 teaspoon finely chopped onion**
- **¾ teaspoon ground mustard**
- **¼ teaspoon Worcestershire sauce**

1. In a small saucepan, combine butter and garlic; cook and stir over medium heat until butter is melted. Drizzle 2 tablespoons butter mixture over salmon; top with lemon slices. Set aside remaining butter mixture for basting.
2. Using long-handled tongs, moisten a paper towel with cooking oil and lightly coat the grill rack. Add wood chips to grill according to manufacturer's directions. Place salmon skin side down on grill rack. Grill, covered, over medium heat or 4 in. from the heat for 5 minutes.
3. Carefully spoon some reserved butter mixture over salmon. Cover and grill or broil 15-20 minutes longer or until fish flakes easily with a fork, basting occasionally with remaining butter mixture.
4. Meanwhile, in a small bowl, combine the tartar sauce ingredients. Serve with salmon.

GRAND PRIZE

Spicy Pork with Ginger-Maple Sauce

My physical therapist shared this recipe with me and said it was completely foolproof. She was right. It's a real winner! I serve it with sauteed green beans.

—JUANITA MOORE DANA POINT, CALIFORNIA

PREP: 25 MIN. **BAKE:** 20 MIN. **MAKES:** 2 SERVINGS

- **2 teaspoons chili powder**
- **1 teaspoon ground cinnamon**
- **1 teaspoon pepper**
- **½ teaspoon salt**
- **¼ teaspoon ground allspice**
- **1 pork tenderloin (¾ pound)**
- **½ teaspoon olive oil**

SAUCE

- **½ cup chopped onion**
- **1 tablespoon butter**
- **1 teaspoon minced fresh gingerroot**
- **½ cup chicken broth**
- **¼ cup maple syrup**
- **1 tablespoon diced crystallized ginger**

1. In a small bowl, combine the chili powder, cinnamon, pepper, salt and allspice. Rub over pork. In a large skillet, brown pork in oil on all sides.
2. Transfer to an 11-in. x 7-in. baking dish coated with cooking spray. Bake, uncovered, at 375° for 15 minutes.
3. Meanwhile, in a small skillet, saute onion in butter until tender. Add fresh ginger; saute 1-2 minutes longer. Stir in the broth, syrup and candied ginger. Bring to a boil; cook until sauce is reduced to about ½ cup. Pour over pork.
4. Bake 5-10 minutes longer or until a meat thermometer reads 160°. Let stand for 5 minutes before slicing.

GINGERROOT

Fresh gingerroot is available in your grocer's produce section. It should have a smooth skin. If wrinkled and cracked, the root is dry and past its prime. When stored in a heavy-duty resealable plastic bag, unpeeled gingerroot can be frozen for up to 1 year. When needed, simply peel and mince or grate.

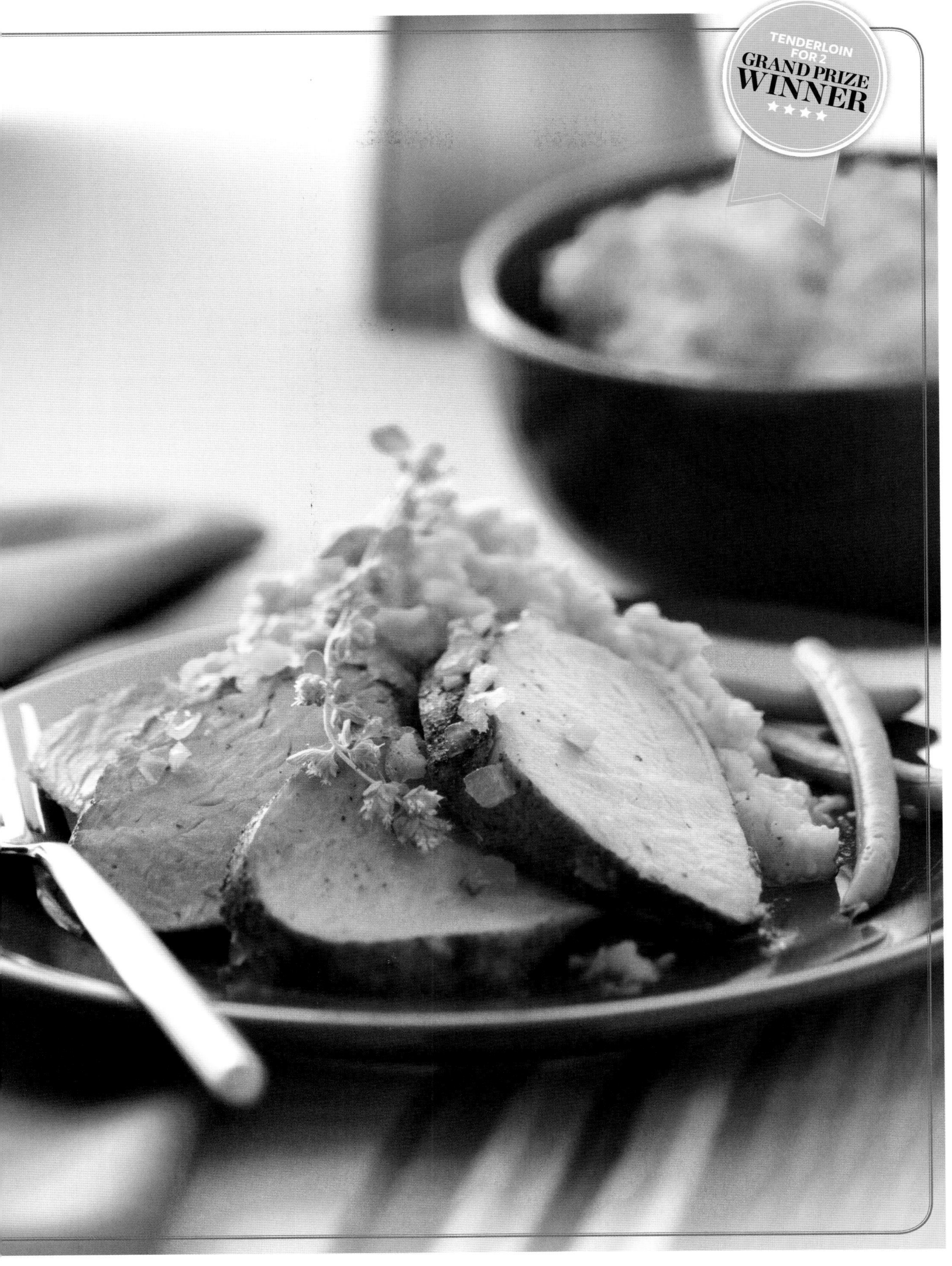
TENDERLOIN FOR 2
GRAND PRIZE
WINNER

Halibut Enchiladas

To create a dish where the North meets South of the Border, I roll our local Alaskan halibut into tortillas. It's one of my most requested recipes and a mainstay for potlucks.

—CAROLE DERIFIELD VALDEZ, ALASKA

PREP: 45 MIN. **BAKE:** 40 MIN. **MAKES:** 12 SERVINGS

- **3 pounds halibut fillets**
- **½ teaspoon salt**
- **⅛ teaspoon pepper**
- **⅛ teaspoon cayenne pepper**
- **1 medium onion, finely chopped**
- **1 medium green pepper, finely chopped**
- **1 tablespoon canola oil**
- **2 garlic cloves, minced**
- **1 can (10 ounces) hot enchilada sauce**
- **1 can (10 ounces) green enchilada sauce**
- **1 cup (8 ounces) sour cream**
- **1 cup mayonnaise**
- **2 cans (4 ounces each) chopped green chilies**
- **2 cans (10 ounces each) mild enchilada sauce**
- **4 cups (16 ounces) shredded Colby-Monterey Jack cheese**
- **24 flour tortillas (6 inches), warmed**
- **1 bunch green onions, thinly sliced**
- **2 tablespoons chopped ripe olives**

1. Place fillets on a greased baking sheet. Sprinkle with salt, pepper and cayenne. Bake, uncovered, at 350° for 15-20 minutes or until fish flakes easily with a fork.
2. Meanwhile, in a large skillet, saute onion and green pepper in oil until tender. Add garlic; cook 1 minute longer.
3. Flake fish with two forks; set aside. In a large bowl, combine the hot enchilada sauce, green enchilada sauce, sour cream, mayonnaise, chilies, onion mixture and fish. Spread ½ cup mild enchilada sauce into each of two greased 13-in. x 9-in. baking dishes. Sprinkle each with 1 cup cheese.
4. Place a heaping ⅓ cup halibut mixture down the center of each tortilla. Roll up each and place seam side down over cheese. Pour remaining sauce over top.
5. Cover and bake at 350° for 30 minutes. Sprinkle with the green onions, olives and remaining cheese. Bake, uncovered, for 10-15 minutes longer or until cheese is melted.

Salmon with Orange Vinaigrette

This is my favorite way to add zip to classic salmon. The tangy vinaigrette complements the naturally sweet fish, and the golden orange color is so appealing on the plate.

—LORIE RICE LIVERPOOL, NEW YORK

PREP/TOTAL TIME: 25 MIN. **MAKES:** 4 SERVINGS

- **1 cup orange juice**
- **4½ teaspoons finely chopped red onion**
- **4½ teaspoons lime juice**
- **1 teaspoon chili powder**
- **1 teaspoon honey Dijon mustard**
- **½ cup fat-free Italian salad dressing**
- **4 salmon fillets (6 ounces each)**
- **Salt and pepper to taste**
- **1 tablespoon olive oil**
- **4 teaspoons minced fresh cilantro**

1. Place orange juice in a small saucepan. Bring to a boil; cook until liquid is reduced to ¼ cup. Cool slightly. Transfer to a blender. Add the onion, lime juice, chili powder and mustard; cover and process until blended. While processing, gradually add salad dressing in a steady stream; process until blended.
2. Season fillets with salt and pepper. In a large skillet, cook fillets in oil over medium-high heat for 2 minutes on each side or until golden brown.
3. Transfer to a greased 15-in. x 10-in. x 1-in. baking pan. Bake at 400° for 5-10 minutes or until fish flakes easily with a fork. Serve with orange vinaigrette. Garnish with cilantro.

Nutrition Facts: *1 fillet with 3 tablespoons vinaigrette equals 397 calories, 22 g fat (4 g saturated fat), 101 mg cholesterol, 547 mg sodium, 12 g carbohydrate, 1 g fiber, 35 g protein.*

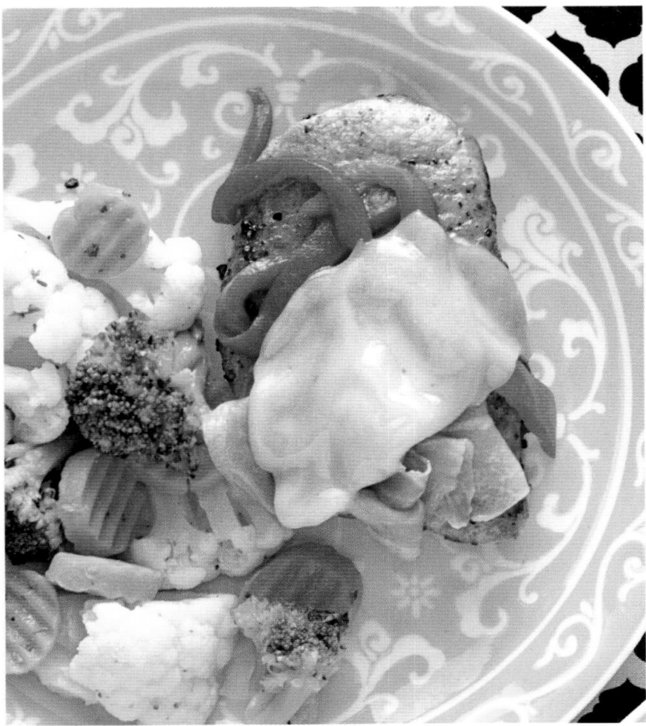

Prosciutto-Pepper Pork Chops

Here's a dish that's simple, fast and delicious. It's easy to make for two, six or even eight. Serve these chops with a medley of veggies or pasta salad for a light and satisfying meal.

—**DONNA PRISCO** RANDOLPH, NEW JERSEY

PREP/TOTAL TIME: 20 MIN. **MAKES:** 4 SERVINGS

- **4 boneless pork loin chops (4 ounces each)**
- **1/8 teaspoon garlic powder**
- **1/8 teaspoon pepper**
- **2 teaspoons canola oil**
- **4 thin slices prosciutto or deli ham**
- **1/2 cup julienned roasted sweet red peppers**
- **2 slices reduced-fat provolone cheese, cut in half**

1. Sprinkle pork chops with garlic powder and pepper. In a large nonstick skillet, cook chops in oil over medium heat for 4-5 minutes on each side or until a thermometer reads 145°.
2. Top each pork chop with prosciutto, red peppers and cheese. Cover and cook for 1-2 minutes or until cheese is melted. Let stand 5 minutes before serving.
Nutrition Facts: *1 pork chop equals 237 calories, 12 g fat (4 g saturated fat), 72 mg cholesterol, 483 mg sodium, 1 g carbohydrate, trace fiber, 28 g protein.* **Diabetic Exchanges:** *4 lean meat, 1/2 fat.*

Cheese-Stuffed Shells

When I was living in California, I tasted this rich, cheesy pasta dish at a neighborhood Italian restaurant. I got the recipe and made a few slight changes to make it my own.

—**LORI MECCA** GRANTS PASS, OREGON

PREP: 35 MIN. **BAKE:** 50 MIN. **MAKES:** 12 SERVINGS

- **1 pound bulk Italian sausage**
- **1 large onion, chopped**
- **1 package (10 ounces) frozen chopped spinach, thawed and squeezed dry**
- **1 package (8 ounces) cream cheese, cubed**
- **1 egg, lightly beaten**
- **2 cups (8 ounces) shredded part-skim mozzarella cheese, divided**
- **2 cups (8 ounces) shredded cheddar cheese**
- **1 cup 4% cottage cheese**
- **1 cup grated Parmesan cheese**
- **1/4 teaspoon salt**
- **1/4 teaspoon pepper**
- **1/8 teaspoon ground cinnamon, optional**
- **24 jumbo pasta shells, cooked and drained**

SAUCE

- **1 can (29 ounces) tomato sauce**
- **1 tablespoon dried minced onion**
- **1 1/2 teaspoons dried basil**
- **1 1/2 teaspoons dried parsley flakes**
- **2 garlic cloves, minced**
- **1 teaspoon sugar**
- **1 teaspoon dried oregano**
- **1/2 teaspoon salt**
- **1/4 teaspoon pepper**

1. In a large skillet, cook sausage and onion over medium heat until meat is no longer pink; drain. Transfer to a large bowl. Stir in the spinach, cream cheese and egg. Add 1 cup mozzarella cheese, cheddar cheese, cottage cheese, Parmesan cheese, salt, pepper and cinnamon if desired.
2. Stuff pasta shells with sausage mixture. Arrange in two 11-in. x 7-in. baking dishes coated with cooking spray. Combine the sauce ingredients; spoon over shells.
3. Cover and bake at 350° for 45 minutes. Uncover; sprinkle with remaining mozzarella. Bake 5-10 minutes longer or until bubbly and cheese is melted. Let stand for 5 minutes before serving.
Nutrition Facts: *2 stuffed shells equals 397 calories, 23 g fat (14 g saturated fat), 94 mg cholesterol, 1,097 mg sodium, 24 g carbohydrate, 2 g fiber, 24 g protein.*

MASHED POTATOES SUPREME, PAGE 165

Sides, Breads & Condiments

Round out any meal with a few of the special side dishes and fresh-baked goodies featured here. Whether you're craving sweet or savory, these award winners make for **memorable munching.**

Sweet Potato Sausage Casserole

Most people never consider combining sweet potatoes with pasta and kielbasa, but I adapted this recipe from several others and received several compliments on it. You can adjust any of the ingredient amounts to suit your taste.

—**RICKEY MADDEN** CLINTON, SOUTH CAROLINA

PREP: 20 MIN. **BAKE:** 25 MIN. **MAKES:** 8 SERVINGS

- **8 ounces uncooked spiral pasta**
- **8 ounces smoked sausage, cut into ¼-inch slices**
- **2 medium sweet potatoes, peeled and cut into ½-inch cubes**
- **1 cup chopped green pepper**
- **½ cup chopped onion**
- **2 tablespoons olive oil**
- **1 teaspoon minced garlic**
- **1 can (14½ ounces) diced tomatoes, undrained**
- **1 cup heavy whipping cream**
- **¼ teaspoon salt**
- **¼ teaspoon pepper**
- **1 cup (4 ounces) shredded cheddar cheese**

1. Cook pasta according to package directions. Meanwhile, in a large skillet, cook the sausage, sweet potatoes, green pepper and onion in oil over medium heat for 5 minutes or until vegetables are tender. Add garlic; cook 1 minute longer. Drain.
2. Add the tomatoes, cream, salt and pepper. Bring to a boil; remove from the heat. Drain pasta; combine with the sausage mixture. Transfer to a greased 13-in. x 9-in. baking dish. Sprinkle with cheese.
3. Bake, uncovered, at 350° for 25-30 minutes or until bubbly. Let stand for 5 minutes before serving.

Grilled Sweet Onions

These onions are so delicious, we prepare them all year long—on the grill in summer, or in an oven preheated to 350° for the same amount of time in winter. A small salad, a slice of bread—and you've got a great light meal. This recipe is sure to become a family favorite at your house, too!

—**MARY BILKE** EAGLE RIVER, WISCONSIN

PREP: 15 MIN. **GRILL:** 35 MIN. **MAKES:** 4 SERVINGS

- **4 large sweet onions**
- **4 teaspoons beef bouillon granules**
- **4 tablespoons butter**
- **½ teaspoon dried thyme**
- **¼ teaspoon salt**
- **¼ teaspoon pepper**
- **4 teaspoons white wine or beef broth, optional**

1. With a sharp knife, carefully remove a 1-in. core from the center of each onion. Cut each onion into four wedges to within ½ in. of root end.
2. Place each onion on a double thickness of heavy-duty foil (about 12 in. square). Place bouillon granules in the center of each onion; top with the butter, thyme, salt and pepper. Drizzle with white wine if desired. Fold foil around the onions and seal tightly.
3. Prepare grill for indirect heat. Grill onions, covered, over indirect medium heat for 35-40 minutes or until tender. Open foil carefully to allow steam to escape.

Nutrition Facts: *1 onion (calculated without wine or broth) equals 172 calories, 12 g fat (7 g saturated fat), 30 mg cholesterol, 1,099 mg sodium, 15 g carbohydrate, 3 g fiber, 2 g protein.*

Streusel-Topped Plum Muffins

Living on a fruit farm, I had plenty of fresh ingredients on hand when I found this muffin recipe. Originally, it called for cherries, but my husband and I agree it's delicious made with our homegrown plums.
—BETTY TIMMRECK EAU CLAIRE, MICHIGAN

PREP: 25 MIN. **BAKE:** 20 MIN.
MAKES: 15 MUFFINS

- **½ cup butter, softened**
- **1 cup sugar**
- **2 eggs**
- **1 teaspoon almond extract**
- **½ teaspoon vanilla extract**
- **2 cups all-purpose flour**
- **2 teaspoons baking powder**
- **½ teaspoon salt**
- **½ cup heavy whipping cream**
- **1½ cups chopped fresh plums**

TOPPING

- **3 tablespoons brown sugar**
- **2 tablespoons all-purpose flour**
- **1 teaspoon ground cinnamon**
- **1 tablespoon cold butter**
- **⅓ cup chopped walnuts**
- **1 tablespoon coarse sugar**

1. In a large bowl, cream the butter and sugar until light and fluffy. Add eggs, one at a time, beating well after each addition. Beat in the extracts. Combine the flour, baking powder and salt; add to the creamed mixture alternately with cream. Fold in the plums. Fill greased or paper-lined muffin cups three-fourths full with batter.
2. For topping, in a small bowl, combine the brown sugar, flour and cinnamon; cut in butter until crumbly. Stir in walnuts. Sprinkle over batter; sprinkle with coarse sugar.
3. Bake at 350° for 20-25 minutes or until a toothpick inserted near the center comes out clean. Cool muffins for 5 minutes before removing from pans to wire racks. Serve warm.

Lemon Crumb Muffins

I always keep the dough for these muffins ready and waiting in the fridge for when unexpected company arrives. They bake up in 20 minutes and taste delicious right out of the oven. Their cake-like texture makes them perfect for a sweet breakfast, side or snack.

—CLAUDETTE BROWNLEE KINGFISHER, OKLAHOMA

PREP: 25 MIN. **BAKE:** 20 MIN./BATCH **MAKES:** 40 MUFFINS

- **6 cups all-purpose flour**
- **4 cups sugar**
- **¾ teaspoon baking soda**
- **¾ teaspoon salt**
- **8 eggs**
- **2 cups (16 ounces) sour cream**
- **2 cups butter, melted**
- **3 tablespoons grated lemon peel**
- **2 tablespoons lemon juice**

TOPPING

- **¾ cup all-purpose flour**
- **¾ cup sugar**
- **¼ cup cold butter, cubed**

GLAZE

- **½ cup sugar**
- **⅓ cup lemon juice**

1. In a large bowl, combine the flour, sugar, baking soda and salt. In another bowl, combine the eggs, sour cream, butter, lemon peel and juice. Stir into dry ingredients just until moistened. Fill greased or paper-lined muffin cups three-fourths full.
2. In a small bowl, combine flour and sugar; cut in butter until mixture resembles coarse crumbs. Sprinkle over batter.
3. Bake at 350° for 20-25 minutes or until a toothpick inserted near the center comes out clean. Cool for 5 minutes before removing from pans to wire racks. In a small bowl, whisk glaze ingredients; drizzle over warm muffins. Serve warm.

Marvelous Shells 'n' Cheese

I made a few changes to my mother's mac 'n' cheese recipe, and even she agrees that my version is rich and heavenly. Just pop it in the oven, and dinner will be ready shortly!

—LAUREN VERSWEYVELD DELAVAN, WISCONSIN

PREP: 25 MIN. **BAKE:** 30 MIN. **MAKES:** 6 SERVINGS

- **1 package (16 ounces) medium pasta shells**
- **1 package (8 ounces) process cheese (Velveeta), cubed**
- **⅓ cup 2% milk**
- **2 cups (16 ounces) 2% cottage cheese**
- **1 can (10¾ ounces) condensed cream of onion soup, undiluted**
- **3 cups (12 ounces) shredded Mexican cheese blend**
- **⅔ cup dry bread crumbs**
- **¼ cup butter, melted**

1. Cook pasta according to package directions. Meanwhile, in a large saucepan, combine process cheese and milk; cook and stir over low heat until melted. Remove from the heat. Stir in cottage cheese and soup.
2. Drain pasta and add to cheese sauce; stir until coated. Transfer to a greased 13-in. x 9-in. baking dish. Sprinkle with Mexican cheese blend. Toss bread crumbs with butter; sprinkle over the top.
3. Bake, uncovered, at 350° for 30-35 minutes or until heated through. Serve immediately.
4. Or before baking, cover and freeze casserole for up to 3 months.

To use frozen casserole: *Thaw in the refrigerator overnight. Remove from the refrigerator 30 minutes before baking. Bake according to directions.*

Smoky Onion Biscuit Squares

Whip up a batch of my savory, biscuit-like squares to complement dinner—or whenever you need a yummy bite of comfort.

—DONNA MARIE RYAN TOPSFIELD, MASSACHUSETTS

PREP: 20 MIN. **BAKE:** 20 MIN. **MAKES:** 16 SERVINGS

- **1 small onion, chopped**
- **2 tablespoons butter**
- **¼ teaspoon sugar**
- **1 garlic clove, minced**
- **1½ cups biscuit/baking mix**
- **½ cup 2% milk**
- **1 egg**
- **¼ pound smoked mozzarella cheese, shredded, divided**
- **1 teaspoon salt-free Southwest chipotle seasoning blend**

1. In a small skillet, cook onion in butter over medium heat until tender. Add sugar; cook 10-15 minutes longer or until golden brown. Add garlic; cook for 1 minute. Cool slightly.
2. In a small bowl, combine the biscuit mix, milk and egg. Fold in ½ cup cheese, seasoning blend and onion mixture. Transfer to an 8-in. square baking dish coated with cooking spray. Sprinkle with remaining cheese.
3. Bake at 400° for 18-22 minutes or until a toothpick inserted near the center comes out clean. Cut into squares; serve warm.

Nutrition Facts: *1 piece equals 91 calories, 5 g fat (2 g saturated fat), 22 mg cholesterol, 197 mg sodium, 8 g carbohydrate, trace fiber, 3 g protein.* **Diabetic Exchanges:** *1 fat, ½ starch.*

ONION ADVICE

If a recipe calls for sauteed onions, make extra and refrigerate in a covered container. Over the next few days, you can save time preparing other dishes that use sauteed onion, or enhance your own kitchen creations with a savory kick.

Tomato 'n' Corn Risotto

I enjoy making this recipe because it uses items from my garden. Milk and Parmesan cheese lend a rich creaminess that everyone at your table is sure to enjoy.

—ANGELA LIVELY BAXTER, TENNESSEE

PREP: 15 MIN. **COOK:** 35 MIN. **MAKES:** 5 SERVINGS

- **2½ cups water**
- **2 cups whole milk**
- **3 tablespoons chicken broth**
- **1 large onion, finely chopped**
- **2 tablespoons butter**
- **1 garlic clove, minced**
- **¾ cup uncooked arborio rice**
- **1⅓ cups fresh corn (about 5 ears of corn)**
- **1 medium tomato, peeled, seeded and chopped**
- **½ cup grated Parmesan cheese**
- **½ cup fresh basil leaves, thinly sliced**
- **½ teaspoon salt**
- **Pepper to taste**

1. In a large saucepan, heat the water, milk and broth; keep mixture warm.
2. In a large skillet, saute onion in butter until tender. Add garlic; cook 1 minute longer. Add rice; cook and stir for 2-3 minutes. Stir in 1 cup of the hot water mixture. Cook and stir until all liquid is absorbed.
3. Add remaining water mixture, ½ cup at a time, stirring constantly. Allow the liquid to absorb between additions. Cook until risotto is creamy and rice is almost tender. (Cooking time is about 20 minutes.) Stir in the remaining ingredients; heat through and serve immediately.

Nutrition Facts: *¾ cup equals 295 calories, 11 g fat (6 g saturated fat), 29 mg cholesterol, 476 mg sodium, 41 g carbohydrate, 2 g fiber, 10 g protein.*

Vidalia Onion Bake

PREP: 25 MIN. **BAKE:** 20 MIN.
MAKES: 8 SERVINGS

- **6 large sweet onions, sliced (about 12 cups)**
- **½ cup butter, cubed**
- **2 cups crushed butter-flavored crackers**
- **1 cup shredded Parmesan cheese**
- **½ cup shredded cheddar cheese**
- **¼ cup shredded Romano cheese**

1. In a large skillet, saute the onions in butter until tender and liquid has evaporated. Place half of the onions in a greased 2-qt. baking dish; sprinkle with half of the cracker crumbs and cheeses. Repeat layers.
2. Bake, uncovered, at 325° for 20-25 minutes or until golden brown.

"The mild taste of Vidalias makes this bake appealing to onion lovers and skeptics alike. It's an excellent accompaniment to beef, pork or chicken."

—**KATRINA STITT** ZEPHYR HILLS, FLORIDA

CHEESE, PLEASE!

When a recipe calls for a cheese blend, like this one does, there's plenty of room for home cooks to experiment! Consider using other firm cheeses like Asiago, aged Gouda or Gruyere. Have a bit of provolone on hand? Throw some in the mix and adjust the measurements accordingly. When it comes to cheese substitutions, anything goes!

Sweet Potato Casserole

I'm always looking for ways to enjoy our abundant supply of sweet potatoes. This recipe is my own creation, and I've made it many times. When I take the spiced and nutty casserole to family potlucks, it never fails to earn praise.
—KATHY RAIRIGH MILFORD, INDIANA

PREP: 30 MIN. **BAKE:** 35 MIN. **MAKES:** 8 SERVINGS

- **2¼ pounds sweet potatoes (about 3 large), peeled and cubed**
- **3 egg whites, lightly beaten**
- **3 tablespoons maple syrup**
- **1 teaspoon vanilla extract**

TOPPING

- **¼ cup chopped pecans**
- **1 tablespoon brown sugar**
- **1 tablespoon butter, melted**
- **⅛ teaspoon ground cinnamon**
- **⅓ cup dried apricots, chopped**
- **⅓ cup dried cherries, chopped**

1. Place sweet potatoes in a Dutch oven and cover with water. Bring to a boil. Reduce heat; cover and simmer for 15-20 minutes or until tender. Drain and place in a large bowl; mash. Cool slightly. Stir in the egg whites, syrup and vanilla.
2. Transfer to an 8-in. square baking dish coated with cooking spray. Combine the pecans, brown sugar, butter and cinnamon; sprinkle over the top.
3. Bake, uncovered, at 350° for 30 minutes. Sprinkle with apricots and cherries. Bake 5-7 minutes longer or until a thermometer reads 160° and the fruits are heated through.

Nutrition Facts: *½ cup equals 186 calories, 4 g fat (1 g saturated fat), 4 mg cholesterol, 40 mg sodium, 34 g carbohydrate, 3 g fiber, 3 g protein.* **Diabetic Exchanges:** *1½ starch, 1 fat, ½ fruit.*

Surprise Monkey Bread

A glorified monkey bread, this finger-lickin' good recipe conceals cheesy goodness inside. I also make a savory version with garlic and cheese for dinner sometimes.
—LOIS RUTHERFORD ELKTON, FLORIDA

PREP: 25 MIN. **BAKE:** 40 MIN. **MAKES:** 1 LOAF (12 SERVINGS)

- **1 cup packed brown sugar**
- **½ cup butter, cubed**
- **2 tubes (12 ounces each) refrigerated flaky buttermilk biscuits**
- **½ cup sugar**
- **1 tablespoon ground cinnamon**
- **1 package (8 ounces) cream cheese, cut into 20 cubes**
- **1½ cups chopped walnuts**

1. In a small microwave-safe bowl, heat brown sugar and butter on high for 1 minute or until sugar is dissolved; set aside.
2. Flatten each biscuit into a 3-in. circle. Combine sugar and cinnamon; sprinkle ½ teaspoon in the center of each biscuit. Top with a cream cheese cube. Fold dough over filling; pinch edges to seal tightly.
3. Sprinkle ½ cup walnuts into a 10-in. fluted tube pan coated with cooking spray. Layer with half of the biscuits, cinnamon-sugar and butter mixture and ½ cup walnuts. Repeat layers.
4. Bake at 350° for 40-45 minutes or until golden brown. Invert onto a serving platter and serve. Refrigerate leftovers.

Broccoli Rice Casserole

When I was little, this dish was the only way my mother could get me to eat broccoli. It's an excellent recipe and tastes especially good alongside a poultry entree.

—JENNIFER FULLER BALLSTON SPA, NEW YORK

PREP: 15 MIN. **BAKE:** 30 MIN. **MAKES:** 8 SERVINGS

- **1½ cups water**
- **½ cup butter, cubed**
- **1 tablespoon dried minced onion**
- **2 cups uncooked instant rice**
- **1 package (16 ounces) frozen chopped broccoli, thawed**
- **1 can (10¾ ounces) condensed cream of mushroom soup, undiluted**
- **1 jar (8 ounces) process cheese sauce**

1. In a large saucepan, bring the water, butter and onion to a boil. Stir in rice. Remove from the heat; cover and let stand for 5 minutes or until water is absorbed.
2. Stir in the broccoli, soup and cheese sauce. Transfer to a greased 2-qt. baking dish. Bake, uncovered, at 350° for 30-35 minutes or until bubbly.

GRAND PRIZE

Pumpkin Scones with Berry Butter

These delightful scones, alongside a cup of hot tea, can brighten any chilly day. They also make a pretty hostess gift arranged in a basket with the cranberry butter packed in a small jar.

—JUDY WILSON SUN CITY WEST, ARIZONA

PREP: 25 MIN. + CHILLING **BAKE:** 15 MIN.
MAKES: 8 SCONES (ABOUT ½ CUP BUTTER)

- **2 tablespoons dried cranberries**
- **½ cup boiling water**
- **½ cup butter, softened**
- **3 tablespoons confectioners' sugar**

DOUGH

- **2¼ cups all-purpose flour**
- **¼ cup packed brown sugar**
- **2 teaspoons baking powder**
- **1½ teaspoons pumpkin pie spice**
- **¼ teaspoon salt**
- **¼ teaspoon baking soda**
- **½ cup cold butter, cubed**
- **1 egg**
- **½ cup canned pumpkin**
- **⅓ cup 2% milk**
- **2 tablespoons chopped pecans, optional**

1. Place dried cranberries in a small bowl; add boiling water. Let stand for 5 minutes; drain and chop. In another small bowl, beat butter until light and fluffy. Add confectioners' sugar and cranberries; mix well. Cover and refrigerate for at least 1 hour.
2. In a large bowl, combine the flour, brown sugar, baking powder, pie spice, salt and baking soda. Cut in butter until the mixture resembles coarse crumbs. In a small bowl, whisk the egg, pumpkin and milk; add to crumb mixture just until moistened. Stir in pecans if desired.
3. Turn dough onto a floured surface; knead 10 times. Pat into an 8-in. circle. Cut into eight wedges; separate the wedges and place on a greased baking sheet.
4. Bake at 400° for 12-15 minutes or until golden brown. Serve warm with the berry butter.

CRAVING CRANBERRIES?

For some quick and tasty results, try these easy ideas: Mix a little cranberry juice with some hot apple cider for a zingy beverage. Add a half cup (or more) of chopped cranberries to your favorite bread, muffin or stuffing mix. Lend variety to baked apples by filling the center with cranberries and a dash of sugar and cinnamon. At the grocery store, look for firm, plump berries with a lustrous color. You'll find fresh cranberries in the produce section from September through December. They freeze well, so buy extra.

PUMPKIN PATCH SPECIALTIES
GRAND PRIZE
WINNER

Roasted Garlic Mashed Potatoes

Yukon Gold potatoes give this dish a rich, buttery color and hearty texture. I've taken the recipe to many potlucks, always with great success. Sometimes, I wish it wasn't so popular because I never have any leftovers to take home!

—MARILYN GEARY-SYMONS PORTLAND, OREGON

PREP: 20 MIN. **BAKE:** 30 MIN. + COOLING **MAKES:** 8 SERVINGS

1 whole garlic bulb
1 teaspoon olive oil
2½ pounds Yukon Gold potatoes, peeled and quartered
2 cups chicken broth, divided
¼ cup butter, softened
¼ teaspoon pepper
⅛ teaspoon salt

1. Remove papery outer skin from garlic bulb (do not peel or separate cloves). Cut top off bulb; brush with olive oil. Wrap in heavy-duty foil. Bake at 425° for 30-35 minutes or until softened. Cool for 10-15 minutes.
2. Meanwhile, place potatoes in a large saucepan and cover with water. Bring to a boil. Reduce heat; cover and cook for 15-20 minutes or until tender.
3. Place 1 cup broth in a blender. Squeeze softened garlic into blender; cover and process until blended. Drain potatoes; place in a large bowl. Add the butter, pepper, salt, garlic mixture and remaining broth; beat until smooth.

Glazed Carrots and Green Beans

Even non-vegetable eaters will devour this simple, tasty side dish. I've used frozen green beans when I didn't have any fresh on hand, and it still tastes wonderful!

—SUSAN KAKUK PLYMOUTH, MINNESOTA

PREP/TOTAL TIME: 20 MIN. **MAKES:** 6 SERVINGS

6 cups water
½ pound fresh baby carrots
½ pound fresh green beans, trimmed
½ cup chicken broth
1 tablespoon butter
1 teaspoon sugar
Salt and pepper to taste

1. In a large saucepan, bring water to a boil. Add carrots; cover and cook for 1 minute. Add beans; cover and cook 2 minutes longer. Drain and immediately place vegetables in ice water. Drain and pat dry.
2. Place the vegetables in a large skillet; add broth and butter. Bring to a boil; cook, uncovered, for 2-3 minutes or until liquid is reduced to about 2 teaspoons. Add the sugar, salt and pepper; cook and stir for 1 minute.

Blue Cheese Onions

When tangy cheese softens and melds with baked onions and butter, you have a side dish fit for company. This one's delicious—straight from the oven—and can be served with any meat.

—NORMA REYNOLDS YORK, PENNSYLVANIA

PREP: 15 MIN. **BAKE:** 20 MIN. **MAKES:** 2 CUPS

1½ cups (6 ounces) crumbled blue cheese
2 tablespoons Worcestershire sauce
½ teaspoon dill weed
¼ teaspoon pepper
2 large onions, thinly sliced
6 tablespoons butter, melted

1. In a food processor, combine the crumbled blue cheese, Worcestershire sauce, dill weed and pepper; cover and process until blended.
2. Place the onions in an ungreased 13-in. x 9-in. baking dish. Drizzle with butter; top with tablespoonfuls of the blue cheese mixture.
3. Bake, uncovered, at 425° for 20-25 minutes or until golden brown. Serve immediately.

Mashed Potatoes Supreme

I received this recipe from my sister some 60 years ago, and many people have requested it since. The potatoes are creamy and taste like twice-baked. You can make it ahead for convenience, so it's the ideal contribution to a potluck.

—JULIA DAUBRESSE SUN CITY CENTER, FLORIDA

PREP: 40 MIN. **BAKE:** 20 MIN. **MAKES:** 8 SERVINGS

3 pounds medium red potatoes, quartered
2 packages (3 ounces each) cream cheese, cubed
½ cup butter, cubed
½ cup half-and-half cream or milk
1 medium green pepper, chopped
4 green onions, thinly sliced
1 jar (2 ounces) sliced pimientos, drained
½ teaspoon salt
¼ teaspoon pepper
½ cup shredded cheddar cheese, divided
½ cup grated Parmesan cheese, divided

1. Place potatoes in a large saucepan; cover with water. Bring to a boil. Reduce heat; cover and cook for 10-15 minutes or until tender. Drain.
2. In a large bowl, mash the potatoes. Add the cream cheese, butter and cream; beat until blended. Stir in the green pepper, onions, pimientos, salt and pepper. Stir in ⅓ cup cheddar cheese and ⅓ cup Parmesan cheese.
3. Transfer to a greased 11-in. x 7-in. baking dish. Sprinkle with remaining cheeses. Bake, uncovered, at 350° for 20-25 minutes or until heated through.

Mini Toffee Rolls

I found this quick and easy recipe in a magazine years ago and adapted the original to make it my own. The bite-size morsels are packed with comforting cinnamon flavor!

—CAROL GILLESPIE CHAMBERSBURG, PENNSYLVANIA

PREP: 20 MIN. **BAKE:** 15 MIN. **MAKES:** 4 DOZEN

- **6 tablespoons butter, softened**
- **½ cup packed brown sugar**
- **1 teaspoon ground cinnamon**
- **⅓ cup milk chocolate English toffee bits**
- **2 tubes (8 ounces each) refrigerated crescent rolls**
- **1 cup confectioners' sugar**
- **4½ teaspoons 2% milk**
- **¼ teaspoon vanilla extract**

1. In a small bowl, cream the butter, brown sugar and cinnamon until light and fluffy. Stir in toffee bits.
2. Separate each tube of crescent dough into four rectangles; seal perforations. Spread evenly with butter mixture. Roll up each rectangle jelly-roll style, starting with a long side.
3. Cut each into six 1-in. slices; place cut side down into two greased 8-in. square baking dishes. Bake at 375° for 14-16 minutes or until golden brown.
4. In a small bowl, combine the confectioners' sugar, milk and vanilla until smooth. Drizzle over warm rolls.

"I developed this recipe to give as a Christmas present to family and friends. I package it in fun cups from garage sales and wrap them in bright cellophane bags, along with an easy chili recipe. Now, I'm filling requests all year!"

—CAROLINE MUNOZ AUSTIN, MINNESOTA

Chili Seasoning Mix

PREP/TOTAL TIME: 10 MIN. **MAKES:** 1¾ CUPS

- **½ cup dried parsley flakes**
- **½ cup chili powder**
- **¼ cup dried minced onion**
- **2 tablespoons salt**
- **2 tablespoons cornstarch**
- **2 tablespoons dried minced garlic**
- **2 tablespoons ground cumin**
- **1 tablespoon ground coriander**
- **1 tablespoon each dried cilantro flakes, basil and oregano**
- **1 tablespoon crushed red pepper flakes**
- **1½ teaspoons pepper**

In a small bowl, combine all ingredients. Store in an airtight container for up to 6 months. Use as a pork rub or seasoning for chili, or sprinkle on fish.

Nutrition Facts: *1 tablespoon equals 18 calories, 1 g fat (trace saturated fat), 0 cholesterol, 531 mg sodium, 3 g carbohydrate, 1 g fiber, 1 g protein.*

Mashed Potato Artichoke Bake

These jazzed-up mashed potatoes make a welcome side dish for any entree. My husband loves this bake.

—LAURA MCALLISTER
MORGANTON, NORTH CAROLINA

PREP: 30 MIN. **BAKE:** 15 MIN.
MAKES: 2 SERVINGS

- **2 medium potatoes, peeled and quartered**
- **¼ cup sour cream**
- **2 tablespoons 2% milk**
- **2 tablespoons mayonnaise**
- **1 tablespoon butter**
- **½ teaspoon snipped fresh dill or ⅛ teaspoon dill weed**
- **Dash salt**
- **Dash pepper**
- **¾ cup frozen artichoke hearts, thawed and chopped**
- **1 green onion, chopped**
- **2 bacon strips, cooked and crumbled**
- **⅓ cup shredded cheddar cheese**

1. Place potatoes in a small saucepan and cover with water. Bring to a boil. Reduce heat; cover and cook for 10-15 minutes or until tender. Mash potatoes with the sour cream, milk, mayonnaise, butter and seasonings. Stir in artichokes and onion.
2. Transfer to a 1-qt. baking dish coated with cooking spray. Sprinkle with bacon and cheese. Bake, uncovered, at 400° for 15-20 minutes or until heated through and cheese is melted.

Nutrition Facts: *1½ cups (prepared with reduced-fat sour cream, reduced-fat mayonnaise and reduced-fat cheese) equals 362 calories, 18 g fat (8 g saturated fat), 44 mg cholesterol, 569 mg sodium, 40 g carbohydrate, 5 g fiber, 14 g protein.*

SPUD SCIENCE

Russet or Idaho potatoes are oblong and thick-skinned. Their light, fluffy texture makes them perfect for baking and mashing. Due to their crumbly flesh, russets do not hold their shape when cooked, so skip them in salads or casseroles. When fried, russets stay crispy on the outside, soft on the inside and don't absorb too much oil.

IT'S ALL ABOUT THE DOUGH
GRAND PRIZE
WINNER

GRAND PRIZE

Pull-Apart Caramel Coffee Cake

PREP: 10 MIN. **BAKE:** 25 MIN. **MAKES:** 12 SERVINGS

- **2 tubes (12 ounces each) refrigerated flaky buttermilk biscuits**
- **1 cup packed brown sugar**
- **½ cup heavy whipping cream**
- **1 teaspoon ground cinnamon**

1. Cut each biscuit into four pieces; arrange evenly in a 10-in. fluted tube pan coated with cooking spray. Combine the brown sugar, cream and cinnamon; pour over the biscuits.
2. Bake at 350° for 25-30 minutes or until golden brown. Cool for 5 minutes before inverting onto a serving platter.

Nutrition Facts: *1 slice equals 240 calories, 5 g fat (3 g saturated fat), 14 mg cholesterol, 496 mg sodium, 45 g carbohydrate, trace fiber, 5 g protein.*

"This luscious treat was a huge hit the first time I made it for a brunch. Now I get requests every time family or friends host morning gatherings. I always keep the four easy ingredients on hand."

—**JAIME KEELING** KEIZER, OREGON

SPICING THINGS UP

With its mildly sweet-to-bittersweet flavor, cinnamon is a common addition to baked goods, but is also found in stews and curries, as well as fruit, squash, pork and beef dishes. If you'd like to add some depth to the flavor of the recipe above, consider warm, sweet nutmeg or rich, earthy cloves—both perfect partners for cinnamon. You could also opt for allspice, a combination of all three. Cardamom has a tart, floral flavor that pairs nicely with cinnamon, too. Just follow your palate!

Jumbo Pumpkin Pecan Muffins

Perk up breakfast or snack time with one of these hearty muffins. You'll really enjoy the pumpkin-spice flavor and crumbly nut topping—no matter what the season!

—**JANICE CHRISTOFFERSON** EAGLE RIVER, WISCONSIN

PREP: 25 MIN. **BAKE:** 25 MIN. **MAKES:** 6 MUFFINS

- **2½ cups all-purpose flour**
- **½ cup sugar**
- **¼ cup packed brown sugar**
- **2 teaspoons pumpkin pie spice**
- **1 teaspoon baking powder**
- **1 teaspoon baking soda**
- **½ teaspoon salt**
- **2 eggs**
- **1 cup canned pumpkin**
- **½ cup buttermilk**
- **¼ cup canola oil**
- **1 teaspoon vanilla extract**
- **½ cup chopped pecans**

TOPPING

- **⅓ cup packed brown sugar**
- **⅓ cup finely chopped pecans**
- **¼ cup all-purpose flour**
- **¼ cup cold butter, cubed**

1. In a large bowl, combine the first seven ingredients. In another bowl, combine the eggs, pumpkin, buttermilk, oil and vanilla. Stir into dry ingredients just until moistened. Fold in the pecans. Fill six greased or paper-lined jumbo muffin cups three-fourths full.
2. In a small bowl, combine the brown sugar, pecans and flour; cut in butter until crumbly. Sprinkle over batter.
3. Bake at 375° for 25-30 minutes or until a toothpick inserted near the center comes out clean. Cool for 5 minutes before removing from pan to a wire rack. Serve warm.

Glazed Orange Carrots

Want your kids to eat more carrots? This tender side dish has a pleasant citrus flavor and a pretty orange glaze. It's a "must" at all our family gatherings.

—**MARILYN HASH** ENUMCLAW, WASHINGTON

PREP/TOTAL TIME: 25 MIN. **MAKES:** 6 SERVINGS

- **2 pounds fresh carrots, sliced**
- **2 tablespoons butter**
- **¼ cup thawed orange juice concentrate**
- **2 tablespoons brown sugar**
- **2 tablespoons minced fresh parsley**

1. Place 1 in. of water in a saucepan; add carrots. Bring to a boil. Reduce heat; cover and simmer for 7-9 minutes or until crisp-tender. Drain.
2. Melt butter in a large skillet; stir in orange juice concentrate and brown sugar. Add carrots and parsley; stir to coat. Cook and stir 1-2 minutes or until glaze is thickened.

Fruit-Nut Pumpkin Bread

PREP: 30 MIN. **BAKE:** 1 HOUR + COOLING
MAKES: 2 LOAVES (12 SLICES EACH) AND 1 CUP SPREAD

- **2⅔ cups sugar**
- **1 can (15 ounces) solid-pack pumpkin**
- **1 cup canola oil**
- **4 eggs**
- **1 teaspoon vanilla extract**
- **3½ cups all-purpose flour**
- **1½ teaspoons ground cinnamon**
- **1 teaspoon salt**
- **1 teaspoon baking soda**
- **¼ teaspoon ground cloves**
- **1½ cups coarsely chopped walnuts**
- **⅔ cup golden raisins**
- **⅔ cup raisins**
- **⅔ cup dried cranberries**

CRANBERRY CREAM CHEESE SPREAD

- **½ cup dried cranberries**
- **1½ cups boiling water**
- **1 package (8 ounces) cream cheese, softened**
- **⅓ cup chopped walnuts**

1. In a large bowl, beat the sugar, pumpkin, oil, eggs and vanilla until well blended. Combine the flour, cinnamon, salt, baking soda and cloves; gradually beat into pumpkin mixture until blended. Fold in the walnuts, raisins and cranberries.
2. Transfer to two greased 9-in. x 5-in. loaf pans. Bake at 350° for 60-70 minutes or until a toothpick inserted near the center comes out clean. Cool for 10 minutes before removing from pans to wire racks.
3. For spread, place the cranberries in a small bowl; add boiling water. Let stand for 5 minutes; drain. In a small bowl, beat cream cheese until smooth. Beat in cranberries and walnuts until blended. Serve with the bread.

"Our family dinners wouldn't be complete without this simple bread. I bake a variety to suit everyone—one plain, one with just nuts, one with raisins and dried cranberries, and one with everything."

—**PRISCILLA GILBERT** INDIAN HARBOUR BEACH, FLORIDA

Dijon Scalloped Potatoes

My family really enjoys this creamy and colorful recipe for cheesy potatoes. What's not to love? It features both sweet and russet potatoes, lots of rich, buttery flavor and an enticing, golden crumb topping.
—CAROLYN PUTNAM NORWALK, OHIO

PREP: 25 MIN. **BAKE:** 50 MIN. + STANDING
MAKES: 8 SERVINGS

- **⅔ cup chopped onion**
- **2 teaspoons canola oil**
- **1 can (14½ ounces) chicken broth**
- **2 packages (3 ounces each) cream cheese, cubed**
- **1 tablespoon Dijon mustard**
- **3 medium russet potatoes, peeled and thinly sliced**
- **2 medium sweet potatoes, peeled and thinly sliced**
- **1½ to 2 cups crushed butter-flavored crackers**
- **3 tablespoons grated Parmesan cheese**
- **2 tablespoons butter, melted**
- **2 teaspoons minced fresh parsley**

1. In a Dutch oven, saute onion in oil until tender. Reduce heat to medium; stir in the broth, cream cheese and mustard until blended. Remove from the heat. Stir in the potatoes.
2. Transfer to a 13-in. x 9-in. baking dish coated with cooking spray. In a small bowl, combine the crushed crackers, cheese and butter; sprinkle over the top.
3. Bake, uncovered, at 350° for 50-60 minutes or until potatoes are tender. Sprinkle with parsley. Let stand for 10 minutes before serving.

SWEET POTATO SECRETS

Select firm sweet potatoes without cracks or bruises. If stored in a cool, dark, well-ventilated place, they'll remain fresh for about 2 weeks. Above 60°, they'll sprout or become woody. Once cooked, sweet potatoes can be stored for up to 1 week in the refrigerator.

Cranberry Banana Bread

Studded with cranberries and nuts, these moist, golden loaves make yummy breakfasts and gifts for grateful friends. I experimented for years, and this recipe is now near perfection!

—**EVA RIDER** MONTGOMERY, ALABAMA

PREP: 25 MIN. **BAKE:** 50 MIN. + COOLING
MAKES: 1 LOAF (12 SLICES)

- **⅓ cup shortening**
- **⅔ cup sugar**
- **2 eggs**
- **1 cup mashed ripe bananas (about 2 medium)**
- **1½ cups all-purpose flour**
- **⅓ cup cinnamon graham cracker crumbs (about 2 whole crackers)**
- **1½ teaspoons baking powder**
- **½ teaspoon baking soda**
- **½ teaspoon salt**
- **½ cup chopped walnuts or pecans**
- **½ cup dried cranberries**

1. In a large bowl, cream shortening and sugar until light and fluffy. Add eggs, one at a time, beating well after each addition. Stir in bananas. Combine the flour, cracker crumbs, baking powder, baking soda and salt; gradually add to creamed mixture and mix well. Fold in walnuts and cranberries. Pour into a greased 8-in. x 4-in. loaf pan.
2. Bake at 350° for 50-55 minutes or until a toothpick inserted near the center comes out clean. Cool for 10 minutes before removing from pan to a wire rack.

Herbed Corn

PREP/TOTAL TIME: 25 MIN. **MAKES:** 8 SERVINGS

- **8 cups fresh or frozen corn, thawed**
- **1 cup finely chopped red onion**
- **¾ cup butter, cubed**
- **12 garlic cloves, minced**
- **4 to 6 teaspoons herbes de Provence or Italian seasoning**
- **1 teaspoon salt**

In a Dutch oven over medium-high heat, cook and stir the corn and onion in butter for 5 minutes. Add the garlic; cook 1 minute longer. Add herbes de Provence and salt; cook 2-4 minutes or until vegetables are tender.

Editor's Note: *Look for herbes de Provence in the spice aisle.*

"A pleasant blend of herbs enhances this fast, easy and tasty side dish. It's our family's favorite way to eat fresh corn."

—**TANIA BIKERMAN** PITTSBURGH, PENNSYLVANIA

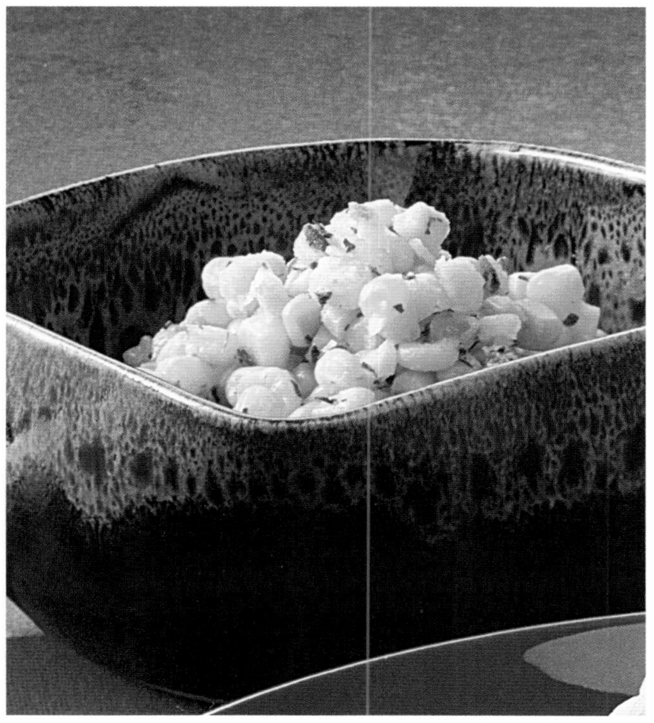

Garlic-Cheese Crescent Rolls

Here's a recipe that couldn't be much quicker or easier, and is sure to add a special touch to any dinner. The garlic and Parmesan flavors really come through on the tender rolls. Enjoy!

—**LORI ABAD** EAST HAVEN, CONNECTICUT

PREP/TOTAL TIME: 20 MIN. **MAKES:** 8 SERVINGS

- **1 tube (8 ounces) refrigerated crescent rolls**
- **3 tablespoons butter, melted**
- **1½ teaspoons garlic powder**
- **1 teaspoon dried oregano**
- **2 tablespoons grated Parmesan cheese**

1. Separate crescent dough into eight triangles. Roll up from the wide end and place point side down 2 in. apart on an ungreased baking sheet. Curve ends to form a crescent.
2. Combine the butter, garlic powder and oregano; brush over rolls. Sprinkle with cheese.
3. Bake at 375° for 10-12 minutes or until rolls are golden brown. Serve warm.

HERBES DE PROVENCE, DECODED

A dried seasoning blend named for the region in France, herbes de Provence (pronounced AIRB deh pro-VANS) blends sweet, aromatic and floral herbs and spices, including rosemary, fennel, savory, basil, thyme, tarragon and lavender. It's typically used to add flavor to vegetables, poultry, beef and pork.

Smoky Grilled Corn

A friend and I cooked up this corn one evening when getting ready to grill. The buttery corn, with its sweet-spicy seasoning, won top honors over our steaks!

—LINDA LANDERS KALISPELL, MONTANA

PREP: 25 MIN. **GRILL:** 10 MIN. **MAKES:** 6 SERVINGS

- **2 tablespoons plus 1½ teaspoons butter**
- **½ cup honey**
- **2 large garlic cloves, minced**
- **2 tablespoons hot pepper sauce**
- **½ teaspoon salt**
- **¼ teaspoon pepper**
- **¼ teaspoon paprika**
- **6 medium ears sweet corn, husks removed**

1. In a small saucepan, melt the butter. Stir in the honey, garlic, pepper sauce and seasonings until blended; heat through. Brush over corn.
2. Moisten a paper towel with cooking oil; using long-handled tongs, lightly coat the grill rack.
3. Grill the corn, covered, over medium heat for 10-12 minutes or until the corn is tender, turning and basting occasionally with the butter mixture. Serve the corn with any remaining butter mixture.

Nutrition Facts: *1 ear of corn equals 208 calories, 6 g fat (3 g saturated fat), 13 mg cholesterol, 275 mg sodium, 41 g carbohydrate, 3 g fiber, 3 g protein.*

Garden Zucchini Chutney

At my wits' end with grating zucchini from my garden, I was determined to make something other than zucchini bread and zucchini cake. Then I found this recipe and altered it to our taste. Now we use the sweet and tangy topping for many dishes!

—TAREN WEYER HUDSON, WISCONSIN

PREP: 20 MIN. **COOK:** 50 MIN. **MAKES:** 4 CUPS

- **6 cups chopped seeded zucchini (about 7 medium)**
- **2 medium tart apples, peeled and chopped**
- **1½ cups raisins or dried currants**
- **1½ cups white vinegar**
- **1 cup honey**
- **1 medium sweet red pepper, chopped**
- **1 small onion, chopped**
- **⅓ cup thawed orange juice concentrate**
- **2 tablespoons lemon juice**

1. In a Dutch oven, bring all ingredients to a boil. Reduce heat; simmer, uncovered, for 45-55 minutes or until thickened.
2. Serve warm or cold. Refrigerate the leftovers.

FRESH CORN

When buying sweet corn, you'll know it's at the peak of freshness if you look for a few characteristics: a mold-free, tightly closed husk; brown, dried silk, and a moist stem end. Then, pull back a small section of the husk and check for even rows of kernels that extend to the end of the cob.

Pecan Lemon Loaf

A lemony glaze gives this tender, nutty bread an extra boost of tangy flavor. For variety, substitute grated orange peel and orange juice for lemon.

—**LAURA COMITZ** ENOLA, PENNSYLVANIA

PREP: 20 MIN. **BAKE:** 50 MIN. + COOLING
MAKES: 1 LOAF (16 SLICES)

- **½ cup butter, softened**
- **1½ cups sugar, divided**
- **2 eggs**
- **2 cups all-purpose flour**
- **1 teaspoon baking powder**
- **½ teaspoon salt**
- **¾ cup sour cream**
- **1 cup chopped pecans, toasted**
- **1 tablespoon grated lemon peel**
- **¼ cup lemon juice**

1. In a large bowl, cream butter and 1 cup sugar until light and fluffy. Beat in eggs. Combine the flour, baking powder and salt; add to creamed mixture alternately with sour cream, beating well after each addition. Fold in pecans and lemon peel.
2. Transfer to a greased 9-in. x 5-in. loaf pan. Bake at 350° for 50-60 minutes or until a toothpick inserted near the center comes out clean.
3. In a small saucepan, combine lemon juice and remaining sugar. Cook and stir over medium heat until sugar is dissolved. Pour over warm bread. Cool completely on a wire rack before removing from the pan.

Fresh Corn Medley

Your family will be sweet on this summery side dish that combines corn "off" the cob with green pepper, bacon, cheddar cheese and honey. It's just as delightful made with frozen corn.

—**SUSAN PADEN** MEXICO, MISSOURI

PREP: 25 MIN. **COOK:** 20 MIN. **MAKES:** 5 SERVINGS

- **1 medium green pepper, chopped**
- **1 small onion, chopped**
- **3 tablespoons butter**
- **4 cups fresh corn (about 9 ears of corn)**
- **¼ cup hot water**
- **1 jar (2 ounces) diced pimientos, drained**
- **1 tablespoon honey**
- **1 teaspoon salt**
- **Dash pepper**
- **½ cup shredded cheddar cheese**
- **4 bacon strips, cooked and crumbled**

1. In a large skillet, saute the green pepper and onion in butter until tender. Add the corn, water, diced pimientos, honey, salt and pepper.
2. Bring to a boil. Reduce the heat; simmer, uncovered, for 8-10 minutes or until the corn is tender. Sprinkle with cheese and bacon.

Nutrition Facts: *¾ cup equals 263 calories, 14 g fat (8 g saturated fat), 35 mg cholesterol, 711 mg sodium, 31 g carbohydrate, 4 g fiber, 8 g protein.*

Double Corn Dressing

I have served this mouthwatering dressing, made with a dry stuffing mix, for years to family and friends, and it always receives compliments. It goes great with pork or poultry.

—BERLIENE GROSH LAKELAND, FLORIDA

PREP: 25 MIN. **BAKE:** 40 MIN. **MAKES:** 16 SERVINGS

- **1 package (12 ounces) unseasoned stuffing cubes**
- **1 medium onion, finely chopped**
- **½ each medium green, sweet yellow and red pepper, chopped**
- **1 teaspoon garlic powder**
- **½ teaspoon salt**
- **¼ teaspoon pepper**
- **3 eggs, lightly beaten**
- **1 can (15¼ ounces) whole kernel corn, drained**
- **1 can (14¾ ounces) cream-style corn**
- **½ cup butter, melted**
- **½ to 1 cup chicken broth**

1. In a large bowl, combine the stuffing, onion, sweet peppers and seasonings. Add the eggs, corn and butter; toss to coat. Stir in enough broth to achieve desired moistness.
2. Spoon into a 3-qt. baking dish coated with cooking spray. Cover and bake at 350° for 25 minutes or until a thermometer inserted into the center reads 160°. Uncover; bake for 15-20 minutes longer or until golden brown.

Nutrition Facts: *¾ cup equals 190 calories, 8 g fat (4 g saturated fat), 55 mg cholesterol, 485 mg sodium, 26 g carbohydrate, 2 g fiber, 5 g protein.* **Diabetic Exchanges:** *2 starch, 1½ fat.*

Mexican Grits

PREP: 20 MIN. **BAKE:** 35 MIN. **MAKES:** 10 SERVINGS

- **4 cups 2% milk**
- **½ cup plus ⅓ cup butter, divided**
- **1 cup quick-cooking grits**
- **2 eggs**
- **1 can (11 ounces) Mexicorn, drained**
- **1 can (4 ounces) chopped green chilies**
- **1 cup (4 ounces) shredded Mexican cheese blend**
- **1 teaspoon salt**
- **¼ teaspoon white pepper**
- **1 cup shredded Parmesan cheese**

1. In a large saucepan, bring milk and ½ cup butter to a boil. Slowly stir in grits. Reduce heat; cook and stir for 5-7 minutes.
2. In a small bowl, whisk the eggs. Stir a small amount of hot grits into the eggs; return all to the pan, stirring constantly. Melt the remaining butter; stir into grits. Add the corn, chilies, cheese, salt and pepper.
3. Transfer to a greased 2-qt. baking dish. Sprinkle with Parmesan cheese. Bake, uncovered, at 350° for 35-40 minutes or until a knife inserted near the center comes out clean.

“I grew up on grits and have fixed them in various ways. I decided to put a new twist on them with this recipe, and my husband says it's a keeper. Even the leftovers are good.”

—BARBARA MOORHEAD GAFFNEY, SOUTH CAROLINA

Crab Cake-Stuffed Portobellos

Served as an appetizer, side dish or a light entree, these stuffed mushrooms are pretty and delicious. Canned crabmeat becomes absolutely elegant.

—JENNIFER CODUTO KENT, OHIO

PREP/TOTAL TIME: 30 MIN.
MAKES: 6 SERVINGS

- **6 large portobello mushrooms**
- **¾ cup finely chopped sweet onion**
- **2 tablespoons olive oil, divided**
- **1 package (8 ounces) cream cheese, softened**
- **1 egg**
- **½ cup seasoned bread crumbs**
- **½ cup plus 1 teaspoon grated Parmesan cheese, divided**
- **1 teaspoon seafood seasoning**
- **2 cans (6½ ounces each) lump crabmeat, drained**
- **¼ teaspoon paprika**

1. Remove stems from mushrooms (discard or save for another use); set caps aside. In a small skillet, saute onion in 1 tablespoon oil until tender. In a small bowl, combine the cream cheese, egg, bread crumbs, ½ cup cheese and seafood seasoning. Gently stir in crab and onion.
2. Spoon ½ cup crab mixture into each mushroom cap; drizzle with remaining oil. Sprinkle with paprika and remaining cheese. Place in a greased 15-in. x 10-in. x 1-in. baking pan.
3. Bake, uncovered, at 400° for 15-20 minutes or until mushrooms are tender.

HOW TO CLEAN A MUSHROOM

First, gently remove any dirt from the mushroom. You could rub it with a mushroom brush, wipe it with a damp paper towel or rinse the mushroom quickly under cold water, drain and pat dry with paper towels. Once it's clean, trim the mushroom's stem and any bruised flesh.

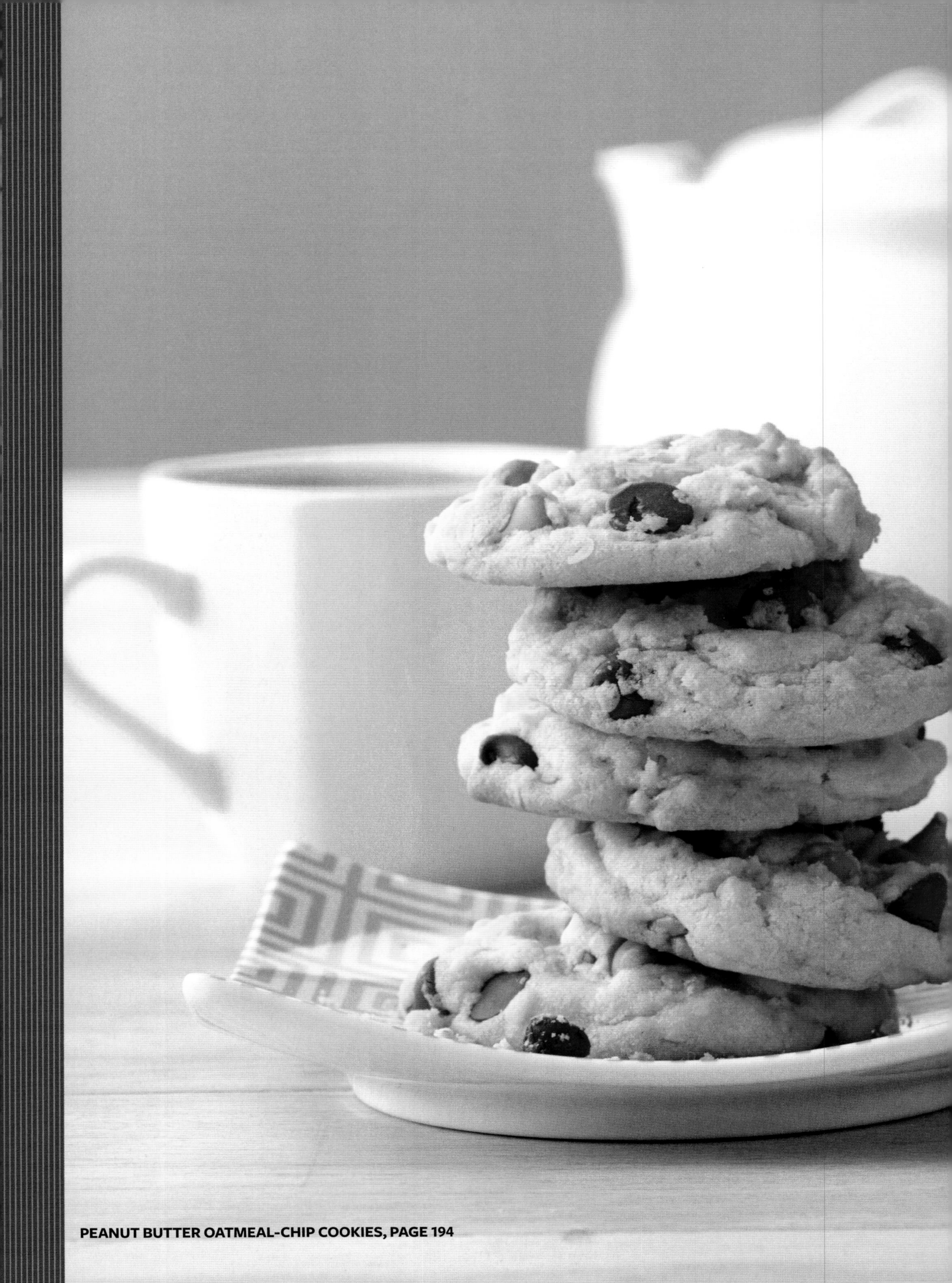
PEANUT BUTTER OATMEAL-CHIP COOKIES, PAGE 194

Cookies, Bars & Candy

For **simple prep, easy gift-giving, delightful holiday fun** or just a bit of love to tuck into a lunch box, try any one of the **irresistible little sweets** on the following pages.

Black Cat Brownie

My mom made this treat for my brother and me every Halloween as we were growing up. Now my daughter enjoys it each year, too. It's so easy to make and a fun tradition to pass on.

—JANICE KORSMEYER HIGHLAND, ILLINOIS

PREP: 25 MIN. **BAKE:** 20 MIN. + COOLING **MAKES:** 20 SERVINGS

- **1 package fudge brownie mix (13-inch x 9-inch pan size)**
- **1 can (16 ounces) chocolate frosting**
- **2 large yellow gumdrops**
- **1 large green gumdrop**
- **1 large black gumdrop**
- **2 pieces black shoestring licorice**
- **6 candy corns**

1. Line two 9-in. round baking pans with parchment paper; coat with cooking spray and set aside.

2. Prepare brownie mix batter according to package directions. Pour into prepared pans. Bake at 350° for 20-25 minutes or until a toothpick comes out clean. Cool for 10 minutes before removing from pans to wire racks to cool completely; remove parchment paper.

3. For cat's body, place one brownie circle on a covered board. From one side of the remaining brownie, cut a 1-in.-wide crescent-shaped slice; position tail on board. From the center of the opposite side, measure 2¾ in. toward the center. Make a vertical cut, forming a small half circle; cut in half and trim if desired, forming two ears. Position brownie with the flat side against the cat's body; trim sides of brownie as needed, forming the head. Add the ears.

4. Frost cat. Flatten yellow gumdrops. Cut two thin rounds from green gumdrop; position yellow and green gumdrops for eyes. Press black gumdrop into frosting for nose. Cut licorice into desired lengths for whiskers and a mouth; press lightly into frosting. Arrange candy corns at base of cat for toes.

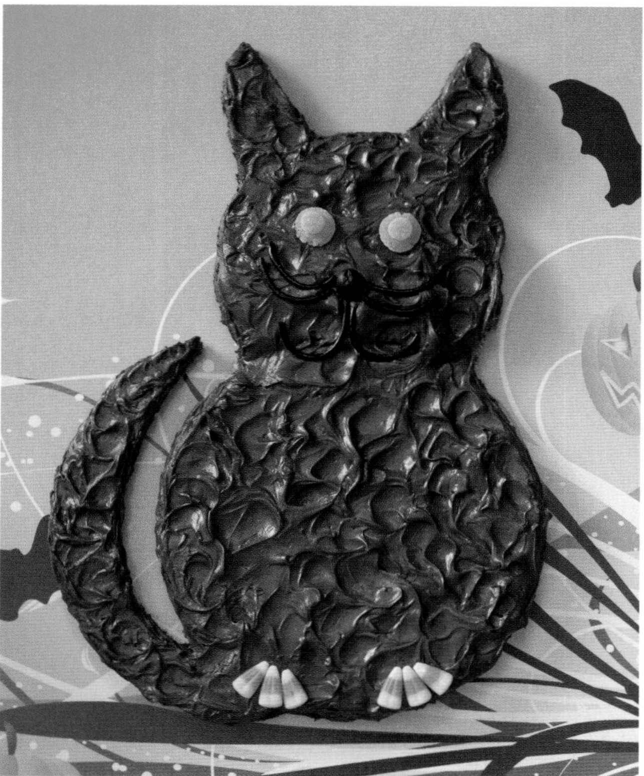

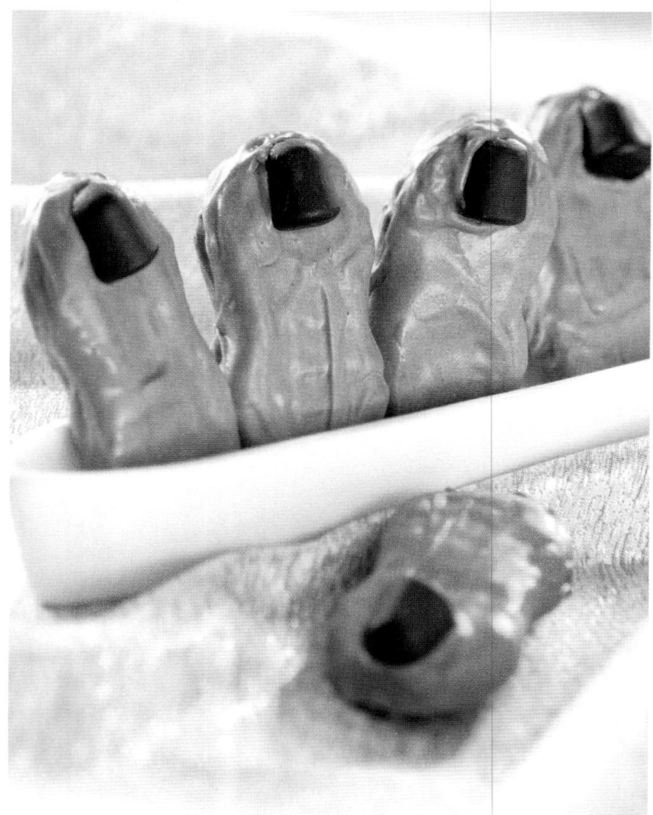

"With only four ingredients and no baking, my cute cookies will have you in and out of the kitchen in no time. Children will have fun helping attach the black candy toenails!"

—JAMEY JACKSON GILE, WISCONSIN

Gruesome Green Toes

PREP: 25 MIN. + STANDING **MAKES:** 22 COOKIES

- **12 ounces white candy coating, coarsely chopped**
- **Green paste food coloring**
- **22 Nutter Butter cookies**
- **11 Crows candies, halved lengthwise**

1. In a microwave, melt the candy coating; stir until smooth. Tint green.

2. Dip one cookie into candy coating. Let excess drip off; place cookie on waxed paper. Immediately place a candy half, cut side down, on the cookie. Repeat. Let stand for 15 minutes or until set.

Nutrition Facts: *1 cookie equals 155 calories, 7 g fat (5 g saturated fat), trace cholesterol, 52 mg sodium, 22 g carbohydrate, trace fiber, 1 g protein.* **Diabetic Exchanges:** *1½ starch, 1 fat.*

Ghostly Graveyard

I came up with this idea for my youngest daughter's October birthday. Then my son requested it for a school treat. But I knew it was a hit when my oldest daughter took it to a class Halloween party and even her teacher asked for the recipe!

—ANGIE DIERIKX TAYLOR RIDGE, ILLINOIS

PREP: 30 MIN. **COOK:** 10 MIN.
MAKES: 12 SERVINGS

- **4 cups miniature marshmallows**
- **¼ cup butter, cubed**
- **6 cups crisp rice cereal**
- **12 oval cream-filled chocolate sandwich cookies**
- **1 tube white decorating gel**
- **1 can (16 ounces) chocolate frosting**
- **Halloween sprinkles**

1. In a large saucepan, combine the marshmallows and butter. Cook and stir over medium-low heat until melted and blended. Remove from the heat; stir in cereal. Press into a greased 13-in. x 9-in. dish; cool.

2. Cut cooled bars into 12 squares and set aside.

3. Cut a ½-in. piece from the bottom of each sandwich cookie. Crush removed cookie pieces; set aside. Write "RIP" on each cookie, using white decorating gel.

4. Position the cereal squares on a large serving tray. With 2 tablespoons frosting, form a circle on each cereal square; top each with a decorated cookie.

5. Sprinkle reserved cookie crumbs around the tombstones and top with Halloween sprinkles.

SPOOKY PARTY PUNCH

Hosting a Halloween party? You can make a tasty black punch by mixing grape and orange Kool-Aid. I like to use the unsweetened kind.

—MERRILL P. SPEARVILLE, KANSAS

Coconut Clouds

Coconut lovers will have reason to celebrate when they taste these cake-like drop cookies. The generous frosting and toasted coconut topping make these gems a hit at holiday cookie parties.

—DONNA SCOFIELD YAKIMA, WASHINGTON

PREP: 45 MIN. **BAKE:** 10 MIN./BATCH + COOLING
MAKES: ABOUT 5½ DOZEN

- **¼ cup butter, softened**
- **¼ cup shortening**
- **1 cup sugar**
- **½ cup packed brown sugar**
- **2 eggs**
- **1 teaspoon coconut extract**
- **1 teaspoon vanilla extract**
- **1 cup (8 ounces) sour cream**
- **2¾ cups all-purpose flour**
- **1 teaspoon salt**
- **½ teaspoon baking soda**
- **1 cup flaked coconut, toasted**

FROSTING

- **⅓ cup butter, cubed**
- **3 cups confectioners' sugar**
- **3 tablespoons evaporated milk**
- **1 teaspoon coconut extract**
- **1 teaspoon vanilla extract**
- **2 cups flaked coconut, toasted**

1. In a large bowl, cream the butter, shortening and sugars until light and fluffy. Beat in eggs and extracts. Stir in sour cream. Combine the flour, salt and baking soda; gradually add to creamed mixture and mix well. Fold in coconut.
2. Drop by tablespoonfuls 2 in. apart onto lightly greased baking sheets. Bake at 375° for 8-10 minutes or until set. Remove to wire racks to cool.
3. In a small heavy saucepan, heat butter over medium heat for 5-7 minutes or until golden brown. Pour into a small bowl; beat in the confectioners' sugar, milk and extracts.
4. Frost cookies; dip in coconut. Let stand until completely dry. Store in an airtight container.

Nutrition Facts: *1 cookie equals 110 calories, 5 g fat (3 g saturated fat), 13 mg cholesterol, 72 mg sodium, 16 g carbohydrate, trace fiber, 1 g protein.*

Christmas Mice Cookies

These whimsical little mice taste like truffles, have been a family favorite for years and bring lots of laughs and smiles. Every Christmas, we make sure to have enough for friends, neighbors and get-togethers.

—DEBORAH ZABOR FORT ERIE, ONTARIO

PREP: 30 MIN. + CHILLING **MAKES:** 1½ DOZEN

- **⅔ cup semisweet chocolate chips**
- **2 cups chocolate wafer crumbs, divided**
- **⅓ cup sour cream**
- **36 red nonpareils**
- **¼ cup sliced almonds**
- **18 pieces black shoestring licorice (2 inches each)**

1. In a microwave, melt chocolate chips; stir until smooth. Stir in 1 cup crumbs and sour cream. Cover and refrigerate mixture for 1 hour or until easy to handle.
2. For each mouse, roll about 1 tablespoon chocolate mixture into a ball, tapering one end to resemble a mouse. Roll in remaining wafer crumbs to coat. Position nonpareils for eyes, almond slices for ears and licorice pieces for tails.

Nutrition Facts: *1 cookie equals 135 calories, 5 g fat (2 g saturated fat), 3 mg cholesterol, 89 mg sodium, 22 g carbohydrate, 1 g fiber, 2 g protein.* **Diabetic Exchanges:** *1½ starch, ½ fat.*

Apricot Bars

I created this recipe one winter's day and shared it with a good friend. Since then, I've had many favorable comments from those who have sampled it. Great apricot flavor and a sprinkling of coconut make these bars special.

—BARBARA ROHLF SPIRIT LAKE, IOWA

PREP: 25 MIN. **BAKE:** 25 MIN. + COOLING **MAKES:** 2 DOZEN

- **1 package (16 ounces) pound cake mix**
- **4 eggs**
- **½ cup butter, melted**
- **2 teaspoons vanilla extract, divided**
- **1 cup chopped dried apricots**
- **1 package (8 ounces) cream cheese, softened**
- **2 cups confectioners' sugar**
- **½ cup apricot preserves**
- **¾ cup flaked coconut**
- **¾ cup sliced almonds**

1. In a large bowl, combine the cake mix, 2 eggs, butter and 1 teaspoon vanilla; beat until well blended. Fold in dried apricots. Spread into a greased 15-in. x 10-in. x 1-in. baking pan; set aside.
2. In another bowl, beat the cream cheese, confectioners' sugar, preserves and remaining vanilla. Add remaining eggs; beat on low speed just until combined. Gently spread over cake batter. Sprinkle with coconut and almonds.
3. Bake at 350° for 25-30 minutes or until golden brown. Cool on a wire rack. Cut into bars. Refrigerate leftovers.

Chocolate-Cherry Cheesecake Bars

My luscious bars are wonderful for Christmas, Valentine's Day or any occasion that calls for a bite-size celebration. I've had the recipe longer than I can remember.

—DARLENE BRENDEN SALEM, OREGON

PREP: 20 MIN. **BAKE:** 20 MIN. + CHILLING **MAKES:** 15 BARS

- **1 cup all-purpose flour**
- **½ cup packed brown sugar**
- **⅓ cup cold butter, cubed**
- **½ cup finely chopped walnuts**
- **1 package (8 ounces) cream cheese, softened**
- **½ cup sugar**
- **⅓ cup baking cocoa**
- **1 egg, lightly beaten**
- **¼ cup 2% milk**
- **½ teaspoon vanilla extract**
- **½ cup chopped maraschino cherries**
- **Additional maraschino cherries, halved**

1. Place the flour, brown sugar and butter in a food processor; cover and process until fine crumbs form. Stir in walnuts. Set aside ¾ cup for topping.
2. Press remaining crumb mixture onto the bottom of an ungreased 8-in. square baking dish. Bake the crust at 350° for 10 minutes or until set.
3. Meanwhile, in a small bowl, beat the cream cheese, sugar and cocoa until smooth. Add the egg, milk and vanilla; beat on low speed just until combined. Stir in chopped cherries. Pour over crust; sprinkle with reserved crumb mixture.
4. Bake for 20-25 minutes or until center is almost set. Cool on a wire rack for 1 hour. Refrigerate for at least 2 hours.
5. Cut into bars; top each with a cherry half. Store in the refrigerator.

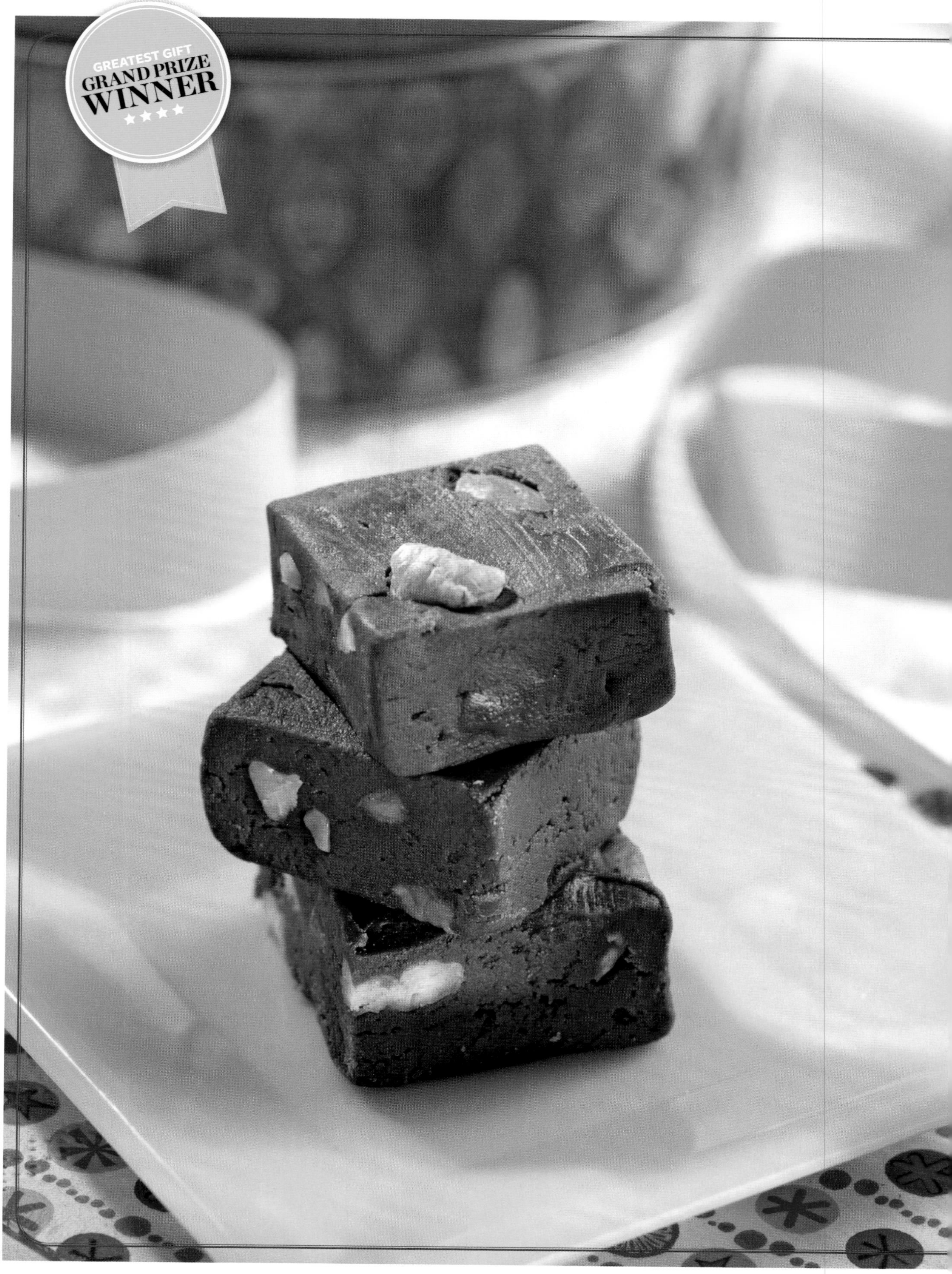
GREATEST GIFT
GRAND PRIZE
WINNER

GRAND PRIZE

Pecan Toffee Fudge

My fudge is always popular wherever I take it, and it makes great gifts for loved ones and friends. The toffee bits add a special touch. And it's so easy, even young children can help make it—with a little supervision!

—**DIANE WILLEY** BOZMAN, MARYLAND

PREP: 20 MIN. + CHILLING **MAKES:** 2½ POUNDS

- **1 teaspoon butter**
- **1 package (8 ounces) cream cheese, softened**
- **3¾ cups confectioners' sugar**
- **6 ounces unsweetened chocolate, melted and cooled**
- **¼ teaspoon almond extract**
- **Dash salt**
- **¼ cup coarsely chopped pecans**
- **¼ cup English toffee bits**

1. Line a 9-in. square pan with foil and grease the foil with butter; set aside. In a large bowl, beat cream cheese until fluffy. Gradually beat in confectioners' sugar. Beat in the melted chocolate, extract and salt until smooth. Stir in pecans and toffee bits.

2. Spread into prepared pan. Cover and refrigerate overnight or until firm. Using foil, lift fudge out of pan. Gently peel off foil; cut fudge into 1-in. squares. Store in an airtight container in the refrigerator.

Nutrition Facts: *1 piece equals 49 calories, 3 g fat (1 g saturated fat), 3 mg cholesterol, 15 mg sodium, 7 g carbohydrate, trace fiber, 1 g protein.* **Diabetic Exchanges:** *½ starch, ½ fat.*

FOIL-LINED PANS GIVE PERFECT RESULTS

Lining a pan with foil allows you to lift cooled fudge out of the pan in one piece. This makes it easy and quick to cut the candy into uniform pieces with nice, clean edges. You also avoid scratching or damaging your pan.

Line the pan with a piece of foil that extends over all sides. Press foil firmly into the bottom edges and corners to ensure the fudge will have a neat appearance. Lightly grease the foil with butter or use nonstick cooking spray.

When the candy is firm, grasp the foil on opposite sides and gently lift the fudge out of the pan. Place it on a cutting board, discard the foil and cut the candy into small squares.

Peanut Butter Clusters

PREP: 20 MIN. + CHILLING **MAKES:** ABOUT 3½ DOZEN

- **2 cups peanut butter chips**
- **1 cup milk chocolate chips**
- **1½ cups dry roasted peanuts**
- **1 cup crushed ridged potato chips**

1. In a microwave-safe bowl, melt peanut butter chips and chocolate chips; stir until smooth. Stir in the peanuts and potato chips.

2. Drop by level tablespoonfuls onto waxed paper-lined baking sheets. Refrigerate until firm. Store the candy in an airtight container.

Nutrition Facts: *1 piece equals 96 calories, 6 g fat (2 g saturated fat), 1 mg cholesterol, 70 mg sodium, 8 g carbohydrate, 1 g fiber, 3 g protein.* **Diabetic Exchanges:** *1 fat, ½ starch.*

"Four ingredients and 20 minutes make for one fabulous treat! This chocolate-coated crunch also freezes well, so try keeping some on hand."

—**PAT MAXWELL** TAFT, CALIFORNIA

Santa Claus Cutouts

Santa turns out to be a handsome fellow when I use my favorite cutout cookie recipe. Painting on the candy coating allows for detailed decorating. My 14 shoe boxes of shaped cutters are a testament to how much I enjoy making cookies.

—**JANE BROWN** GREENSBURG, INDIANA

PREP: 30 MIN. + CHILLING **BAKE:** 10 MIN./BATCH + COOLING
MAKES: ABOUT 3 DOZEN

- **1 cup butter, softened**
- **1 package (3 ounces) cream cheese, softened**
- **1 cup sugar**
- **1 egg**
- **1 teaspoon vanilla extract**
- **2½ cups all-purpose flour**
- **¼ teaspoon salt**
- **White, red and blue candy coating disks**

1. In a large bowl, cream the butter, cream cheese and sugar until light and fluffy. Beat in egg and vanilla. Combine flour and salt; gradually add to creamed mixture and mix well. Cover and refrigerate for 1-2 hours or until firm.

2. On a lightly floured surface, roll out dough to ¼-in. thickness. Cut with a floured 3-in. Santa cookie cutter. Place 1 in. apart on greased baking sheets. Bake at 375° for 6-8 minutes or until edges are lightly browned. Cool for 1 minute before removing to wire racks to cool completely.

3. Melt white candy coating; using a clean new paintbrush, add a beard, mustache, eyebrows, hat brim and pom-pom to each Santa. Melt red coating; add hat, nose and mouth. Melt blue coating; add eyes. Let stand until set. Store cookies in an airtight container.

Oatmeal Cranberry Cookie Mix

Who wouldn't want to find a jar of this simply delicious cookie mix, loaded with cranberries and walnuts, under the Christmas tree? Be sure to include a list of added ingredients and instructions for baking. Yum!

—**SARAH WILSON** REPUBLIC, WASHINGTON

PREP: 15 MIN. **BAKE:** 10 MIN./BATCH **MAKES:** ABOUT 2½ DOZEN

- **½ cup all-purpose flour**
- **¼ teaspoon baking soda**
- **¼ teaspoon salt**
- **¼ cup sugar**
- **¼ cup packed brown sugar**
- **1 cup old-fashioned oats**
- **1 cup chopped walnuts**
- **½ cup Shredded Wheat, crushed**
- **½ cup dried cranberries**

ADDITIONAL INGREDIENTS

- **½ cup butter, softened**
- **1 egg**
- **2 tablespoons water**
- **½ teaspoon vanilla extract**

1. In a small bowl, combine the flour, baking soda and salt. In a 1-qt. glass container, layer the flour mixture, sugar, brown sugar, oats, walnuts, cereal and cranberries. Cover and store in a cool dry place for up to 6 months. **Yield:** 1 batch (about 4 cups total).

To prepare cookies: *In a large bowl, beat the butter, egg, water and vanilla until blended. Add cookie mix and mix well. Drop by rounded tablespoonfuls 2 in. apart onto ungreased baking sheets. Bake at 350° for 10-12 minutes or until golden brown. Cool for 1 minute before removing from pans to wire racks. Store in an airtight container.*

Nutrition Facts: *1 cookie equals 89 calories, 5 g fat (2 g saturated fat), 14 mg cholesterol, 51 mg sodium, 9 g carbohydrate, 1 g fiber, 2 g protein.* **Diabetic Exchanges:** *1 fat, ½ starch.*

Pretzel Cereal Crunch

PREP: 20 MIN. + COOLING **MAKES:** ABOUT 9 CUPS

- **1¼ cups Golden Grahams**
- **1¼ cups Apple Cinnamon Cheerios**
- **1¼ cups miniature pretzels**
- **1 cup chopped pecans, toasted**
- **1 package (10 to 12 ounces) white baking chips**
- **2 tablespoons creamy peanut butter**

1. In a large bowl, combine the cereals, pretzels and pecans.
2. In a microwave-safe bowl, melt chips; stir until smooth. Stir in peanut butter. Drizzle over cereal mixture; toss to coat.
3. Spread evenly on a waxed paper-lined baking sheet. Cool candy completely, then break into pieces. Store candy in an airtight container.

Nutrition Facts: *½ cup equals 190 calories, 12 g fat (4 g saturated fat), 3 mg cholesterol, 105 mg sodium, 19 g carbohydrate, 1 g fiber, 3 g protein.*

"A fancy container of this salty-sweet treat was left in my mailbox several Christmases ago—and disappeared in a heartbeat! My neighbor also shared the quick and easy recipe. I've since added peanut butter because I love the flavor."

—**CINDY LUND** VALLEY CENTER, CALIFORNIA

Peppermint Meltaways

These minty little bites look so pretty and festive on a holiday cookie platter. I often cover a plate with red or green plastic wrap and tuck a bright bow in one corner. And yes, they really do melt in your mouth!

—**DENISE WHEELER** NEWAYGO, MICHIGAN

PREP: 30 MIN. **BAKE:** 10 MIN./BATCH + COOLING
MAKES: 3½ DOZEN

- **1 cup butter, softened**
- **½ cup confectioners' sugar**
- **½ teaspoon peppermint extract**
- **1¼ cups all-purpose flour**
- **½ cup cornstarch**

FROSTING

- **2 tablespoons butter, softened**
- **1½ cups confectioners' sugar**
- **2 tablespoons 2% milk**
- **¼ teaspoon peppermint extract**
- **2 to 3 drops red food coloring, optional**
- **½ cup crushed peppermint candies**

1. In a small bowl, cream butter and confectioners' sugar until light and fluffy. Beat in extract. Combine flour and cornstarch; gradually add to creamed mixture and mix well.
2. Shape into 1-in. balls. Place 2 in. apart on ungreased baking sheets. Bake at 350° for 10-12 minutes or until bottoms are lightly browned. Remove to wire racks to cool.
3. In a small bowl, beat butter until fluffy. Add confectioners' sugar, milk, extract and food coloring if desired; beat until smooth. Spread over cooled cookies; sprinkle with crushed candies. Store in an airtight container.

Nutrition Facts: *1 cookie equals 90 calories, 5 g fat (3 g saturated fat), 13 mg cholesterol, 36 mg sodium, 11 g carbohydrate, trace fiber, trace protein.* **Diabetic Exchanges:** *1 fat, ½ starch.*

Raspberry Coconut Bars

I've been whipping up these delicious bars for years, recently with help from my young daughter. I bake them every Christmas and always receive many compliments and recipe requests. The chocolate toppings create such a lovely lacy effect.

—**BARB BOVBERG** FORT COLLINS, COLORADO

PREP: 20 MIN. **BAKE:** 20 MIN. + CHILLING **MAKES:** 3 DOZEN

- **1⅔ cups graham cracker crumbs**
- **½ cup butter, melted**
- **2⅔ cups flaked coconut**
- **1 can (14 ounces) sweetened condensed milk**
- **1 cup seedless raspberry preserves**
- **⅓ cup chopped walnuts, toasted**
- **½ cup semisweet chocolate chips**
- **¼ cup white baking chips**

1. In a small bowl, combine cracker crumbs and butter. Press into a 13-in. x 9-in. baking dish coated with cooking spray. Sprinkle with coconut; drizzle with milk.

2. Bake at 350° for 20-25 minutes or until lightly browned. Cool completely on a wire rack.

3. Spread preserves over crust. Sprinkle with walnuts. In a microwave, melt chocolate chips; stir until smooth. Drizzle over walnuts. Repeat with white chips. Cut into bars. Refrigerate for 30 minutes or until chocolate is set.

Nutrition Facts: *1 piece equals 155 calories, 8 g fat (5 g saturated fat), 11 mg cholesterol, 83 mg sodium, 20 g carbohydrate, 1 g fiber, 2 g protein.*

GRAND PRIZE

Double-Drizzle Pecan Cookies

Here's a recipe for chewy pecan treats that are a must with my cookie munchers every holiday. Caramel and chocolate drizzle make them doubly delicious and so pretty on the cookie plate.

—**PAULA MARCHESI** LENHARTSVILLE, PENNSYLVANIA

PREP: 25 MIN. **BAKE:** 10 MIN./BATCH + COOLING
MAKES: ABOUT 3½ DOZEN

- **½ cup butter, softened**
- **1½ cups packed brown sugar**
- **1 egg**
- **1 teaspoon vanilla extract**
- **1½ cups all-purpose flour**
- **1½ teaspoons baking powder**
- **¼ teaspoon salt**
- **1¼ cups chopped pecans**

CARAMEL DRIZZLE

- **½ cup packed brown sugar**
- **¼ cup heavy whipping cream**
- **½ cup confectioners' sugar**

CHOCOLATE DRIZZLE

- **1 ounce semisweet chocolate, chopped**
- **1 tablespoon butter**

1. In a large bowl, cream butter and brown sugar until light and fluffy. Beat in egg and vanilla. Combine the flour, baking powder and salt; gradually add to the creamed mixture and mix well.

2. Shape dough into 1-in. balls; roll in pecans. Place 2 in. apart on ungreased baking sheets; flatten slightly. Bake at 350° for 8-10 minutes or until lightly browned. Cool for 2 minutes before removing to wire racks to cool completely.

3. In a small saucepan, bring brown sugar and cream to a boil. Remove from the heat; whisk in confectioners' sugar. Immediately drizzle over cookies.

4. In a microwave, melt chocolate and butter; stir until smooth. Drizzle over cookies. Let stand until set. Store in an airtight container.

Nutrition Facts: *1 cookie equals 118 calories, 6 g fat (2 g saturated fat), 13 mg cholesterol, 52 mg sodium, 16 g carbohydrate, 1 g fiber, 1 g protein.*

IRRESISTIBLE BAKE-SALE BUY

Taking your favorite cookies to a bake sale? Thoughtful packaging can increase sales and help set your cookies apart. Consider wrapping some cookies in pairs with their bottoms together at once price point. Wrap others in short stacks of four or six as an option for bake sale customers who don't need a dozen or who might want to try a few of each kind. This is also great for those who want a snack right away!

SANTA'S FAVORITE COOKIES
GRAND PRIZE WINNER

White Chocolate Raspberry Thumbprints

When I pass around the cookie tray, all eyes land on these fancy thumbprints. The white chocolate filling and dab of jewel-toned jam will satisfy the most discriminating sweet tooth.

—**AGNES WARD** STRATFORD, ONTARIO

PREP: 25 MIN. + CHILLING **BAKE:** 10 MIN./BATCH + COOLING
MAKES: ABOUT 3 DOZEN

- **¾ cup butter, softened**
- **½ cup packed brown sugar**
- **2 eggs, separated**
- **1¼ cups all-purpose flour**
- **¼ cup baking cocoa**
- **1¼ cups finely chopped pecans or walnuts**

FILLING

- **4 ounces white baking chocolate, coarsely chopped**
- **2 tablespoons butter**
- **¼ cup seedless raspberry jam**

1. In a large bowl, cream butter and brown sugar until light and fluffy. Beat in egg yolks. Combine flour and cocoa; gradually add to creamed mixture and mix well. Cover and refrigerate for 1-2 hours or until easy to handle.
2. In a shallow bowl, whisk egg whites until foamy. Place nuts in another shallow bowl. Shape dough into 1-in. balls. Dip in egg whites, then roll in nuts.
3. Using a wooden spoon handle, make an indentation in center of each cookie. Place 1 in. apart on greased baking sheets. Bake at 350° for 8-10 minutes or until set. Remove to wire racks to cool.
4. In a microwave, melt white chocolate and butter; stir until smooth. Spoon about 1/2 teaspoon into each cookie. Top each with about 1/4 teaspoon jam. Store in an airtight container.

Browned-Butter Sandwich Spritz

A heavenly sweet maple filling sets these scrumptious spritz cookies apart. You can count on them to come out buttery and tender. They're almost too pretty to eat.

—**DEIRDRE DEE COX** KANSAS CITY, KANSAS

PREP: 50 MIN. + CHILLING **BAKE:** 10 MIN./BATCH + COOLING
MAKES: ABOUT 3 DOZEN

- **1 cup plus 2 tablespoons butter, cubed**
- **1¼ cups confectioners' sugar, divided**
- **1 egg**
- **1 egg yolk**
- **2 teaspoons vanilla extract**
- **2¼ cups all-purpose flour**
- **½ teaspoon salt**
- **½ cup maple syrup**

1. In a small heavy saucepan, cook and stir butter over medium heat for 8-10 minutes or until golden brown. Transfer to a small bowl; refrigerate until firm, about 1 hour.
2. Set aside 2 tablespoons browned butter for filling. In a large bowl, beat 1/2 cup confectioners' sugar and remaining browned butter until smooth. Beat in the egg, yolk and vanilla. Combine flour and salt; gradually add to creamed mixture and mix well.
3. Using a cookie press fitted with the disk of your choice, press dough 2 in. apart onto parchment paper-lined baking sheets. Bake at 375° for 8-9 minutes or until set (do not brown). Remove to wire racks to cool.
4. In a small heavy saucepan, bring syrup to a boil. Cool slightly. Whisk in remaining confectioners' sugar until smooth. Beat reserved browned butter until light and fluffy. Beat in syrup mixture until smooth.
5. Spread 1 teaspoon of filling over the bottom of half of the cookies. Top with remaining cookies.

Vanilla Walnut Crescents

My friends look forward to receiving these crescents as a gift. The pastry is tender and flaky, and the vanilla flavor comes through beautifully. It's my all-time favorite cookie!

—BETTY LAWTON PENNINGTON, NEW JERSEY

PREP: 30 MIN. + CHILLING **BAKE:** 20 MIN./BATCH
MAKES: 3 DOZEN

- **2 cups all-purpose flour**
- **⅛ teaspoon salt**
- **1 cup cold butter, cubed**
- **1 egg, separated**
- **⅔ cup sour cream**
- **½ teaspoon vanilla extract**
- **⅔ cup finely chopped walnuts**
- **⅔ cup sugar**
- **1 teaspoon ground cinnamon**

1. In a large bowl, combine flour and salt; cut in butter until mixture resembles coarse crumbs. In a small bowl, whisk the egg yolk, sour cream and vanilla; add to crumb mixture and mix well. Cover and refrigerate for 4 hours or overnight.
2. Divide dough into thirds. On a lightly floured surface, roll each portion into a 10-in. circle. Combine the walnuts, sugar and cinnamon; sprinkle ¼ cup over each circle. Cut each circle into 12 wedges.
3. Roll up each wedge from the wide end and place point side down 1 in. apart on greased baking sheets. Curve ends to form crescents. Whisk egg white until foamy; brush over crescents. Sprinkle with remaining nut mixture.
4. Bake at 350° for 18-20 minutes or until lightly browned. Remove to wire racks to cool. Store in an airtight container.

Nutrition Facts: *1 cookie equals 110 calories, 7 g fat (4 g saturated fat), 22 mg cholesterol, 48 mg sodium, 10 g carbohydrate, trace fiber, 1 g protein.*

Dipped Cherry Cookies

Our children and grandchildren declared this festive, flavorful cookie to be a keeper. We gave a batch to our mail carrier to thank her for trudging through so much snow, and she requested the recipe!

—RUTH ANNE DALE TITUSVILLE, PENNSYLVANIA

PREP: 30 MIN. **BAKE:** 10 MIN./BATCH + STANDING
MAKES: ABOUT 4 DOZEN

- **2½ cups all-purpose flour**
- **¾ cup sugar, divided**
- **1 cup cold butter, cubed**
- **½ cup finely chopped maraschino cherries, patted dry**
- **12 ounces white baking chocolate, finely chopped, divided**
- **½ teaspoon almond extract**
- **2 teaspoons shortening**
- **Coarse sugar and red edible glitter**

1. In a large bowl, combine flour and ½ cup sugar; cut in butter until crumbly. Knead in the cherries, ⅔ cup chopped white chocolate and extract until dough forms a ball.
2. Shape into ¾-in. balls. Place 2 in. apart on ungreased baking sheets. Flatten slightly with a glass dipped in remaining sugar. Bake at 325° for 10-12 minutes or until edges are lightly browned. Remove to wire racks to cool completely.
3. In a microwave, melt shortening and remaining white chocolate; stir until smooth.
4. Dip half of each cookie into chocolate; allow excess to drip off. Place on waxed paper; sprinkle with coarse sugar and edible glitter. Let stand until set. Store in an airtight container.

Editor's Note: *Edible glitter is available from Wilton Industries. Call 800-794-5866 or visit wilton.com.*

Nutrition Facts: *1 cookie equals 108 calories, 6 g fat (4 g saturated fat), 11 mg cholesterol, 34 mg sodium, 12 g carbohydrate, trace fiber, 1 g protein.*

Triple-Chocolate Peppermint Treats

Santa is sure to stop by your house if you leave these minty chocolate cookies waiting for him! They're quick and easy for the whole family to make together.

—**TERESA RALSTON** NEW ALBANY, OHIO

PREP: 40 MIN.
BAKE: 10 MIN./BATCH + COOLING
MAKES: ABOUT 6½ DOZEN

- **1 cup butter, softened**
- **1 cup packed brown sugar**
- **½ cup sugar**
- **2 eggs**
- **2 teaspoons vanilla extract**
- **2½ cups all-purpose flour**
- **¾ cup baking cocoa**
- **1 teaspoon salt**
- **1 teaspoon baking soda**
- **1 cup (6 ounces) semisweet chocolate chips**
- **½ cup 60% cacao bittersweet chocolate baking chips**

WHITE CHOCOLATE FROSTING

- **½ cup white baking chips**
- **4 ounces cream cheese, softened**
- **3 cups confectioners' sugar**
- **⅓ to ½ cup crushed peppermint candies**

1. In a large bowl, cream butter and sugars until light and fluffy. Beat in eggs and vanilla. Combine the flour, cocoa, salt and baking soda; gradually add to creamed mixture and mix well. Stir in the chocolate chips.

2. Drop by rounded teaspoonfuls 2 in. apart onto ungreased baking sheets. Bake at 375° for 8-10 minutes or until set. Cool for 2 minutes before removing to wire racks to cool completely.

3. In a microwave, melt baking chips; stir until smooth. Cool.

4. In a small bowl, beat cream cheese and confectioners' sugar until smooth. Beat in melted chips. Frost cookies; sprinkle with peppermint candies.

Pecan Shortbread Diamonds

My mother and I used to make these rich, buttery shortbread cookies every year for holiday gift-giving. With a hint of chocolate and a chewy pecan filling, they are exceptionally good. The diamond shape adds a special touch.

—JANE ELLEN BENROTH BLUFFTON, OHIO

PREP: 40 MIN. **BAKE:** 20 MIN. + COOLING **MAKES:** 5 DOZEN

- **¾ cup butter, softened**
- **½ cup confectioners' sugar**
- **2 cups all-purpose flour**
- **½ teaspoon salt**

FILLING

- **2 ounces unsweetened chocolate, chopped**
- **4 eggs**
- **1½ cups packed brown sugar**
- **2 teaspoons vanilla extract**
- **½ teaspoon salt**
- **3 cups chopped pecans**

1. In a large bowl, cream butter and confectioners' sugar until light and fluffy. Combine flour and salt; gradually add to creamed mixture and mix well. Press into an ungreased 15-in. x 10-in. x 1-in. baking pan. Bake at 375° for 12-15 minutes or until lightly browned. Cool for 5 minutes on a wire rack. Reduce temperature to 350°.

2. To make filling, in a microwave-safe bowl, melt chocolate; stir until smooth. Cool. In a large bowl, combine the eggs, brown sugar, vanilla, salt and melted chocolate; fold in pecans.

3. Pour filling over crust. Bake for 18-20 minutes or until filling is set. Cool completely on a wire rack. Cut into diamond-shaped bars.

Nutrition Facts: *1 piece equals 111 calories, 7 g fat (2 g saturated fat), 20 mg cholesterol, 63 mg sodium, 11 g carbohydrate, 1 g fiber, 2 g protein.* **Diabetic Exchanges:** *1 starch, 1 fat.*

Fluffy Lemon Squares

A few handy convenience items hurry along preparation of these bright-tasting lemon bars. They're not only fun to create with children, they're also delectable!

—JOYCE SPEERBRECHER GRAFTON, WISCONSIN

PREP: 25 MIN. + CHILLING **MAKES:** 12 SERVINGS

- **1½ cups crushed vanilla wafers (about 45 wafers)**
- **⅓ cup chopped pecans**
- **6 tablespoons butter, melted**
- **½ cup heavy whipping cream**
- **2 packages (3 ounces each) lemon gelatin**
- **1¼ cups boiling water**
- **1 package (3.4 ounces) instant lemon pudding mix**
- **1 pint lemon sherbet, softened**

1. In a small bowl, combine the wafer crumbs, pecans and butter; set aside ¼ cup for topping. Press remaining crumb mixture into an ungreased 11-in. x 7-in. dish. Refrigerate crust for 30 minutes.

2. Meanwhile, in a small bowl, beat cream until stiff peaks form; set aside. In a large bowl, dissolve gelatin in boiling water. Add pudding mix; beat on low speed for 2 minutes. Add sherbet; beat on low for 1 minute or until soft-set. Fold in whipped cream.

3. Spread over crust; sprinkle with reserved crumb mixture. Chill for 1 hour or until set. Refrigerate leftovers.

NUTS FOR BAKING

Since I use lots of nuts in my baking, I buy large bags from wholesale stores, pour them into freezer bags, label and store them in the freezer. When preparing a recipe, I just pour out the amount of nuts called for and put the rest back in the freezer.

—DORIS R. FALLSTON, MARYLAND

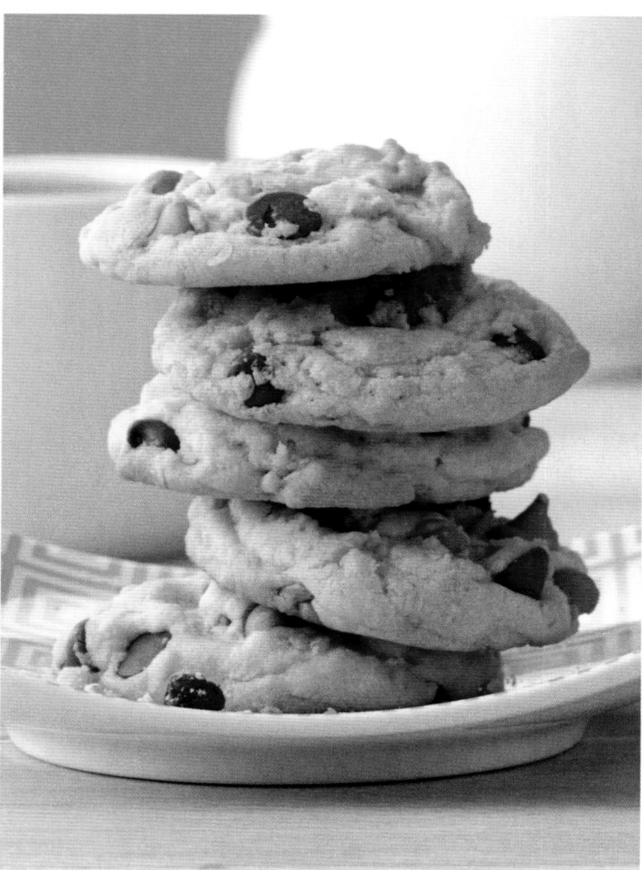

Peanut Butter Oatmeal-Chip Cookies

This cookie is my husband's favorite, my classes' favorite, my colleagues' favorite and, frankly, it's my favorite, too. It's just plain yummy. It also makes about 11 dozen...bake sale, here we come!

—DANA CHEW OKEMAH, OKLAHOMA

PREP: 35 MIN. **BAKE:** 10 MIN./BATCH **MAKES:** 11 DOZEN

- **2½ cups butter, softened**
- **2 cups sugar**
- **2 cups packed brown sugar**
- **½ cup creamy peanut butter**
- **4 eggs**
- **2 teaspoons vanilla extract**
- **6 cups all-purpose flour**
- **2 teaspoons salt**
- **2 teaspoons baking soda**
- **½ teaspoon baking powder**
- **1 package (12 ounces) semisweet chocolate chips**
- **1 package (11 ounces) peanut butter and milk chocolate chips**
- **1 cup quick-cooking oats**

1. In a large bowl, cream the butter, sugars and peanut butter until light and fluffy. Beat in eggs and vanilla. Combine the flour, salt, baking soda and baking powder; gradually add to creamed mixture and mix well.
2. Stir in the chips and oats. Drop by rounded tablespoonfuls 2 in. apart onto ungreased baking sheets. Bake at 375° for 9-12 minutes or until golden brown.
3. Cool for 2 minutes before removing from pans to wire racks. Store in an airtight container.

Slice 'n' Bake Lemon Gems

Rolled in colorful sprinkles, these melt-in-your-mouth cookies are pretty enough for any party.

—DELORES EDGECOMB ATLANTA, NEW YORK

PREP: 25 MIN. + CHILLING **BAKE:** 10 MIN./BATCH + COOLING **MAKES:** 28 COOKIES

- **¾ cup butter, softened**
- **½ cup confectioners' sugar**
- **1 tablespoon grated lemon peel**
- **1 cup all-purpose flour**
- **½ cup cornstarch**
- **¼ cup colored nonpareils**

LEMON ICING

- **1 cup confectioners' sugar**
- **2 tablespoons lemon juice**
- **½ teaspoon grated lemon peel**

1. In a small bowl, cream butter and confectioners' sugar until light and fluffy. Beat in lemon peel. Combine flour and cornstarch; gradually add to creamed mixture and mix well. Cover and refrigerate for 1 hour or until easy to handle.
2. Shape into a 1¾-in.-diameter roll; roll in nonpareils. Wrap in plastic wrap. Refrigerate for 2-3 hours or until firm.
3. Unwrap and cut into ¼-in. slices. Place 1 in. apart on ungreased baking sheets. Bake at 375° for 9-11 minutes or until set and edges are lightly browned. Cool for 1 minute before removing to wire racks to cool completely.
4. In a small bowl, beat icing ingredients until smooth. Spread over cookies.

Nutrition Facts: *1 cookie equals 102 calories, 5 g fat (3 g saturated fat), 13 mg cholesterol, 35 mg sodium, 13 g carbohydrate, trace fiber, 1 g protein.* **Diabetic Exchanges:** *1 starch, 1 fat.*

Hawaiian Turtle Cups

My mother-in-law loves macadamia nuts, and my daughter is partial to white chocolate. So I came up with this fun twist on classic turtle candy that incorporates both ingredients.

—**LARISA SARVER** LASALLE, ILLINOIS

PREP: 20 MIN. + CHILLING
MAKES: 1 DOZEN

- **1½ cups white baking chips**
- **½ cup macadamia nuts, chopped**
- **18 caramels**
- **2 teaspoons heavy whipping cream**
- **12 dried pineapple pieces, chopped**

1. In a microwave, melt white chips; stir until smooth. Pour by teaspoonfuls into greased miniature muffin cups until each muffin cup is about half full; set aside remaining melted chips. Sprinkle the center of each muffin cup with nuts.
2. In a microwave, melt caramels and cream; stir until smooth. Pour over nuts. Reheat reserved chips if necessary; pour over caramel mixture. Top each with pineapple.
3. Chill for 30 minutes or until set. Carefully run a knife around the edge of each muffin cup to loosen candy.

PRETTY PACKAGES

You don't have to spend a fortune or valuable time at the mall in search of that perfect gift. Quite often the most priceless treasures are your own homemade cookies and candies presented in decorative tins, baskets, papier-mache boxes, jars, plates or candy dishes. Another fun idea is to wrap cookies in plastic wrap, place a bow on top and tuck inside a pretty coffee mug or teacup.

LEMONY WHITE CHOCOLATE CHEESECAKE, PAGE 206

Cakes & Pies

Nothing crowns off a special occasion like **gorgeous, taste-tempting** cakes, cheesecakes, cupcakes and pies. No matter the time of year, you'll find **delightful new reasons to celebrate!**

Frozen Raspberry Cheesecake

I got this recipe from my sister years ago and like it for entertaining because I can make it ahead. It's fancy enough for special occasions but so easy to make with ingredients I usually have on hand. Try varying the juices and fruits.

—DONNA REAR RED DEER, ALBERTA

PREP: 20 MIN. + FREEZING **MAKES:** 12 SERVINGS

- **1½ cups Oreo cookie crumbs**
- **¼ cup butter, melted**
- **1 package (8 ounces) cream cheese, softened**
- **¾ cup confectioners' sugar**
- **1 package (10 ounces) frozen sweetened raspberries, thawed**
- **¾ cup cranberry-raspberry juice, divided**
- **1 teaspoon lemon juice**
- **2 cups heavy whipping cream, whipped**

1. Combine cookie crumbs and butter; press onto the bottom of an ungreased 9-in. springform pan. In a large bowl, beat cream cheese and confectioners' sugar until smooth. Beat in the raspberries, 1/2 cup cranberry-raspberry juice and lemon juice until blended. Fold in whipped cream. Pour onto crust.
2. Spoon remaining juice over cheesecake; cut through batter with a knife to swirl. Cover and freeze overnight. Remove from the freezer 15 minutes before serving.

Spiced Plum Pie

If you're craving some good comfort food, give this pie a try. Served warm and a la mode, it can't be beat!

—LUCILLE MEAD ILION, NEW YORK

PREP: 20 MIN. **BAKE:** 45 MIN. + COOLING **MAKES:** 8 SERVINGS

- **Pastry for double-crust pie (9 inches)**
- **4½ cups sliced fresh plums**
- **⅔ cup sugar**
- **¼ cup all-purpose flour**
- **1 teaspoon ground cinnamon**
- **¼ teaspoon salt**
- **¼ teaspoon ground nutmeg**
- **1 egg, lightly beaten**
- **½ cup orange juice**
- **1 teaspoon grated orange peel**
- **2 tablespoons butter**
- **Vanilla ice cream, optional**

1. Line a 9-in. pie plate with bottom pastry; trim even with edge. Arrange plums in crust. In a small bowl, combine the sugar, flour, cinnamon, salt and nutmeg. Stir in the egg, orange juice and peel. Pour over plums; dot with butter.
2. Roll out remaining pastry to fit top of pie; place over filling. Trim, seal and flute edges. Cut slits in pastry.
3. Bake at 400° for 45-50 minutes or until crust is golden brown and filling is bubbly (cover edges with foil during the last 15 minutes to prevent overbrowning if necessary). Cool on a wire rack for 10 minutes before cutting. Serve warm with ice cream if desired.

"This dessert is fancy and fun enough to make hamburgers and fries a meal to remember! It's so tall and pretty and just like eating a frozen banana split. Make it ahead to save time."

—**JOY COLLINS** BIRMINGHAM, ALABAMA

Frozen Banana Split Pie

PREP: 25 MIN. + FREEZING **MAKES:** 8 SERVINGS

- **3 tablespoons chocolate hard-shell ice cream topping**
- **1 graham cracker crust (9 inches)**
- **2 medium bananas, sliced**
- **½ teaspoon lemon juice**
- **½ cup pineapple ice cream topping**
- **1 quart strawberry ice cream, softened**
- **2 cups whipped topping**
- **½ cup chopped walnuts, toasted**
- **Chocolate syrup**
- **8 maraschino cherries with stems**

1. Pour chocolate topping into crust; freeze for 5 minutes or until chocolate is firm.
2. Meanwhile, place bananas in a small bowl; toss with lemon juice. Arrange bananas over chocolate topping. Layer with pineapple topping, ice cream, whipped topping and walnuts.
3. Cover and freeze until firm. Remove from the freezer 15 minutes before cutting. Garnish with chocolate syrup and maraschino cherries.

Chocolate Shoofly Pie

If you like traditional shoofly pie, I think you'll agree this chocolate version is even better! I sometimes serve it with vanilla ice cream, but it's just as good on its own.

—**GWEN BROUNCE WIDDOWSON** FLEETWOOD, PENNSYLVANIA

PREP: 20 MIN. **BAKE:** 45 MIN. + COOLING **MAKES:** 6-8 SERVINGS

- **Pastry for single-crust pie (9 inches)**
- **½ cup semisweet chocolate chips**
- **1½ cups all-purpose flour**
- **½ cup packed brown sugar**
- **3 tablespoons butter-flavored shortening**
- **1 teaspoon baking soda**
- **1½ cups water**
- **1 egg, lightly beaten**
- **1 cup molasses**

1. Line a 9-in. deep-dish pie plate with pastry. Trim to ½ in. beyond edge of plate; flute edges. Sprinkle chocolate chips into shell; set aside.
2. In a large bowl, combine flour and brown sugar; cut in shortening until crumbly. Set aside 1 cup for topping. Add the baking soda, water, egg and molasses to remaining crumb mixture and mix well. Pour over chips. Sprinkle with reserved crumb mixture.
3. Bake at 350° for 45-55 minutes or until a knife inserted near the center comes out clean. Cool the pie on a wire rack for 20 minutes before cutting. Serve warm.

MEASURING TRICK

I wipe a little bit of cooking oil inside my measuring cup when I'm making recipes that call for molasses or peanut butter. This keeps the sticky ingredients from clinging to the cup and makes cleanup a snap.

—**LYNN H.** ST. JOHN, NEW BRUNSWICK

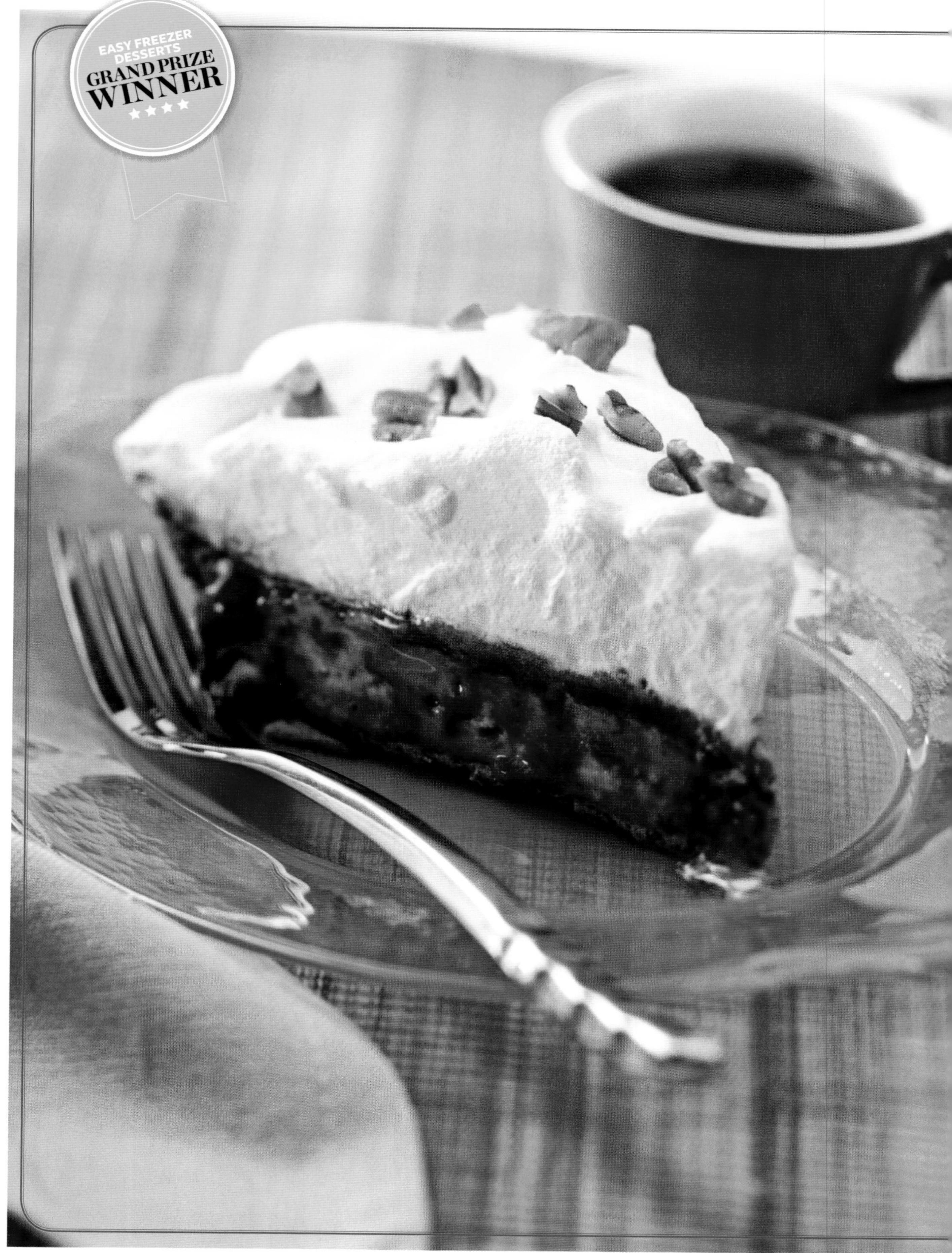
EASY FREEZER DESSERTS
GRAND PRIZE
WINNER

GRAND PRIZE

Winning Coffee Ice Cream Pie

I love me a good cup of joe, and this dreamy creation allows me to enjoy the flavor my favorite beverage inside a dessert. Feel free to vary the flavor of ice cream if you like.

—VELMA BROWN TURNER STATION, KENTUCKY

PREP: 30 MIN. + FREEZING **MAKES:** 8 SERVINGS

- **2 ounces unsweetened chocolate, chopped**
- **¼ cup butter, cubed**
- **1 can (5 ounces) evaporated milk**
- **½ cup sugar**
- **1 pint coffee ice cream, softened**
- **1 chocolate crumb crust (8 inches)**
- **1 carton (8 ounces) frozen whipped topping, thawed**
- **¼ cup chopped pecans**

1. In a heavy saucepan, melt chocolate and butter over low heat. Stir in milk and sugar. Bring to a boil over medium heat, stirring constantly. Cook and stir for 3-4 minutes or until thickened. Remove from the heat; cool completely.

2. Spoon ice cream into crust. Stir sauce; spread over ice cream. Top with whipped topping; sprinkle with pecans. Freeze until firm. Remove from the freezer 15 minutes before serving.

BE AN ICE CREAM PIE ARTIST

Whip up a crowd-pleasing treat in no time with these ideas:

- Start with a store-bought graham, chocolate crumb or shortbread crust.
- Mix chocolate ice cream with chopped pecans; top pie with caramel, whipped cream and more pecans.
- Stir chopped peanut butter cups into vanilla ice cream; drizzle top of pie with chocolate sauce.
- Top strawberry ice cream pie with lemon curd and garnish with fresh strawberries.

Bat Cupcakes

Even my adult children love these Halloween cupcakes. We serve them every year at our pumpkin-carving party. You can also make them with the fudge stripes on their wings facing up for variety.

—JOYCE MOYNIHAN LAKEVILLE, MINNESOTA

PREP: 25 MIN. **BAKE:** 20 MIN. + COOLING **MAKES:** 2 DOZEN

- **1 package chocolate cake mix (regular size)**
- **1 can (16 ounces) chocolate frosting**
- **24 fudge-striped cookies**
- **24 milk chocolate kisses**
- **Red decorating icing**

1. Prepare and bake cake batter according to package directions for cupcakes; cool completely.

2. Set aside 2 tablespoons chocolate frosting. Frost cupcakes with remaining frosting. For bat wings, cut cookies in half and add scalloped edges if desired. Insert two cookie halves into each cupcake. Gently press chocolate kisses into frosting for heads. Pipe ears with reserved frosting; add eyes with decorating icing.

Eggnog Pumpkin Pie

This family classic is a combination of our favorite holiday flavors. With its flaky crust, creamy filling and crunchy topping, it's the perfect finale to a special meal!

—LYN DILWORTH RANCHO CORDOVA, CALIFORNIA

PREP: 40 MIN. + CHILLING **BAKE:** 50 MIN. + COOLING
MAKES: 8 SERVINGS

- **1¼ cups all-purpose flour**
- **¼ teaspoon salt**
- **3 tablespoons shortening, cubed**
- **3 tablespoons cold butter, cubed**
- **3 to 4 tablespoons cold water**

FILLING

- **2 eggs**
- **1 can (15 ounces) solid-pack pumpkin**
- **1 cup eggnog**
- **½ cup sugar**
- **1 teaspoon ground cinnamon**
- **½ teaspoon salt**
- **½ teaspoon ground ginger**
- **½ teaspoon ground nutmeg**
- **¼ teaspoon ground cloves**

TOPPING

- **½ cup packed brown sugar**
- **2 tablespoons butter, softened**
- **½ cup chopped pecans**

1. In a food processor, combine flour and salt; cover and pulse to blend. Add shortening and butter; cover and pulse until mixture resembles coarse crumbs. While processing, gradually add water until dough forms a ball. Wrap in plastic wrap. Refrigerate for 1 to 1½ hours or until easy to handle.
2. Roll out pastry to fit a 9-in. pie plate. Transfer pastry to pie plate. Trim pastry to ½ in. beyond edge of plate; flute edges.
3. In a large bowl, whisk the eggs, pumpkin, eggnog, sugar, cinnamon, salt, ginger, nutmeg and cloves until blended. Pour into crust.
4. In a small bowl, beat brown sugar and butter until crumbly, about 2 minutes. Stir in pecans; sprinkle over filling.
5. Bake at 350° for 50-60 minutes or until a knife inserted near the center comes out clean. Cool on a wire rack. Refrigerate leftovers.
Editor's Note: *This recipe was tested with commercially prepared eggnog.*

Buttermilk Torte

I grew up on a farm, and our family enjoyed delicious down-home food. It was always a special treat when my mother prepared her buttermilk torte. It hit the spot after a long day of chores.

—CAROL LEDVINA MISHICOT, WISCONSIN

PREP: 25 MIN. **BAKE:** 80 MIN. + COOLING **MAKES:** 12 SERVINGS

- **¾ cup butter-flavored shortening**
- **1¾ cups sugar, divided**
- **2 eggs, separated**
- **1 teaspoon vanilla extract**
- **2½ cups all-purpose flour**
- **1 teaspoon baking soda**
- **1 teaspoon ground cinnamon**
- **½ teaspoon salt**
- **1¼ cups buttermilk**
- **¼ teaspoon cream of tartar**
- **½ cup semisweet chocolate chips**
- **½ cup flaked coconut**

1. Grease the bottom only of a 10-in. springform pan; set aside. In a large bowl, cream shortening and 1½ cups sugar until light and fluffy. Beat in egg yolks and vanilla. Combine the flour, baking soda, cinnamon and salt; add to the creamed mixture alternately with buttermilk, beating well after each addition. Transfer to prepared pan.
2. Bake at 325° for 50-55 minutes or until a toothpick inserted near the center comes out clean. Remove from the oven; increase heat to 375°.
3. In a small bowl, beat egg whites and cream of tartar on medium speed until soft peaks form. Gradually add the remaining sugar, 1 tablespoon at time, beating on high until stiff glossy peaks form.
4. Spread evenly over warm cake, sealing edges to sides of pan. Sprinkle chips and coconut over the top. Bake for 15 minutes or until coconut and meringue are golden brown. Run a knife around edge of pan; remove sides. Cool completely on a wire rack. Refrigerate leftovers.

Lemonade Meringue Pie

Here's a beautiful pie with excellent citrus flavor. I like to add some lemon zest on top of the meringue for even more lemony zing.

—**KAY SEILER** GREENVILLE, OHIO

PREP: 30 MIN. **BAKE:** 15 MIN. + CHILLING **MAKES:** 8 SERVINGS

- **Pastry for single-crust pie (9 inches)**
- **3 eggs, separated**
- **1¼ cups 2% milk**
- **1 cup (8 ounces) sour cream**
- **1 package (4.6 ounces) cook-and-serve vanilla pudding mix**
- **⅓ cup thawed lemonade concentrate**
- **1 teaspoon lemon juice**
- **¼ teaspoon cream of tartar**
- **6 tablespoons sugar**

1. Line a 9-in. pie plate with pastry; trim and flute edges. Line unpricked pastry with a double thickness of heavy-duty foil. Bake at 450° for 8 minutes. Remove foil; bake 5-7 minutes longer or until lightly browned. Cool on a wire rack.

2. Place egg whites in a large bowl; let stand at room temperature for 30 minutes. Meanwhile, in a large saucepan, combine the milk, sour cream and pudding mix until smooth. Cook and stir over medium heat until thickened and bubbly. Reduce heat; cook and stir 2 minutes longer.

3. Remove from the heat. Stir a small amount of hot mixture into egg yolks; return all to the pan, stirring constantly. Bring to a gentle boil; cook and stir for 2 minutes longer. Remove mixture from the heat. Gently stir in lemonade concentrate; keep warm.

4. Add lemon juice and cream of tartar to egg whites; beat on medium speed until soft peaks form. Gradually beat in sugar, 1 tablespoon at a time, on high until stiff glossy peaks form and sugar is dissolved.

5. Pour warm filling into pastry shell. Spread meringue evenly over filling, sealing edges to crust.

6. Bake at 350° for 15-20 minutes or until the meringue is golden brown. Cool on a wire rack for 1 hour. Refrigerate for at least 3 hours before serving. Store leftovers in the refrigerator.

Butterscotch Peach Pie

When peach season arrives, this old-fashioned pie is sure to be on the table. The recipe has been in our family for more than 60 years, and I still make it every summer. Butterscotch buffs love it.

—**BARBARA MOYER** TIFFIN, OHIO

PREP: 30 MIN. + CHILLING **BAKE:** 45 MIN. + COOLING
MAKES: 8 SERVINGS

- **2 cups all-purpose flour**
- **1 teaspoon salt**
- **¾ cup shortening**
- **4 to 5 tablespoons cold water**

FILLING

- **¾ cup packed brown sugar**
- **2 tablespoons all-purpose flour**
- **⅓ cup light corn syrup**
- **3 tablespoons butter, melted**
- **2 tablespoons lemon juice**
- **¼ teaspoon almond extract**
- **8 medium peaches, peeled and sliced**

1. In a large bowl, combine flour and salt; cut in shortening until crumbly. Gradually add water, tossing with a fork until dough forms a ball. Cover and refrigerate for 30 minutes or until easy to handle.

2. For filling, in a small saucepan, combine brown sugar and flour. Stir in corn syrup and butter until blended. Bring to a boil; cook and stir for 2 minutes or until thickened. Remove from the heat; stir in lemon juice and extract. Place peaches in a large bowl; add syrup mixture and toss to coat.

3. Divide dough in half so one ball is slightly larger than the other. Roll out larger ball to fit a 9-in. pie plate. Transfer to pie plate; trim pastry to ½ in. beyond rim of plate. Add filling. Roll out remaining pastry; make a lattice crust. Trim, seal and flute edges. Cover edges loosely with foil.

4. Bake at 375° for 25 minutes. Uncover; bake 20-25 minutes longer or until crust is golden brown and filling is bubbly. Cool on a wire rack.

Italian Cream Cake

Here's a scrumptious cake that melts in your mouth. Pecan lovers will eagerly accept a second slice.

—**MARILYN MOREL** KEENE, NEW HAMPSHIRE

PREP: 40 MIN.
BAKE: 20 MIN. + COOLING
MAKES: 12 SERVINGS

- **½ cup butter, softened**
- **½ cup shortening**
- **2 cups sugar**
- **5 eggs**
- **1 teaspoon vanilla extract**
- **2 cups all-purpose flour**
- **1 teaspoon baking soda**
- **¼ teaspoon salt**
- **1 cup buttermilk**
- **1 cup chopped pecans**
- **½ cup flaked coconut**

CREAM CHEESE FROSTING

- **2 packages (one 8 ounces, one 3 ounces) cream cheese, softened**
- **½ cup butter, softened**
- **3¾ cups confectioners' sugar**
- **1 teaspoon vanilla extract**
- **1 cup coarsely chopped pecans**

1. In a large bowl, cream the butter, shortening and sugar until light and fluffy. Add eggs, one at a time, beating well after each addition. Beat in vanilla.

2. Combine the flour, baking soda and salt; add to creamed mixture alternately with buttermilk, beating well after each addition. Fold in pecans and coconut.

3. Pour into three greased and floured 9-in. round baking pans. Bake at 350° for 20-25 minutes or until a toothpick inserted near the center comes out clean. Cool the cakes for 10 minutes before removing from pans to wire racks to cool completely.

4. For frosting, in a large bowl, beat cream cheese and butter until fluffy. Add confectioners' sugar and vanilla; beat until smooth. Spread frosting between layers and over top and sides of cake. Press pecans onto sides of cake. Store in the refrigerator.

Pumpkin Cupcakes

A unique mix of pineapple and pumpkin creates moist cupcakes with mouthwatering flavor and texture. Cap them off with the accompanying cream cheese frosting.

—**MARY RELYEA** CANASTOTA, NEW YORK

PREP: 30 MIN. **BAKE:** 20 MIN. + COOLING **MAKES:** 16 CUPCAKES

- **2/3 cup shortening**
- **2 eggs**
- **3/4 cup maple syrup**
- **1/2 cup 2% milk**
- **1 1/2 cups all-purpose flour**
- **1 1/4 teaspoons baking powder**
- **1/2 teaspoon salt**
- **1/2 teaspoon baking soda**
- **1/2 teaspoon ground ginger**
- **1/2 teaspoon ground allspice**
- **1 cup canned pumpkin**
- **1 can (8 ounces) crushed pineapple, drained**
- **1 package (8 ounces) cream cheese, softened**
- **1/4 cup butter, softened**
- **1 1/2 cups confectioners' sugar**

1. In a large bowl, beat shortening until light and fluffy. Add eggs, one at a time, beating well after each addition (mixture will appear curdled). Beat in syrup and milk. Combine the flour, baking powder, salt, baking soda, ginger and allspice; add to shortening mixture and beat just until moistened. Stir in pumpkin and pineapple.

2. Fill paper-lined muffin cups two-thirds full. Bake at 350° for 20-25 minutes or until a toothpick inserted near the center comes out clean. Cool cupcakes for 10 minutes before removing from pans to a wire rack to cool completely.

3. For frosting, in a small bowl, beat cream cheese and butter until fluffy. Add confectioners' sugar and beat until smooth. Frost cupcakes.

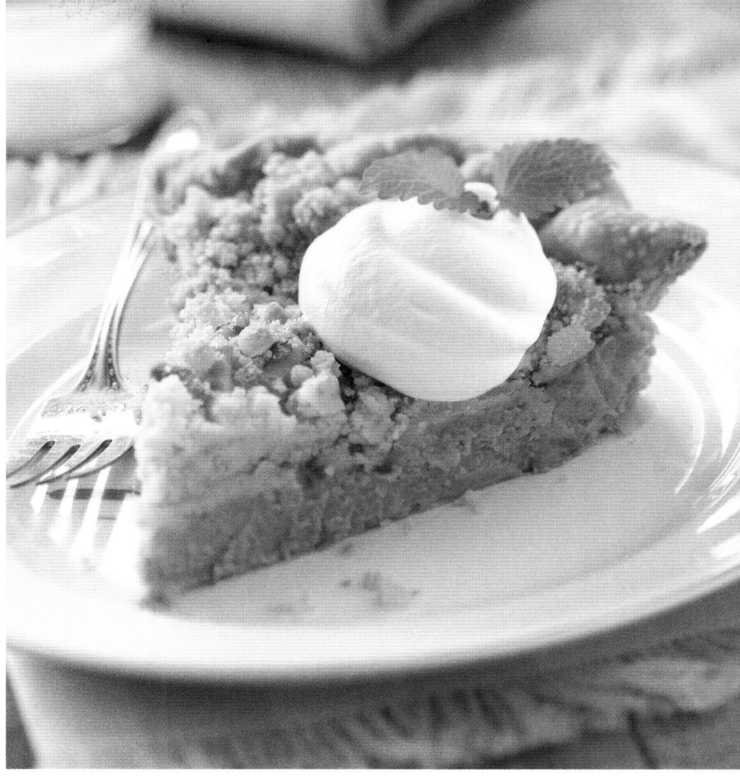

Ginger-Streusel Pumpkin Pie

I love to bake and have spent a lot of time making goodies for my family and friends. The streusel topping gives this pie a special touch your family will love.

—**SONIA PARVU** SHERRILL, NEW YORK

PREP: 25 MIN. **BAKE:** 55 MIN. + COOLING **MAKES:** 8 SERVINGS

- **1 sheet refrigerated pie pastry**
- **3 eggs**
- **1 can (15 ounces) solid-pack pumpkin**
- **1 1/2 cups heavy whipping cream**
- **1/2 cup sugar**
- **1/4 cup packed brown sugar**
- **1 1/2 teaspoons ground cinnamon**
- **1/2 teaspoon salt**
- **1/4 teaspoon ground allspice**
- **1/4 teaspoon ground nutmeg**
- **1/4 teaspoon ground cloves**

STREUSEL

- **1 cup all-purpose flour**
- **1/2 cup packed brown sugar**
- **1/2 cup cold butter, cubed**
- **1/2 cup chopped walnuts**
- **1/3 cup finely chopped crystallized ginger**

1. On a lightly floured surface, unroll pastry. Transfer pastry to a 9-in. pie plate. Trim pastry to 1/2 in. beyond edge of plate; flute edges.

2. In a large bowl, whisk the eggs, pumpkin, cream, sugars, cinnamon, salt, allspice, nutmeg and cloves. Pour into pastry shell. Bake at 350° for 40 minutes.

3. In a small bowl, combine flour and brown sugar; cut in butter until crumbly. Stir in walnuts and ginger. Gently sprinkle over filling.

4. Bake 15-25 minutes longer or until a knife inserted near the center comes out clean. Cool on a wire rack. Refrigerate leftovers.

Lemony White Chocolate Cheesecake

Although it takes some time to prepare this eye-catching cheesecake, the combination of tangy lemon and rich white chocolate is hard to beat. It's always a hit!

—MARLENE SCHOLLENBERGER BLOOMINGTON, INDIANA

PREP: 30 MIN. **BAKE:** 65 MIN. + CHILLING **MAKES:** 12 SERVINGS

- **1¼ cups all-purpose flour**
- **2 tablespoons confectioners' sugar**
- **1 teaspoon grated lemon peel**
- **½ cup cold butter, cubed**

FILLING

- **4 packages (8 ounces each) cream cheese, softened**
- **1¼ cups sugar**
- **10 ounces white baking chocolate, melted and cooled**
- **2 tablespoons all-purpose flour**
- **2 tablespoons heavy whipping cream**
- **2 tablespoons lemon juice**
- **2 teaspoons grated lemon peel**
- **2 teaspoons vanilla extract**
- **4 eggs, lightly beaten**
- **White baking chocolate curls and lemon peel strips, optional**

1. Place a 9-in. springform pan on a double thickness of heavy-duty foil (about 18 in. square). Securely wrap foil around pan; set aside.

2. In a small bowl, combine the flour, confectioners' sugar and peel; cut in butter until crumbly. Press onto the bottom and 1 in. up the sides of prepared pan. Place on a baking sheet. Bake at 325° for 25-30 minutes or until golden brown. Cool crust on a wire rack.

3. In a large bowl, beat cream cheese and sugar until smooth. Beat in the white chocolate, flour, cream, lemon juice, lemon peel and vanilla. Add eggs; beat on low speed just until combined. Pour into crust.

4. Place pan in a large baking pan; add 1 in. of hot water to larger pan. Bake at 325° for 65-85 minutes or until center is just set and top appears dull.

5. Remove pan from water bath. Cool on a wire rack for 10 minutes. Carefully run a knife around edge of pan to loosen; cool 1 hour longer. Refrigerate overnight. Remove sides of pan. Garnish with white chocolate and lemon peel if desired.

Pumpkin Cheesecake Deluxe

I developed this recipe to combine my love for cheesecake and my family's love for pumpkin pie. Whenever I serve it, we devour every last morsel!

—ANDREA QUIROZ CHICAGO, ILLINOIS

PREP: 35 MIN. **BAKE:** 1 HOUR + CHILLING **MAKES:** 12 SERVINGS

- **¾ cup chopped pecans, toasted**
- **32 gingersnap cookies, coarsely crushed**
- **3 tablespoons brown sugar**
- **6 tablespoons butter, melted**

FILLING

- **3 packages (8 ounces each) cream cheese, softened**
- **1 cup packed brown sugar**
- **1½ cups canned pumpkin**
- **½ cup heavy whipping cream**
- **¼ cup maple syrup**
- **3 teaspoons vanilla extract**
- **1 teaspoon ground cinnamon**
- **½ teaspoon ground ginger**
- **¼ teaspoon ground cloves**
- **4 eggs, lightly beaten**
- **Sweetened whipped cream, optional**
- **Pecan brittle, optional**

1. Place a greased 9-in. springform pan on a double thickness of heavy-duty foil; securely wrap foil around pan. Place pecans in a food processor; cover and process until ground. Add the gingersnaps, brown sugar and butter; cover and pulse until blended. Press onto the bottom and 2 in. up the sides of prepared pan; set aside.

2. In a large bowl, beat cream cheese and brown sugar until smooth. Beat in the pumpkin, cream, syrup, vanilla and spices. Add eggs; beat on low speed just until combined. Pour into crust. Place springform pan in a large baking pan; add 1 in. of hot water to larger pan.

3. Bake at 325° for 60-70 minutes or until center is just set and top appears dull. Remove pan from water bath. Cool on a wire rack for 10 minutes. Carefully run a knife around edge of pan to loosen; cool 1 hour longer. Chill overnight. Remove sides of pan.

4. Garnish with whipped cream and pecan brittle if desired.

White Chocolate-Coconut Layer Cake

Over the years I've added my own special touches to this impressive three-layer cake. I incorporated fresh peaches and macadamia nuts into the batter and also switched from dark to white chocolate. My family gave my creation a thumbs-up!

—DARL COLLINS MARKLEVILLE, INDIANA

PREP: 25 MIN. **BAKE:** 35 MIN. + COOLING **MAKES:** 12 SERVINGS

- **8 ounces white baking chocolate, chopped**
- **¾ cup butter, softened**
- **1½ cups sugar**
- **⅛ teaspoon salt**
- **4 eggs**
- **1 teaspoon coconut extract**
- **2½ cups cake flour**
- **6 teaspoons baking powder**
- **1¼ cups 2% milk**
- **1 cup frozen unsweetened sliced peaches, thawed and finely chopped**
- **½ cup macadamia nuts, chopped, toasted**

FROSTING

- **6 ounces white baking chocolate, chopped**
- **¼ cup heavy whipping cream**
- **1 cup butter, softened**
- **½ teaspoon coconut extract**
- **4 cups confectioners' sugar**
- **1 cup flaked coconut, toasted**
- **¼ cup macadamia nuts, chopped, toasted**

1. Line three 8-in. round baking pans with parchment paper; coat paper with cooking spray and set aside.
2. In a small bowl, melt chocolate; set aside.
3. In a large bowl, cream butter, sugar and salt until light and fluffy. Add eggs, one at a time, beating well after each addition. Beat in extract. Sift flour and baking powder; add to the creamed mixture alternately with milk, beating well after each addition.
4. Pat peaches dry with paper towels. Fold peaches, chocolate and macadamia nuts into batter. Divide among prepared pans.
5. Bake at 350° for 35-40 minutes or until a toothpick inserted near the center comes out clean. Cool for 15 minutes before removing from pans to wire racks to cool completely.
6. For frosting, in a microwave, melt chocolate with cream; cool to room temperature. In a large bowl, beat butter and extract until fluffy; add cooled chocolate mixture. Gradually beat in confectioners' sugar.
7. Spread between layers and over top and sides of cake. Sprinkle with coconut and macadamia nuts.

Gingerbread Pudding Cake

A handful of spices and a half cup of molasses give my dessert a wonderful old-fashioned flavor. It's pretty, too, with a dollop of whipped cream on top.

—BARBARA COOK YUMA, ARIZONA

PREP: 20 MIN. **COOK:** 2 HOURS + STANDING
MAKES: 6-8 SERVINGS

- **¼ cup butter, softened**
- **¼ cup sugar**
- **1 egg white**
- **1 teaspoon vanilla extract**
- **½ cup molasses**
- **1 cup water**
- **1¼ cups all-purpose flour**
- **¾ teaspoon baking soda**
- **½ teaspoon ground cinnamon**
- **½ teaspoon ground ginger**
- **¼ teaspoon salt**
- **¼ teaspoon ground allspice**
- **⅛ teaspoon ground nutmeg**
- **½ cup chopped pecans**

TOPPING

- **6 tablespoons brown sugar**
- **¾ cup hot water**
- **⅔ cup butter, melted**

1. In a large bowl, cream butter and sugar until light and fluffy. Beat in egg white and vanilla. Combine molasses and water. Combine the flour, baking soda, cinnamon, ginger, salt, allspice and nutmeg; gradually add to creamed mixture alternately with molasses mixture, beating well after each addition. Fold in pecans.
2. Pour into a greased 3-qt. slow cooker. Sprinkle with brown sugar. Combine hot water and butter; pour over batter (do not stir).
3. Cover and cook on high for 2 to 2½ hours or until a toothpick inserted near center of cake comes out clean. Turn off heat. Let stand for 15 minutes. Serve warm.

Lemon Chess Pie

My lemony, old-fashioned pie cuts beautifully and has a smooth texture. It's a perennial favorite.

—HANNAH LARUE RIDER EAST POINT, KENTUCKY

PREP: 15 MIN. **BAKE:** 35 MIN. + CHILLING **MAKES:** 6 SERVINGS

- **1 sheet refrigerated pie pastry**
- **4 eggs**
- **1½ cups sugar**
- **½ cup lemon juice**
- **¼ cup butter, melted**
- **1 tablespoon cornmeal**
- **2 teaspoons all-purpose flour**
- **⅛ teaspoon salt**

1. Unroll pastry on a lightly floured surface. Transfer to a 9-in. pie plate. Trim pastry to ½ in. beyond edge of plate; flute edges.
2. In a large bowl, beat eggs for 3 minutes. Gradually add sugar; beat for 2 minutes or until mixture becomes thick and lemon-colored. Beat in the lemon juice, butter, cornmeal, flour and salt.
3. Pour mixture into pastry shell. Bake at 350° for 35-40 minutes or until a knife inserted near the center comes out clean. Cool on a wire rack for 1 hour. Refrigerate pie for at least 3 hours before serving.

GRAND PRIZE

Lemon Chiffon Cake

This moist and airy cake was my dad's favorite. Mom revamped the original recipe to include lemons. Now I make it for my own family when I want to treat them to something special.

—TRISHA KAMMERS CLARKSTON, WASHINGTON

PREP: 25 MIN. **BAKE:** 50 MIN. + COOLING
MAKES: 12-16 SERVINGS

- **7 eggs, separated**
- **2 cups all-purpose flour**
- **1½ cups sugar**
- **3 teaspoons baking powder**
- **1 teaspoon salt**
- **¾ cup water**
- **½ cup canola oil**
- **4 teaspoons grated lemon peel**
- **2 teaspoons vanilla extract**
- **½ teaspoon cream of tartar**

LEMON FROSTING

- **⅓ cup butter, softened**
- **3 cups confectioners' sugar**
- **¼ cup lemon juice**
- **4½ teaspoons grated lemon peel**
- **Dash salt**

1. Place egg whites in a large bowl; let stand at room temperature for 30 minutes.
2. In a large bowl, combine the flour, sugar, baking powder and salt. In another bowl, whisk the egg yolks, water, oil, lemon peel and vanilla; add to dry ingredients and beat until well blended. Add cream of tartar to egg whites; beat on medium speed until stiff peaks form. Fold into batter.
3. Gently spoon into an ungreased 10-in. tube pan. Cut through batter with a knife to remove air pockets. Bake on the lowest oven rack at 325° for 50-55 minutes or until cake springs back when lightly touched. Immediately invert pan; cool completely, about 1 hour.
4. Run a knife around side and center tube of pan. Remove cake to a serving plate. In a small bowl, combine frosting ingredients; beat until smooth. Spread over top of cake, allowing frosting to drape down the sides.

ABOUT CHIFFON CAKES

Chiffon cakes are moist, light and airy, with a springy texture similar to sponge cake, but with the rich flavor of a butter cake. Although prepared similarly to a butter cake, chiffon cake uses oil instead of butter. The dry ingredients are mixed together. Then, the oil, egg yolks, water and flavorings are beaten in. Egg whites, used for leavening, are beaten until stiff and gently folded into the batter.

LEMON LOVERS
GRAND PRIZE
WINNER

WATERMELON BOMBE, PAGE 213

212
225
228

Just Desserts

With this **heavenly assortment** of tortes, cobblers, trifles, creamy sensations, frozen delights and other unforgettable pleasures, it doesn't matter how full you are...there's **always room for dessert!**

Lemon Bar Trifle

My sweet hubby gave me a mixer for my birthday when I was his new bride over 50 years ago. This lemon dessert was in the small booklet that came with it. The tangy flavor always takes me back to those cherished days of experimenting with new recipes.

—ALYCE MCCRARY LEIGHTON, ALABAMA

PREP: 35 MIN. + CHILLING **MAKES:** 9 SERVINGS

- **2 cups all-purpose flour**
- **1 cup chopped pecans**
- **1 cup butter, melted**

LEMON LAYER

- **1½ cups sugar**
- **¼ cup cornstarch**
- **¼ cup all-purpose flour**
- **1¾ cups cold water**
- **3 egg yolks, beaten**
- **⅔ cup lemon juice**
- **2 tablespoons butter**
- **4 teaspoons grated lemon peel**

CREAM CHEESE LAYER

- **1 package (8 ounces) cream cheese, softened**
- **3 cups confectioners' sugar**
- **1 carton (8 ounces) frozen whipped topping, thawed**

1. In a small bowl, combine flour and pecans; stir in butter. Press into an ungreased 13-in. x 9-in. baking dish. Bake at 350° for 18-20 minutes or until light golden brown. Cool on a wire rack.
2. In a small heavy saucepan, combine the sugar, cornstarch and flour. Stir in water until smooth. Cook and stir over medium-high heat until thickened and bubbly. Reduce heat; cook and stir 2 minutes longer.
3. Remove from the heat. Stir a small amount of hot mixture into egg yolks; return all to the pan, stirring constantly. Bring to a gentle boil; cook and stir 2 minutes longer. Remove from the heat. Gently stir in the lemon juice, butter and lemon peel.
4. Transfer mixture to a large bowl. Cool to room temperature without stirring. Cover surface with waxed paper; refrigerate until chilled.
5. In a large bowl, beat cream cheese and confectioners' sugar until smooth. Fold in whipped topping. Crumble the baked pecan mixture; set aside ½ cup for topping.
6. Just before serving, in a 3-qt. trifle bowl, layer 1 cup each pecan mixture, lemon mixture and cream cheese mixture. Repeat layers twice. Sprinkle with reserved pecan mixture. Refrigerate leftovers.

Swirled Sherbet Dessert

Lemon and orange sherbet are swirled over a coconut and pecan crust in this refreshing frozen dessert. It has a tropical appeal that makes it perfect for dining alfresco on sultry summer nights.

—AGNES WARD STRATFORD, ONTARIO

PREP: 25 MIN. + FREEZING **MAKES:** 12 SERVINGS

- **1 cup crushed vanilla wafers (about 30 wafers)**
- **⅓ cup flaked coconut**
- **⅓ cup chopped pecans**
- **¼ cup butter, melted**
- **1 pint lemon sherbet, softened**
- **1 pint orange sherbet, softened**

1. In a small bowl, combine the wafer crumbs, coconut, pecans and butter; press onto the bottom of an ungreased 9-in. springform pan. Bake at 350° for 10-12 minutes or until lightly browned. Cool for 10 minutes on a wire rack.
2. Arrange scoops of sherbet over crust, alternating flavors. Cut through sherbet with a knife to swirl. Cover and freeze overnight. Remove from the freezer 15 minutes before serving.

Nutrition Facts: *1 slice equals 181 calories, 10 g fat (4 g saturated fat), 11 mg cholesterol, 86 mg sodium, 24 g carbohydrate, 2 g fiber, 1 g protein.*

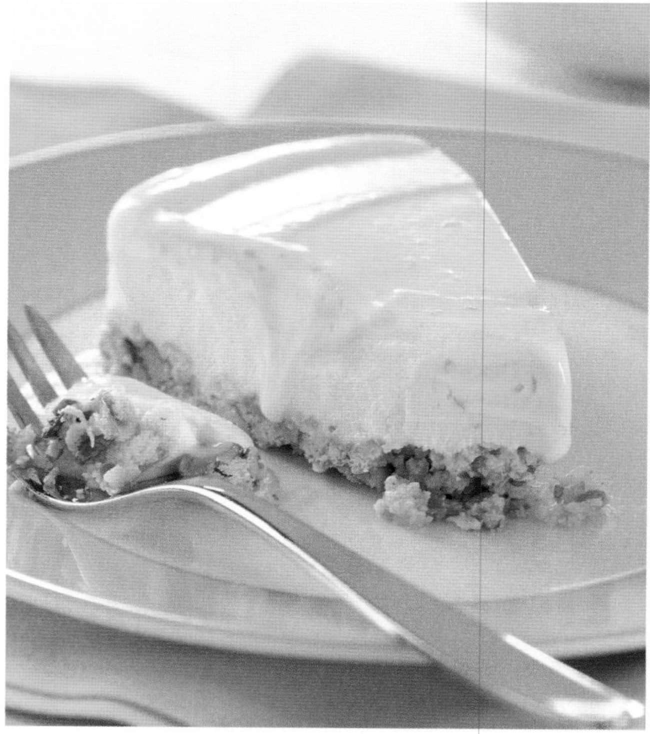

> "I can't count the times I've made this frosty delight. It's a favorite at our family barbecues. People think you really fussed, but it couldn't be easier—and there are never any leftovers!"
>
> —**MARY ANN DELL** PHOENIXVILLE, PENNSYLVANIA

Watermelon Bombe

PREP: 25 MIN. + FREEZING **MAKES:** 8 SERVINGS

- **1 pint pistachio ice cream, softened**
- **6 drops green food coloring**
- **1 pint vanilla ice cream, softened**
- **1 pint strawberry ice cream, softened**
- **6 drops red food coloring**
- **½ cup miniature semisweet chocolate chips**

1. Line a 2-qt. freezer-safe bowl with plastic wrap. Place in the freezer for 30 minutes. In a small bowl, combine pistachio ice cream and green food coloring. Quickly spread pistachio ice cream over the bottom and up the sides to within ½ in. of the top of bowl. Freeze for 1 hour or until firm. Repeat with vanilla ice cream. Freeze for 2 hours or until firm.
2. In a small bowl, combine strawberry ice cream and red food coloring; stir in chocolate chips. Spoon into ice cream shell. Cover and freeze overnight.
3. Remove from the freezer and invert onto a serving plate. Remove bowl and plastic wrap. Cut into wedges.

Lemon Cheesecake Dessert

Everyone will know spring is here when you serve these yummy, yellow cheesecake squares. I like to garnish this cool and refreshing dessert with lemon slices.

—**PATTY AUXIER** ROYALTON, KENTUCKY

PREP: 25 MIN. **BAKE:** 30 MIN. + CHILLING
MAKES: 12 SERVINGS (2 CUPS SAUCE)

- **2 cups graham cracker crumbs**
- **¼ cup sugar**
- **½ cup butter, melted**

FILLING

- **4 packages (8 ounces each) cream cheese, softened**
- **1¼ cups sugar**
- **1 package (3 ounces) lemon gelatin**
- **1 teaspoon lemon extract**
- **5 eggs, lightly beaten**

LEMON SAUCE

- **1 package (2.9 ounces) cook-and-serve lemon pudding mix**
- **¼ cup sugar**
- **2½ cups cold water**

1. In a small bowl, combine cracker crumbs, sugar and butter. Press onto the bottom and 1 in. up the sides of a greased 13-in. x 9-in. baking dish. Refrigerate.
2. In a large bowl, beat cream cheese and sugar until smooth. Add dry gelatin and lemon extract; beat 3 minutes longer. Add eggs; beat on low speed just until combined. Pour into crust.
3. Bake at 325° for 30-40 minutes or until center is almost set. Cool on a wire rack for 1 hour. Cover and refrigerate overnight.
4. In a small saucepan, combine pudding mix and sugar. Gradually stir in water. Cook and stir over medium heat until mixture comes to a boil. Cook and stir 1-2 minutes longer or until thickened. Transfer to a bowl. Cover surface with waxed paper; refrigerate until chilled. Serve with dessert.

Caramel Apple Pizza

I made this favorite recipe lighter by making my own cookie crust. I used less fat and sugar, and part whole wheat pastry flour. I also used a combination of fat-free and low-fat cream cheese as well as fat-free caramel sauce. My family doesn't even notice the difference!

—**TARI AMBLER** SHOREWOOD, ILLINOIS

PREP: 40 MIN. + COOLING
MAKES: 12 SLICES

- **¼ cup butter, softened**
- **¼ cup sugar**
- **¼ cup packed brown sugar**
- **1 egg**
- **2 tablespoons canola oil**
- **1 tablespoon light corn syrup**
- **1 teaspoon vanilla extract**
- **1 cup whole wheat pastry flour**
- **¾ cup all-purpose flour**
- **½ teaspoon baking powder**
- **¼ teaspoon salt**
- **¼ teaspoon ground cinnamon**

TOPPING

- **1 package (8 ounces) fat-free cream cheese**
- **¼ cup packed brown sugar**
- **½ teaspoon ground cinnamon**
- **½ teaspoon vanilla extract**
- **3 medium tart apples, thinly sliced**
- **¼ cup fat-free caramel ice cream topping**
- **¼ cup chopped unsalted dry roasted peanuts**

1. In a large bowl, cream butter and sugars until light and fluffy. Beat in the egg, oil, corn syrup and vanilla. Combine the flours, baking powder, salt and cinnamon; gradually add to creamed mixture and mix well.

2. Press dough onto a 14-in. pizza pan coated with cooking spray. Bake at 350° for 12-15 minutes or until lightly browned. Cool on a wire rack.

3. In a small bowl, beat the cream cheese, brown sugar, cinnamon and vanilla until smooth. Spread over crust. Arrange apples over the top. Drizzle with caramel topping; sprinkle with peanuts. Serve immediately.

Nutrition Facts: *1 slice equals 238 calories, 9 g fat (3 g saturated fat), 29 mg cholesterol, 228 mg sodium, 36 g carbohydrate, 2 g fiber, 6 g protein.*

Lemon Custard Ice Cream

Several years ago, I found this recipe and now I make it whenever I have the opportunity. One thing I like about this ice cream—besides the lemony taste—is that it doesn't turn icy the next day.

—SUSAN LITWAK BELLEVUE, NEBRASKA

PREP: 15 MIN. + CHILLING **PROCESS:** 20 MIN./BATCH + FREEZING **MAKES:** 2 QUARTS

- **2 cups sugar**
- **¼ cup all-purpose flour**
- **¼ teaspoon salt**
- **4 cups milk**
- **4 eggs, lightly beaten**
- **3 cups heavy whipping cream**
- **1 cup lemon juice**

1. In a large saucepan, combine the sugar, flour and salt. Gradually add milk. Bring to a boil over medium heat; cook and stir for 2 minutes or until thickened. Remove from the heat; cool slightly.

2. Whisk a small amount of hot milk mixture into the eggs. Return all to the pan, whisking constantly. Cook and stir until mixture reaches 160° and coats the back of a metal spoon.

3. Remove from the heat; stir in cream and lemon juice. Cool quickly by placing pan in a bowl of ice water; stir for 2 minutes. Press waxed paper onto surface of custard. Refrigerate for several hours or overnight.

4. Fill cylinder of ice cream freezer two-thirds full; freeze according to the manufacturer's directions. Refrigerate remaining mixture until ready to freeze. When ice cream is frozen, transfer to a freezer container; freeze for 2-4 hours before serving.

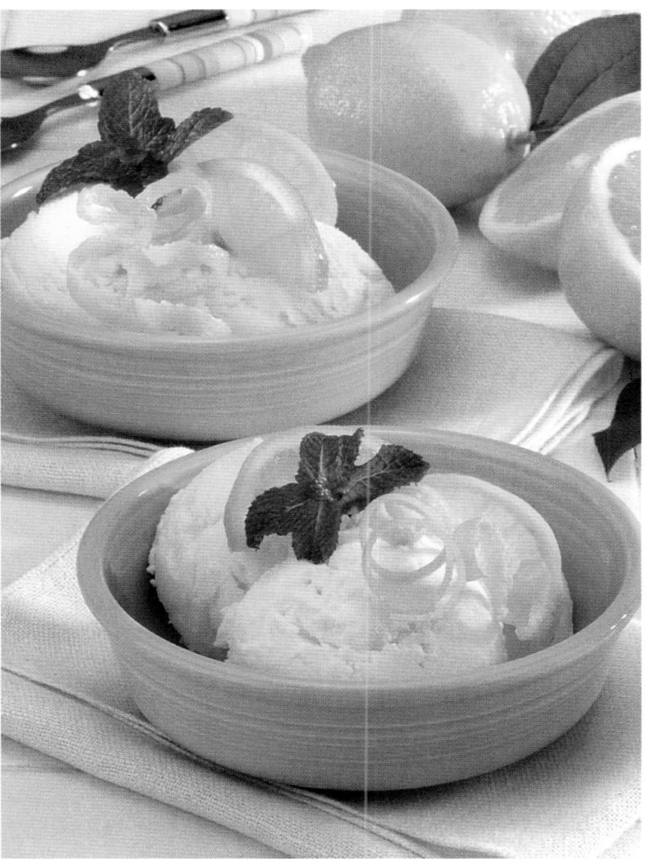

Tiramisu Cheesecake Dessert

I wasn't a big fan of tiramisu until I tried this recipe with its distinctive cheesecake- and-coffee-flavored layers. It's one of my favorite desserts to bring to potlucks.

—CHRISTIE NELSON TAYLORVILLE, ILLINOIS

PREP: 20 MIN. **BAKE:** 40 MIN. + CHILLING **MAKES:** 12 SERVINGS

- **1 package (12 ounces) vanilla wafers**
- **5 teaspoons instant coffee granules, divided**
- **3 tablespoons hot water, divided**
- **4 packages (8 ounces each) cream cheese, softened**
- **1 cup sugar**
- **1 cup (8 ounces) sour cream**
- **4 eggs, lightly beaten**
- **1 cup whipped topping**
- **1 tablespoon baking cocoa**

1. Layer half of wafers in a greased 13-in. x 9-in. baking dish. In a small bowl, dissolve 2 teaspoons coffee granules in 2 tablespoons hot water. Brush wafers with half of coffee; set remaining mixture aside.

2. In a large bowl, beat cream cheese and sugar until smooth. Beat in sour cream. Add eggs; beat on low speed just until combined. Divide batter in half. Dissolve remaining coffee granules in remaining hot water; stir into one portion of batter. Spread over wafers. Layer with remaining wafers; brush with reserved coffee. Top with remaining batter.

3. Bake at 325° for 40-45 minutes or until center is almost set. Cool on a wire rack for 10 minutes. Carefully run a knife around edge of dish to loosen; cool 1 hour longer. Refrigerate overnight.

4. Spread with whipped topping; dust with cocoa. Refrigerate leftovers.

Lemon Noodle Kugel

Comforting kugel is a traditional dessert at our family's Polish Christmas Eve supper. Rich with butter, sugar, sour cream and cinnamon, it suits any special-occasion meal.

—**ROMAINE SMITH** GARDEN GROVE, IOWA

PREP: 25 MIN. **BAKE:** 55 MIN. + STANDING **MAKES:** 12 SERVINGS

- **5 cups uncooked egg noodles**
- **2 tablespoons butter**
- **4 eggs**
- **2 cups (16 ounces) sour cream**
- **2 cups (16 ounces) 4% cottage cheese**
- **1 cup milk**
- **¾ cup plus 1½ teaspoons sugar, divided**
- **1½ teaspoons lemon extract**
- **1 teaspoon vanilla extract**
- **½ teaspoon ground cinnamon**

1. Cook noodles according to package directions; drain and return to the pan. Toss with butter; set aside.

2. In a large bowl, beat the eggs, sour cream, cottage cheese, milk, ¾ cup sugar and extracts until well blended. Stir in the noodles.

3. Transfer to a 13-in. x 9-in. baking dish coated with cooking spray. Combine cinnamon and remaining sugar; sprinkle over noodle mixture.

4. Bake, uncovered, at 350° for 55-60 minutes or until a thermometer reads 160°. Let stand for 10 minutes before cutting. Serve warm or cold. Refrigerate leftovers.

GRAND PRIZE

Peaches and Cream Torte

This is the dessert I make when I'm craving something cool and fruity. It's a lovely ending to any meal. The cream cheese adds richness to the fluffy filling.

—**ELVA ROBERTS** SUMMERSIDE, PRINCE EDWARD ISLAND

PREP: 40 MIN. + CHILLING **MAKES:** 12 SERVINGS

- **2 cups graham cracker crumbs**
- **⅓ cup packed brown sugar**
- **½ cup butter, melted**

FILLING

- **1 can (29 ounces) sliced peaches**
- **1¼ cups sugar, divided**
- **2 tablespoons cornstarch**
- **1 package (8 ounces) cream cheese, softened**
- **2 cups heavy whipping cream**

1. In a small bowl, combine graham cracker crumbs and brown sugar; stir in butter. Set aside ¼ cup for topping. Press remaining crumb mixture onto the bottom and 1 in. up the sides of a greased 9-in. springform pan.

2. Place pan on a baking sheet. Bake at 350° for 10 minutes. Cool on a wire rack.

3. Drain peaches, reserving syrup in a 2-cup measuring cup. Add enough water to measure 1½ cups. In a large saucepan, combine ¼ cup sugar and cornstarch; stir in syrup mixture until smooth. Add peaches. Bring to a boil over medium heat; cook and stir for 2 minutes or until thickened. Cool to room temperature, stirring occasionally.

4. Meanwhile, in a large bowl, beat cream cheese and remaining sugar until smooth. In a small bowl, beat cream until stiff peaks form; fold into cream cheese mixture.

5. Spread half of the cream cheese mixture over crust. Top with half of the peach mixture; repeat layers. Sprinkle with reserved crumb mixture. Cover and refrigerate for 8 hours or overnight. Remove sides of pan before slicing.

PEACH POINTERS

If you like, replace the canned peaches in this torte with fresh peaches. Purchase peaches that have an intense fragrance and that give slightly to palm pressure. Avoid those that are hard or have soft spots. A half pound will yield about 1 cup chopped peaches. To ripen peaches, place in a brown paper bag and store at room temperature for about 2 days. To easily remove the pit, cut the fruit from stem to stem all the way around; twist the peach halves in opposite directions and lift out the pit.

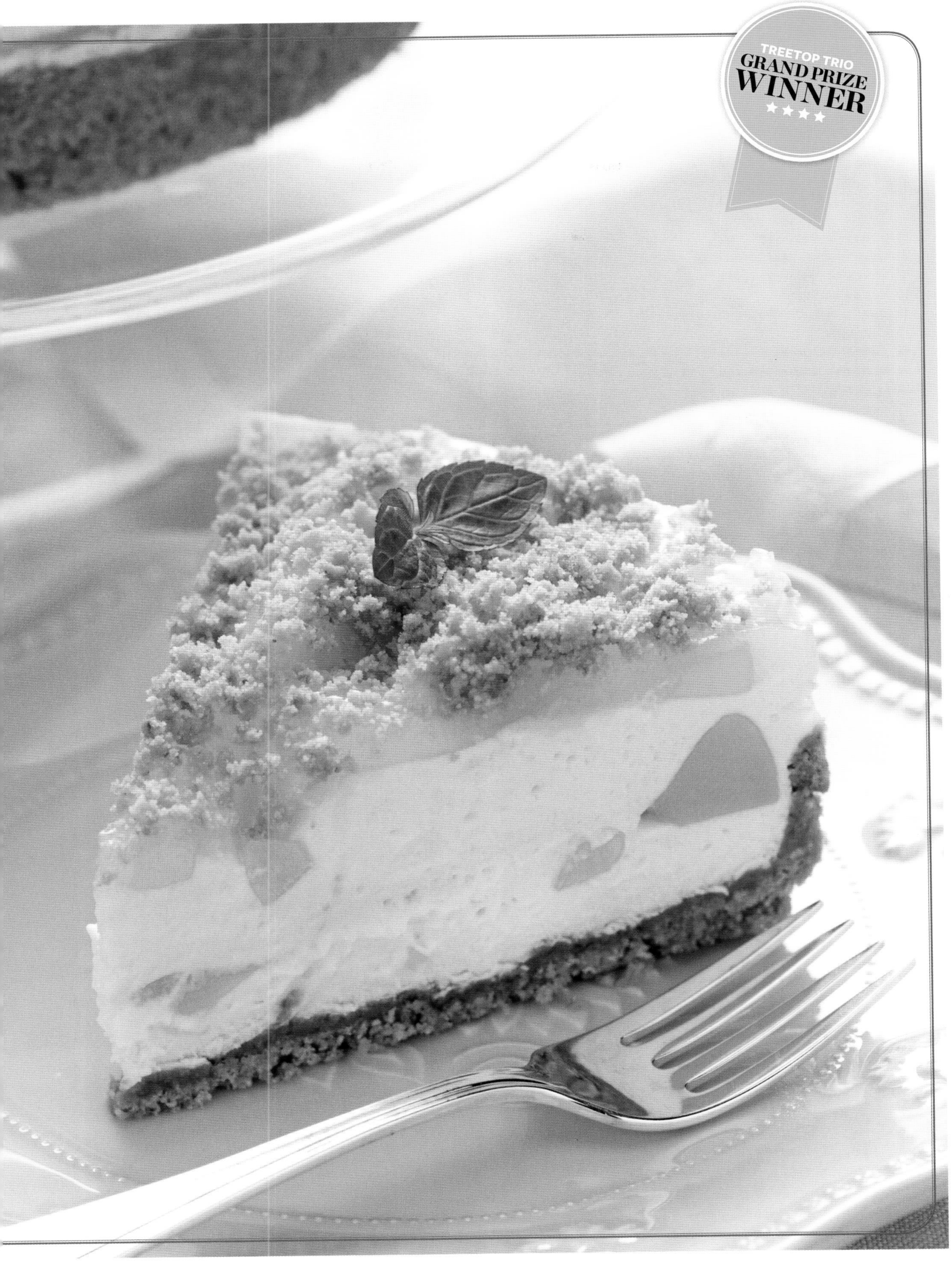
TREETOP TRIO
GRAND PRIZE
WINNER

Frozen Almond-Cream Desserts

These little, frozen cheesecakes are a surefire crowd-pleaser, particularly when served with the peach puree.

—EVA WRIGHT GRANT, ALABAMA

PREP: 30 MIN. + FREEZING
MAKES: 12 SERVINGS

- **¾ cup ground almonds**
- **1 tablespoon butter, melted**
- **1 envelope unflavored gelatin**
- **¼ cup cold water**
- **12 ounces reduced-fat cream cheese**
- **⅓ cup sugar**
- **¾ cup fat-free milk**
- **¼ teaspoon almond extract**

PEACH SAUCE

- **3 cups sliced peeled peaches**
- **2 tablespoons sugar**
- **⅛ teaspoon salt**

1. In a small bowl, combine almonds and butter. Press onto the bottom of 12 paper- or foil-lined muffin cups. Cover and freeze for 10 minutes.

2. Meanwhile, in a small saucepan, sprinkle gelatin over cold water; let stand for 1 minute. Cook over low heat, stirring until gelatin is completely dissolved; set aside.

3. In a small bowl, beat cream cheese and sugar until smooth. Gradually beat in milk and extract. Stir in gelatin mixture. Spoon into muffin cups; freeze until firm.

4. Remove desserts from the freezer 10 minutes before serving. Place the sauce ingredients in a blender; cover and process until pureed. Spoon onto dessert plates. Peel liners off desserts; invert onto peach sauce.

Nutrition Facts: *1 dessert with 3 tablespoons sauce equals 170 calories, 10 g fat (5 g saturated fat), 23 mg cholesterol, 163 mg sodium, 16 g carbohydrate, 2 g fiber, 6 g protein.* **Diabetic Exchanges:** *2 fat, 1/2 starch, 1/2 fruit.*

ADD GELATIN

Reduced-fat cream cheese doesn't get as firm as its full-fat counterpart in cheesecake recipes. To remedy this, use one envelope of unflavored gelatin for every 8-12 ounces of reduced-fat cream cheese. The gelatin adds no flavor but firms up the cheesecake nicely.

Mascarpone Cheesecake

This rich dessert is sure to delight with its creamy filling, whipped topping and sweet caramel drizzle. It makes an ideal ending to a special meal.

—**DEANNA POLITO-LAUGHINGHOUSE** RALEIGH, NORTH CAROLINA

PREP: 30 MIN. **BAKE:** 50 MIN. + CHILLING **MAKES:** 12 SERVINGS

- **¾ cup graham cracker crumbs**
- **3 tablespoons sugar**
- **3 tablespoons butter, melted**

FILLING

- **2 packages (8 ounces each) cream cheese, softened**
- **2 cartons (8 ounces each) Mascarpone cheese**
- **1 cup sugar**
- **1 tablespoon lemon juice**
- **1 tablespoon vanilla extract**
- **4 eggs, lightly beaten**

TOPPING

- **1 envelope whipped topping mix**
- **1 tablespoon caramel ice cream topping**

1. Place a greased 9-in. springform pan on a double thickness of heavy-duty foil (about 18 in. square). Securely wrap foil around pan.
2. In a small bowl, combine cracker crumbs and sugar; stir in butter. Press onto the bottom of prepared pan. Place pan on a baking sheet. Bake at 325° for 10 minutes. Cool on a wire rack.
3. For filling, in a large bowl, beat the cheeses, sugar, lemon juice and vanilla until smooth. Add eggs; beat on low speed just until combined. Pour over crust. Place springform pan in a large baking pan; add 1 in. of hot water to larger pan.
4. Bake at 325° for 50-60 minutes or until center is just set and top appears dull. Remove springform pan from water bath. Cool on a wire rack for 10 minutes. Carefully run a knife around the edge of pan to loosen; cool 1 hour longer.
5. Refrigerate overnight. Remove sides of pan. Before serving, prepare topping mix according to package directions. Garnish cheesecake with whipped topping; drizzle with caramel. Refrigerate leftovers.

Apricot Sherbet

PREP: 10 MIN. **PROCESS:** 20 MIN. + FREEZING
MAKES: 1½ QUARTS

- **2¼ cups apricot nectar**
- **1½ cups milk**
- **¾ cup heavy whipping cream**
- **1½ cups sugar**
- **3 tablespoons lemon juice**

1. In a large bowl, combine all ingredients. Fill cylinder of ice cream freezer; freeze according to manufacturer's directions.
2. Transfer to a freezer container; freeze sherbet for 4 hours or until firm.

“Searching for a light and refreshing dessert that you can make ahead? Try this pretty sherbet that bursts with the invigorating flavor of apricot. It's the perfect summertime treat.”

—**ORPHA CAMPBELL** MIDLAND, TEXAS

Baked Apple Dumplings

These versatile dumplings can be made with peaches or mixed berries in place of apples, and drizzled with hot caramel sauce instead of icing. Add vanilla custard or ice cream, and it's the perfect dessert!

—EVANGELINE BRADFORD ERLANGER, KENTUCKY

PREP: 35 MIN. **BAKE:** 15 MIN. **MAKES:** 1½ DOZEN

- **½ cup sugar**
- **3 tablespoons dry bread crumbs**
- **4½ teaspoons ground cinnamon**
- **Dash ground nutmeg**
- **1 package (17.3 ounces) frozen puff pastry, thawed**
- **1 egg, beaten**
- **2¼ cups chopped peeled tart apples**

STREUSEL

- **⅓ cup chopped pecans, toasted**
- **⅓ cup packed brown sugar**
- **⅓ cup all-purpose flour**
- **2 tablespoons plus 1½ teaspoons butter, melted**

ICING

- **1 cup confectioners' sugar**
- **2 tablespoons 2% milk**
- **1 teaspoon vanilla extract**

1. In a small bowl, combine the sugar, bread crumbs, cinnamon and nutmeg. On a lightly floured surface, roll pastry into two 12-in. squares. Cut each sheet into nine 4-in. squares.
2. Brush squares with egg. Place 1 teaspoon sugar mixture in the center of a square; top with 2 tablespoons chopped apples and 1 teaspoon sugar mixture. Gently bring up corners of pastry to center; pinch edges to seal. Repeat with remaining pastry, crumb mixture and apples. Place dumplings on greased baking sheets.
3. In a small bowl, combine the streusel ingredients. Brush remaining egg over dumplings; press streusel over tops.
4. Bake at 400° for 14-18 minutes or until golden brown. Place pans on wire racks. Combine icing ingredients; drizzle over dumplings.

Nutrition Facts: *1 dumpling equals 252 calories, 11 g fat (3 g saturated fat), 16 mg cholesterol, 116 mg sodium, 37 g carbohydrate, 3 g fiber, 3 g protein.*

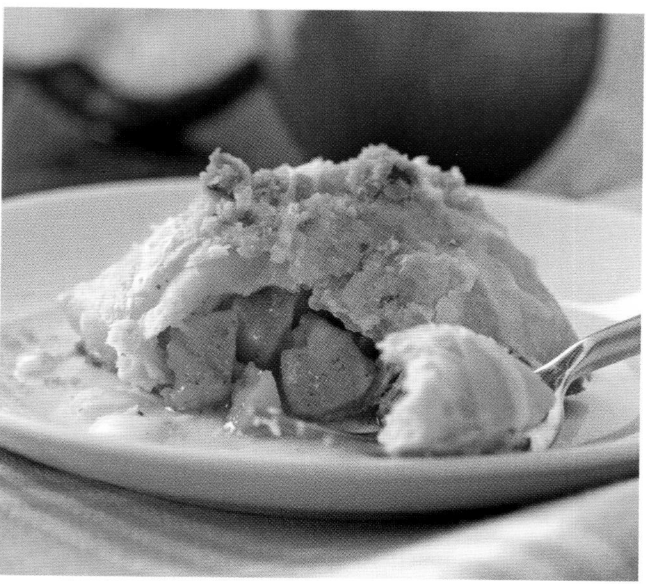

Cherry Cobbler

Berries, peaches or any fruit can be used for this simple recipe, but the cheery bright color of cherries makes it especially nice for gray, winter days.

—ELEANOR JACOBY EUREKA, KANSAS

PREP: 15 MIN. **BAKE:** 25 MIN. **MAKES:** 3 SERVINGS

- **1 cup canned pitted tart cherries**
- **⅓ cup plus 3 tablespoons sugar, divided**
- **½ cup all-purpose flour**
- **½ teaspoon baking powder**
- **1 tablespoon cold butter**
- **¼ cup 2% milk**

1. In a small saucepan over medium heat, bring cherries and ⅓ cup sugar to a boil. Remove from the heat; set aside.
2. In a small bowl, combine the flour, baking powder and remaining sugar. Cut in butter until mixture resembles coarse crumbs. Stir in milk just until moistened. Spread into a greased 3-cup baking dish; pour cherries over the top.
3. Bake at 375° for 25-30 minutes or until bubbly and edges are golden brown. Serve warm.

COBBLERS FOR ANY SEASON

To make a cobbler fit any occasion, use seasonal cookie cutters to cut sheets of puff pastry dough. Arrange the cutouts over the fruit mixture, brush with butter, sprinkle with sugar, and bake until a perfect golden brown.

Strawberry Cheesecake Mousse

"Heaven on a spoon" is one way to describe my lightened-up mousse. It's like a crustless no-bake cheesecake. For a pretty presentation, serve in glass dishes garnished with strawberries.

—VIRGINIA ANTHONY JACKSONVILLE, FLORIDA

PREP: 20 MIN. + CHILLING **MAKES:** 6 SERVINGS

- **½ teaspoon unflavored gelatin**
- **¼ cup cold water**
- **1 quart fresh strawberries, halved**
- **2 tablespoons reduced-sugar strawberry preserves**
- **1 package (8 ounces) reduced-fat cream cheese**
- **½ cup sugar, divided**
- **¼ cup reduced-fat sour cream, divided**
- **½ cup heavy whipping cream**

1. Sprinkle gelatin over cold water; let stand for 1 minute. Microwave on high for 20 seconds. Stir and let stand for 1 minute or until gelatin is completely dissolved. Meanwhile, combine strawberries and preserves; set aside.

2. In a large bowl, beat the cream cheese, 1/4 cup sugar and 2 tablespoons sour cream until blended; set aside.

3. In another bowl, beat whipping cream and remaining sour cream until it begins to thicken. Add the gelatin mixture and remaining sugar; beat until stiff peaks form. Fold into cream cheese mixture.

4. In each of six dessert dishes, layer 1/2 cup strawberry mixture and 1/3 cup cream cheese mixture. Refrigerate until chilled.

Nutrition Facts: *1 serving equals 279 calories, 16 g fat (10 g saturated fat), 57 mg cholesterol, 176 mg sodium, 29 g carbohydrate, 2 g fiber, 6 g protein.*

Chocolate-Fruit Crepes

These special dessert crepes are delicate, delightful and simple to make. They are great for dessert or as a lovely addition to brunch.

—LAURA MCDOWELL LAKE VILLA, ILLINOIS

PREP: 30 MIN. + CHILLING **COOK:** 5 MIN./BATCH
MAKES: 10 SERVINGS

- **1½ cups buttermilk**
- **3 eggs**
- **3 tablespoons butter, melted**
- **1 cup all-purpose flour**
- **2 tablespoons sugar**
- **2 tablespoons baking cocoa**

FILLING

- **1 can (21 ounces) cherry pie filling**
- **1 can (8½ ounces) sliced peaches, drained and chopped**
- **½ teaspoon ground cinnamon**
- **⅛ teaspoon almond extract**
- **⅓ cup hot fudge ice cream topping, warmed**
- **Whipped cream, optional**

1. In a large bowl, combine the buttermilk, eggs and butter. Combine the flour, sugar and cocoa; add to buttermilk mixture and mix well. Cover and refrigerate for 1 hour.

2. Heat a lightly greased 8-in. nonstick skillet over medium heat; pour 2 tablespoons batter into the center of skillet. Lift and tilt pan to coat bottom evenly. Cook until top appears dry; turn and cook 15-20 seconds longer. Remove to a wire rack. Repeat with remaining batter, greasing skillet as needed. When cool, stack crepes with waxed paper or paper towels in between.

3. In a microwave-safe bowl, combine the pie filling, peaches and cinnamon. Microwave, uncovered, on high for 3-4 minutes or until heated through, stirring once. Stir in extract. Spoon 2 tablespoons filling down the center of each crepe. Fold sides of crepe over filling. Drizzle with ice cream topping and garnish with whipped cream if desired.

Nutrition Facts: *2 filled crepes (calculated without whipped cream) equals 241 calories, 6 g fat (3 g saturated fat), 74 mg cholesterol, 109 mg sodium, 41 g carbohydrate, 1 g fiber, 5 g protein.*

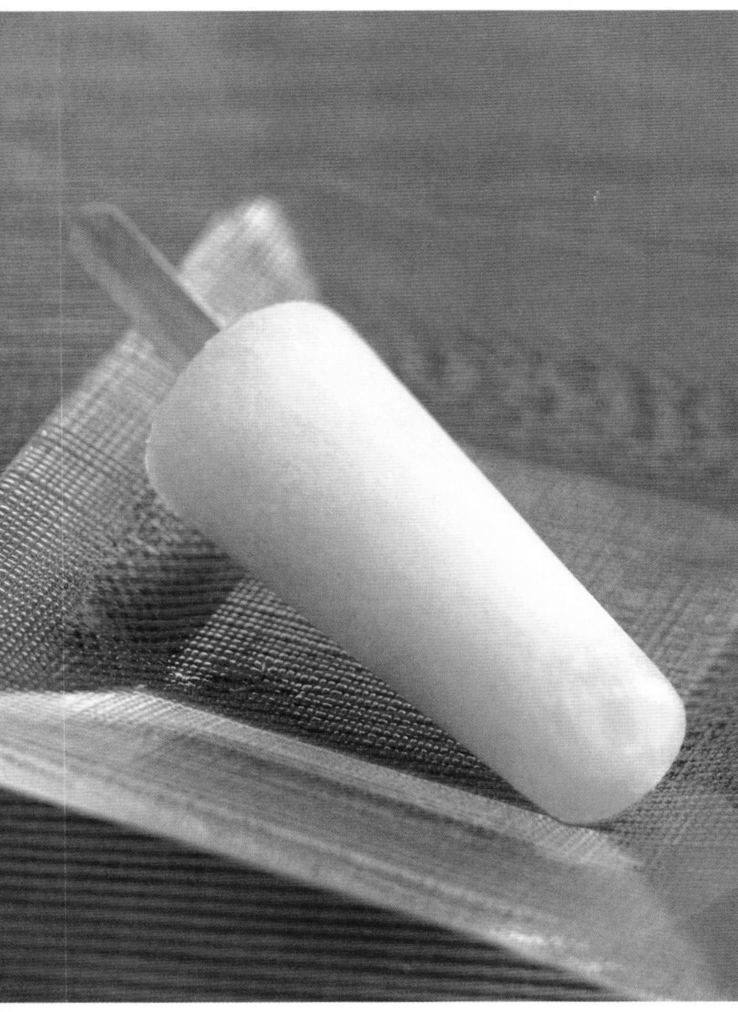

Nutty Cookies & Cream Dessert

PREP: 25 MIN. + FREEZING **MAKES:** 15 SERVINGS

- **1 package (15½ ounces) Oreo cookies**
- **½ cup butter, melted**
- **½ gallon cookies and cream ice cream, softened**
- **1½ cups salted peanuts, coarsely chopped**
- **⅔ cup hot fudge ice cream topping**
- **⅔ cup caramel ice cream topping**
- **1 carton (8 ounces) frozen whipped topping, thawed**

1. In a large bowl, combine cookie crumbs and butter; set aside 1 cup. Press remaining crumbs into an ungreased 13-in. x 9-in. dish. Spread with ice cream. Layer with peanuts, ice cream toppings and whipped topping; sprinkle with reserved crumbs. Cover and freeze until firm.
2. Remove from the freezer 15 minutes before serving.

"The flavors of hot fudge, caramel, chocolate cookies and ice cream combine in every mouthful of this fabulous frozen dessert. No matter how big the meal, you'll always find room for this treat!"

—CHERYL MELERSKI HARBORCREEK, PENNSYLVANIA

Fruit Juice Pops

This is one of my go-to recipes whenever my kids have a hankering for a refreshing treat. We enjoy these pops more than store-bought ones, and they taste great with either pineapple or orange juice. For a fun twist, freeze and serve in cups made from hollowed-out oranges.

—BARBARA STEWART GARLAND, TEXAS

PREP: 25 MIN. + FREEZING **MAKES:** 1 DOZEN

- **2 cups water**
- **1½ cups sugar**
- **4 cups unsweetened apple juice**
- **1 cup unsweetened pineapple or orange juice**
- **½ cup lemon juice**
- **12 Popsicle molds or paper cups (3 ounces each) and Popsicle sticks**

1. In a large saucepan, combine water and sugar; bring to a boil. Reduce heat; simmer, uncovered, for 3-4 minutes or until sugar is dissolved, stirring occasionally. Remove from the heat; stir in juices.
2. Fill molds or cups with ¼ cup juice mixture; top with holders or insert sticks into cups. Freeze.

Nutrition Facts: *1 juice pop equals 149 calories, trace fat (trace saturated fat), 0 cholesterol, 3 mg sodium, 38 g carbohydrate, trace fiber, trace protein.*

Rainbow Sherbet Dessert

Macaroons, pecans and layers of cool, fruity sherbet combine in this three-tone dessert. Garnish with fresh strawberries for a summertime treat that's simply out of this world!

—KATHRYN DUNN AXTON, VIRGINIA

PREP: 30 MIN. + FREEZING
MAKES: 12 SERVINGS

- **12 macaroon cookies, crumbled**
- **2 cups heavy whipping cream**
- **3 tablespoons confectioners' sugar**
- **1 teaspoon vanilla extract**
- **¾ cup chopped pecans, toasted**
- **1 pint each raspberry, lime and orange sherbet, softened**

1. Sprinkle cookie crumbs onto an ungreased baking sheet. Bake at 350° for 5-8 minutes or until golden brown. Cool completely.

2. In a large bowl, beat cream until it begins to thicken. Add confectioners' sugar and vanilla; beat until stiff peaks form. Combine cookie crumbs and pecans; fold in whipped cream. Spread half of cream mixture onto the bottom of an ungreased 9-in. springform pan. Freeze for 30 minutes.

3. Gently spread raspberry sherbet over cream layer. Layer with lime and orange sherbets; spread with remaining cream mixture. Cover and freeze until firm. Remove from the freezer 10 minutes before serving. Remove sides of pan.

TOASTED PECANS

While you can toast chopped nuts in the microwave or in a dry skillet on your stovetop, it's easiest to toast them in the oven. Simply spread them in a baking pan and bake at 350° until golden brown, stirring often. Generally, nuts will be toasted in 6-10 minutes. Timing will depend on how finely the nuts are chopped and the thickness of your baking pan.

Bing Cherry Sherbet

I need only four ingredients to whip up this pretty, cherry-studded sherbet in my ice cream maker. The recipe is great made with sliced peaches and peach soda, too.

—**HELEN HUMBLE** LONGVIEW, TEXAS

PREP: 30 MIN. **PROCESS:** 20 MIN./BATCH + FREEZING
MAKES: ABOUT 3 QUARTS

- **4 cups fresh or frozen pitted dark sweet cherries, quartered**
- **1 cup sugar**
- **2 liters black cherry soda, chilled**
- **1 can (14 ounces) sweetened condensed milk**

1. In a large saucepan, bring cherries and sugar to a boil over medium heat, stirring constantly. Reduce heat; cover and simmer for 10 minutes, stirring occasionally. Cool slightly. Transfer to a large bowl; cover and refrigerate until chilled.
2. Stir in soda and milk. Fill ice cream freezer cylinder two-thirds full; freeze according to manufacturer's directions. Refrigerate remaining mixture until ready to freeze. Transfer to a freezer container; freeze for 2-4 hours or until firm. Remove from the freezer 10 minutes before serving.

Nutrition Facts: *3/4 cup equals 201 calories, 2 g fat (1 g saturated fat), 8 mg cholesterol, 45 mg sodium, 44 g carbohydrate, 1 g fiber, 2 g protein.*

Frosty Mallow Fruit Dessert

This recipe came from my husband's relatives in Holland and has been a favorite for many years. It's fancy, frosty, and goes together in just 10 minutes!

—**PATRICIA SWART** GALLOWAY, NEW JERSEY

PREP: 10 MIN. + FREEZING **MAKES:** 8 SERVINGS

- **1 package (8 ounces) cream cheese, softened**
- **1 cup (8 ounces) sour cream**
- **¼ cup sugar**
- **1 can (15 ounces) apricot halves, drained and coarsely chopped**
- **1 can (8 ounces) crushed pineapple, drained**
- **1 cup miniature marshmallows**
- **1 can (15 ounces) pitted dark sweet cherries, drained**

1. In a large bowl, beat the cream cheese, sour cream and sugar until smooth. Fold in the apricots, pineapple and marshmallows. Gently fold in cherries. Spoon into a 5-cup ring mold coated with cooking spray.
2. Cover and freeze for 4 hours or until firm. Just before serving, invert onto a platter.

Strawberry Sundae Sauce

My clan simply loves this fruity sauce over their ice cream. It's also delicious served in banana splits.

—**PEGGY TOWNSEND** FLORENCE, COLORADO

PREP: 25 MIN. + STANDING **MAKES:** 8 CUPS

- **2 quarts fresh strawberries**
- **6 cups sugar**
- **1 pouch (3 ounces) liquid fruit pectin**
- **⅓ cup chocolate syrup**
- **⅓ cup raspberry liqueur, optional**
- **Vanilla ice cream**

1. Wash and mash strawberries, measuring out enough mashed berries to make 4 cups. In a Dutch oven, combine strawberries and sugar. Bring to a full rolling boil over high heat, stirring constantly. Stir in pectin. Boil 1 minute longer, stirring constantly. Remove from the heat. Stir in syrup and liqueur if desired. Skim off foam.

2. Pour into jars or freezer containers, leaving a ½-in. headspace. Cool to room temperature, about 1 hour. Cover and let stand overnight or until set. Refrigerate for up to 3 weeks or freeze for up to 1 year. Serve with ice cream.

Nutrition Facts: *¼ cup (calculated without liqueur and ice cream) equals 174 calories, trace fat (trace saturated fat), 0 cholesterol, 3 mg sodium, 43 g carbohydrate, 1 g fiber, trace protein.*

Maple Mocha Pops

My husband says one is just not enough of these creamy pops. They're a breeze to make, and kids love them, too. For a more grown-up presentation, freeze them in pretty serving cups and add a dollop of whipped cream.

—**CAROLINE SPERRY** ALLENTOWN, MICHIGAN

PREP: 15 MIN. + FREEZING **MAKES:** 1 DOZEN

- **2 cups heavy whipping cream**
- **½ cup half-and-half cream**
- **¼ cup maple syrup**
- **¼ cup chocolate syrup**
- **1 tablespoon instant coffee granules**
- **12 Popsicle molds or paper cups (3 ounces each) and Popsicle sticks**

1. In a large bowl, whisk the whipping cream, half-and-half, maple syrup, chocolate syrup and coffee granules until coffee is dissolved.

2. Fill molds or cups with ¼ cup cream mixture; top with holders or insert sticks into cups. Freeze.

Nutrition Facts: *1 mocha pop equals 185 calories, 16 g fat (10 g saturated fat), 59 mg cholesterol, 25 mg sodium, 10 g carbohydrate, 0 fiber, 1 g protein.*

Spiced Pumpkin Mousse

Gingersnaps add a nice crunch to this creamy, smooth-as-silk spiced mousse.

—LARA PENNELL
MAULDIN, SOUTH CAROLINA

PREP: 30 MIN. + CHILLING
MAKES: 6 SERVINGS

- **1½ teaspoons unflavored gelatin**
- **4½ teaspoons cold water**
- **3 egg yolks**
- **¾ cup sugar**
- **1½ cups canned pumpkin**
- **¾ teaspoon ground cinnamon**
- **¼ teaspoon ground ginger**
- **⅛ teaspoon ground cloves**
- **1½ cups heavy whipping cream**
- **1½ teaspoons vanilla extract**
- **18 gingersnap cookies, divided**

1. In a small saucepan, sprinkle gelatin over water; let stand for 1 minute or until softened. Beat in egg yolks and sugar. Cook and stir over medium heat until a thermometer reads 160° and mixture has thickened, about 5 minutes.

2. Transfer to a small bowl; beat until cool and thickened, about 3 minutes. Beat in pumpkin and spices. Refrigerate for 1 hour or until set.

3. In a small bowl, beat cream and vanilla until stiff peaks form. Fold into pumpkin mixture.

4. Coarsely crumble 12 gingersnaps; sprinkle into six parfait or dessert dishes. Spoon or pipe mousse over the top. Cover and refrigerate for 1 hour or until set. Just before serving, garnish with remaining gingersnaps.

PIE PUMPKINS

Pie pumpkins—small, dense, flavorful pumpkins intended for eating—can be substituted for canned pumpkin. Pick pie pumpkins when they are fully ripened. Wash, peel and remove seeds. Cut pumpkin into chunks and steam until soft. Puree using a food mill or processor. Cool and pack into freezer bags or containers in the amounts needed for recipes. Use cup-for-cup in place of canned pumpkin.

Peach Tartlets

Tarts are special treats that make any fruit a showstopper. The crust is rich, tender and crunchy, almost like a cookie. I love this pastry recipe so much, I use it for every type of tart or pie I make.
—LEANNE WHELESS BORGER, TEXAS

PREP: 30 MIN. **BAKE:** 15 MIN. + COOLING **MAKES:** 8 SERVINGS

- **3⅓ cups all-purpose flour**
- **¼ cup sugar**
- **½ teaspoon salt**
- **1 cup cold butter, cubed**
- **½ cup plus 2 tablespoons cold water**
- **2 egg yolks**

FILLING

- **⅔ cup sugar**
- **2 tablespoons cornstarch**
- **Dash salt**
- **1 cup water**
- **1 can (29 ounces) sliced peaches, drained**
- **1 teaspoon lemon juice**
- **Whipped cream, optional**

1. In a large bowl, combine the flour, sugar and salt; cut in butter until mixture resembles coarse crumbs. Add water and egg yolks; stir until dough forms a ball.
2. Divide into eight portions; press onto the bottom and up the sides of eight 4-in. tart pans. Bake at 400° for 15-20 minutes or until golden brown. Cool on wire racks.
3. For filling, in a large saucepan, combine the sugar, cornstarch and salt. Stir in water until smooth. Bring to a boil; cook and stir for 2 minutes or until thickened. Remove from the heat. Stir in peaches and lemon juice.
4. Spoon into tart shells. Chill until serving. Garnish with whipped cream if desired.
Editor's Note: *To make Apricot Tartlets, substitute canned apricot halves for the peaches. For Pear Tartlets, substitute canned sliced pears for the peaches.*

Crescent Apple Dessert

My family loves any dessert that tastes like apple pie, and this one's so easy, even children can help make it. My grandchildren love helping MawMaw in the kitchen making yummy treats like this.
—JUDY TAYLOR KENNA, WEST VIRGINIA

PREP: 25 MIN. **BAKE:** 20 MIN. + COOLING **MAKES:** 12 SERVINGS

- **1 tube (8 ounces) refrigerated crescent rolls**
- **1 cup chopped walnuts**
- **¾ cup sugar**
- **½ teaspoon ground cinnamon**
- **¼ teaspoon ground nutmeg**
- **1 can (21 ounces) apple pie filling, chopped**

TOPPING

- **½ cup all-purpose flour**
- **½ cup packed brown sugar**
- **¼ cup cold butter**
- **1 cup flaked coconut**
- **¼ cup chopped walnuts**

1. Unroll crescent dough into an ungreased 13-in. x 9-in. baking pan; seal seams and perforations. Bake dough at 375° for 10 minutes.
2. Combine the walnuts, sugar, cinnamon and nutmeg; sprinkle over crust. Spread with pie filling.
3. In a small bowl, combine flour and brown sugar; cut in butter until mixture resembles coarse crumbs. Stir in coconut and walnuts. Sprinkle over filling.
4. Bake at 375° for 18-22 minutes or until golden brown. Cool on a wire rack.

Mint Sundae Brownie Squares

I love the classic pairing of chocolate and mint. This recipe makes a luscious, after-dinner dessert that's sure to cleanse the palate.

—EDIE DESPAIN LOGAN, UTAH

PREP: 20 MIN. + FREEZING **BAKE:** 25 MIN. + COOLING
MAKES: 15 SERVINGS

- **1 package fudge brownie mix (13-inch x 9-inch pan size)**
- **¾ cup chopped walnuts**
- **1 can (14 ounces) sweetened condensed milk**
- **2 teaspoons peppermint extract**
- **4 drops green food coloring, optional**
- **2 cups heavy whipping cream, whipped**
- **½ cup miniature semisweet chocolate chips**
- **1 jar (16 ounces) hot fudge ice cream topping, warmed**
- **⅓ cup chopped salted peanuts**

1. Prepare brownie mix according to package directions. Stir in walnuts. Pour into a greased 13-in. x 9-in. baking pan. Bake at 325° for 23-27 minutes or until a toothpick inserted in the center comes out clean (do not overbake). Cool on a wire rack.
2. Meanwhile, in a large bowl, combine the milk, extract and food coloring if desired. Fold in whipped cream and chocolate chips. Spread over brownie layer. Cover and freeze for several hours or overnight.
3. Let stand at room temperature for 10 minutes before cutting. Drizzle with ice cream topping; sprinkle with peanuts.

Peppermint Cheesecake

Just wait until you take the first sweet bite of this rich, velvety cheesecake. I like to go all out with a showstopping garnish made of hardened melted chocolate studded with Andes candies.

—CARRIE PRICE OTTAWA, ILLINOIS

PREP: 40 MIN. **BAKE:** 1¼ HOURS + CHILLING
MAKES: 16 SERVINGS

- **2½ cups cream-filled chocolate sandwich cookie crumbs**
- **⅓ cup butter, melted**
- **5 packages (8 ounces each) cream cheese, softened**
- **1 cup sugar**
- **1 cup (8 ounces) sour cream**
- **3 tablespoons all-purpose flour**
- **3 teaspoons vanilla extract**
- **1 teaspoon peppermint extract**
- **3 eggs, lightly beaten**
- **1 package (10 ounces) Andes creme de menthe baking chips or 2 packages (4.67 ounces each) mint Andes candies, chopped**

TOPPING

- **1 package (8 ounces) cream cheese, softened**
- **⅓ cup sugar**
- **1 carton (12 ounces) frozen whipped topping, thawed**
- **Miniature candy canes, optional**

1. Place a greased 9-in. springform pan on a double thickness of heavy-duty foil (about 18 in. square). Securely wrap foil around pan.
2. In a small bowl, combine cookie crumbs and butter. Press onto the bottom and 1 in. up the sides of prepared pan. Place pan on a baking sheet. Bake at 325° for 12-14 minutes or until set. Cool on a wire rack.
3. In a large bowl, beat cream cheese and sugar until smooth. Beat in the sour cream, flour and extracts. Add eggs; beat on low speed just until combined. Fold in chips. Pour into crust. (Pan will be full.) Place springform pan in a large baking pan; add 1 in. of hot water to larger pan.
4. Bake at 325° for 1¼ to 1½ hours or until center is just set and top appears dull. Remove springform pan from water bath. Cool on a wire rack for 10 minutes. Carefully run a knife around edge of pan to loosen; cool 1 hour longer. Refrigerate overnight. Remove sides of pan.
5. For topping, in a large bowl, beat cream cheese and sugar until smooth. Stir one-fourth whipped topping into mixture; fold in remaining whipped topping. Spread or pipe onto cheesecake. Garnish with miniature candy canes if desired.

Meringues with Fresh Berries

Juicy ripe berries and a dollop of light cream fill these cloudlike meringues. I sometimes double the recipe to serve friends, and they always rave about it.

—AGNES WARD STRATFORD, ONTARIO

PREP: 20 MIN. **BAKE:** 1 HOUR + COOLING **MAKES:** 2 SERVINGS

- **2 egg whites**
- **1/8 teaspoon cream of tartar**
- **Dash salt**
- **1/4 cup sugar**
- **1/4 teaspoon vanilla extract**
- **1 cup mixed fresh berries**
- **1/2 teaspoon sugar, optional**
- **1/3 cup sour cream**
- **1/8 to 1/4 teaspoon rum extract**

1. Place egg whites in a small bowl; let stand at room temperature for 30 minutes. Add cream of tartar and salt; beat on medium speed until soft peaks form. Gradually beat in sugar, 1 tablespoon at a time, on high until stiff peaks form. Beat in vanilla.

2. Drop meringue into two mounds on a parchment paper-lined baking sheet. Shape into 3½-in. cups with the back of a spoon.

3. Bake at 225° for 1 to 1¼ hours or until set and dry. Turn oven off; leave meringues in oven for 1 hour. Remove to wire racks to cool.

4. In a small bowl, combine berries and sugar if desired; let stand for 5 minutes. Combine sour cream and extract; spoon into meringue shells. Top with berries.

Nutrition Facts: *1 serving (calculated without optional sugar) equals 222 calories, 7 g fat (5 g saturated fat), 27 mg cholesterol, 149 mg sodium, 33 g carbohydrate, 2 g fiber, 5 g protein.* **Diabetic Exchanges:** *2 starch, 1½ fat, ½ fruit.*

Ginger Fruit Crisp

Our bed-and-breakfast guests tell us this fun crisp is one of the most enjoyable parts of their stay. There's seldom a crumb left.

—ELINOR STABILE CANMORE, ALBERTA

PREP: 20 MIN. **BAKE:** 30 MIN. **MAKES:** 9 SERVINGS

- **1/3 cup packed brown sugar**
- **2 tablespoons plus 1½ teaspoons cornstarch**
- **2 cups sliced fresh plums**
- **1 cup sliced peeled peaches**
- **1 cup sliced nectarines**

TOPPING

- **1 cup crushed gingersnap cookies (about 20 cookies)**
- **1/2 cup old-fashioned oats**
- **1/3 cup packed brown sugar**
- **1/2 teaspoon ground ginger**
- **1/2 teaspoon ground cinnamon**
- **1/4 teaspoon salt**
- **1/3 cup cold butter, cubed**
- **1/2 cup sliced almonds**
- **Whipped cream, optional**

1. In a large bowl, combine brown sugar and cornstarch. Add the plums, peaches and nectarines; gently toss to coat. Transfer to a greased 8-in. square baking dish.

2. For topping, in a small bowl, combine the gingersnap crumbs, oats, brown sugar, ginger, cinnamon and salt. Cut in butter until crumbly. Stir in almonds; sprinkle over fruit.

3. Bake at 350° for 30-35 minutes or until filling is bubbly and topping is browned. Serve warm with whipped cream if desired.

Nutrition Facts: *1 serving (calculated without whipped cream) equals 276 calories, 12 g fat (5 g saturated fat), 18 mg cholesterol, 222 mg sodium, 42 g carbohydrate, 3 g fiber, 3 g protein.*

General Recipe Index

This handy index lists every recipe by food category, major ingredient and/or cooking method, so you can easily locate recipes to suit your needs.

MANGOES

MAPLE

MARSHMALLOWS

MEATBALLS

MEATLESS ENTREES

MOUSSE & TRIFLES

MUSHROOMS

NUTS & PEANUT BUTTER

OATS & OATMEAL

OLIVES

ONIONS

ORANGES & TANGERINES

OVEN ENTREES

Alphabetical Recipe Index

This handy index lists every recipe in alphabetical order, so you can easily find your favorite recipes.